UNDERSTANDING CONFLICT RESOLUTION

3RD EDITION

UNDERSTANDING CONFLICT RESOLUTION

PETER WALLENSTEEN

Los Angeles | London | New Delhi
Singapore | Washington DC

First published 2012

First edition published 2002
Second edition published 2007
Reprinted 2009 (twice)

SAGE Publications Ltd
1 Oliver's Yard
55 City Road
London EC1Y 1SP

SAGE Publications Inc.
2455 Teller Road
Thousand Oaks, California 91320

SAGE Publications India Pvt Ltd
B 1/I 1 Mohan Cooperative Industrial Area
Mathura Road
New Delhi 110 044

SAGE Publications Asia-Pacific Pte Ltd
33 Pekin Street #02-01
Far East Square
Singapore 048763

Library of Congress Control Number: 201192440

British Library Cataloguing in Publication data

A catalogue record for this book is available from the British Library

ISBN 978-0-85702-049-9
ISBN 978-0-85702-050-5 (pbk)

Typeset by C&M Digitals (P) Ltd, Chennai, India
Printed and bound by CPI Group (UK) Ltd, Croydon, CR0 4YY
Printed on paper from sustainable resources

To Lena

Contents

List of Figures

List of Tables

About the Author

Peter Wallensteen is the Dag Hammarskjöld Professor of Peace and Conflict Research, Uppsala University (since 1985) as well as the Richard G. Starmann, Sr. Research Professor of Peace Studies at the Kroc Institute for International Peace Studies, University of Notre Dame, Indiana, USA (since 2006). He directs the Uppsala Conflict Data Program (UCDP) and the Special Program on sanctions (SPITS). His *Understanding Conflict Resolution: War, Peace and the Global System* (Sage, 3rd edition 2007, also in an Arabic translation) is used in teaching around the world. His book *Peace Research: Theory and Practice* has recently been published demonstrating his range of research (Routledge 2011). In 2010 he published a study on mediation with Isak Svensson *The Go-Between* on the renown Swedish diplomat Jan Eliasson. Wallensteen has published widely on conflict trends, conflict resolution, mediation, prevention, sanctions and the United Nations.

Preface to the First Edition

The abundance of conflicts and wars since the end of the Cold War has created scepticism about the prospects for peace, security, dialogue and discussion among parties in conflict. We have, however, also had other developments: peacemaking paralleled warmaking. Wars have actually been terminated without the physical or political elimination of the opponent. This book focuses on the ability of opposing parties to negotiate durable agreements in spite of the fact that they have fought a bitter war. In many ways, this is historically a new phenomenon, indicating that the hopes of success in peacemaking have to be realistic. There is much to be learnt and it is my hope that this work can contribute to that process.

This book draws heavily on the facts and figures retrieved by the Uppsala Conflict Data Project at the Department of Peace and Conflict Research, Uppsala University. Its many collaborators throughout the years have had considerable impact on my thinking. Indeed, the Department as such has served as a productive environment for increasing our understanding of the perplexing realities emerging since the end of the Cold War. I am grateful for inputs from my colleagues, notably Thomas Ohlson, Margareta Sollenberg, Birger Heldt, Kjell-Åke Nordquist and the many active members of the research seminar. I have also benefited a great deal from two longer periods away from the Department. I spent the autumn semester 1999 at Yale University, New Haven, Connecticut, under the auspices of the Department of Political Science. For this period I was affiliated with the unit for UN Studies. Discussions with Bruce M. Russett, James Sutterlin, Jean Krasno and Leonard Wantchekon were most rewarding, as were inputs from students I was teaching. A stay at the Joan B. Kroc Institute of International Peace Studies at the University of Notre Dame, South Bend, Indiana, during the spring semester of 2001 was also important. It was made possible by the Institute and a grant from the American-Scandinavian Foundation. I am particularly grateful to Robert Johansen, Raimo Väyrynen and Scott Appelby for this. The book received its final touches during a short period as Visiting Canterbury Fellow at the University of Canterbury, Christchurch, New Zealand, organized by Jacob Bercovitch.

Finally, I owe a particular gratitude to Bill Montross, for having carefully, critically and constructively read the entire manuscript in his spare time and to my wife Lena for being such a wonderful support. I am happy to dedicate this book to Lena.

Peter Wallensteen

Preface to the Second Edition

Recent political events, as well as progress in peace research, have affected the agenda for conflict resolution. Thus, this thoroughly revised second edition has included material on aspects of global terrorism as well as dimensions of human security. In particular, this edition has benefited from the creation of the Uppsala Conflict Database, as part of the Uppsala Conflict Data Program, with its detailed information on all armed conflicts since 1989, as well as a dataset covering the period after 1946. This has required the reconstruction of tables, particularly in Chapters 2 and 4–7. The graphs in Chapter 3 have also been improved. The basic tenets of the discussions are intact, however. In spite of some political developments, the ability to solve conflicts with peaceful means remains a key concern and a way to build durable peace.

In the revisions I have had assistance from the team associated with the Uppsala Conflict Data Program and with the Department of Peace and Conflict Research at Uppsala University: Lotta Harbom, Stina Högbladh, Roland Kostic, Joakim Kreutz, Hanna Matti, Erik Melander, Frida Möller, Margareta Sollenberg, Maria Wold-Troell and Magnus Öberg.

I am particularly grateful to Bill Montross who, once again, has read the entire manuscript with sharp eyes and perceptive observations on language and logics. Again, I dedicate this work to my wife Lena for her great understanding and support.

Peter Wallensteen
Uppsala, Sweden

Preface to the Third Edition

Current upheavals against authoritarian regimes in the Arab world are changing the political landscape in this key region – and provide yet another testimony to the continued importance of finding ways of solving conflicts in a peaceful manner and of building durable quality peace.

Retaining the structure of previous editions, this volume presents fresh research achievements in fields such as regional conflicts, mediation, peacebuilding and social justice. Recent information from the Uppsala Conflict Data Program (UCDP) has led to further updating of tables and graphs.

In these efforts I have been assisted by researchers associated with the UCDP at the Department of Peace and Conflict Research at Uppsala University, notably Lotta Themnér, Stina Högbladh, Joakim Kreutz and Ralph Sundberg. At the Kroc Institute, University of Notre Dame, South Bend, Indiana, Rachel Miller provided a valuable contribution.

As usual I am grateful to Bill Montross, who once again, has read the entire manuscript resulting in creative observations and comments. This edition is dedicated to my principal supporter – my wife Lena.

Peter Wallensteen
Uppsala, Sweden, May 2011

PART ONE
THE PROBLEM AND
HOW TO APPROACH IT

1 Understanding Conflict Resolution

2 Armed Conflicts and Peace Agreements

3 Approaching Conflict Resolution

4 Analysing Conflict Resolution

UNDERSTANDING CONFLICT RESOLUTION 1

1.1 Peacemaking as a New Experience

Since the Cold War ended there have been more peace agreements than in any period after the termination of the Second World War. Many of these accords curtailed violence successfully and transformed conflicts into more constructive relations between states, peoples and groups. Others failed utterly and remained signatures on paper with no effect in the lives of human beings exposed to the dangers of warfare. There is, consequently, a need to understand conflict resolution in a new way. It is not enough for the outside world to ask for negotiations and contacts between warring parties. There is also a need to suggest what the parties should discuss, how they may agree, how agreements can be made a reality and, not least, how settlements can be made to endure so that new generations can be raised without repeating bitter war experiences. It is, furthermore, important to ask what can be learned for effective conflict prevention, allowing for just aspirations to develop without systematic and deliberate violence.

In the early 1990s knowledge in conflict resolution for war conditions was limited. There was considerable insight in negotiations in domestic political affairs, the art of deal-making. Understanding was generated from societies and conditions, which involved little violence and war. It referred to situations of shared values and norms, where few cultural borders were transgressed. However, conflict resolution takes on an entirely different dimension when parties have been trying to kill each other. In the management of conflict between employers and employees there is the threat of strikes and lockouts. This is not the same as when negotiators, their families, relatives, friends and colleagues have been under armed attack by the other side. Involving issues of life and death, war is a qualitatively different form of conflict. Negotiation and peacemaking in ending wars can learn from other experiences but face unique problems. The issues at hand – the incompatibilities – are central to such an analysis and are likely to concern major questions of society and its direction. Also crucial are the ways to end the fighting. This has to be done without inviting a repetition of war. It also has to meet standards of justice and, at the same time, provide physical security for the opposing sides. There is a need to compensate for sufferings that cannot be compensated or redressed. Norms of human relations have been violently broken, leaving the difficult task of finding sufficiently shared grounds on which to build a new relationship. There is the requirement that the opposing sides be equally committed to viewing an agreement as *theirs*, and to taking responsibility for implementing it under conditions which may be novel to the society. Thus, there are reasons for analysts to believe that peacemaking after war is a losing proposition. Still, it takes place and it seems to be working. How this is possible is what this book is all about.

Only in the early 1990s did the world start seriously to attend to peacemaking after war. During the Cold War, negotiations and agreements on issues that involved the use of weapons were few and limited. There was a peace agreement on Indochina in 1954, but, like its successor in 1973, it was quickly undermined. There were also settlements between India and Pakistan after the 1965 and 1971 wars, achieving a reduction in tension, but not an end to the incompatibility. The emphasis in the major power confrontation of the time, the Cold War, was victory, not compromise. The ideological components and the historical record made the Cold War an existential battle. It was waged between right and wrong, democracy and dictatorship, capitalism and socialism, liberation and imperialism. Compromise was seen as morally questionable. The same attitude was reflected in other disputes of the period, whether related to the Cold War or not.

There were reasons for this aversion to negotiated resolution. The memory of the flawed and failed agreement at Munich in September 1938 haunted some of the actors. At that time, the democratic countries (Britain and France) agreed with a totalitarian one (Nazi Germany) on the dissolution, rather than the protection, of a small, democratic country, Czechoslovakia. Even so, Hitler chose not to honour the agreement. It became part of a rapid series of developments towards major war. To Western leaders it showed the futility of compromising with dictatorships. Appeasement became a synonym for negotiations. The Soviet leadership may have drawn similar conclusions from its deal with Nazi Germany in August 1939, the agreement that made the Second World War inevitable. Although it aimed at preventing a war between the two, by dividing influence in Eastern Europe and the Baltic region, Germany attacked the Soviet Union less than two years later. Thus, both sides in the Cold War that followed the joint defeat of Nazi Germany could agree on the dangers of making peace with an opponent. For both, the conclusion was that lasting peace required solid victory. Consequently, there were few agreements on political issues in conflict in the decades that followed.

It is, then, remarkable to find that negotiations were still possible in a particular sphere: arms control and disarmament. There were agreements banning nuclear weapons tests, restricting the production of missiles, and even eliminating whole categories of weaponry. These negotiations aimed to reduce the risk of inadvertent war between the major powers, without settling their fundamental incompatibilities. This was an effort at conflict management, making sure the relationships between the major powers would not unintentionally get out of hand. In spite of this, the Cold War continually led to new crises. Basic distrust and confrontation, though contained from becoming nuclear conflict, guided the leaderships. All other types of conflict were allowed: wars were waged by proxy, in secret, as interventions. The danger of local conflicts escalating into nuclear war was an element of most serious analysis. An important Cold War lesson is that the reduction of weaponry has limited value in conflict resolution. After all, the 'political' issues involved in forming the conflict are primary, and weapons are used to pursue such interests. Conflict management can help to reduce the dangers of crisis, creating some confidence and lessening (potential or actual) suffering. Conflict resolution is more ambitious as it tries to affect the basic issues, the incompatibilities that direct the conflicting parties. This book is devoted to this difficult and delicate material.

1.2 Peace Research and Conflict Resolution

Conflict resolution is approached on the basis of the insights generated in contemporary peace research. This means drawing conclusions from the study of causes of war, issues of disarmament and arms control, and conflict dynamics. This involves quantitative and qualitative studies. Although conflict resolution in armed conflict has been part of the peace research agenda, it has yet to develop a consistent set of research-based propositions. The methodological approach taken by most scholars today is comparative. History-oriented methods have dominated. Systematic quantitative research has begun to emerge. The basis for this book is, consequently, not a consolidated set of insights on which strategies work or why agreements endure. Rather, it brings together plausible understandings which, it is hoped, help to highlight policy dilemmas and further more study.

Peace research, like any other field of inquiry that deals with societal affairs, is, of course, coloured by major historical changes and events. Peace research, with its ambition to understand the causes of violence and to find ways to reduce/remove violence, has been sensitive to such changes. Sometimes they have constituted challenges to the existing research paradigms, thus leading to new fields of inquiry. At other times, the historical developments have confirmed the importance of the existing agenda. Either way, the dialogue with realities remains a constant feature. As can be seen from Table 1.1, peace research has developed agendas resting on the traumatic experiences of the past century, but also from hopeful developments that are integral to the flow of events (Wallensteen 2001b, 2011a, 2011b).

Table 1.1 identifies 17 major themes that have served to enlarge the agenda of what was originally a limited topic. Peace research arose as a

Table 1.1 Traumas and hopes forming the agenda of peace research

Event		Understanding of event	Peace research topics
First World War	**Trauma**	Loss of crisis control, 1914	History, causes of war
League of Nations	*Hope*	Aggression, need for rules	International law
Second World War	**Trauma**	Again, lost control	Strategic study v. peace research
Hiroshima	**Trauma**	Science used for war	Disarmament, arms control
Gandhi in India	*Hope*	Use of non-violent means	History, cases of non-violence
United Nations	*Hope*	International cooperation	International organization
Holocaust	**Trauma**	Genocide, ethnic violence	Human and collective rights
Cold War	**Trauma**	Danger of polarization, escalation	Conflict theory, gaming
European Unity	*Hope*	Overcoming enmity	Integration and democracy theory
Vietnam War	**Trauma**	Dependence, imperialism	Structural violence
Totalitarian dissidents	*Hope*	Popular moves for democracy	NGOs, popular attitudes
Détente	*Hope*	Confidence-building	Cooperation, common themes
Environmental threats	**Trauma**	Hope or cause of conflict	Scarcity, conflict and cooperation
Bosnia	**Trauma**	Ethnic identities as element	Ethnic security dilemmas
Peacemaking	*Hope*	Ending of wars	Conflict resolution and peacebuilding
Emancipation	*Hope*	Gender and peace	Gender as variable/paradigm
September 11, 2001	**Trauma**	Terrorism	Pre-emption v. human security

field devoted to understanding the causes of war by systematic analyses of the historical experiences of war. Pioneering studies integrated many dimensions, notably the works of Pitirim Sorokin (1937) and Quincy Wright (1942). The causes of war remain, to this day, fundamental questions for peace research. The solution to the problem of the origins of war has since then been enlarged to involve a vast array of analytical questions. Table 1.1 indicates how such issues have come to take a central role.

There are almost equal numbers of traumatic and negative experiences and hopes, creative events that point to new possibilities. The *traumas* are connected with human suffering on a large scale affecting many parts of the world. The same is true for the *hopes*, which are not only isolated events, but also developments that have drawn global attention. The common feature of traumas and hopes is that they both challenge conventional wisdom and, thus, result in breaks in trends, or even paradigm shifts. The traumas suggest limits to established thinking that clearly have to be overcome, and where research can play a role in the process. The hopes suggest that reality offers many surprises. Some of them stem from theoretical thoughts of 'utopian' character, which 'suddenly' take material forms. This closeness of reality to research is a feature of social science in general but, in peace research, a culture of openness and willingness to challenge one's assumptions has been particularly central.

Certainly, none of the topics mentioned in Table 1.1 is exclusive to peace research. In spite of a vigorous development, peace research *per se* continues to be organizationally distinct and a financially limited field of the full study of war and peace, international relations, foreign policy, sociology, economics, international law, etc. Many of the topics mentioned as subjects for peace research are administratively and intellectually embraced in other disciplines. The debate during the Cold War, positing strategic studies against peace research, subsided, but re-emerged in a softer form following September 11, 2001. More comprehensive concepts of security are common on both sides, and their shared understanding has increased to the point where there is today little necessity to draw a sharp line. If there is one, however, it has to do with the close connection to political decision-making in leading countries and views of the use of force. The calculated use of violence remains, as a strategy, alien to peace research. The idea is instead to search, as far as is possible, for 'peace with peaceful means' (Galtung 1996). War-fighting strategies are not likely to be developed at peace research institutions. Even so, the ideas of an international responsibility to protect populations exposed to the risk of genocide or ethnic persecution are debated in peace research institutions, but without the formulation of practical strategies for such operations. This fits, however, with the broader concern of human security as a means of reducing the risk of future terrorism.

Conflict resolution, as Table 1.1 makes clear, is a more recent concept. It certainly has roots, as evidenced by the reference to international law, conflict theory, cooperation and integration. During the 1990s it has taken on a new, more significant and central meaning. Systematic study is found only from the middle of the 1980s, and the literature has grown in recent years. There certainly are – as will be seen throughout this book – mixed experiences in the field. Collecting such lessons, systematizing and making them explicit, is a way to move forward. This book aims at understanding when peace agreements are likely to become durable settlements. This requires an analysis of different types of conflict. Agreements, it will be argued, are particularly dependent on the central issues of contention, the incompatibilities. Furthermore, emphasis will be given to the significance of the ways agreements are derived, as the processes themselves can explain some of the agreements, but also are important for assessing their durability. In addition, it is important to observe the interconnections between conflicts in the same region and the role of the international community. The analysis builds on the conflict resolution agreements concluded after the Cold War but also draws on general theories of conflict, negotiation and mediation. It is a book reporting on a record, in a way which is hoped will stimulate practice as well as research in the field.

1.3 Defining Conflict Resolution

Before we can proceed further, there is a need to establish a preliminary definition of conflict resolution. The definition will be discussed in more detail in Chapter 2. A distinction between conflict management and conflict resolution has already been cited. We have also mentioned the recent phenomenon of peace agreements. Peace agreements are an integral part of conflict resolution. Without some form of agreement among the conflicting parties, it is hard to talk about conflict resolution. However, an agreement, even if implemented, may not be sufficient to establish a durable peace. Peace requires more than an agreement among the parties. The peace agreement is, however, a necessary step to a lasting arrangement. Thus, we can preliminarily define conflict resolution as a situation *where the conflicting parties enter into an agreement that solves their central incompatibilities, accept each other's continued existence as parties and cease all violent action against each other*. This means, of course, that conflict resolution is something that necessarily comes after conflict. It means that we first need to have concepts and tools for the analysis of conflict. This is what conflict theory is all about. Conflict resolution in the context of conflict theory is the theme of Chapter 2.

Let us scrutinize key elements in this definition. The *agreement* is normally a formal understanding, a document signed under more or less solemn conditions. However, there can be more informal, implicit understandings worked out between the parties. Such agreements may exist in secret documents, for instance, a crucial promise made as a precondition for the formal arrangements, or as deals about which the parties have been more or less explicit. Many cases are likely to see as much dispute around such informal understandings as over the formalized documents. Furthermore, such informal pacts require considerable trust between the parties. They are, most likely, not made without there being a formal arrangement. Thus, the formal document is important for any peace process.

The definition talks about the parties accepting *each other's continued existence as parties*. This is an important element as it distinguishes a peace agreement from an agreement of capitulation. An agreement of capitulation is the strongest agreed expression of victory and defeat. It means that one side lays down its struggle, dissolves its organization, departs from the disputed territory and, in short, ceases to be an actor of influence and significance. An example is a withdrawal agreement. This is an arrangement where one side agrees to remove its troops from an area of dispute and where this is the only matter the agreement regulates. The withdrawing party is not likely, however, to see it as a matter of capitulation, although the essence of the agreement is to end that party's participation in the conflict. An example is the Soviet withdrawal from Afghanistan that was agreed in 1988 and implemented by 1989. It ended the dominant role of the Soviet Union in internal Afghan affairs. Another example is the resignation of a party leader from the government, where he/she also leaves the country. This was the case with the departure of Charles Taylor from Liberia in 2003, thus ending a civil war and opening a chance for long-term peacebuilding in the war-torn country. Lately, there have also been victories without agreements or acts of capitulation. The USA declared the defeat of Iraq to be 'one victory in a war on terror', on May 1, 2003. The government of Sri Lanka won over the Tamil Tigers in May 2009, without a formal consent (i.e. capitulation) from the losing party.

However, the conflict resolution agreements of interest here are more complex. Peace agreements refer to documents in which the fighting parties accept each other also as parties in future dealings with one another. It means that nobody wins all that there is to win, but no one loses all that there is to lose. Such arrangements are more difficult to maintain, no doubt, but they are more frequent than perhaps recognized at first. Of course, the word 'accept' in the definition does not imply that the parties agree to everything or that they like each other. It only means that they accept the other as much as they need for the agreement to be implemented by the opposing sides.

The formulation that the parties *cease all violent action against each other* is most important. Many times it is part of the same treaty but it can be done as a separate undertaking. Often the cessation of violence is made public at about the same time as the peace agreement is concluded. To the public at large, it means that the war ends and the dangers of being killed are reduced. Sometimes, however, cease-fire agreements can precede the actual conclusion of the agreement regulating the incompatibilities between the parties. There is debate whether cease-fires should precede, be simultaneous with, or come after the more political agreements. There are a number of truce agreements that have lasted a long time, without resulting in peace accords. The armistice lines drawn in 1949 separating Israel from its Arab neighbours were used in the agreements with Egypt 30 years later. The same territorial divisions are relevant for a final agreement between Israel and Palestine. The lines have now existed for more than 60 years. The separation lines between Korea's two states in 1953 will soon reach a similarly venerable age. Perhaps an agreement will be achieved earlier on Cyprus, where the territorial divisions that are the references for today's discussions date from the war in 1974. The line separating Georgia from South Ossetia today dates to the cease-fire of 1992. Cease-fire agreements, in other words, are closer to conflict management, a way of freezing a military *status quo*, and do not necessarily result in peace efforts. It is safe to conclude that a peace agreement, solving the central incompatibilities between the parties, which does not include a simultaneous undertaking to cease fighting, is not likely to be credible. Thus, the agreements included as conflict resolution measures are those which both solve incompatibilities and end fighting.

1.4 Limits of Conflict Resolution

Conflict resolution is not necessarily identical with peace. There is considerable overlap, however, as most notions of peace are based on the *absence or ending of war*. A conflict, we have just made clear, is not resolved if it does not include an end to armed struggle. At the same time, it is not sufficient that it *only* contains the ending of fighting. Conflict resolution is more than the limited definition of peace. It is more than the absence of war. The parties are agreeing to respect each other and prepare for living together with one another. However, there are broader understandings of what peace is, such as the presence of cooperation, justice and integration. Conflict resolution may or may not include such larger values. It will depend on the situation. The preferred definition does not, a priori, include such elements. The definition is dependent on what the parties want or can agree to include. Conflict resolution may, or may not, contain broader aspects.

In the worst circumstances, a peace agreement may negate widely held values. The accords studied here have been concluded between parties with arms. They are militarily stronger than other parties in their societies. Thus, there is a danger that the agreed form of conflict resolution will contain *privileges for the armed parties*, at the expense of other interests in the society. There are many examples of this, even where persons who have been responsible for a lot of destruction take up government positions, thus becoming legal powerholders. Such developments create fear in parts of society. From a conflict resolution perspective, it is necessary to warn against such arrangements. They may contain the seeds of renewed conflict or initiate entirely new conflict dynamics. The deal, from the population's point of view, is that granting privileges will stop a war. The hope may be that these privileges can be challenged by a stronger civil society once the war is over. The conditions of peace may require new types of leadership, and thus, the hope may be borne out. A minimum conclusion is to ensure that the peace agreement does not prevent such developments; a better position is that it actually encourages it.

A question that has gained increased importance is the issue of *crimes* committed during a war, as part of the fighting or under the protection of the war. The international war crimes tribunal was set up in 1993 for the conflict in former Yugoslavia, followed by a similar tribunal for Rwanda a year later. By the summer of 1998 a fully-fledged International Criminal Court (ICC) was created through an international treaty. With enough ratifications by 2004, the ICC became operational (although the USA chose to remain outside and initially tried to reduce its international reach). The ICC is a dramatic new development. After the Second World War, war crime tribunals were set up for the responsible actors in Germany and Japan. They were not permanent institutions and war crimes were seldom pursued internationally in the following decades. The only consistent effort taken up by some countries and some non-governmental organizations was to bring to trial those involved in the Holocaust. The Cold War precluded an international consensus on the pursuit of war crimes.

Thus, only after the Cold War could a shared understanding again develop on war crimes, necessary procedures and punishments. Nevertheless, there are recent peace agreements which include different forms of amnesty to leaders and decision-makers. Amnesty has been seen as necessary by negotiators for any agreement at all to be concluded. Leaders could, in other words, protect themselves from legal procedures, the opposing sides and the legitimate anger of their own populations. Developments during the 1990s make such agreements increasingly unlikely. They are not easily accepted internationally. In that sense, conflict resolution today has become more demanding than it was immediately after the Cold War. The first indictment from the ICC concerned the leader of a rebellion in Uganda, at the same time making further negotiations for an end to the civil war more complicated. Thus, the effects of the focus on war crimes can be discussed. Some argue that it threatens to prolong conflict, as parties fearing to be brought to trial have little incentive to make agreements which endanger their own means of control. Others argue that it deters parties from getting into war in the first place, as the ICC increases the likelihood that war crimes will be pursued, thus, in the long run, preventing new wars.

Finally, we should also note that conflict resolution is not the same as complete *disarmament*. The agreement may allow the parties to retain a certain arsenal. It is likely, however, that this will be lower than what has been put to use in the war itself. The parties may, nevertheless, maintain that they need special protection. Clearly, the higher the level of protection required and agreed, the more likely it is that this creates renewed insecurity in a society. Thus, it is probable that peace agreements will only be durable if they result in some disarmament, as well as changes in all security sectors towards transparency, integrity and a professionalism that includes human rights. Particularly, disarming and demobilization need to be coupled with reintegration and rehabilitation of soldiers, not the least child soldiers. In recent years, such disarmament, demobilization and reintegration (DDR) programmes have become central efforts in peacebuilding following the ending of wars.

There are also other aspects of peace. Conflict resolution finds itself at a bridge between a very narrow concept of peace (no war) and a very broad one (justice). By leaving conflict resolution as a concept defined by the parties, it may become difficult to compare one situation to another. However, the fact is that there are increasingly established norms for the content of internationally acceptable peace agreements. International law has set some standards for conflict resolution between states. The end of the Cold War has also led to signposts for the settlement of internal conflicts: principles of democracy, human rights, criminal justice, reconciliation and economic cooperation are part of this. In this sense, an international understanding of conflict resolution is developing. It contributes to pushing the concept further in the direction of justice, or what could be termed quality peace, not simply cessation of violence.

1.5 Outlining This Book

The existing peace agreements are important inputs to this work. The analysis, however, has to start with the phenomenon that precedes any peace agreement and may eventually replace it: conflict. It requires some tools for understanding the extent of armed conflict and types of outcome. This is covered in Chapter 2, which gives information on patterns of conflict and peacemaking. Then we will go into the theoretical underpinnings, to review some of the elements of contemporary conflict theory, in order to be able to appreciate what goes into peacemaking (Chapter 3). From this, we will proceed to develop the necessary instruments for basic conflict analysis. This is done in Chapter 4, where we will see that three types of prevalent conflict, constituting a trichotomy of conflict, require different types of agreement. This completes Part One. In Part Two the peace agreements since the end of the Cold War, as well as previous experiences, are married to this structure to show how the distinctions serve to highlight features of consequence for durable agreements (Chapters 5, 6 and 7). Part Three examines particularly complex issues in conflict analysis. These relate to the linkages between different conflicts into conflict complexes, within regions, with or without major power involvement (Chapter 8). In Chapter 9 the roles of the United Nations in conflict resolution are assessed. Finally, in Chapter 10, the new action communities, conflict prevention, mediation and structural changes for reducing armed conflict are discussed.

Further Readings

Go to the *Understanding Conflict Resolution* web page at www.sagepub.co.uk for free access to journal articles listed.

Galtung, J. 1964. 'An Editorial', *Journal of Peace Research*, 1 (1): 1–4.
Galtung, J. 1969. 'Violence, Peace and Peace Research', *Journal of Peace Research*, 6 (3): 167–91.
Galtung, J. 1971. 'A Structural Theory of Imperialism', *Journal of Peace Research*, 8 (2): 81–117.
Höglund, K. and Söderberg Kovacs, M. 2010. 'Beyond the Absence of War: The Diversity of Peace in Post-Settlement Societies', *Review of International Studies*, 36 (2): 367–90.
Kant, I. 1795. *Perpetual Peace: A Philosophical Sketch*.
Machiavelli, N. 1532. *The Prince*.
More, T. 1516. *Utopia*.
Wallensteen, P. 2011. 'The Origins of Contemporary Peace Research', in K. Höglund and M. Öberg (eds), *Understanding Peace Research*. London: Routledge. pp. 14–32.
Wallensteen, P. 2011. *Peace Research: Theory and Practice*. London: Routledge. pp. 4–22.

ARMED CONFLICTS AND PEACE AGREEMENTS 2

2.1 The Concept of Conflict

A strong statement is that conflicts *are* solvable. This is not necessarily an idealistic or optimistic position. As this book will show, it is a realistic proposition. Most actors in conflicts will find themselves in need of negotiations at one time or another. Even if a conflict results in war and destruction, there may have been other options and alternative paths for the conflict. There are frequent statements on the inevitability of conflict, violence and war. Indeed, finding solutions may often be difficult. This difficulty not only arises out of political constraints, but can also be due to a lack of insight or imagination. There are also views of the desirability and even necessity of violence and war. Unbearable conditions or overwhelming threats may make such opinions understandable. Too often, however, the results of war negate the very hope for a better future that may initially have motivated the war. Few wars follow the paths anticipated by the actors. Short wars may avoid such pitfalls, but who is to guarantee that a war will be short? Many wars have started from this premise. Afterwards, it will be asked: were all avenues used to find a peaceful solution prior to the initiation of war? Only after this can be convincingly proven do the arguments of inevitability and desirability approach validity. The determined search for a solution is not only a moral question; it is also a rational one. This is the sole way in which a free society will be prepared to accept the strains of war. Indeed, if conflicts are exposed to such early challenges, solutions may actually be found, even in unexpected situations. Thus, conflicts are solvable and there are many and varied experiences of such solutions.

If conflicts *are* solvable is it also true that conflicts – sooner or later – *will be* solved? Clearly, once a conflict has developed into a war the options are fewer. At that moment, the primary actors will pursue victory rather than a joint solution. The victory of one side over the other is, then, a possible outcome, even to the point of the other's capitulation, dissolution and disappearance as an actor. The record shows that this is what happens in some conflicts, but by no means all. Conflicts will come to an end at some point. Whether that ending is a solution, a victory or a stalemate has to be scrutinized. To this should be added the question of whether the conflict is likely again to be armed and violent.

Victory is the outcome preferred by most actors. If achieved, it may solve parts of an issue, but often not the entire problem at hand. The victory of the allied countries over Nazi Germany is a case in point. After the failure of the agreement reached in Munich in 1938, it was no longer possible for the Western powers to consider negotiations with Adolf Hitler and the Nazi regime. The end of the Second World War meant the implementation of the demand for unconditional surrender and the elimination of the Nazis as an actor. This was as clear-cut a victory as can be. It did not, however, mean the end of Germany. The issue of Germany's position in the international system still had to be settled. Conflict among the victors arose over this question. It became one of the few core issues in the Cold War. A solution developed as new leaders emerged in West Germany. They were democratically inclined, conscientiously building on pre-1933 democratic traditions and new ideas from the Western powers. A reintegration of Germany into the international system took place, ultimately even allowing for its reunification in 1990, but only 45 years after the end of the Second World War. It was only possible with a new Germany, willing to admit its responsibility for the past and able to accommodate to the present. If the Second World War had been a question solely of Germany's role in the international system, there was a route through peaceful dialogue and development. A solution within a democratic framework among democratic countries was found. It could have been found before the Nazis took power. For any country, there are, in other words, always alternatives to a war strategy for achieving goals. Regimes, however, may deliberately narrow their options and construct situations where the choice becomes defeat or victory. Nazi Germany chose such a path.

Conflict precedes conflict resolution. There is already considerable analysis of the origin and the pursuit of conflict. Machiavelli and Clausewitz are important writers in one Western tradition of conflict analysis. Adam Smith and Karl Marx offered competition and class analysis as other tools for understanding. In classical Chinese discourse Sun Tzu is a central writer, as is Kautilya in India or Ibn Khaldun in the Arab world. Military-strategic thinking has become universally shared, and there is often, among military officers, a surprising degree of common understanding across battle lines. Also, the analysis of societal contradiction has such cross-cultural traits, Smith and Marx being influential in different quarters across the globe. The same, however, is not true for conflict resolution thinking. It is a novel topic. It is less developed and less coherent. Thus, it is important to introduce the ideas of modern thinkers. It is also necessary to relate them to trends of social science thinking.

'Conflict' has many meanings in everyday life. To some it refers to *behaviour* or *action*. There is conflict when a trade union goes on strike or an employer locks out its employees. It is also conflict when two states are at war with one another, and where battlefield events determine their relations. The actions constitute the conflict. If this were all, however, it would mean that a conflict ends once this behaviour ends. Few would agree to this. A cease-fire is not the end of a conflict. Even the cession of verbal statements, non-violent actions, the mobilization of petitions, demonstrations, boycotts and sanctions may only indicate that there is an interlude in the conflict. Actions may resume at some later stage. There may still be dissatisfaction. Obviously, conflict is more than the behaviour of the parties.

A closer look indicates that the parties in an industrial dispute will not cease their actions until there is some movement on the issues which sparked the dispute. The 'issue' refers to the incompatible positions taken by the parties, motivating their actions. This, then, is a deeper understanding of what a conflict is. It contains a severe disagreement between at least two sides, where their demands cannot be met by the same resources at the same time. This is an *incompatibility*. Positions are incompatible. There is some form of scarcity. If there is an abundance of resources, the demands from the various sides may easily be met. The incompatibility can be solved. If there are limited resources, however, problems will arise. The easy solutions are no longer available and more ingenious ways have to be found. How this can be done will be discussed later. For the time being it is sufficient to note that when the parties adjust their demands so that there is no longer scarcity, the conflict disappears. The incompatible demands have been handled. Incompatibility appears to be a key to the existence of conflict. If there are no actions, although it is possible for an outsider to point to incompatibilities, there is a latent conflict. Manifest conflict requires both action and incompatibility.

This is still not enough to get an initial understanding of the concept of conflict. We need to include the actors as well. Many would say that trade unions are created by employees to deal with an existing incompatibility from a stronger position, which may result in conflict. This is why they have a membership. Members expect to be protected even to the point where a manifest conflict becomes a distinct possibility. This means that there is a tension built into the relationship between the employer and the employees. 'Conflict' does exist, even if there are no actions taken or demands formulated. The conflict is internal to the system. Similar descriptions can be found for the interstate system. It is argued that sovereign states are inevitably locked into conflict with one another. States are continuously preparing to defend themselves from possible attack in order to protect their own survival. Such preparations only confirm to others that there are real dangers, thus they do the same. These are the dynamics of the well-known security dilemma (Herz 1950; Waltz 1959, 1979). This perspective suggests that the existence of one state is a danger to any other state. As long as there is unpredictability in the system, there will be fear and, thus, conflict. For our purposes it means that *actors* or *parties* are fundamental for conflict to exist. If the actors are formed, and if they make an analysis where their needs for survival are in conflict with others, then there is conflict built into the system. The history of the actors, the actors' understanding of their own role and their resources are important elements in conflict analysis. From this we can conclude that conflict consists of three components: incompatibility, action and actors. Combining them, we arrive at a complete definition of a conflict as *a social situation in which a minimum of two actors (parties) strive to acquire at the same moment in time an available set of scarce resources*. This definition brings together essential elements from a number of commonly used definitions. It includes the actors or 'parties' in the definition which, as we have just seen, is basic. In many definitions the actor is left as a separate item. However, the preceding arguments make clear that it is integral to the analysis and to the definition.

The word 'strive' in the defining sentence requires a comment. It is a vague term, but the point is that when the parties are acting, they are doing something (however minimal) to acquire the resources. 'Strive' may even include warfare. It covers a wide range of activities.

An additional phrase needs some reflection. It is said that the parties are striving to acquire the resources 'at the same moment in time'. This is sometimes overlooked in definitions and may, again, be self-evident. If one actor is satisfied with having its demands met a year from now, other actors may be able to meet their goals today. There is no conflict today. Perhaps the first actor will worry for the future – will there be anything left? – but if the party believes it has guarantees, the incompatibility is gone. It is clearly a different matter when the demands are geared to the same moment in time. It is conventional wisdom that only one person can be prime minister at a time and that only one country can have formal jurisdiction over a particular piece of territory at a time. These resources are regarded as indivisible, for the time being. If this is what the parties believe, then this is their reality. In actual life there are solutions even to such problems, for instance, the creation of posts as first and second prime minister (as in Cambodia in the 1990s) or finding forms of shared rule for a territory. Such solutions emerge only if the parties perceive an incompatibility to be divisible. Time, as we notice every day, is scarce but still has this quality of divisibility, something that our calendars make clear. Schedules may dissolve incompatibilities.

The notion of an 'available set of scarce resources' should not be taken to include only economic matters. The term 'resources' covers all kinds of positions that are of interest to an actor. To be a prime minister, to control a particular piece of territory, to be able to propagate a particular idea in the media can all be covered by the notion of 'available resources'. This definition demands that something is desired which is scarce, be it positions of power, attractive land, or access to airwaves. Such resources can sometimes be estimated in money, square metres or other measures, but often they are intangible. For instance, demands for recognition, acceptance of responsibility for destructive actions or psychological retribution exemplify intangible values. They are still highly important. They may involve admissions that have implications for an actor's standing nationally or internationally, but only indirectly relate to material resources. Thus, there are incompatibilities relating to matters of justice, moral norms and guilt.

Hopefully, with the conflict concept clarified, we move to the most difficult of all conflicts: wars. They are different from all other conflicts in that they are irreversible actions. Wars involve the taking of territory, the eviction of inhabitants, the death of soldiers and civilians, the destruction of property, resources and the environment, and the disruption of people's mental, physical, economic and cultural development. War is among the most destructive phenomena that one human group can inflict on another. In the same category of extreme conflict we can also locate systematic repression, totalitarianism and genocide. These are actions initiated by human beings. These are matters that can be ended and remedied by humans, but not undone. They become strong and conscious elements in the history of peoples, groups and individuals. Let us first look more closely at the exact meaning of war and then proceed to study recent trends in armed conflict and war.

2.2 Identifying Armed Conflict

Three projects

A commonly asked question is whether conflict and war have become more frequent and are more destructive today than they used to be. It is a question about quantity, where it is assumed that conflicts are easily comparable. The question is asked to reach an understanding of where the world is headed, as a whole, for a particular region or for a particular phenomenon (for instance, arms production). It is often a question about the future, not only about history. At the same time, there are those who resent having 'their' conflict compared to other situations. Each conflict is unique and has its own characteristics. There are qualities which make them different. The question of frequency makes little sense to those who are parties in conflict. Why should they worry, it is bad enough with one conflict, they would say.

Both perspectives are valid. The projects that exist within the peace research community all aim at understanding why conflicts occur or how they can be terminated. Their answers to the questions of frequency of wars are actually by-products of other ambitions. The questions are nevertheless important and contribute to the development of deeper answers. If there are general patterns recurring over a large number of different conflicts, it suggests something that can possibly explain why wars begin. By implication, it may yield ideas for improving the situation. Certain factors can be singled out for closer analysis. Questions of frequency interest the media and the public for other reasons. Today, it is frequently asked if there is a difference between the post-Cold War years and the Cold War period, or before/after September 11, 2001. Changes in the international system or in domestic policies, associated with the ending of this confrontation, may explain our present predicament. There are many other candidates for possible causation, however, and the impact of each may be difficult to disentangle. In the analysis, many factors are mentioned, such as bipolarity, the deterrent effect of nuclear weapons, the changed roles of international organizations, democratization, the spread of free market mechanisms, changes in media access, concern for human rights, the growth of non-governmental organizations, etc. Comparisons across time can illustrate a number of effects. However, they do not necessarily prove them. To be scientific, evidence, cases and periods have to be selected with rigour and there have to be many observations. For the purpose of this book, it is important to have a general idea of the frequency and severity of armed conflicts in the world. It helps to set the topics of conflict resolution in perspective. Thus, let us review some ongoing efforts.

Armed conflict patterns are mapped continuously by several projects. This book uses the work of the Uppsala Conflict Data Program, based at the Department of Peace and Conflict Research, Uppsala University, in Sweden. Data are published by the department in the annual publication *States in Armed Conflict*. Information is also available through the yearbooks of the Stockholm International Peace Research Institute (SIPRI) (for major armed conflicts in the last ten years); the *Journal of Peace Research* (*JPR*); from the International Peace Research Institute, Oslo (PRIO) (all armed conflicts, backdated to 1946); the *Human Security Report* (from the Simon Fraser University); and, most fully, through accessing the Uppsala Conflict Data Program itself and its database (www.ucdp.uu.se).

Second, there is the project on wars and armed conflict by the Causes of War project at the University of Hamburg (AKUF, from its name in German), mapping the global record of local wars since 1945. This is also published in annual reports and books (Gantzel and Schwinghammer 2000). The third enduring project is the Correlates of War project (known as COW), originating at the University of Michigan, Ann Arbor, Michigan, carrying information on wars since 1816. This information is normally available in the form of datasets, sometimes also in printed publications (Sarkees and Wayman 2010). It has found a wide usage in research projects and the findings have been systematized (Geller and Singer 1998; Vasquez 2000). There are additional important projects that aim to highlight the present dilemmas of war and violence. Among these is the Minorities at Risk project, University of Maryland, College Park, Maryland, focusing on a subset of conflict: those involving ethnic minorities around the world. It contains data for minority groups which have been involved in some form of conflict since 1945. From this has also developed a biannual report on peace and conflict (Gurr 1993, 2000a; Marshall 1999; Marshall and Gurr 2005). Crisis behaviour between states can also be used to discuss questions of frequency (Brecher 1993). A number of researchers have their own systematic collections of conflict-related information which are reported in international journals (Bercovitch 1996; Carment 1993; Carment and James 1995; Gibler 1999a, 1999b; Goldstein 1992; Holsti 1991; Levy 1983; Licklider 1995; Luard 1986; Morton and Starr 2001; Tillema 1989). For an update, see the conflict project directory by Kristine Eck, the Uppsala Conflict Data Program (Eck 2005, www.ucdp.uu.se). The annual *Human Security Report* makes use of these and other sources.

The first three projects stand out, however, as the most consistent specifically addressing armed conflicts of all categories, whether between or within states. They contain additional information which is useful for theorizing on the war phenomenon. Two are oriented towards understanding the causes of conflict, as can be surmised from their names (the Hamburg and Michigan projects). One deals specifically with conflict resolution (the Uppsala project). What, then, do they tell us about trends in armed conflict and war?

The question is simple but requires an understanding of key definitions before an answer can be given. The definitions of conflict and war guide the types of information any project will collect. Potentially, conflict data projects can show different global tendencies, depending on what categories of conflict they focus on. The comparability, in other words, can be limited. Furthermore, there are several criteria that have to be met for a conflict dataset to be reliable. First, it must have a definition that is sufficiently general to go beyond what is important only to a particular period in history. The definitions in these projects meet these criteria: they do not vary with time or with the phenomena studied. The projects may still be relevant for other concerns as well. For instance, although ethnic conflict is not used as a category in these three projects, it is possible to retrieve information from them which is relevant for the study of ethnic conflict. They have, for example, separate categories of internal war. In this way, the projects cover a wider range of conflict than does, for instance, the Minorities at Risk project.

Second, there has to be a definition that captures conflict between as well as within states. It means that it has to tap the general issue of violence, cutting across particular legal categories. This allows for an understanding of war beyond the category of interstate events. Clearly, data on interstate conflicts are more easily compiled. What two states do to one another that might lead to war is of interest to the surrounding community as well. Thus, such disputes will have more attention. Conflicts inside a state, however, are not as likely to immediately affect neighbours, thus threatening to make the international recording of such conflicts more sporadic. A full study might require intimate knowledge of all countries in the world. Thus, it still has to be the ambition to include *all* conflicts. This is a third criterion which is necessary if changes in armed conflict over time are to be discussed meaningfully. Fourth, the definitions have to be precise, so as to guide data collection (operationalization) and delimit a particular conflict in time and space (beginning, ending) from other conflicts. Finally, the data must be open to scrutiny by other researchers.

The Michigan and Hamburg projects

The Michigan project is the oldest and serves as a reference point for many projects. It was initiated in the middle of the 1960s by J. David Singer and Melvin Small and is still maintained, something which is an achievement in itself. It has now turned into an inter-university cooperation programme and is physically located in Pennsylvania State University. Since 2005 Paul Diehl, University of Illinois, Urbana, is the Director. It contains data on wars since 1816 and its record is constantly updated. A major review has been undertaken during the 2000s, resulting in a more consistent war definition and, thus, a more coherent list of wars (Sarkees and Wayman 2010).

Basic to COW is the delineation of an international system consisting of states. Thus, wars are conflicts between states where at least two are members of the international system. In addition, there are extra-systemic conflicts ('extra-state wars') between one system member and another entity (such as colonial and liberation wars). Furthermore, there are intra-state conflicts where most of the military action takes place within a state that is a member of the system ('intra-state wars'). Innovatively, COW has now also included a category of wars between non-state actors ('non-state wars'). For all conflicts there is the requirement of 1,000 battle-related fatalities. COW also now has included the parties' motives for engaging in war, thus borrowing a feature from the Uppsala Conflict Data Program, however, it is only applied to the category of intra-state wars. For the period 1816–2007, COW reports 95 interstate wars, 163 extra-state wars, 335 intra-state wars and 62 non-state wars (Sarkees and Wayman 2010: 75–7, 193–7, 337–46, 485–7). It therefore identifies a total of 655 wars for the period, meaning an average of more than three wars of some kind starting somewhere in the world every year. War, in other words, is shown to be a pervasive and global phenomenon.

The Hamburg project was initiated by Istvan Kende in Budapest. It was later modified and developed at the University of Hamburg, through the efforts of Klaus Jürgen Gantzel. Its results are different. Its definition does not require that a party be a member in the international system for a conflict to be included. The AKUF project, however, has the criterion that a state should be the actor on one side in a conflict. The actors should have, at a minimum, central command and practical control over the fighting. It is also stipulated that there has to be a measure of continuity in battle. There is no requirement for a particular number of deaths, which is an important consideration in the Michigan project (and in the Uppsala project as well, as we shall see). The Hamburg project, in fact, regards this criterion as a questionable indicator for practical, theoretical and ethical reasons. For instance, it is argued that information on deaths is unreliable and that there is no reason to include only those who have died from battle, but not those who have suffered from other consequences of the war (Gantzel and Meyer-Stamer 1986: 4–5; Jung et al. 1996: 52). Instead, the 'continuity' in the struggle is decisive for inclusion of a particular conflict. This criterion, of course, results in a problem of judging continuity in a reliable way.

These criteria mean that AKUF covers a broader set of cases than COW. The project has data on all wars since 1945. For the period to 2007, the project reported 238 wars (AKUF webpages www. sozialwiss.uni hamburg. de/publish/Ipw/Akuf/kriege_archiv.htm, accessed on August 31, 2010). On average this gives almost four new wars per year. The effect of the definitions can be seen more clearly by comparing the years where the projects overlap and where the state is an actor in the conflict. For the same period, COW reports 38 interstate wars, 23 extra-state wars and 118 intra-state wars, a total of 179 wars. It gives an average of close to three new wars per year. The two projects clearly overlap, but still AKUF reports more activity. It could mean that the projects do not include the same major conflicts, although this should not have such a strong impact, as the number is limited. More likely is that many armed conflicts are below the threshold of 1,000 battle-related deaths. As would be expected, a considerable number of conflicts with lower intensity levels are not covered in the COW project.

In its studies of a separate category of conflicts, militarized interstate disputes, COW has accumulated information, which corrects for this effect. This category, which is also of great theoretical significance, covers relations between states. It includes more confined events, such as military interventions, limited wars and threats of war. Together with the war data, this gives a more comprehensive picture for relations between states. There is no record, however, in the COW project of militarized disputes *within* states. For both projects, internal or civil conflicts take up a large percentage of all events recorded. To develop a definition that parallels militarized interstate disputes for intra-state conditions is a cumbersome task. A very large number of episodes would have to be scrutinized for possible inclusion. It would, needless to say, be difficult to make a global comparison, as unbiased information is harder to obtain the more limited the episodes are. For instance, threats to use force in internal affairs may involve military as well as police forces. Such threats can also be issued by opposition groups with limited credibility and representativity. Thus, drawing the lines of inclusion will require additional distinctions. It is, however, possible to do, for instance, by relying on data on human rights violations or other indicators of repression.

Both AKUF and COW are oriented to searching for the origins of violent conflict. The difference in approach is partly a reflection of distinct theoretical concerns. COW focuses on understanding interstate conflict, and particularly aims at questioning or modifying so-called realist thinking. This means it is designed to understand factors such as the balance of power, military capabilities, interdependence and other variables of importance for the working of the international system. There is, deliberately, no coherent theoretical perspective guiding the project. Instead, there is a conscious methodological approach. Reality, as expressed in the data, will speak for itself. It shows how the world actually functions: correlations are important, thus the name of the project. This is an empirical approach, where theory development will build on what has been proven to be repeated and verified ways in which states really behave. Theoretical assumptions that are common in realist thinking are tested against observable patterns of conduct. An advantage with this open position is that it also makes COW data useful for other purposes. The concepts and their operationalization are explicit and simple, constructed to reflect world developments over close to 200 years. COW's information has been used for very different investigations. For instance, there is research on whether arms races lead to war (this can be studied by using the militarized disputes and comparing them to the war data, with the original work done by Michael Wallace in 1979 and Diehl in 1983). The data are also used for analysis of the hypothesis on peace among democratic states, resulting in the much debated democratic peace proposition (a large number of articles is devoted to this puzzle, the early phases of which were crystallized in work by Bruce Russett in 1993 (see also Russett and Oneal 2001).

The Hamburg project departs from a fairly coherent theoretical approach. It relates the onset of war to the development of capitalist societies, and sees conflict as a result of the new forms of production, monetarization of the economy and the resulting dissolution of traditional forms of social integration. The large number of conflicts in the Third World fits with this relationship. As the project reports that there is an increasing frequency of conflicts since 1945, researchers also conclude that 'the contradictions in world society are increasing'. In an interesting twist, relevant here, the authors point out that even a phenomenon such as 'ethnic' conflict is a result of processes in 'which all social mechanisms that previously allowed us to live together are destroyed' (Jung et al. 1996: 52–61). In other words, conflict resolution instruments are being eliminated and this makes armed conflict more frequent. The issue of such social breakdown has lately captured considerable attention, with the term 'state failure' as a central concept (Esty et al. 1998; Zartman 1995b, 2000a, 2000b; more on this in Section 6.5 below).

This perspective points to the difference between the two projects. The Correlates of War project departs from the notion of a system that consists of a larger number of independent states. It is a system that does not have central institutions and lacks means to maintain or enforce decisions for all. Thus, it is a picture of an uncoordinated world that is the point of departure. In this world, states maintain some predictability through their actions. When war breaks out, it is not the result of an international society breaking down, as there is no assumption about such a society in the first place. The problem is found in the strategies for survival used by different states. War is a result of failed choices, but also the conditions which make it difficult for states to pursue other options. In some writings inspired by the project, the importance of norms comes forth as an important conclusion, based on the experiences that peace nevertheless exists in the system (Vasquez 2000). An implication may eventually be the need for constructing an organized international order.

The Hamburg project, on the contrary, departs from an understanding of an international system that is fairly integrated, almost having a purpose of its own, which is to promote market economy and democracy. It is a highly hierarchical world, centred on the strongest actors in the system, the Western countries. These actors are also influenced by the strength of the system. They are all capitalist, market-oriented and expansive, furthering a system of asymmetrical linkages. This international system penetrates into all parts of the world, creating instability and pushing aside traditional forms of social relations. There is an asymmetry between stronger actors that benefit from this development, and weaker actors that risk becoming marginalized. The project has a critical attitude to the basis of the existing international system. In this way, the disagreement on whether fatalities should be used as a criterion has a deeper meaning. The Hamburg project could argue as follows: if one side is vastly superior, it can win an armed conflict within a short period of time, and thus the casualties will be limited. It is still a military operation for purposes that might be the same as those found in more protracted and devastating conflicts. From the point of view of causes of war, in other words, the magnitude may not be so significant. For the Michigan project, with its elaborate measurements of battle-related deaths per month, for instance, very large confrontations are the most interesting. The destruction in itself makes them more important. They suggest inadequacies in balance-of-power thinking and deterrence strategies. Such realist theories are developed exactly to prevent major disasters. If these still occur, the project can show this, and take a critical attitude to this particular aspect of the international system and its interpreters. The two projects contrast on important points of departure, their epistemology. This affects their definitions for data collection and interpretation of the resulting data. Thus, both projects are needed and valuable. Together they highlight different sides of the contemporary global system.

2.3 Trends in Armed Conflicts

The Uppsala Conflict Data Program (UCDP)

The Uppsala program (UCDP) uses the concept of 'armed conflict' and focuses on conflict resolution. Like AKUF, it reports annually on ongoing conflicts and has much current information. Its definitions and understandings of conflict put it somewhere between the Michigan and Hamburg projects. From the beginning it treated all conflicts in an identical way, as did the Hamburg project and as COW now does, whether they take place between or within states. The same definition applies to both situations. For UCDP, it means that the distinction between an international system and an intra-state system is not of primary importance. What counts is the use of violence. The conflicts included are those that have at least one state or government as a party. This is also the case for the other two projects.

It covers conflicts from a threshold level of 25 battle-related deaths in a conflict in a year. This is an easily identifiable criterion and requires less evaluation by the researchers than, for instance, the continuity criterion used in the Hamburg project. It means also that there is a way of discussing intensity in conflict, as is done in the Michigan project. There are two thresholds (25 and 1,000 battle-related deaths, respectively), resulting in two categories of intensity: 'minor armed conflicts', conflicts with more than 25 deaths but fewer than 1,000 for the year and for the duration of the conflict; and 'wars', conflicts with more than 1,000 battle-related deaths in one year. The casualties are significant in a study of conflict resolution. The more destruction, the more difficult will be peacemaking, reconstruction and the creation of a new post-war relationship. These distinctions are also relevant from a conflict prevention perspective. It is a common belief that it is in the early phases of a conflict that it can be brought to an end most successfully. Thus, conflicts with lower levels of casualties may reflect preventive efforts, not just superiority. It becomes important to understand which conflicts remain on a low level and which ones do not. The criteria make this possible.

The Uppsala project adds an element which originally was not found in COW nor in AKUF, and it is introduced for theoretical as well as practical reasons. It requires that the conflict should have an issue, an incompatibility. This is derived from the theoretical considerations that guide this book. In the definition of conflict given in Section 2.1, this is an important element and it is, as a consequence, reflected in the data collection. The two other projects are satisfied once they have identified the actors and the actions. Still, there is an implicit understanding that only political violence is included. The Uppsala project handles this openly by requiring that there should be an explicit issue of contention, defined in political terms. In this way, a clear line is drawn between political and non-political violence.

The project includes as armed conflicts only those events that concern control over government or control over territory. These are in turn defined as two exclusive categories. Control over government means that the issue is who should rule a particular state, and that demands for change include the change of rulers. The incumbents are not likely to abide by such a demand easily. Thus, an incompatibility exists. This means that interventions from abroad to remove a leadership in a country are recorded as armed conflicts (for instance, the United States intervening in Panama in 1989 or in Iraq in 2003). So are rebellions against a government by internal forces (for instance, the uprising against the Mobutu regime in Zaire in 1997 or against the successor Kabila regime a year later). Control over territory means that demands by one state for territory in another state, even the occupation of another state, are included. So are rebellions inside a state to achieve autonomy, independence or the joining of a particular territory to the neighbouring state. This has an international dimension (for instance, Iraq's claim on Kuwait, occupying the country in 1990 and being forced out by 1991) as well as an intra-state one (Kosovo Albanians aspiring to leave the Federal Republic of Yugoslavia, 1997–98, expressed also in violent form).

There are theoretical reasons for bringing incompatibility into the con-flict definition. Conflict theory suggests that parties act for particular pur-poses. Thus, they need initially to be taken at face value. In other analyses such purposes are regarded as secondary. The Correlates of War project in Michigan originally focused on armed behaviour, the war. It aims at understanding what triggers this particular type of behaviour. The project design focuses on structural conditions as potential explanations, such as balance of power and other elements in the international system. At first it did not include the party's own perception of why the conflict is there. In the latest version, however, such a distinction is made for intra-state wars, where the project now separates conflicts for control of the central govern-ment from conflicts over local or regional interests (Sarkees and Wayman 2010: 339). The terminology is close to the one used in the Uppsala project for two decades. Thus, the Hamburg project is nearer the original COW definition in this regard and its perspective is equally structural (notably, capitalism or globalization) as are those of COW (the international system). However, if the focus is shifted to conflict resolution, as is the case for the Uppsala project, the parties' intentions become more important. Conflict exists, the parties will say, because there are particular grievances and, thus, the conflict cannot end until such grievances are resolved, ended or at least attended to. With its categories, the Uppsala project attempts to capture basic grievances. This approach receives interesting support from other studies, pointing to the importance of territory, for instance, by Holsti (1991) and Vasquez (1993, 1995). The Uppsala project aims at connect-ing its data to the development of conflict theory, in particular, theories of conflict resolution.

There is also a practical consideration, alluded to in the Hamburg project (Jung et al. 1996: 51), that a line has to be drawn between politi-cal violence and sheer banditry, mutinies and other forms of collective violence. There are cases where drug dealers clearly are behind the assas-sination of presidential candidates. Colombia had such an experience in the 1990s. However, the purpose is seldom for the assassin and his/her bosses to take control of the government. The aim is rather to prevent actors from taking power, if they might affect the government's policy on drug trade (changes in laws, operations and effectiveness of the policy). This type of violence is different, as it reflects criminal concerns. Such matters require police strategies, not peace research. There are delicate borderlines to observe, however. It is known that regular armed serv-ices, grey-zone paramilitary groups as well as many so-called liberation movements sustain themselves through the drug trade or other smuggling operations. There are also warlords who draw a thin line between politics and commerce.

The UCDP has expanded considerably and now operates an Internet-based database, that is available free of charge, for all armed conflicts since 1975 (www.ucdp.uu.se). It also cooperates with other institutions: With the International Peace Research Institute, Oslo (PRIO), the definitions have been applied back to 1946, a dataset that is available on the UCDP website; and with the Human Security Project at Simon Fraser University, Vancouver, Canada, additional aspects are studied, such as conflicts between non-state actors and one-sided violence against unorganized populations (for example, genocide and ethnic cleansing). Thus, the types of political violence included in UCDP go beyond those reported by AKUF. As mentioned, COW has introduced a category of non-state war. For the period since 1946, there are ten such wars according to COW. It should be noted that the UCDP category of non-state conflict contains 361 conflicts for the period 1989–2008, of which 14 had more than 1,000 battle-related deaths for a year (Pettersson 2010). For non-state conflict, the inclusion threshold of 1,000 deaths may be particularly problematic. In this volume, however, the focus is on the armed conflicts where the state is one party.

Patterns of armed conflict

The number of armed conflicts for the period 1989–2009 with the Uppsala definition is 130 (Harbom and Wallensteen 2010). For the 21-year period, this means that the average number of new conflicts per year is more than six, a higher ratio than reported in the two other projects. Adding information on non-state conflicts (361 conflicts for the period 1989–2008) and actors involved in one-sided violence, we see that politically motivated violence is considerably higher (Pettersson and Themnér 2010). For the longer period 1946–2007, COW reports 179 wars, AKUF 238 conflicts and Uppsala/PRIO 244 armed conflicts. Figure 2.1 shows the trends in armed conflict for the entire period of 1946–2009 using UCDP definitions.

Given the discussion on wars, the bottom area of Figure 2.1 is most interesting to follow. The trends are not linear. During the Cold War period there was a constant increase in overall conflict frequency. The number of about 20 ongoing wars also parallels what is reported by the Correlates of War for these years. By the middle of the 1990s the total numbers as well as the numbers of wars declined somewhat. Several wars were brought to a halt or settled by peace agreements. However, by the late 1990s the number of severe conflicts was again higher, only to be brought down in the first years of the new millennium, again followed by a gradual increase in later years.

This pattern is even more pronounced when studying different regions. Europe, which for a large part of the Cold War saw little manifest armed conflict, was the first region to experience a sharp rise in conflicts. These were associated with the break-up of the Soviet and Yugoslav unions. The numbers went from two armed conflicts in 1989 to ten by 1993. By 1997 they were down to zero, only to see two conflicts in 1998 (Northern Ireland and Kosovo) and three in 1999 (Kosovo, Dagestan and Chechnya). Since then, minor conflicts have been recorded in Macedonia, Georgia and Chechnya. The conflicts in Georgia and Chechnya had heavy Russian involvement. For the coming years, the Balkans and the Caucasus stand out as the areas most in need of conflict resolution arrangements and political solutions.

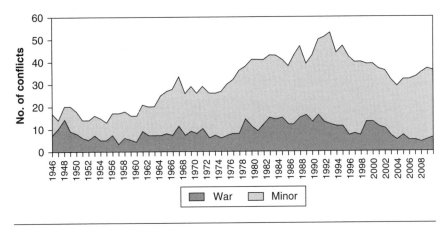

Figure 2.1 Armed conflicts by intensity, 1946–2009

For Africa, there is another pattern. By the middle of the 1990s, this continent appeared to be a beneficiary of the end of the Cold War. Wars on the continent that had been sustained by the Cold War, as well as by South African polarization, were ending. This could be observed for the Horn of Africa and Southern Africa. West Africa and the Sudan seemed to be the only conflict areas left. From 12 armed conflicts in 1989 and 16 in 1991 the numbers were down to 11 in 1995–96, only to be back up to 15 or 16 for 1997–2002. New wars were experienced in the Horn of Africa (Eritrea v. Ethiopia) and, most challenging, in Central Africa, connecting conflicts over a vast, highly populated and resource-rich region. Conflicts in this area became increasingly difficult to disentangle. A regional conflict complex was created, initially centred on the Hutu–Tutsi conflict which, by way of refugee flows, guerrilla movements and interventions, came to engulf a number of states.[1] Similarly, regionally related wars took place in Western Africa. There were, however, also concerted efforts to deal with the violence and, by 2003, they began to pay off. The war in the Democratic Republic of Congo tapered off, although Rwandan troops were battling Hutu groups in the territory. The protracted war in Sudan ended in a peace agreement in 2005, with an uncertain future. By 2011, Somalia remained the most notorious conflict on the African continent, but there were serious dangers of a return to war in Southern Sudan. The West African state of Côte d'Ivoire also remained in a fragile condition after an armed conflict in March and April 2011.

In comparison to the dramatic developments in Europe and Africa, other regions show a surprisingly permanent pattern of conflict. The Gulf War of 1990–91 saw a continuation in the US-led intervention in 2003, leading to civil war in the country. By 2010, US combat forces were withdrawn, still leaving 50,000 soldiers on other missions in the country. The Arab spring of 2011 resulted in armed battles between the government and the democratic opposition in Libya, a new development for the region. The tensions in South Asia between India and Pakistan gradually increased, adding a nuclear dimension.

The peace process attempted in 2004 stalled, but there was no sustained direct violence between the two. The long war in Sri Lanka ended with government victory in 2009. The situation in Afghanistan became increasingly complicated, drawing in Pakistan as well as a host of allies to the United States and the Afghan government led by Hamid Karzai. In the USA, the Obama administration gave the conflict priority, acting under the lingering impact of the attacks on September 11, 2001. In the Americas, Colombia remained the major battlefield, although Mexico saw a dramatic escalation of drug-related violence, much of which UCDP would categorize as non-state violence.

For the world as a whole, the total number of armed conflicts going on is staggering. Despite great efforts at conflict resolution, it appears that, for each conflict solved between parties with international efforts, a new one emerges, often pursued by splinter groups, requiring the same mix of improvisation and standard operating procedures by the international community. This repeated experience of inadequacy fuels the interest in preventive conflict management as well as post-conflict peacebuilding. Also, it shows the need to search for the underlying causes in order to find remedies that combine conflict prevention with social change and popular participation. In a longer perspective, however, none of the armed conflicts initiated in the 1990s has been as devastating as some of the older conflicts. The protracted war in Afghanistan, which began in 1978, has more than 1 million battle-related deaths. The 1980s also witnessed the Iran–Iraq War with 1.2 million deaths. The Vietnam War or, more appropriately, the Second Indochina War, ended in 1975, with possibly 2 million deaths. The Nigerian Civil War in the 1960s was a disaster, with 1 million deaths. The Korean War in the 1950s reportedly led to 2 million deaths. The civil war in the 1940s in China, ending with the Communist Party taking control, saw 1 million battle-related deaths (Singer 1991; Small and Singer 1982). The war scenarios since the Cold War are serious enough. Still, it might be suggested that there is a greater ambition to reduce human suffering. There are examples of humanitarian support even in the midst of war, in Bosnia, for instance. Principles containing a responsibility to protect exposed populations have gained adherence. There is also a willingness from the outside community to act earlier in a serious conflict to prevent it from becoming more destructive. This means that the reported reduction in battle deaths and risks of death in armed conflict since 1946 – surprising as it might be to the normal consumer of daily news – is plausible (Lacina and Gleditsch 2005; Lacina et al. 2006).

2.4 Outcomes of Armed Conflict

The concept of conflict resolution was given a preliminary definition in Chapter 1. It will be further refined in Chapter 3. Having delineated armed conflict and war, peacemaking is easier to encircle. It is something done by the warring parties, expressed in the form of an agreement, implemented by first ending the fighting and then followed through in all other respects. The value of agreements has been challenged. It is, however, not easy to end a war and start a process of forging a post-war order without having some shared awareness of what the new arrangement should look like. An agreement expresses such a joint understanding. It may not include everything that needs settlement, and there are likely to develop different interpretations of what has been concluded. Still, an agreement provides a basis for a new relationship. It is not easy to make accords after a war, even when the parties have been allies, as was the case of the USA, Britain and the Soviet Union during the Second World War. Even before the war ended, the allies had serious disagreements on the post-war world, although they had made agreements (in Yalta in January 1945, for instance). If victors cannot agree among themselves, it is probably even more difficult for enemies to develop a shared document on the future of their interaction. A peace agreement, in other words, is a particular result in a process that began before the agreement was signed and continues after the ink has dried.

The Uppsala program is collecting data on peace agreements and the information is available in its database for the period after 1975. It makes possible closer scrutiny of frequencies of different types of war ending. For instance, for the period 1989–2009, with a total of 130 armed conflicts, 95 had actually been terminated by early 2010, that is close to three-quarters of the total. This supports the statement in Section 2.1 that conflicts and wars actually do end.

However, a peace agreement may not be the ending of a conflict. Agreements may not be implemented, or only implemented by some. This means that conflict may continue. The same is true for victory and other outcomes as well. Thus, the information on peace agreements needs to be complemented with data on conflict terminations, that is, situations where there has been no fighting for a period of time, for instance during one year. This will give us a fuller picture of the intricacy of conflict. For instance, such terminations may be due to a victory or to a peace agreement, but could also be the result of other arrangements (cease-fires, unilateral withdrawals, etc.).

Table 2.1 overleaf shows that the number of conflicts terminated through victories are more than double the number of peace agreements, but even so more than half of all conflicts end in other ways (cease-fires and other outcomes, which includes unilateral withdrawal, for instance). Furthermore, peace agreements fail earlier than victories but in the long run the recurrence of armed conflict is somewhat less frequent. In fact, the failure rates are much higher for cease-fires and other outcomes, both in the short run and in the longer perspective. It is also so that victory outcomes are often seen in short conflicts. Kreutz (2010: 246) observes that 'parties often manage to quickly defeat their opponents through military superiority in the beginning of a conflict. If neither party is able to do so, the conflict is more likely to be settled through a negotiated process'. In fact, Table 2.1 demonstrates that peace agreements and cease-fires are almost as common as victories, and both are examples of negotiated arrangements.

The variety of possible outcomes displayed in Table 2.1 is probably not what the initiators have normally planned for. The preference is for durable victory within a reasonably short period. Many conflicts are deeply entrenched, have witnessed broken negotiations, failed cease-fire arrangements, and abandoned peace agreements. They are probably increasingly

Table 2.1   Duration and types of conflict termination, 1946–2009

	Number of conflict terminations	Percentage of conflicts recurring within 3 years	Percentage of conflicts recurring at all during the period
Peace agreement	59	14	36
Victory	125	12	42
Cease-fire	55	18	47
Other outcomes	176	36	61
Total	415	23	50

Source: Kreutz 2010; UCDP Conflict Termination Dataset v 2010–1, www.ucdp.uu.se

Note: There is a total of 415 terminated conflict episodes in 244 armed conflicts that took place in this period, that is, fighting ceased for at least one year. The endings have been coded according to four categories. Status by end of 2009.

difficult to settle. For many initiators, however, what was originally planned may no longer be possible to accomplish.

One of the most protracted conflicts has been the one in Afghanistan. The war began as an attempt by a communist party to reform the feudal society, change the land distribution and give women a stronger standing. After 20 years of war with many special features – Soviet invasion, US support to opposition movements and involvement from a host of neighbouring and Middle Eastern countries – the communist party was eliminated and many of its leaders brutally murdered. The conflict was then pursued along traditional divisions, and the dominating group until November 2001 (the Taliban) was unusually Islamic and anti-women. The conflict dynamics have become entirely different from what the originators had anticipated. The rule of the Taliban was effectively ended by December 2001, when a local and international alliance led by the United States, escalated the war in order to rout the al-Qaida organization based in the country. Resistance linked to the Taliban regrouped and returned, however, and, by 2010, the conflict was one of the four wars recorded in the world.

Victory is difficult to achieve. It does occur, however. The most obvious example is the USA intervening in Panama, capturing the 'strongman' of the leadership, General Noriega, bringing him to trial in Florida, convicting him for drug-trade offences and putting him in a US prison until 2010 when he was extradited to France for further sentencing. The Gulf War is also a victory: Iraqi forces had to withdraw and Kuwait was restored as a sovereign country. In 1997 a rebellion against the incumbent regime in Zaire ended with victory. The war lasted eight months. The new regime faced another rebellion less than nine months later. A peace agreement concluded in July 1999, and signed in September the same year, was meant to end the war, without accomplishing this by the end of 2000. The US victory over the regime in Iraq in 2003 seemed swift. The statue of Saddam Hussein was brought down on April 9, 2003 and major combat was declared to be over by May 1. The continued fighting illustrates the difficulty of sustaining victory. By 2010, 4,400 US servicemen had been killed in an internal war which was 'won' more than seven years earlier.

The dynamics of victory and defeat are known from history. The large number of peace agreements is a most novel aspect, and part of the experience since the Cold War. A recent review of conflict terminations shows that peace agreements have become more common since 1990 (27 compared to 12 for the 1946–89 period) and more common than victories (Kreutz 2010). Also, 46 conflicts had a total of 139 such agreements and that violence remained ended for at least five years following 78 of these agreements (Högbladh 2006).

Furthermore, some agreements outlined processes towards a solution (Israel v. Palestine since 1993) where other parties nevertheless pursued a violent ending. There are even cases of a complete settlement concluded between the main parties, where other actors took up or continued armed struggle nevertheless (Mindanao in 1996). Of course, there are also agreements that have been functioning for a period of time but then have been undermined by the parties. This is true for the settlements for Angola in 1991 and 1994, Chechnya in 1996 and Sierra Leone 1996 and again in 1999. However, all peace agreement failures do not have to result in renewed war. Côte d'Ivoire saw a series of failed agreements from 2003 to 2010, but no renewed fighting (Wallensteen et al. 2011). A short armed conflict erupted in March–April 2011.

The record of successful peacemaking is as varied as can be expected from the difficulties of ending long-lasting wars. Still, the ambition to do so with the help of negotiation and agreement makes the period since the end of the Cold War an interesting object of study. The developments of the post-Cold War period can legitimately be compared to the very few peace agreements ending wars that were concluded during the entirety of the Cold War. There were cease-fire agreements, no doubt, but very few peace agreements. As we noted already in Chapter 1, some of the cease-fire lines drawn during the Cold War still constitute the main territorial divisions in many conflicts. To the cases mentioned previously we can also add the territorial division between India and Pakistan in Kashmir in 1949 that ended their first war. New wars in the area in 1965 and 1971 led to a return to the previous cease-fire lines. The conflict remains unresolved.

Among the few real peace agreements concluded during the Cold War, the Geneva peace agreement for Indochina in 1954 was effectively undermined within two years. The war between Malaysia and Indonesia, which began in 1963, was concluded through a peace pact in 1966, and the conflict has not resumed. A short war in 1963 between Algeria and Morocco found a mediated agreement the same year. An agreement in 1972 to end the war in the Sudan was shattered in 1983 and war returned. The Camp David agreement between Israel and Egypt in 1979 has stood the test of time. For the 45 years of Cold War, the peace agreements are few, probably 12 by the latest account (Kreutz 2010; Licklider 1995; Mason and Fett 1996; Stedman 1991). This is not a particularly striking record at peacemaking. It contrasts the many arms control agreements made, where one source lists 27 international accords from 1963 to 1991 (Goldstein 1992). This also makes the large number of peace agreements during the turbulent period since 1989 valuable and worth a close analysis.

Since 1989 peace agreements have been concluded in all regions of the world. This means that peacemaking has a global meaning. Without the peacemaking efforts the number of wars would probably increase significantly. The agreements may have been concluded between parties too exhausted to find resources to win the wars, but sometimes they are also not capable of concluding agreements on their own. The Dayton Agreement on Bosnia-Herzegovina may fit in this category, as the warring parties only accepted the deal under strong international pressure. Thus, we will proceed to the theme of conflict resolution by departing from the peace agreements concluded or implemented since 1989. With this in mind, it is first necessary to turn to a more theoretical discussion on conflict theory and its implications for conflict resolution. This is done in Chapter 3.

Further Readings

Go to the *Understanding Conflict Resolution* web page at www.sagepub.co.uk for free access to journal articles listed.

Dixon, J. 2009. 'What Causes Civil Wars? Integrating Quantitative Research Findings', *International Studies Review*, 11 (4): 707–35.

Duffield, M. 2000. 'Globalization, Transborder Trade, and War Economies', in M. Berdal and D. Malone (eds), *Greed and Grievance: Economic Agendas in Civil Wars*. International Peace Academy, Boulder, CO, and London: Lynne Rienner. pp. 69–89.

Haas, E. B., R. L. Butterworth and J. S. Nye 1972. *Conflict Management by International Organizations*. Morristown, NJ: General Learning Press.

Harbom, L. and R. Sundberg 2009 (eds). *States in Armed Conflict 2008*. Uppsala University: Department of Peace and Conflict Research.

Richardson, L. F., Q. Wright and C.C. Lienau 1960. *Statistics of Deadly Quarrels*. Pittsburgh: Boxwood Press.

Singer, J. D. 1970. 'From A Study of War to Peace Research', *Journal of Conflict Resolution*, 14 (4): 527–42.

Singer, J. D. 1972. 'The Correlates of War Project', *World Politics*, 24: 243–70.

Sorokin, P. 1957. *Social and Cultural Dynamics. A Study of Change in Major Systems of Art, Truth, Ethics, Law and Social Relationships*. Boston, MA: Porter Sargent.

Themnér, L. and P. Wallensteen 2011. 'Armed Conflicts 1946–2010', *Journal of Peace Research*, 48 (4): 525–36.

Tickner, A. 1993. *Gender in International Relations*. New York: Colombia University Press.

Tickner, A. 1997. 'You Just Don't Understand: Troubled Engagements Between Feminists and IR Theorists', *International Studies Quarterly*, 41 (4): 611–32.

Vasquez, J. A. and M. T. Henehan 2001.'Territorial Issues and the Probability of War, 1816–1992', *Journal of Peace Research*, 38 (1): 123–38.

Wallensteen, P. 2011. *Peace Research: Theory and Practice*. London: Routledge. pp. 105–24.

Wright, Q. 1942. *A Study of War*. Chicago: Chicago University Press.

Note

1   The genocide in Rwanda in 1994 is separated from armed conflict in the Uppsala Conflict Data Program. It is located in a category of one-sided violence as it is directed against unorganized civilians by a state or a non-state actor.

APPROACHING CONFLICT RESOLUTION 3

3.1 The Evolution of Conflict Analysis

During the Cold War conflict analysis was developed largely to handle the understanding of the East–West conflict. It used tools such as system analysis and game theory. Game theory could illustrate the dangers inherent in a prisoner's dilemma game, but it could also be used to sharpen strategic thinking. To some, conflict theory could also be used for conflict resolution studies (Kriesberg 1997). Pertinent questions were how it was possible that three major powers (the USA, Britain and the Soviet Union), which had been united in the greatest war ever fought on this planet, only a couple of years later found themselves in a mortal conflagration. How could allies become deadly enemies so quickly? There were ready-made answers drawn from 'realist' power calculations, but there were also fears and misunderstandings arising from closed decision-making. The threats of the nuclear confrontation and the global reach of the Cold War made it urgent to understand the dynamics of conflict. The focus was on escalation and polarization, and how to manage and contain the violence built into such processes.

The simultaneous and surprising experience of the integration of the two former enemies, Germany and France, illustrated the potential of reversing dynamics. It showed that it was possible to move from being enemies to allies, in a relationship that was closer than traditional alliances of convenience. Again this took place in a short period of time. Thus, it was necessary to develop conflict analysis as well as integration studies. Considerable work was done in the 1950s and 1960s.

Soon, the perspectives began to deepen. Conflicts in the global South not only reflected the dynamics of polarization and integration; there were other forces at play as well. The leading power, the United States, saw intense, even armed, internal disputes in the 1960s and 1970s with riots and militant parties. The analysis had to focus on grievances that could drive conflicts. Scholars saw a role in contributing to a process of solving conflicts, in forms which the academics were used to (workshops and seminars). Towards the end of the 1980s and in the 1990s, the experience of settlement of local conflicts, as well as the ending of the Cold War, again strengthened the interest in conflict resolution. September 11, 2001, may have led to a return of strategic analysis, at least in conflicts relating to terrorism. However, many pointed to the needs for social change and conflict resolution for dealing also with such conflicts, particularly in a longer perspective. The divergent origins have resulted in different approaches which all need to be understood. To this task we devote this chapter.

The different modes of analysis are brought together under three headings. There are approaches which emphasize (1) conflict dynamics, (2) needs-based conflict origins, and (3) rational, strategic calculations. These constitute distinct forms of analysis. However, they do intersect and many writers use them interchangeably. They are presented with reference to the work of particular researchers, but should not necessarily be seen as coherent 'schools of thinking' or as the exclusive approach of a particular writer. They are tools which are needed for any researcher, something that will be made clear in the synthesizing section of this chapter.

3.2 Focusing on Conflict Dynamics

A classic understanding of conflict sees it as a dynamic phenomenon: one actor is reacting to what another actor is doing, which leads to further action. Quickly, the stakes in the conflict escalate. One sequence of events follows another, and it is difficult to decipher which party is more responsible for what happens. In popular understanding, it is expressed as 'it takes two to conflict'. There are many observations which evoke this theme, notably the prevalence of mirror images, that parties and issues are seeing the conflict in the same way, only reversing the picture. There are also dynamics pushing the actors in conflicts into two camps (polarization), creating commanding leadership (centralization), and forming institutions with particular responsibilities and little insight (secrecy and protection). The conflict takes on a life of its own, engulfing the actors and, seemingly irresistibly, pushing them into ever increasing conflict. The idea of conflict as a social phenomenon moving by itself is powerful. It is invoked when parties say that they have no alternatives. The dynamics of the conflict have removed all other possible actions, and are said to give a party no choice but to continue to react at increasing levels of threat and violence.

For the analysis of such dynamics, some tools have been developed. Game theory is a way of illustrating how parties act within the confines set up by the game itself. If the parties follow the rules, the outcomes are predictable. But it also raises the possibility that actors can change the dynamics by making particular moves or even breaking some of the 'rules' that the conflict has generated. Such an analysis was developed in the 1960s for the polarized East–West conflict, suggesting credible de-escalating steps that could lead to positive responses. The idea was that if one actor begins to act on its own, the other(s) may follow, and thus the dynamics change direction. Some of these ideas were used for the US–Soviet relations in early periods of *détente* (Etzioni 1967; Osgood 1962).

In a slightly more complicated version, the conflict triangle – introduced by Johan Galtung in the 1960s – provides a helpful analytical tool (Galtung 1969, 1996; Mitchell 1981; Wiberg 1976/1990). It suggests that a conflict moves among the triangle's three corners, where corner A refers to conflict attitudes, B to conflict behaviour and C to the conflict or contradiction itself (the incompatibility). A conflict sequence can begin in any of these corners. In later writings, Galtung gives somewhat more emphasis to C as a more frequent – or even logical – starting point. The dynamics are still most important, however, even expressed in conflicts having life-cycles. From this it follows that the resolution of conflict, conflict transformation, is a 'never-ending process'. A solution 'in the sense of a steady-state, durable formation is at best a temporary goal'. The conflict is transformed, for instance, through transcendence (where the goals are met fully for the conflict parties), compromise (goals are met less than fully for the sides) and withdrawals (goals are given up) (Galtung 1996: 72, 81–90, 96).

Although structural features, such as frustration and structural violence, are mentioned in this approach, dynamics are more central. The dynamics can be affected and steered in ways that make conflict creative. This is achieved by the parties themselves or with contributions from outsiders, intervening in a benign way. In Galtung's version of conflict dynamics, finding agreements through diplomatic means is less important, but not excluded. In fact, his examples point to the importance of procedures for changing conflict dynamics. Ingenious conference arrangements can help make complexity more manageable, as exemplified by the Law of the Sea Conference in Caracas in 1974 and the Helsinki process for *détente* in the East–West conflict in Europe, initiated in 1972 (Galtung 1996: 92–3). Such examples might be surprising as these conferences did not involve a solution to the substance of the conflicts, but only provided a reasonable process through which the issues could be handled. It points out, however, that negotiations are ways in which conflicts can be transformed. Finding a mutually acceptable process may be a necessary precursor to a solution.

In the end, Galtung concedes, agreements on substance are also needed. They may be informal, as in the examples of how children divide an orange and spouses solve a dispute over vacation plans, or formal, as is the case when ending a multilateral conference (the Convention on the Law of the Sea, the Helsinki Final Act). Transcendence means finding an agreement on who divides the orange and chooses among the parts, or finding a place where one family member can climb in the mountains and another remain on the beach (one place is clearly Taormina, Sicily; others might be found in California and New Zealand!). Accords concluded in such disputes do not need to be written into a document, as there is considerable confidence and integration among the parties. But Galtung's third example, the creation of a confederation between Israel and Palestine (Galtung 1996: 98), is unthinkable without negotiations and a signed agreement, constitution or other mutually understood arrangements. This illustrates that conflict resolution after war cannot be thought of in the same way as solving conflicts between parties with a high level of mutual trust. It is not without reason that wars tend to end with documents, signatures and ceremonies. It is a way for the parties to make sure that the other side is committed to the process and to the agreement. An agreement may help to transform the conflict from a destructive, divisive experience to a constructive, shared endeavour.

The work by Galtung has here been used as an example of the dynamic perspective on conflict analysis. There is a considerable body of thinking along similar lines (Kriesberg 1992a, 1992b; Mitchell 1981; Pruitt and Rubin 1986; Wiberg 1976/1990). It represents an early perspective in the development of conflict analysis and parallels game theory advances (Axelrod 1984; Rapoport 1960). It remains rich in its emphasis on the changing and powerful dynamics of conflict. Without insight into such dynamics, conflict analysis misses an important aspect. Central is the understanding of how difficult it is to break the dynamics. Conflict resolution is about changing the direction of the flow of events, so that escalation is turned into de-escalation and polarization into positive interaction.

Particularly fruitful is Galtung's depiction of incompatibility as central to the dynamics of conflict. A way to do an incompatibility analysis is reproduced in Figure 3.1 which shows two actors, A and B, with contradictory goals. What the dispute is about is not significant. It could concern a piece of territory, a sum of money, an attractive government post, or other scarce valuables. If A gets 100 per cent of the available resources, there is nothing left for B, and vice versa. If either one wins, the situation finds itself at point A or point B, respectively, meaning complete victory for one actor and complete defeat for the other. It is an outcome an actor is not likely to abide by easily and voluntarily. Anything beyond these points may, however, be more acceptable and possible. Along the diagonal there are positions at which the parties may meet. C marks a classical point, where the parties divide the resources 50–50, equally much (or little) for each side. The parties may also agree on going to point E, none of them takes anything, but instead the valuables are handed over to actor C, also an agreed solution. In a more sinister scenario, C may enter the conflict and take the valuables from the fighting parties – an opportunistic move by an outsider. The resources may also have been destroyed during the fighting. In the space to the left and below the diagonal in Figure 3.1, there are many outcomes. Different forms of compromise may be found here. To the right and above the line, however, there are other complications. This is where Galtung's ideas lead: transcendence. The hope is to find points of type D, where both parties can get what they want at the same time (again, the example of Taormina, Sicily!). The mathematical formulation is, of course, impossible. There cannot be 200 per cent of something, but this space indicates the challenge of finding solutions beyond established rules and thinking. Creativity is needed for transcendence. Political battle often stifles innovation and reduces the options perceived by the actors. Sometimes, the strains of the effort may result in imaginative actions. In all, Figure 3.1 is a useful device to describe an incompatibility. It will be used later in this book.

The dynamic approach to conflict analysis points to the significance of *establishing a dialogue* between the parties. This is where, for instance, finding a conference format is important. It requires that the parties can participate, but together with others who can serve as practical go-betweens and add issues which may unlock positions. It also points to the importance of *confidence-building measures*, not only in the military field, but also in social, cultural, economic and other areas, as they can be instrumental in changing the dynamics of a conflict. Conferences and confidence-building are mostly multilateral, and in this approach the injection of mediators and facilitators is important. Third parties take a particular role in such settings.

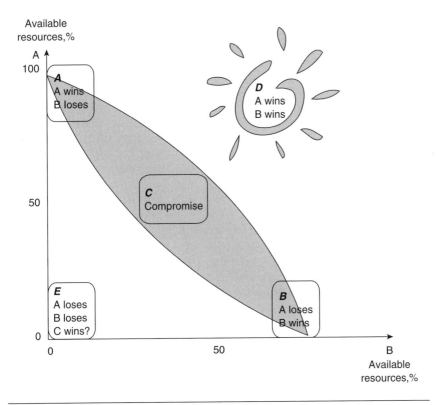

Figure 3.1   Analysis of incompatibility (following Galtung 1996)

An original idea is the one of *conflict resolution mechanisms*. This refers to the creation of independent procedures in which the parties can have confidence. These are formal or informal arrangements to which they can agree to hand over their conflict, whose solution they can accept and which can define the termination of a conflict (Coser 1967; Galtung 1965; Schelling 1960). Such mechanisms exist in internal affairs, for instance, courts, democratic procedures, and elections called to solve a parliamentary stalemate. They are scarce in international relations, where court systems are weak and political fora easily become arenas of dispute, rather than frameworks for handling conflicts. In internal affairs, the possibilities of appeal are important, creating opportunities to review what has been done on lower levels. As part of a future conflict resolution mechanism this can also be a useful device in the international system.

Finally, it follows from this perspective that *parties with non-violent methods* are potentially efficient in changing the dynamics. This gives a role to peace movements, but also to other groups, non-governmental organizations (NGOs) and civil society at large (including academic institutions) that work for conciliation and understanding across divides. Such parties can even be involved in conflicts and take sides, but they pursue their goals with peaceful means, not with violence. They constitute an alternative approach for a community wishing to achieve change, but not convinced that violence is an appropriate action. For instance, in Western Europe, social democratic ways of impacting capitalist systems seem to have achieved more welfare, enjoyed stronger support in the public and lasted longer than did the bitterly competing communist parties. This particular divide focused on the possibility of peaceful versus violent change. Similarly, the non-violent party representing the Nationalist community in Northern Ireland (SDLP) for a long time drew a larger share of the Catholic vote than the party closer to the IRA (Sinn Fein). These non-violent actors may be important in bridging the dynamics, giving space for alternative actions and, thus, be central in a transition from war to peace.

Still, this perspective is weak in its understanding of why conflicts start. Is it reasonable to assume that conflicts really begin with conflict attitudes, or are such attitudes a result of previous behaviour and pre-existing incompatibilities? Can there be a more complex background that also has to be part of the analysis? What if the parties who often are modelled to be of equal strength are, in fact, highly unequal? These are critical challenges to conflict theory. This gives reason for considering alternative approaches.

3.3 Focusing on Basic Needs

A classic writer in social conflict theory is Lewis A. Coser. His book, *The Functions of Social Conflict* (1956), contains a series of statements on how conflicts can contribute positively to the functioning of society. There are also dysfunctional effects, but by devoting his work entirely to the functions, the book stimulated research, influencing all three perspectives that are presented here. Coser's work cannot be easily categorized. His functional approach indicates a dynamic perspective on conflict. It is noteworthy that he has very little to say on the ending of conflict, for instance. However, his definition of what he calls 'realistic conflicts' points in a different direction. These are conflicts 'which arise from frustration of specific demands … and … are directed at the presumed frustrating object' (1956: 49). Thus they are instrumental actions, not just a form of tension release, or 'anger' (Fry and Björkqvist 1997: 27–8).

In a later work, Coser analysed the 1965 Watts riots in Los Angeles, California, demonstrating empirically what this approach would mean. What happened in Watts, he says, 'was an effort of an active minority … to announce their unwillingness to continue accepting indignity and frustration without fighting back. In particular, they were communicating their desperation through violent acts since no other channels of communication seemed open to them' (1967: 103). Thus, Coser argues that the conflicts as well as the violent actions stem from not being accepted in society, a matter of dignity, political access and power. The rioters struck, in particular, against those who had treated members of their ethnic community in a condescending way. Coser points to a remedy: access to the political system. He writes that 'only where there exist open channels of political communication through which all groups can articulate their demands, are the chances high that the political exercise of violence can be successfully minimized' (1967: 106). This means that violent conflict can be terminated by satisfying needs for access. Furthermore, this has to be maintained over time. The solution, in other words, is likely to be found in building new institutions, whether formal or informal.

In his work on 'protracted social conflict' 20 years later, Edward Azar outlined ideas for explaining the duration of conflicts and the repeated failure of conflict resolution. He was concerned, for instance, with the civil war in Lebanon which, by the time of writing, had raged for more than a decade. This and other protracted conflicts dealt with such needs as security, identity, recognition and participation, factors which are identical to those that Coser singled out (Azar and Burton 1986: 29). These contributions by Coser and Azar result in a different approach to conflict resolution. If the basis of a conflict is the denial of particular needs, then the resolution process must identify those needs and include ways of answering them. Negotiations have a tendency to give advantages to elites, and if agreements 'do not touch upon the underlying issues in the conflict [agreements] do not last'. Instead, Azar finds, conflict resolution requires decentralized structures and ways in which psychological, economic and relational needs can be satisfied (Azar and Burton 1986: 30–9).

This thinking is part of a materialist theoretical tradition and constitutes a significant element in class analysis. But Marxist theorists seldom have come to an understanding of conflict resolution. On the contrary, much Marxist thinking is based on the idea of continuous conflict, ending only with the defeat of the oppressive system – at this time, capitalism. Negotiation and compromise were not part of the political formula, or of the academic study. Only in the reformist, social democratic version, as we have just seen, was conflict within capitalism manageable. Another root of the idea of conflict stemming from frustration is the approach of analysing revolution as emerging from unsatisfied needs. Theories of deprivation have been given thoughtful consideration in a number of works and been exposed to empirical tests (Davies 1971; Gurr 1970). The results are mixed. In his elaborate treatment of relative deprivation, Ted R. Gurr found support for 'relative deprivation' as a systematic way for conflicts to become violent. In his later work on ethnic groups, Gurr reports factors that were associated with escalation into violent conflict, most notably the negative effects of the removal of autonomy for a particular group. It often becomes an important reason for the group to revolt (Gurr 1993). This observation is linked to Coser's reflections on dignity and political access. The removal of channels of influence may spark violence. Thus, the creation of such channels can be important in terminating violence and making non-armed conflict a constructive part of the political process.

These theorists refer to concepts such as frustration and deprivation. What they provide is an analysis of social frustration. Basic needs are not met in a particular society; instead they are out of reach for a group, which thus becomes frustrated. The conflict originates in or feeds on this frustration. It comes close to classical studies on frustration as resulting in aggression, and aggression as stemming from frustration (Dollard et al. 1939), which has given rise to considerable debate and revision. For instance, it has been asked if aggression is the only way to direct frustration, and whether there are other possible explanations for frustration and conflict behaviour (Fry and Björkqvist 1997: 26–32).

The sequence is captured in James C. Davies' figure on revolution, as shown in Figure 3.2. It shows pointedly how a gap emerges and when the difference between expectations and frustration becomes obvious. As the figure is constructed, expectations are always higher than what is accomplished. A certain difference is, therefore, manageable. The achievements are seen as the lower line in the figure. When the gap becomes too large, however, it is likely to be unacceptable. This may happen, for instance, if the economy ceases to grow after a period of sustained growth. The actual achievement becomes considerably lower than was expected and thus discontent rises. This, it has been argued, leads to a revolution of rising expectations. Interestingly, Davies finds in his study that this pattern fits with the economic performance of several countries before a revolution breaks out. However, this does not settle the issue. For instance, a question is whether or not the same experience has occurred in a number of other countries, but without revolution. Frustration, as described by Davies, may be theoretically interesting, but does it hold up empirically? Gurr's initial study

Figure 3.2   Satisfaction of needs and revolution (following Davies 1971)

(1970) did not result in strong correlations, but his work focusing on what we may call political frustration (1993) suggests intriguing relationships.

The model in Figure 3.2 is confined to internal, or intra-state, situations. Revolutions are directed at the leaders in the same society. How can frustration result in international conflict? John W. Burton, who has written extensively on conflict resolution, suggests there is a 'spillover' effect. Conflicts, 'especially at the international level', he says, 'are a spillover of some internal institutional or personal problem'. These are ways in which leaders 'divert attention' (Burton 1996: 41). Thus, internal conflict may arise from a group's reaction to discrimination, and the resulting disturbances are diverted by the government into international conflict. This is a popular theory. Theoretically, however, there are a number of other ways in which frustration can be diverted or covered, for instance, in the Roman slogan of 'Bread and Circus', meaning that basic economic necessities were met and that spectacular shows were arranged to give the populations interests other than politics. Today this may be seen in the form of food price subsidies and Olympic Games. There is also the possibility that leaders actually attempt to solve the grievance. As Heldt points out, adding an international problem to an internal one will actually risk making the leader's position even more precarious. Thus, the diversion hypothesis needs to specify how a certain type of frustration may lead to an attack on another group, or even another state. Empirically, the evidence for a systematic spillover effect is not strong (Heldt 1996). It continues to be an attractive idea, however, and thus has an impact on conflict resolution strategies. As we saw in the conflict dynamics perspective, ending of conflict is not necessarily part of the approach; conflicts are transformed, not eliminated. Similarly, we may ask, is it at all possible to meet all the needs that humans and human groups may have? If not, then conflict resolution becomes but a way of managing conflict, possibly channelling it, but not ending it. Alternatively, we may ask if there are some needs that are possible to meet, and if so, are these the ones which are important to handle in order to reduce the amount of violent conflict in the world? The researchers using this approach still owe us answers to such questions.

There are distinct conflict resolution techniques that follow from this, no matter what the origins of the conflict. One is the *problem-solving workshop,* which, according to Burton, was first used in the middle of the 1960s for the Confrontation Crisis and involved representatives from Indonesia, Malaysia and Singapore (Azar and Burton 1986: 46–7; Burton 1987). The three governments nominated participants to a workshop in London. The meeting lasted for ten days and was controlled by a group of scholars. With this, a tradition of workshops was initiated. There is now a broad array of different approaches (Broome 1997; Doob 1970; Fisher 1983; Kelman and Cohen 1976; Mitchell and Banks 1996) and assessments of their importance (Fisher 1997). It has been argued that they can contribute to changes in political culture between the opposing sides. Assessing effects is difficult as the impact can be 'outweighed by other forces' and thus special evaluation methods have to be developed (Kelman 2008).

The original purpose of the workshop was to go beyond the parties' stated positions and reach the underlying needs (Rouhana 1995). Theoretically, such an analysis should not necessarily assume that all parties are equally responsible for a conflict. In practice, the workshops have included the opposing sides, trying to make them understand each other's needs. Thus, the approach becomes quite symmetric (Rouhana 1995). If one side were defined as the more aggressive, as analysis of conflict causes might suggest, workshops would actually be designed to work with only one side.

However, the problem-solving workshops cannot, by themselves, lead to the solutions. It is more likely that they set an agenda and, thus, inform the parties on the needs of the other side. They will be able to act on a more complete understanding of each other's preferences. Still, needs may not be met in a society, due to a lack of resources or the way scarce resources are managed. Thus, *equitable economic policies* become central, as a way of preventing future conflicts as well as handling acute crises within a society. Although this is easily said, there may be unexpected effects. It may, for instance, result in serious conflict with other actors who fear to lose their positions. Solutions to the frustrations of one actor can lead to fears and frustrations of others. There are also arguments against economic equality. Discrepancies are said to be the way in which economies develop. Certain differences in income and wealth are important as they give incentives to work hard (Olson 1971). However, with the same logic, too large and growing differences would create a revolutionary potential and that is, of course, the starting point for Marxist analysis. It is expressed in Figure 3.2 above. It is reasonable to assume that a society, in order to sustain itself, needs to distribute economic resources relatively equitably to all citizens. This may be equally true whether the economy as a whole is growing or declining.

This, then, relates to conflict inside one society. Does it also translate into an international community, where a few countries are very wealthy and many are very poor? Certainly, resentment exists, and forms of terrorism build on this fact. The logic of the argument would not halt at the border of states. It does not require spillover arguments either, as frustration emerges once the differences and injustices are seen. In today's world they are apparent. But, a sceptic could ask, is this manageable through a problem-solving workshop? Also, is a global policy for a fair economy feasible?

Such considerations make Coser's ideas of *open channels* interesting. The most important would be to have access, thus giving hope for a positive change. The argument speaks in favour of democratization, but also for a democracy to be efficient in delivering desired change. The same logic follows from Gurr's conclusion on autonomy. The democratic system would make it possible for grievances to be heard. It gives a chance to all groups, perhaps more than any other system. This would also be true for the international system as a whole, if frustrated needs of relevance can be channelled through legitimate procedures. This requires radical change of the world, combining conflict resolution with a quest for development and dignity.

A final point: aggression has victims and perpetrators. When needs and grievances are seen by actors to coincide with ethnic, linguistic, religious, cultural or historical lines, they add elements which make a situation even more explosive. In many riots, it is not the distant leaders who feel the direct impact of rage, but those who are closest to the mobs, be they shop owners, the weak, poor, women or children. They have to face the destruction, as was the case in Watts and repeated elsewhere, for instance, in Indonesia in 1998 (targeting property of the Chinese population, but also the Suharto family) or France in the autumn of 2005 (in areas dominated by immigrant populations). The dynamics of the conflict may be reflected in the targeted groups. Examples are Kosovo in 1999 (first targeting Albanians, then Serbs, Romas), East Timor in 1999 (first pro-independence groups, later leaving pro-Indonesia groups in fear) and Iraq since 2003 (first American troops, then Westerners, Iraqi police recruits, later Shiites, then Sunnis and mosques whether Shiite or Sunni, and, most recently, Christians). The aggressive group, the perpetrators, needs a closer analysis, not only the societal relationship. One may ask: why did this group think that atrocities against another group would improve its lot? Were there alternative thoughts? Are there outside incentives for pursuing these actions? Who is actually participating in actions? There are many and legitimate questions asked about this form of mobilization of popular energy and why it takes a particular direction. Such questions, furthermore, lead to ideas about the possibility of *non-aggressive reactions* for more constructive uses of accumulated energy. In most revolutionary situations, there are groups that share the sentiments of the militants, but find other courses of action to be more effective. Internal debates on the appropriate course of action within a particular group are important. The outside world can impact on this debate in ways which may favour conflict resolution.

With the needs-based approach, it is the difficulty of meeting an individual party's need that is the origin of the conflict and the key to its solution. The analysis aims at locating unmet needs. It may then be more important to work with one particular actor than another, although different sides are represented. In an asymmetric situation, it is a matter of conveying to the dominant group the perspective of the dominated, but also to clarify to the dominated constraints on the dominating side. In the conflict dynamics approach, it is basic that the actors are treated in a similar, symmetric fashion, as all have some responsibility for the conflict and, thus, also for the solution of the conflict. The two perspectives contrast with each other, but they do not necessarily exclude each other. Let us see if this is also true for the third perspective on conflict resolution.

3.4 Focusing on Rational Calculations

The perspectives we have presented so far see actors, incompatibilities and actions as stemming from the circumstances in which actors find themselves. The actors individually or as a system of actors have to handle conditions that drive them apart. The third perspective assumes that actors have their own rationality, form their own judgements, make decisions, pursue strategies and, thus, initiate the chain of events that lead to war. The reversal of this, that is, ending wars and reaching agreements, has to be seen in the same light. There is a need for actors to make calculations that can terminate a conflict, but at the same time, ending war is not the actor's only interest. A good presentation of this thinking is found in the many publications of I. William Zartman, but many have worked in similar directions (Fisher and Ury 1981; Stedman 1991).

The idea that wars rise from a rational calculation is, of course, not novel. It is part of established realist and neorealist thinking about the origins of wars. The new twist is to see the ending of wars in such terms. Paul Pillar did pioneering work (1983). The ideas of Zartman have brought the approach further, without leading to the construction of formal models and illustrative diagrams. Zartman outlined such ideas before the end of the Cold War, and continues to adhere to them (Zartman 1989, 1995a; Zartman and Berman 1982; Zartman and Rasmussen 1997; Zartman and de Soto 2010). The literature of the type presented by *Getting to Yes* (Fisher and Ury 1981) rests less on explicit calculation, but still applies a rationalist perspective. The purpose is to understand the real interests of the parties, and thus look beyond their stated positions. Roger Fisher and William Ury introduced a set of notions which were primarily geared to negotiations in general, although the authors were clearly thinking of their utility for armed conflicts and war. In later work, Charles W. Kegley and Gregory A. Raymond state that such calculations have to include moral arguments, to provide a basis for justice in ending war and increasing the chances of durable settlements (Kegley and Raymond 1999). The rational approach, which focuses on the ending of war, appears fruitful and politically relevant. Its main assertions need a closer inspection.

It is assumed that the parties, which may be states, groups or movements, initiate wars to win them. This means that the parties, or at least the initiator, make internal calculations showing that the benefits outweigh the losses when escalating a conflict to a violent confrontation. Such calculations may look different for the opposing sides, but, in principle, the variables and their values are the same. One side makes a calculation for starting the violence, the other for defending itself against the attack. As time passes and nobody wins, the initial calculations are affected and have to be revised. The potential benefits from victory are reduced as the costs increase. The fact that so much time, energy, resources and human life have been invested – destroyed – makes it difficult not to continue, until the final moment of victory is reached. Otherwise the investment would be lost and the suffering meaningless. The parties, in Zartman's analysis, look towards the future. If that does not include a reasonably early chance of victory, but instead suggests a continued stalemate, perhaps even a catastrophe for the fighting sides, then there are elements of a 'ripe moment' for resolution. In Zartman's illuminating words, the conflict offers nothing but a 'flat, unpleasant terrain stretching into the future' (Zartman 1989: 268).

If the parties find this stalemate to be painful, what Zartman calls a 'hurting stalemate', it may lead them to strategic rethinking. There may be a chance for peace. Not necessarily, however. If none of the sides is comfortable with the present and can see no way forward to win the dispute – perhaps only fearing more destruction, without breakthrough – this is likely to be a moment requiring a change of action. At this point the parties might agree on a cease-fire, to reduce the pain, have a chance of recuperation, even getting an opportunity for buying new weapons. It could be time for a pause, perhaps calculated on what is needed before a new offensive. It is a limited strategic rethinking, where the goals are maintained. A cease-fire, in other words, may slow down the move towards a settlement, and instead prolong the fighting. This is an important dilemma in conflict termination. Many have strong opinions on this, but there is little empirical study on the merits of cease-fires for conflict resolution. However, the hurting stalemate can also be turned into, as Zartman has termed it, an 'enticing opportunity'. It can be used for a move forward to settlement, not simply freezing the present situation, the *status quo*. Here enters another of Zartman's concepts, the need for 'finding the formula'. There must be a way out for the parties, the weaker as well as the stronger. This line of argument gives an important role to outside powers. They can point out that there is a stalemate, and a danger of catastrophe in the near future – 'precipice' in Zartman's words – and they can suggest alternatives for settling the conflict (Ohlson 2011; Zartman 1989).

The calculations that go into the decision-making of the warring parties are, by necessity, complex. Let us attempt to project the situation for two sides at different times in a conflict. In the first stage, the dominant side, A, expects to be able to prevail by defeating the other side, B, and keep control over the resources in dispute, be it governmental power, territory, or something else. Actor B at this time expects considerable sacrifice, as B knows it is challenging a dominant actor, threatening to change the *status quo*, to achieve an improved standing in the long run. Thus, the expectations are different. Side A may be less psychologically prepared to manage a sustained battle than is B, for whom this has been a plan for a longer period of time. In terms of casualties, for instance, B may be prepared to accept more pain than A.[1] At a certain moment in time, however, the equation changes. The war has become longer than planned. A has had to invest more and all of A's other policies are affected. The gains from the conflict are decreasing, the costs are mounting. For B, the expectation of victory in a reasonably short period of time was not fulfilled. The *status quo*, the challenger learns, is more entrenched than expected. Victory and associated gains are postponed into the future. The balance between benefits and costs of war may not break evenly. This is one of the appropriate moments for ending the war, a ripe moment. Neither side is winning within the time framework it had expected nor with the resources it had at its disposal. The prognoses are gloomy for both sides. A stalemate exists in the minds of the leaders. If it is reflected on the battlefield, in the form of trenches and unbreakable defensive lines, there is a stalemate in the war, and it might be the right opportunity for interjecting ideas of conflict resolution. It may come, for instance, right after one side has tried and failed to break the military stalemate with an offensive. In more recent studies, the developments on the battlefield are seen as information to the parties about the strength and resources of the opponent, as well as the parties' ability to win. The longer the conflict continues the more willing the parties seem to be to accept offers of mediation (Greig and Regan 2008).

However, the same information can pull the equation in a different direction. It may be argued that one side, be it A or B, has now used so much of its resources that the effect of making a 'final' offensive is only a marginal additional cost, and the gains from such an offensive could be so much greater. Some of the losses could be regained. Failed negotiations, Zartman observes, mean that at least one party 'saw the cost of concessions as being greater than the cost of continuing conflict' (Zartman 1995a: 33). The calculations become increasingly geared to marginal utilities. With a particular, measured, military or political move, A might be able to strengthen its position, so that A will not have to make this particular concession. In a negotiation, in other words, a party may have alternative actions that rest outside the realm of the talks. The term used by Fisher and Ury for this is BATNA, the 'best alternative to negotiated agreement'.[2] In the same way, of course, there might be a 'best alternative' to continued warfare. There are always choices. Each of them carries different costs and benefits. At a certain point, however, terminating the war becomes rational to the warring parties, and an agreed ending can be reached.

The rational calculations are difficult to see from the outside, the information is kept private and not willingly revealed to the other side. At a certain moment in time, it may be possible to argue rationally for a continuation of war as well as a search for peace. This makes it difficult at a particular time to determine, with any certainty, that there *is* a ripe moment. This approach attempts to specify something that goes further than we have seen in either the dynamic or the needs-based approaches. It tries to specify *when* a conflict can be brought to an agreed ending. Neither dynamic approaches nor needs-based analysis can readily point to shifts in the conflict that would signify when and how it can be ended or transformed. The rational calculations are also closer to the practical policy-makers, who see themselves as capable of forming policies and moulding the future. In the previous approaches, such actors are more likely to be regarded as objects of circumstance rather than subjects of will and power.

The policy prescriptions that follow from the rational approach are many. More than the other two approaches, *the outside world* has an active role, particularly when we are concerned with conflicts in smaller countries. It seems legitimate to influence the parties in the direction of conflict management and resolution. Outsiders may be *influencing the calculation* rather than the dynamics or the needs. The calculus for conflict and conflict resolution can be affected, for instance, *by rewards and punishment*. Assistance to one or both sides may be a credible promise made by the outside world. This can be done on condition that the primary parties end the war. It is likely that reconstruction programmes interest the fighting sides. There can also be sanctions for not going into negotiations or for not compromising. This can come in the form of reductions in aid, loss of preferential treatment in trade, a ban on investments, etc. These are measures contributing to the economic constraints for parties already burdened by the war effort. Such steps are generally seen to be legitimate for achieving conflict resolution. It points to the significance of major powers in forcing parties to the negotiation table (Greig and Regan 2008). However, there is some evidence that ongoing wars can be affected by the imposition of monitored UN arms embargoes, making warring actors more interested in negotiations (Fruchart et al. 2007; Strandow 2006).

Even more controversial is whether rewards and punishment can or should be *administered by military means*, in the form of direct military attacks on one party, aiming at tipping the military balance in favour of the other. NATO's bombings in Bosnia in 1995 and in Yugoslavia during the Kosovo crisis in 1999 are in this category. Did they achieve what had been planned? What is the balance of pain inflicted and pain relieved, for instance? Such actions raise legal issues and ethical questions, not only instrumental ones. Also, the decisions to use military arsenals are not taken lightly by the outsiders. They are likely to be available only for some few conflicts, of particular interest to particular outsiders, thus, often involving additional reasons for action not necessarily related only to conflict resolution.

The fact that the outside world can have a strong impact on conflicts involving smaller countries raises an increasingly important question: *who are the parties that should settle a particular conflict?* In line with the dynamic perspective, as many actors as possible should be involved. There is a preference for a broad agenda and liberal rules of invitation. In the needs-based approach, the opposite is favoured. The workshops should be held far from the scene, have little media access, and concentrate on a limited number of parties, who act as representatives, not as individuals. For an approach building on rational calculations, however, the answer is simply that those who count should be in. There is, in Zartman's writing, a repeated observation that not all parties need to be involved in a peace deal. It may be desirable to have as many as possible included, but it is not always necessary. Another calculation can be made: which parties are needed to make an agreement durable? Some parties may create difficulties, and their interests may be better left for later.

In the dynamic approach, the incorporation of as many actors as possible is important. It is not only seen to be more democratic, it is said also to be more fruitful, as there are more issues and there is a larger potential for trade-offs. The outcomes, too, will be more innovative.

From a rational calculation perspective, larger meetings and intensive dialogue can appear as a waste of resources and time. The urgency of solving a conflict, using the ripe moment, may be lost. In the rational calculation perspective, *timing* is very important. Opportunities should be seized, particularly in a situation where a war is ongoing. This requires swift action, often by a few, determined actors. The dynamic and needs-based approaches see conflict resolution as a process and, thus, do not advocate rapid action and political manoeuvring. Ripe moments may come and go. This is not the way conflicts will ever be solved, they would argue.

The question of urgency and timing leads to an observation of which Stedman has given the most elaborate formulation – the issue of *spoilers* and how to handle them (Stedman 1997, 1998). It is not possible to work on the goodwill of the parties, Stedman argues. Experience since the Cold War shows that much violence comes *after* peace agreements are made, not before. There are actors who are dissatisfied with the deal. He gives examples from Rwanda (where the genocide in 1994 was unleashed after the peace agreement was concluded and aimed partly at preventing its implementation). More recently, East Timor could be added. Among Stedman's many observations is that the custodians of the peace agreement have to be united and determined to implement the accords as expeditiously and as unchanged as possible. This is also supported in a comparative study (Höglund 2008). It minimizes the space open to the spoilers and serves to deter them from attacking the agreement. Determined spoilers might quickly exploit even minor disagreements among the custodians. There are also ripe moments for the destruction of peace. The rational calculation approach helps to locate such situations.

The most difficult problem identified by Stedman is whether potential or actual spoilers should be included from the outset in the peace process, as follows from the dynamic approach, or excluded, as the rational calculations approach would often prefer. In the first case, urgency may be lost. Time and energy have to be spent on integrating the recalcitrant party into the process and the outcome would still be uncertain. In the second case, the hope may be that a speedy agreement and its effective implementation may change the local situation in such a way as to erode the support for the spoilers. The first approach, in contrast, may run the risk of legitimizing the spoiler and make the process hostage to spoiler tactics. The second approach, in turn, may rest on the power of the custodians and their ability to marginalize the spoilers. Most likely, the sum of these arguments is in favour of not excluding the (potential or actual) spoilers, but trying to develop a second channel for such groups. Many of them are not likely to participate – as witnessed by the actions of militant unionists and republicans in the Northern Ireland negotiations, sections of Hamas in Palestine, and settlers in Israel – but, in the long run, peacebuilding cannot be accomplished without having such parties involved in the process. In fact, they may have strong followings and in democratic processes achieve parliamentary leading or tipping positions (as has happened in all three cases mentioned).

Spoilers have a capacity to undermine or slow down a peace process by their ability to pressure the custodians on 'their' side. In a democratic framework, peacemakers and spoilers are probably competing for support from the same population, and thus mistakes or problems in implementation will be turned against the custodians and against the peace process. In fact, this makes the management of implementation central to the durability of peace agreements (Stedman et al. 2002). However, this does not exclude the possibility that settlements including only some of the warring rebels can still be lasting. It will be determined by the signatories' commitment when they enter the deal (D. Nilsson 2008). In Burundi, some of the parties entered into the agreement in 2003 and other rebel groups joined in so that by the end of 2008 all warring actors were part of the agreement. The first and partial agreement became a step in an increasingly inclusive peace process.

In the preceding sections we have looked at three perspectives which seemingly contradict each other. They all generate tools for analysis which are important for a complete understanding of ending wars through conflict resolution. In the next section, a synthesis of these approaches is suggested.

3.5 Synthesizing Conflict Resolution

The three approaches yield distinct perspectives of conflict. They carry different understandings of why conflicts emerge, have a particular dynamic and find a distinct resolution. However, one can also see them as complementary. They point to different aspects of the conflict phenomenon. For actors and analysts concerned with conflict resolution, it is an advantage to be accustomed to many approaches rather than only one. These considerations suggest that they can be integrated into one scheme for conflict analysis. Such an attempt will be made here and the utility of this will, hopefully, become apparent when we draw practical conclusions for research and policy.

Refining the definition

The definition needs to be specified. Chapter 1 offered a preliminary definition of conflict resolution. In the review just completed, additional terms have been introduced, such as conflict transformation and conflict management. It becomes necessary to distinguish conflict resolution from these terms. Also, the examination has pointed to a discrepancy between conflicts with and without arms. As the former is our interest, the definition of conflict resolution has to take this into account. These and further considerations, soon to be spelled out, result in the following definition of conflict resolution: it is a *social situation where the armed conflicting parties in a (voluntary) agreement resolve to live peacefully with – and/or dissolve – their basic incompatibilities and henceforth cease to use arms against one another.* This means that the conflict is transformed from violent to non-violent behaviour *by the parties themselves*, not by somebody else, for instance, an outsider or third party. The first test of conflict resolution is that arms are no longer used. This means that a cease-fire and a process of demilitarization are initiated according to agreed plans. To the general public this is *the* sign that the situation has actually changed. Then comes the implementation of the agreement's basic issues, which should follow soon. A second test is that the parties do not resort to violence or to the threat of violence in this phase.

The definition stipulates that the parties enter into agreement. This means that the primary parties take responsibility for the accords, and commit themselves to their implementation and legitimation. In this way, the agreement will have considerable chance of surviving when encountering challenges, as it no doubt will. There are additional arguments for emphasizing the role of the parties in conflict resolution. They are the ones who know the conflict most intimately. Obviously, they were there from the beginning, they have raised the resources and mobilized the people for conflict. This makes them the actors who most legitimately can decide when the conflict is over. All other actors, such as splinter groups, dissidents or civilian groups, will have less authority in this process than the leaders who actually formulated the initial goals for the struggle. Thus, there are reasons for involving these very leaders in any peace process, and for the outsiders to expect that parties initiating conflict are also capable of ending it.

Of course, this leads us into a question of who a *party* actually is. When those who started the war are still leading actors, the identification of responsible parties is easy. Even if the same individuals who started the war are no longer around to sign the peace, there is a continuity that new leaderships take on when assuming power. They build legitimacy on leading a party that has been an actor in the same conflict over a long period of time. They also have to take responsibility for actions that this very party pursued before the incumbent leadership came to power. Recognition of atrocities as well as issues of compensation can be part of the agreement, and builds on this continuity of responsibility. Clearly, the problem is easier to handle when we refer to a state, as it has its laws, decision-making machinery and rules of succession. For popular movements, liberation organizations and many religious communities, continuity is more difficult to establish. Rules of succession are less stable or sometimes non-existent. Splits and mergers change the picture. Thus, there needs to be a careful analysis of each case to determine who actually is a party and who are its leaders.

A delicate situation is the one in which one side does not regard the other as a legitimate party and, consequently, does not want to enter into an agreement with that party. This takes many forms. States may not recognize each other and, thus, have no diplomatic relations (as was the case between the Federal Republic of Yugoslavia and the Republic of Bosnia-Herzegovina, although they were negotiating with one another at Dayton in 1995). There could be a *de facto* recognition, of course, but agreements require a *de jure* arrangement. In the case of an intra-state conflict, governments are reluctant to extend recognition to an armed opposition movement. It regards itself, as we shall see in Chapter 4, as the sole legitimate user of violence. Thus, an agreement with an armed opponent can, in extreme cases, mean the recognition of the indefinite existence of two armies in the same state (as was the outcome of the Dayton negotiations). It can also be that the government regards the opponents as terrorists or bandits and, thus, not on an equal footing. In the case of Mozambique, the Frelimo government faced a South Africa-supported insurgency, Renamo, which it described as 'bandits'. Steven Chan and Moisés Venancio write in favour of recognition of Renamo. The argument is not a legal one but one of commitment: '... people do not fight and risk death as they had no fear, they do not kill as if they had no moral agency at all; they do not do this for a decade for the sake of it, or because they are puppets only' (Chan and Venancio 1998: xiii). Even such movements, in other words, have to be taken seriously. In this book, we include all parties that have armed forces under their control, have a central command and explicitly pursue political goals as parties or actors (these two words are used interchangeably).

There are other elements in the definition that require scrutiny, notably the notion of *a (voluntary) agreement*. How voluntary is an agreement likely to be? The parties have been fighting a war, perhaps over years, and their ambitions have been to win. Thus, accepting something less than this may appear to the parties to be a bitter pill to swallow. This use of force is, however, a part of customary war dynamics. If one party applies force, the fact that the opposite side does the same should not come as a surprise. The force of the opposing side is part of the equation.

More interesting is the pressure from the outside world, notably *secondary parties*. These are actors who do not directly commit their own troops or other regular military resources to the conflict, but still take sides and (openly or not) support a particular primary party. Secondary parties can be extremely important to a primary party, both militarily (providing bases, routes for arms deliveries) and psychologically (making clear to the party that it is 'not alone'). They may also have their own agenda and, thus, use their leverage on the primary parties, if they so wish. If secondary parties on either side agree on how the conflict should be ended, they may very well be in a position to impose this on the parties. This is what many primary parties suspect and fear. They may nervously watch summit meetings between major powers, who may be their main suppliers of weapons. The highly concentrated world trade in major arms gives the five permanent members of the UN Security Council considerable leverage in many conflict situations, if they would act jointly. In this way, a local conflict may in fact become part of a global conflagration, something which was constantly happening during the Cold War. A relatively minor issue, from the point of view of the populations in the major countries, may escalate into a nuclear confrontation (Nincic 1985). A close relationship to outside actors may be necessary but can also be risky for a primary party. Thus, it is noteworthy that agreements made under external pressure tend to be more short-lived than others (Nordquist 1992). The ending of the war 'prematurely' may be blamed on the outsider. Outside pressure may be a good tactic to get support for an agreement at one stage, but when that constraint disappears, the settlement may no longer hold. Thus, agreements with a reasonable amount of voluntary involvement by the parties themselves are likely to last longer.

Conflict resolution here is focused on an *agreement*. It is, as indicated in Section 3.2, difficult to imagine that parties in a war would end their armed conflict and live side by side without some minimum form of understanding. It can be specified in an agreement, highly formalized as a treaty. It may also take other forms. But some arrangement is needed for this to be conflict resolution. It specifies commitments made by the parties, for all to see. The agreement, furthermore, marks the end point of the armed phase of the conflict and the beginning of something new. However, it does not mean that entering an agreement is the same as ending a peace process. Agreement is only one element in a larger process. Concepts such as conflict transformation and peacebuilding bring us into a wider array of concerns. They are all important for the durability of the settlement and for the creation of new, 'normal' conditions. In addition, the focus on agreement distinguishes conflict resolution from conflict management, which often works on implicit, even secret, understandings, or simply ways of 'handling' a problem. Conflict management typically focuses on the armed aspect of the conflict: bringing the fighting to an end, limiting the spread of the conflict and, thus, containing it. Such action may even be regarded as successful. The interest for a particular conflict may disappear. Conflict resolution is more ambitious, as it expects the parties to face jointly their incompatibility and find a way to live with or dissolve it. The significance of entering into an agreement illustrates how 'conflict resolution' differs from other concepts.

One element in the definition requiring further analysis remains – the incompatibility. By studying this, we are also able to isolate a set of resolution methods to be studied more closely in the rest of this book.

Transcending incompatibility: seven mechanisms

The phrase *live with – and/or dissolve – the incompatibility* requires close attention. In the overview of thinking on conflict resolution, different ideas were indicated. These need to be brought together in a more systematic fashion, which can be done by focusing on the incompatibility. The concept of incompatibility is defined as the inability to meet the demands of two or more parties at the same time with the available resources. Giving a certain resource to A will mean that B will not receive its desired share. Resources, of course, may be something less tangible than land, capital, natural resources, military positions or political posts. They can also be the desire to obtain recognition, respect, restitution or restoration (which the party may feel entitled to, due to its historical role or experience of historical injustice). It can concern meeting a historical mission (which in reality is close to the question of recognition or redress of a historical grievance). There is also the question of security, which takes on such significance that it sometimes is not just a means to other goals but a goal in itself.

How can parties with such incompatible positions ever be able to arrive at the stipulation in the definition: live with – and/or dissolve – the incompatibility? As we have noted, there has been a record number of peace agreements since the end of the Cold War. Parties who have been involved in deadly struggles have found ways to live with one another. Their partnership may not be easy but is, by the parties themselves, defined as preferable to the struggle that preceded it. The solutions may sometimes dissolve the incompatibility, which means finding an arrangement that no longer makes this issue a salient one. It disappears. It may, in a way, mean that a party gives up some of its ambitions. For instance, the (white) Nationalist Party agreed to dismantle Apartheid in South Africa. But the Party remained a political party (until its demise for other reasons) and the white population stayed in the country, safeguarded by the state in an equal way, like other citizens. The political rules have been changed with the enfranchising of the majority of the population. In other situations, the parties agree to disagree, but agree to a framework for disagreement. Thus, they are committing themselves to live peacefully with the incompatibility. This frequently means resorting to democratic forms of politics. In these cases, they have not dissolved the disagreement over, for example, land ownership, but created safe channels to the political process for all sides. There is a set of rules through which the conflict can continue, but without use of arms. How can this be done, theoretically and in practice? Here we will attempt to answer the question theoretically, throughout the book we will discuss it empirically.

In theory, there are seven distinct ways in which the parties can live with or dissolve their incompatibility. These are mechanisms, procedures or forms of transcendence that can be derived from Figure 3.1.

First, a party may change its goals, that is, *shift its priorities*. It is rare that a party will completely change its basic positions, but it can display a shift in what it gives highest priority to. This may open ways in which the other side can reciprocate. Leadership changes are particularly pertinent in this respect. With such changes, new possibilities are created. It does not mean that conflict resolution has to wait for a revolution. Leadership is often recruited from a limited segment of the population, and continuity remains important. Still, new leaders think differently and, thus, new leadership matters. There are also other changes that can take place. Changes in the surrounding world may be important, leading to shifts in strategic priorities. Among major powers, the rise of a new power or the fall of an old one may be such a condition. For less powerful actors, changes in major power relations have many implications. Shifts between *détente* and confrontation can be important for conflict resolution, as was clearly seen at the end of the Cold War. Economic crises can change priorities. The costs of pursuing a war may drain important resources and, thus, the chances of a peace dividend may seem more attractive. However, the possibility for such changes should not be overestimated and it would be outright dangerous for a party to hinge a negotiation policy on expectations of change in a particular direction. New leaders may be weaker, major power relations may change for the worse, economic crises may induce less interest in compromise, etc. But it is important for the parties continuously to probe the other side, to find out if there are shifts in priority.

The second way is a classical one: the parties stick to their goals but find a point at which resources can be *divided*. This is point C in Figure 3.1. It is sometimes seen as the essence of compromise, but it is only one form of compromise. It may mean that both sides change priority. However, it is done in such a way that the change by side A is coupled to a change by side B. To meet halfway, at some point which has a symbolic value, is easier for the parties. Then, it is also possible for them to defend the deal to other decision-makers and to the general public. It may appear reasonable and be in accordance with values in the society. If the incompatibility concerns territory, this may mean drawing a border approximately half the distance between the two demands. It makes sense, but only so long as the areas are not inhabited by people who will have their own interests, or if the area contains resources that also should be part of the deal. Compromise is most readily made with monetary resources. Negotiations between employers and employees have a long history of finding optimal points at which to draw the dividing line between the two sides. In many such situations, it is important for the parties to get some resources, rather than nothing. With power positions this may be more difficult, but even so there are ways in which power can be divided, for instance, along the lines of central–regional divisions or along functions (presidency, prime minister, speaker, supreme court, important committees, etc.). As mentioned, there are examples of two prime ministers in the same cabinet (Cambodia). Rotation of the office of Prime Minister was used for a time in Israel, each party getting an equal number of years – an interesting time-sharing arrangement. This is institutionalized in Switzerland, with its annual shifting of presidency.

A third way is *horse-trading*, where one side has all of its demands met on one issue, while the other has all of its goals met on another issue. It means using two separate incompatibility diagrams (Figure 3.1), one for each issue, where each party gets 100 per cent. This can also be described as a compromise, but works in a different way from the division we just described. In horse-trading over territory, the idea would be that A takes area 1 and B takes area 2, although both of them have had demands on areas 1 and 2. Instead of making a complicated division, an entire piece of territory is taken over by one or the other. Again, as we noted before, this assumes that there are no particular features to the territory, or that such features somehow are equal for both (for instance, oil in both). In a contest over political power positions, A may support B in some matters and receive corresponding support from B in others, meaning A and B abandon previous views and together form what is sometimes referred to as 'national pacts' or 'historical compromises'.

A fourth way is *shared control*. In this case the parties decide to rule together over the disputed resource. This comes close to outcome D indicated in Figure 3.1. A territory can be shared by being ruled as a condominium, where decisions require the consent of both parties. An economic resource can be operated by a joint company and a formula devised for investment and profit sharing. A country can be run by a coalition government, a frequent phenomenon in most parliamentary democracies. Shared control may require some degree of trust; it may also be a temporary arrangement for a transition period. Power-sharing arrangements also exemplify this. This is where all parties are represented in government according to a formula agreed upon beforehand (for each 5 per cent of the national vote a party gets one seat in the cabinet, for instance). Even if agreed to only for a predetermined period, it can mean that a conflict is successfully transcended and that, at the end of the period, the conflict situation is very different from what it was at the beginning. This can also be applied to international regimes setting up rules for using water in shared rivers. In international affairs, such arrangements may mean the beginning of regional integration; in internal affairs they can be contributions to the integration of a fragmented society.

A fifth way is to *leave control to somebody else*, which means externalizing control, so that the warring parties agree not to rule the resources themselves. This is outcome E in Figure 3.1. The primary parties agree, or accept, that a third actor takes control. Such solutions have gained prominence in the discussions on international conflicts during the 1990s. The notion of protectorates has returned to serious discussions. There are recent examples of independent countries having had their sovereignty strongly circumscribed. Bosnia-Herzegovina is one case with its complex constitution. In 1999, one part of a sovereign country was placed under international protection, Kosovo, in the south of the Federal Republic of Yugoslavia. In the case of Kosovo, it meant that neither the Yugoslav authorities nor the Kosovo Albanian representatives ran the area, but instead authority resided with the UN, for the following nine years. In these cases, the parties accepted the set-up, but only after considerable warfare (the Bosnian War and NATO's actions in 1995, the Kosovo wars and the aerial bombardments of Yugoslavia in 1999). Similarly, East Timor was under UN administration 1999–2002, neither a part of Indonesia nor an independent country. It was more a trusteeship than a protectorate.

Obviously, there are other, less dramatic, ways of handing control to third parties. Economic resources can be given as concessions to private companies. The cabinet can be taken over by parliamentary minorities or experts in order to detach the official administration from major political divides in the country. The latter can be important, particularly at times of elections. Bangladesh has such a stipulation in its constitution.

Sixth, there is the possibility of resorting to *conflict resolution mechanisms*, notably arbitration or other legal procedures that the parties can accept. It means finding a procedure that can resolve the conflict according to some of the previously mentioned five ways, with the added quality that it is done through a process outside the parties' immediate control. The legal mechanism builds on the idea of neutrality, distance and resort to precedents and history. Among conflict resolution mechanisms we would also include holding new elections and arranging a referendum, which means leaving the issue to a concerned but still non-predetermined audience. For this to be a legitimate way of ending a conflict, the conflicting parties should have a fair chance to present their views. Studies show that if parties believe that they have been given a fair chance, they are more likely to accept defeat (Tyler 2000). A number of border disputes have been resolved with the use of arbitration. A remarkable case is the drawing of the border between Iraq and Kuwait after the Gulf War, settled according to an exchange of documents between the two parties, but under the authorization of the UN Security Council. The democratic system solves some disputes by resorting to new elections or referenda. Territorial issues can also be resolved this way, by giving a voice to the population itself. That was part of the agreement ending the internal conflict between North and South Sudan, through a successful referendum on independence in January 2011.

Seventh, issues can be *left to later* or even to oblivion. By appointing a commission, parties can gain time, and when the commission reports, political conditions and popular attitudes may have changed. Some issues may gain from being delayed, as their significance may pale or their symbolic character may be reduced. This is an argument for not solving all questions at the same time. But it requires that there be a second chance to bring them up. In fact, the second chance is important for a loser to accept defeat or enter into a compromise. If there is a credible way in which one can return to the issue later or run in a new election, then the agreement is more acceptable. The party does not argue that the issue is given less priority, only that its time is not yet ripe. In the case of the first mechanism, in contrast, there is a significant change of position and the party does not return to its previous view.

3.6 Identifying Key Elements in Conflict Analysis

Living with or dissolving the incompatibility is a central element in conflict analysis. This is learned from the dynamic approach to conflict presented in Section 3.2 as well as from the rational calculation approach given in Section 3.4, for instance, in differentiating between positions and interests and getting into the calculations of the parties. The focus on the needs of parties, as given in Section 3.3, brings with it a close look at the parties themselves, their needs, perceptions and the history behind the conflict. These are elements that are also important for an analysis of rational calculations. There is a relationship between conflict behaviour and changing positions, as indicated in terms such as action–reaction, and carefully, rationally calibrated moves. In all, the three approaches have many shared features. They are, as a consequence, all useful. They illustrate different elements in the conflict process and how it can be turned into a peace process. Figure 3.3 describes this and suggests a shared framework for the analysis.

The dynamics of conflict are illustrated by the arrows in Figure 3.3 overleaf. There are no convincing arguments for assuming that a conflict always starts in one corner. It is more fruitful to assume that connections exist and are more fluid. The different boxes require some closer description. First, in the box on conflict formation is located the creation of parties, which we have stipulated to be an integral part of conflict analysis. Some parties are formed deliberately to make conflicts; others may be there for other purposes. When a party is formed, it begins by making itself known, developing its identity and giving itself a role in the conflict to which it adheres. The history, recruitment and financing of a party are important to understand, as well as its internal decision-making. If there are needs in

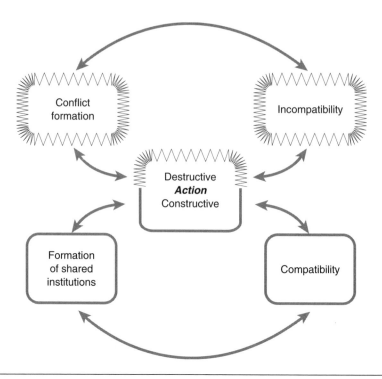

Figure 3.3   Synthesizing concepts in conflict analysis

the society on which its actions purport to be based, then, of course, those needs have to be focused. To this also belongs whether a party really represents the needs of a larger share of the population.

Second, obviously, an analysis of the incompatibility is necessary. What are the conflicting interests, what is the relationship between interests, positions and needs of the actor or of the population it claims to represent? The actors are likely to have an internal priority in terms of issues. Some are more basic than others. It is important for the analyst to have an idea of such hierarchies. Third, there are the actions. Conflicts are fuelled by destructive actions, actions aimed at reducing the influence of the other side, and enhancing the influence of its own side. Thus, this box in Figure 3.3 not only involves actual warfare, but also the making of alliances, finding friends, and locating financiers, as well as preventing the opponent from doing the same. These are seen, by the parties, as integral elements of their struggle. The conflict strategies are important elements in the analysis.

In Figure 3.3, however, a statement of great consequence is made. It is argued, in line with the dynamic approach, that behaviour can be changed, and that such a change is strategic in making a conflict take a different direction. That is described as constructive action. These are actions that aim at bridging the gap to the other side. Included are measures such as confidence-building, but also unilateral actions. The now classical example is the visit by Egypt's President Sadat to Jerusalem in 1977. It was an unexpected action. It was not clear how the Israeli government would receive it. With the support of the Carter administration in the USA, it helped to change the dynamics in the Middle East conflict. Such measures are rare, and risky, but ways out of many recent wars have contained unilateral and constructive moves. Thus, the behaviour of the opposing sides is the element in the conflict that the parties themselves watch most closely. They will ask, for instance, if a positive announcement is followed by positive steps. If not, the former is regarded as propaganda and the latter as the reality. The proof of 'good intentions' is 'good actions'.

Once there is a shift in behaviour, perhaps by separating the parties in a cease-fire through traditional peacekeeping, the lower half of Figure 3.3 comes into operation. A dynamic development may follow and build momentum. The parties may start to search for compatible positions (shared needs or a formula meeting the interests of the primary parties) and, when they find them, there will also be attempts to create new structures through which these can be expressed. This can be simple negotiation fora (multilateral conferences) but also transitory forms of government or even entirely new permanent bodies (the European Union (EU) could be regarded as a way of ending the earlier Franco-German conflict, although it is more often described as a measure to prevent a future one). The detection of compatibilities and the formation of new organizations mean that dynamics are created which may generate more constructive action. Thus, Figure 3.3 describes two processes, a process of conflict formation and escalation in the upper half of the figure and one of peacebuilding and shared interests in the lower half.

The utility of Figure 3.3 can be demonstrated with the phenomenon of spoilers and spoiler management introduced by Stedman. It can now be located theoretically. Spoilers are those actors who have no interest in the conflict process shifting from the higher to the lower level in Figure 3.3. If there is a peace agreement, as postulated by Stedman, then a spoiler aims to prevent the dynamics in the lower level from spinning further. This runs counter to interests held by particular groups. Thus, violent action can be used to attempt to shift the conflict back into the upper level (Höglund 2008). If successful, peace moves are spoiled, for the time being. When a conflict is locked in the upper part of Figure 3.3, most actors are spoilers as long as they all pursue destructive action. Thus, it makes sense to link, as Stedman does, the spoiler phenomenon to a peace agreement or at least a fairly entrenched peace process. In a way, a spoiler is a party still living in the dynamics of the upper level, preferring to be there at least as long as its interests are not met. This also illustrates the importance for the custodians to make clear that the situation has changed and decisively moved into the lower level of Figure 3.3. The custodians have to show in action that they are committed to preventing the conflict from sliding back to the dynamics of the upper level.[3]

The fact that behaviour is the point combining the two dynamics makes clear its dual nature. It may promote one or the other development, but it is also the juncture at which conflict dynamics can change from one loop to the other and back again. It means that conflicts are not unilinear, for instance, moving from frustration to conflict to resolution. Instead they develop through twists and turns, with changes in behaviour, positions and parties, new frustrations and new calculations all affecting the dynamics. It means that conflicts are not simply escalating and de-escalating, or that they are easily predicted and calculated. They are all of these simultaneously and that is the reality with which the analysts have to cope.

In Chapter 4 we will give some additional building blocks for conflict analysis, thus completing Part One and preparing for a closer look at basic as well as complex realities in conflict resolution.

Further Readings

Go to the *Understanding Conflict Resolution* web page at www.sagepub.co.uk for free access to journal articles listed.

Azar, E and Burton, J. 1986. *International Conflict Resolution: Theory and Practice.* Boulder, Colorado: Lynne Rienner.

Bercovitch, J. (ed.) 1996. *Resolving International Conflicts: The Theory and Practice of Mediation.* Boulder, Colorado: Lynne Rienner.

Berdal, M. and D. M. Malone 2000. *Greed and Grievance. Economic Agendas in Civil Wars.* Colorado: Lynne Rienner.

Brown, M. E. et al. 1998. *Theories of War and Peace.* Cambridge, Massachusetts: MIT Press.

Burton, J. 1990. *Conflict: Resolution and Provention.* London: Macmillan.

Collier, P. et al. 2003. *Breaking the Conflict Trap. Civil War and Development Policy.* Washington, D.C.: The World Bank.

Zartman, I. W. (ed.) 1996. *Elusive Peace. Negotiating an End to Civil Wars.* Washington, D.C.: The Brookings Institution.

Notes

1 It is possible that B plans for a surprise attack, which would be swift and, thus, A would be the one who will be prepared for a longer confrontation. A and B simply shift places in the description given in the text.

2 This notion, Daniel Druckman has pointed out, emanates from Thibaut and Kelley, who introduced the comparison level for alternatives (1959: 21–3).

3 Obviously, this can result in the simultaneous pursuit of both upper- and lower-level conflict dynamics, for instance, punishing spoilers according to the upper-level dynamics, while rewarding actors working according to the lower-level dynamics. Indeed, there is even an interplay between the two: acting tough on spoilers may enhance the gains for actors adhering to the peace process. Targeted sanctions may be used this way.

ANALYSING CONFLICT RESOLUTION 4

4.1 Basic and Complex Levels of Analysis

In the preceding chapters we have developed a general understanding of the concept of conflict. This is a necessary initial step in conflict analysis. Here our task is to approach conflicts where arms are used and the role this gives to conflict resolution. Armed conflict is one category of the general phenomenon of social conflict. It has some distinct features. It normally grows out of non-armed conflict, in the sequences illustrated in Figure 3.3, but involves not just a shift in behaviour. It has other aspects associated with the three concepts of parties, incompatibility and action. First, there is a particular role for the state as soon as a conflict becomes armed. The reasons for this are explained in Section 4.2. There are also armed, as well as non-armed, non-state actors in many armed conflicts, and, for a fuller analysis, it is necessary to include them. The conflict analyst not only faces traditional conflict material of states fighting wars among themselves, but also the analytically less well-developed circumstances of intra-state conflicts. This will also be pursued in this chapter. Second, an additional building block is the incompatibility, where the analysis concentrates on two types that are particularly frequently associated with armed conflict. These are incompatibilities dealing with political power (here termed incompatibility over government) and those dealing with control over land (here described as incompatibility over territory). Third, when a conflict shifts from non-armed to predominantly armed conflict behaviour, this may involve a shift of parties and of issues. This makes the task of conflict resolution more cumbersome. It becomes not only a matter of ending violence, but also means affecting relationships between the parties as well as their incompatibilities. Together, these distinctions result in three types of conflict, a trichotomy of conflict. They are the basic units of conflict analysis. Part Two of this book, that is Chapters 5, 6 and 7, is devoted entirely to an analysis of the resolution of such conflicts. There is also a more complex level. Conflicts are often connected to one another, where parties may have alliances or, in fact, be the same across borders or social divides. Incompatibilities may form components in regional or global confrontations. This has to be taken into account. In addition, there is frequent involvement from outside actors, which has to be considered in a complex, comprehensive analysis. The complex level is pursued in Part Three where Chapters 8, 9 and 10 provide tools for an understanding of the full reality in which conflicts arise.

4.2 The Role of the State

Actors in conflict

The definitions of conflict and conflict resolution have so far not said much about who the parties are. In Chapter 3 we have only specified them as 'actors' or 'parties', giving them some general characteristics. However, the definitions used for collecting war statistics in the Michigan, Hamburg and Uppsala programmes described in Chapter 2 limit armed conflict to a considerably smaller cluster of social interactions (although there is also now an increasing interest in non-state violence). They concentrate on conflicts that have a state as one of the parties. The examples used in much of the theorizing on conflict resolution indicate similar restrictions for the selection of cases. The practice of researchers is more restrained than their theories would necessarily require.

In fact, the study of conflict resolution is a merger of two different strands of thought. Conflict theory has the objective of creating a general understanding of conflict. For instance, it takes note of apparent parallels between person-to-person conflicts and state-to-state relations. Thus, it is tempting to search for general understandings. No doubt, interesting lessons can be drawn, building on an intimate knowledge of particular cases and their specific dynamics. The other strand is the causes of war studies, which aim to find general patterns for wars throughout history, ideally by including all wars and empirically thrashing out similarities. Thus, it requires general definitions across time and space in order to arrive at data consisting of comparable phenomena. The value increases with larger numbers and longer time-spans. The state is such a 'stable' actor, providing for comparability, for instance between the end of the Napoleonic Wars (that is, since 1816) or following the Westphalian Peace (that is, since 1648). The merger of these two strands into studies of general conflict resolution theory runs into empirical difficulties. For instance, the cases analysed may be insightful, but how typical are they for the general phenomenon? Can a state be compared to a person, a social group or a social institution? Similarly, data collected for causes of war studies often are not necessarily well designed for conflict theory purposes. Ending of conflicts has seldom been part of the understanding, except, for instance, for finding a termination date. Merging these two strands requires particular efforts.

The Uppsala Conflict Data Program is specifically devoted to conflict resolution. Even so, it initially restricted itself to the types of conflict that the causes of war studies include. The agenda has now been enlarged also to make possible the study of conflicts between non-state actors, and actions of one-sided violence. The solution to such conflicts will enter the agenda and enlarge our understanding of conflict resolution. The non-state relations may take on different qualities, but even so they are likely to be affected by the legal systems of the country, and thus by state authority.

The study of person-to-person relations in state-to-state conflicts, notably the personal relationships between leaders, would be a valuable point of convergence. For instance, the rapport between the very conservative Republican US President Ronald Reagan and the Soviet Secretary-General of the Communist Party, Mikhail Gorbachev, from their first meeting in 1985, appears to have had a profound impact on world developments. A similar understanding between US President George W. Bush and Russian President Vladimir Putin in the early 2000s, however, did not last and had little political consequence. Of course, they met as state leaders, and this is likely to have affected their personal relations as well. From whatever angle we would like to approach the question of conflict resolution in armed conflict, an analysis of the state is unavoidable.

The special roles of the state

There are theoretically valid reasons for having the state as a main actor in the analysis of armed conflict and its resolution. The state is, according to most political science definitions, the only legitimate user of physical violence in a society (Weber 1964: 154–6). Thus, it is almost, by definition, involved whenever there is an armed conflict in society. The control of violence is not the only distinguishing feature. There are also fiscal, territorial and ideological monopolies. The concurrent exercise of these four monopolies provides the state with coherence internally and independence internationally. This requires some further elaboration.

The state has a fiscal monopoly, being the only unit that can collect taxes and tariffs, where the inhabitants have to pay a certain sum of money in return for services whose delivery and quality they cannot immediately inspect and where choice is limited. The fiscal monopoly is unique and distinct from the monopoly that can be exercised by a corporation on a market or a trade union in recruiting members in a company, for instance. A central state may hand over its rights and obligations to others, for instance, to states in a federation, to local communities or even to other units. But this authority derives from the right of the state to collect tax revenue. In the writings of economic historians, the state's fiscal monopoly is seen as particularly important for the state's emergence and growth, compared to other organizational units (Tilly 1990).

The state is the sole legitimate authority within its territory, and is expected by other actors, notably neighbouring states, to maintain that authority. The border is not only a line of territorial separation, but also the geographical space where one legitimate authority is replaced by another. A central governmental task is to uphold authority all the way to the border. However, in an increasingly interdependent world of cross-border transactions, it is in the interest of governments on either side of the border that there also be control on the other side. Otherwise border areas may become bases for non-legitimate actors, such as criminal gangs, drug traders or guerrilla groups directed against one or both governments. The border is no longer only the exposed front line of defence against an unknown or hostile actor on the other side. Borders are increasingly matters of shared interest. In another interesting development, humanitarian concerns change the agenda of the state inside its area of authority, as the state is seen as the guarantor of exposed groups or even a guardian of human rights. One state's failure to pursue this may expose it to international sanctions from other states. Indeed, the 2005 World Summit meeting in New York endorsed the principle that in such cases there is even an international responsibility to protect exposed populations.

In addition to these elements, it is also evident that the state, for instance through its control over the educational system, is the originator of an official view of what the state is all about. There is an ideological function. For each state, the government's interpretation of what the role is of a particular state is likely to be highly influential. It determines the range of debate that is permissible within the state, but it may at the same time restrict the options available to the political leadership. It cannot act easily beyond established parameters of acceptable conduct. Thus, the state determines and expresses the way in which a society describes its history, pursues its values and reproduces the myths that exist for legitimizing its existence. This is an ideological leadership, which is a monopoly in non-democratic states and a more subtle hegemony in many open societies.

All these roles may make the state an actor in conflict as well as an object of conflict. That the state is an actor is obvious. This is the way policy is made, and the instruments available to the state are used (administration, police, military forces, tax collection, etc.). That the state is an object of conflict is also clear. For instance, the access to tax revenue makes it valuable to control the state. It makes the state a resource-rich actor, and is probably perceived to be more so, the poorer a country is. The state may sometimes be the sole provider of wealth in a society. The control over violence indicates that there is a powerful military and police apparatus, with its own interests but also attractive to control. This invites group competition for entry into power. The ideological function means that the state machinery can be used to transmit perspectives and legitimize values directing the society at large. This can be an instrument that groups may value to control. One by one, or taken together, the four functions of a state's monopoly or near-monopoly on force, fiscal resources, territorial control and ideological impact, make the state an asset for those pursuing particular perspectives, be they of left, right, religious, secular, democratic, nationalistic or other orientations.

The one who controls the state acts in its name, and can use the state's legal systems for its own purposes. The state, as a consequence, is a unique actor and cannot be compared to a political party, a guerrilla movement or a business corporation. These may all have resources of different sorts, but will not have the legitimacy that follows with the state. There is a limit, however. If the state is not capable of performing some of these functions, its strength as an actor diminishes, and so does its value as an object. This is the essence of the phenomenon of warlord politics that can be observed in different parts of the world (Duffield 1998; Reno 1998). The phenomenon of state failure – known throughout the history of the state – has received particular attention during the 1990s. This is a matter that affects conflict dynamics and conflict resolution. Thus, we will have to return to it in Parts Two and Three. However, it raises important theoretical and normative issues that we need to dwell on immediately.

Clearly, the state as an institution is caught in a dilemma. If it is too powerful, it is likely to be resented; if it is too weak, it is likely to be dismissed. The former is illustrated by the Soviet Union during its entire existence; the latter is exemplified by Somalia since the 1990s. Both ends of the continuum require some thought. When the state is too strong, it governs through the fear it can instill on the population. Totalitarian systems may survive for considerable periods of time, but do so at a high price of repression and, eventually, face a strong counter-reaction. If central control can be combined with economic growth, the pressure may be deflected, but it may also result in new demands from entrepreneurial groups and other resource-rich constellations. In addition, totalitarian regimes inject fear in neighbouring countries, not only among its own citizens. Even global relations can be affected. Major power relations changed dramatically when the Communist Party under Mao took control over China in 1949. The same happened when a totalitarian regime under Hitler came to power in Germany in 1933. This shows that working interstate relationships are dependent not only on direct interactions between states, but also on the domestic conditions of the parties. The relationship between totalitarian regimes and democratic powers is particularly contentious. This was a feature during the twentieth century and remains for the new century, epitomized by the West's relations to China, Vietnam, North Korea, Burma/Myanmar, the Islamic Republic of Iran, Saddam Hussein's Iraq and Afghanistan under the Taliban.

When the state is too weak a different dynamic can be observed. It means a state cannot maintain law and order within its assigned area, control the flow of arms and pursue the collection of taxes. These functions of the state are, in fact, highly interrelated. To collect revenue, the state needs to have credible legal means and a reliable police system. In order to maintain an efficient police and legal system, it needs revenue. Revenue is collected from citizens, their economic transactions and from border crossings. To be able to do that it needs to have effective control over its territory. This requires police and military resources. It is an interplay that in industrialized, resource-rich countries is robust and entrenched in the minds of people. In a resource-scarce country, other loyalties are stronger. The provider of security and welfare can be a clan leader who, in addition, may want to enlarge the resources at the clan's disposal. Thus, the state faces challenges. Somalia may, to some extent, represent the case of clans in conflict. It is not the full story, however, as there are examples of clan cooperation and the resort to local forms of conflict resolution (Fox 1999, 2000). The competing forces may be other actors, notably companies interested in the extraction of minerals (as seen in other African states, for instance, the Democratic Republic of Congo). State leaders may play religious groups wanting to institute their own order against each other (which can be witnessed in Afghanistan and Iraq). There can also be ethnically based groups searching for control of strategic assets, such as nodes in pipeline systems (a factor in Chechnya, Nigeria and Iraq). Thus, too weak a state invites intra-state wars; too strong a state may do the same. Both, furthermore, may lead to international repercussions. To find the 'ideal' state for peace is not easy. Democracy has been identified as one element (Russett 1993), but it may not be sufficient for handling all the world's conflict material.

The global system

The interactions among the states are described as the international system. According to some writers, it is a self-contained system that can be understood through the lens of the security dilemma. Even a state with defensive purposes may be seen as a threat to other states, whose defensive actions in turn are perceived as threatening. This is a security dilemma to which we have already alluded (Waltz 1979). Although strong theoretically, the notion of the security dilemma builds on some assumptions, most importantly that state survival is the prime motive for states, that states are strong and coherent, and that war between states is of basic concern for security policy. A number of these assumptions are not valid when we look at the entire picture of armed conflicts in the world. It is more common to have war inside states than between them (see Table 4.1 on page 77), states do collapse (as just described) and there are numerous other actors. Thus, the *interstate system*, as instituted in international law and in the UN Charter, is but one subsystem, albeit an important one, in a larger framework – the *global system*. This is a messier, less structured set of relationships that includes a gamut of other actors and interests. In this perspective, the interstate system, often described as anarchic, appears rather structured and based on predictable rules. Let us explore this a little further.

First, *the interstate system* assumes that states can be *fairly easily defined*. The number of states in the world is limited; UN membership (at the end of 2010) is 192. There are some ten additional entities, which are not recognized by the UN majority and, thus, not seated (the Republic of China,

Taipei, also known as Taiwan is one case; Kosovo is another, more successful case, now recognized by one-third of UN member states). There is, in addition, a category of non-recognized states, which exist de facto, but have not been recognized by the central government and, thus, normally not by other states either: Somaliland, Northern Cyprus, Abkhazia, South Ossetia all belong to this category of state-like non-states. In particular Somaliland, which corresponds to the former British Somali colony and was independent for a week in 1960 before it merged with Somalia, the former Italian colony, clearly has managed to keep state authorities functioning and maintain the country's independence, in spite of the collapse of the rest of Somalia (Fox 2000). No country has yet recognized this entity, however. Partly, this is based on the fear that it would stimulate or legitimize secessionism in Africa. In the case of Eritrea, other states did not recognize the new state until after an arrangement had been made with Ethiopia on a procedure for independence, leading to mutually agreed statehood in 1993. The declaration of Northern Cyprus as an independent state in 1983 led to diplomatic recognition by Turkey, whereas the UN defined the declaration as illegal. The Republic of Cyprus does not recognize this entity. There is a tendency of giving the former central, sometimes colonial, power a veto over the recognition of new states emerging from territory nominally under the control of the previous centre. In 1990 several states in the Soviet Union declared themselves independent. At that time, Lithuania was only recognized by Iceland. The major powers did not want to risk undermining Gorbachev's leadership of the Soviet Union as a whole. An agreement on the final status of Kosovo will therefore require the consent of Serbia (the successor to Yugoslavia), but Kosovo nevertheless declared itself independent in 2008. Later the same year Abkhazia and South Ossetia took the same step, immediately being recognized by Russia and three other states. However, the central authority, Georgia, has not agreed. Most states have refused recognition of these two entities, but Kosovo has the stronger international backing.

Thus, the attitude among existing states is less than inviting to the formation of new states. Granted this reluctance, it is still likely that a set of new states will be formed in the coming years, eventually to be seated in the UN. The non-recognized states aspire to receive recognition as a way of protecting their security. On many counts they operate as recognized states, and often model themselves on such states. The process of fragmentation of larger ethnically diverse states, which began during the First World War, is likely to proceed. There are today some 200 state-like entities. The number may grow during the coming years with the addition of one or two states per year. A more dramatic rise is only likely if a major, colonial-type empire is dissolved. The record since 1945 shows that there is at least one such event per decade. The dissolution of the British Empire in South Asia took place in the 1940s. The ending of French control in Indochina and Africa occurred in the 1950s and 1960s. The end of British colonial possessions in Africa can be dated to a decade after 1957 when Ghana became independent.

The crumbling of the Portuguese Empire in Africa in the mid-1970s was achieved through liberation wars. The granting of independence to Pacific islands was a process of the 1980s and the breakdown of the communist empires in Europe was a feature of the early 1990s. The process of formation of new states is not at its end, but it is not an unlimited process either. There are countervailing forces, including the possibility of existing states learning to handle minorities in a more respectful way (Gurr 2000b).

However, in the 130 armed conflicts since 1989 recorded by the Uppsala Conflict Data Program, it can be seen that the state was only one of the actors in most of the conflicts. This means that there were a host of other parties present. They are defined as opposition organizations, or *armed non-state actors*. The Uppsala Conflict Data Program lists 900 such actors. Few of these are recognized by states, and certainly not by the states against which they are fighting. They are instead defined variously as terrorists, gangs, bandits, criminal groups, etc. Such descriptions may sometimes be accurate, sometimes not. Some of these organizations enter into negotiations, or even win wars. Their leaders may then appear as reasonable or even enlightened statespersons despite the labels that have been put on them previously (for instance, Nelson Mandela in South Africa and Xanana Gusmao of Timor-Leste). Sometimes the organizations turn into political parties or legitimate armed structures (the former liberation army UCK/KLA in Kosovo was, by the international community, converted into a civilian protection corps after the 1999 war). Other organizations have instead been recorded in history as uncivilized, cruel and even illogical. A recent example is the al-Qaida network that was led by Osama bin Laden and seen by US authorities as the instigator of the attack on the World Trade Center in New York and the Pentagon in Washington, DC on September 11, 2001. A number of armed groups now claim the al-Qaida mantle, be they located in Morocco, Algeria, Iraq, Somalia, Yemen or Pakistan. There are historical precedents. For instance, the First World War followed on from the assassination of the heir to the throne of the Austro-Hungarian monarchy. This was carried out by a terrorist organization harboured by neighbouring Serbia. Indeed, words such as 'assassins' and 'anarchists' refer to terrorists in European history. Such organizations obviously have to be part of an understanding of wars and armed conflict. How did they emerge, what were their goals, how did they get resources to finance protracted wars? These are pertinent and legitimate questions.

The large number of non-state actors illustrates the shortcomings of focusing only on the interstate system, as if states were in exclusive control even of their own territories. It can be argued, of course, that many of the non-state groups would not have been able to sustain themselves without access to other countries. This may be true, but it does not mean they are always and purely puppets of others. They may in reality be strong enough to coerce regimes and even become involved in wars with the host countries (as happened in Jordan in 1971 and in Lebanon in 1982 with Palestinian groups and the PLO as actors). In the 1990s there has also emerged a market for mercenaries and private security companies, which have played a role in wars in Africa, South America and the Middle East. There are militias or para-military formations, that is, informally or formally organized groups. These are locally recruited, operate with unclear mandates and obscure finances and are often directed by a determined leadership, motivated by political and/or economic gains. Such groups are reported from Colombia, Central Africa, in the Bosnian war, in pre-independent East Timor and in Chechnya. Undoubtedly, their activities affect the work of the international system. In the case of East Timor, it resulted in a UN-authorized peace-keeping operation led by Australia, in mid-September 1999. Thus, we see that insecurity and security dilemmas abound, and they are created also by actors other than states.

Third, the global system includes actors who do not have arms but still have a role in conflict. In the emerging global civil society, *non-governmental organizations* (NGOs), also called civil society organizations (CSOs), have gained in significance since the end of the Cold War. They have an ability to act legitimately in a transnational way that few other actors can. One of the most successful is the Doctors Without Borders, or Médecins Sans Frontières (MSF), the Nobel Peace Prize Laureate 1999, which at the same time delivers humanitarian support and brings global attention to atrocities and disasters. With skilful access to conventional media, use of Internet connections and fax machines, NGOs are able, in a short period of time, to mobilize support globally for particular actions and causes. East Timor is a case in mind, where the UN Secretary-General in his press confer-ence on September 11, 1999, spoke of the thousands of messages he had received on East Timor. This was a quick response to the carnage unleashed by militia groups when they learned that the majority had voted for inde-pendence, not autonomy with Indonesia. The vote took place on August 30, the results were announced by the Secretary-General to the Security Council on September 3. Militia-led violence followed, and the Security Council decided on a peacekeeping operation on September 15. The first peacekeepers were in place on September 20. Such quick action was not possible when the genocide began in Rwanda in April 1994. One has to go back to the swift UN intervention in the Congo in July 1960 to find a paral-lel (Urquhart 1994), then supported by the new African and Asian members of the UN. Remarkably, the events of Darfur in Western Sudan in 2004 did not draw the same global attention and international actions, including sanctions, and peacekeepers were far from satisfactory in ending violence.

Fourth, there are also actors who profit from the messiness of the global system and who operate across borders without any fear of interdiction. This is a category of *trans-state actors*. There are, of course, legitimate multina-tional companies operating all over the globe. They may be involved in the early phases of conflict, as the exploitation of resources may be at the heart of social dynamics leading to armed conflict (as seen in the protracted con-flict over Bougainville, Papua New Guinea). The supply of major weapons involves such trans-state organizations, and some of these transactions may be concealed in obscurity, evading laws, with or without the consent of governments. These actors seldom appear in the armed stages of the conflict, and rarely participate openly in negotiations to end the conflict.[1] Other actors, however, may represent their interests, be they states, non-state actors, NGOs or law firms. In addition, there are less institutionalized actors. Arms dealers trading in small arms, merchants dealing in valuable minerals controlled by governments or non-state actors, drug traders engaged in international cartels and coalitions, or monetary transfers and money laundering to support war efforts. There are reports of entire ships loaded with weapons that have been captured by factions and used in their armed struggles. In addition, support groups may extort 'revolutionary taxes' from compatriots living far from the war scene to demonstrate their professed 'solidarity' with particular causes. Often, such pressures have a mafia-like quality. Support groups for different sides may even fight each other, thousands of kilometres away from the battlegrounds. Thus, linkages may extend globally, in what might be termed ethnic internationals or global 'tribes' (Kotkin 1992). In addition, conditions of lawlessness give rise to human trafficking and enhanced drug trade, not the least organized across borders.

Thus, there are good reasons for using the term 'global system' for these connecting webs with numerous different types of actor. On the basic level of conflict analysis, the focus is on warring parties. This is the relationship that has to be settled for the conflict to be resolved. It is a necessary element and is dealt with in Part Two. It may not be sufficient, however. That is why the global system, with all its actors and its disorder, enters into the complex level of analysis (Part Three).

4.3 Introducing the Trichotomy of Conflict

Our concern is the resolution of conflict. Although the origin and dynamics may be similar for many conflicts, for each party *its* conflict is unique. In many important respects this is also the reality. There are no conflicts which are entirely similar, and special features always have to be kept in mind. Still, there are rules, norms and understandings that try to equalize conflicts so that they can be treated in similar ways. This is true for violence in any society. One murder is not likely to be identical to another; there are still norms which treat them in similar ways. When society wants to contain violence and inflict punishment, it strives to do that in a fair way. Equal punishment for equal crime is a basic rule. These are general rules created for handling unique events. In the process, similarities are emphasized so as to make events comparable. The argument for dealing with conflicts in the global system is parallel. There are large-scale conflicts that are sufficiently similar to allow them to be handled in comparable fashions. Through international law, such a differentiation has already been introduced and has gained considerable acceptance in the international community.

Traditionally, a firm distinction has been drawn between international and internal conflicts. The first can be handled by, for instance, the international institutions, such as the UN, the International Court of Justice and regional organizations. Internal conflicts are, in this thinking, left to the domain of the states themselves, and placed outside the purview of the international bodies. Internal affairs may only become the affairs of the international community if the legitimate authority in the country, that is, its government, asks for such an intervention. This is a basic tenet of the UN Charter and was seen as an untouchable principle during the Cold War. It does not deny, however, the possibility of making rules for internal conflicts. The distinctions drawn have been ones of expediency rather than matters of principle. If interstate conflicts can be compared, this should also be true for internal conflicts. Indeed, otherwise it would not be possible to draw a general distinction between internal and interstate conflicts. Furthermore, the political climate has changed. The lively debate on humanitarian intervention since the Cold War has questioned the validity of the distinction, both normatively and in practice. By the end of the 1990s, humanitarian arguments resulted in large international support for NATO bombings of Yugoslavia during the Kosovo crisis in 1999 as well as for the international involvement in East Timor. The UN extended general support for such actions as part of its new responsibility to protect exposed populations, as agreed in the world summit outcome in 2005. This document gave such authority only to the Security Council. In this way the interstate system was maintained, even if internal conflicts have become central in the debate and policies on international peace. The question of international terrorism has also led the Security Council to make decisions that actually transcend traditional sovereignty, for instance, in decisions on financial sanctions in 2001. However, implementation rests with the member states individually, even if they are exposed to heavy external pressure.

The separation of interstate conflicts from other conflicts is entrenched. It will be maintained here because it is a simple differentiation, which reflects realities of importance for conflict resolution. It needs to be seen, however, together with other conflicts, as well as within a larger framework to lead us to a complete picture. Thus, Chapter 5 is devoted to the interstate conflicts, whereas Chapters 8, 9 and 10 will present the larger picture.

This leaves us with a group of conflicts which are 'internal', but this needs some further discussion. It is a very broad category. Much of what goes on in 'normal' political affairs are interactions among individuals, groups and peoples brought together inside the same borders. The disagreements can be many, as can the conflicts. Internal conflicts, argues Zartman, 'begin with the breakdown of normal politics' (Zartman 1995a: 5). Thus, there is a large number of issues that can be combined in such a way as to make conflict serious and escalatory. There are probably more such concerns inside a particular country than between a given pair of states. Thus, it would be logical to expect more conflict inside states than between them. Decisive for how situations will develop are prevailing and historical social and economic conditions, the governance system for accommodating changes of such conditions, etc. These are matters that will be of concern to the ordinary citizen. To the citizenry, international affairs are often separate and distant. With increasing globalization, their importance may become stronger and more obvious, particularly for small and dependent countries. However, to most inhabitants, what goes on in their own country is likely to be primary as it immediately affects income, well-being and freedom. It is noteworthy that all countries seem to have an internal conflict, which at times is the dominant one. It is also readily identifiable by the citizens of that country. Conflict is a common experience in any society and not necessarily something that is outside 'normal' affairs. Almost to the contrary, as observed already by Coser, conflict may contribute to keeping society together (see Chapter 3 and Coser 1956). What is not 'normal' is the resort to arms. There is likely to be a universal preference for peaceful politics, within as well as between states.

Thus, for the population of this planet, internal conflict is as important a category as international conflict. It needs to get as much attention and to be treated in a similarly thorough way. It may be true that international law instruments have been restricted from dealing with internal issues, but legal rules are becoming more numerous and more intrusive. It is sufficient to remind the reader of the human rights issues, the convention on war crimes tribunals, the many democracy-promoting agencies, as well as the general integration through the global market. Internal affairs are a legitimate object of study and are amenable to conflict resolution that also involves outside parties.

Let us now complement the dichotomy of interstate and intra-state conflict. So far we have presented a dimension which deals with the actors in conflicts – whether they are states or other parties. In Chapter 3 we introduced an equally important notion, incompatibility. This has theoretical and practical implications, particularly for intra-state conflicts. The distinction turned out to be a fruitful dimension in the Uppsala Conflict Data Program. It separates incompatibilities that concern control over territory from those dealing with government. As we have also seen, the Correlates of War project now applies this distinction for intra-state conflicts (Sarkees and Wayman 2010). Territorial conflicts have always been central in interstate conflicts. Military authorities are important for the control of territory. State security often depends on control over particular areas. Such areas are defined as strategic or vital and thus come to justify military action. The same, of course, is true for internal conflicts. If particular groups claim control over certain areas and want to change their status, it affects the inhabitants of the state as a whole. It might mean drawing new borders and altering established rights of all citizens. It impacts on access to particular areas. It has implications for control over resources. The interest in maintaining the existing territorial arrangements is strong in interstate relations. International consensus is highly resistant to territorial changes which do not have the consent of the parties. The government of a state is likely to be equally conservative with respect to the territory it is set to administer. Challenges are likely to be taken very seriously. Thus, territorial issues also acquire a particular meaning in internal affairs. Studies point to the significance of territory in explanations of interstate war (Vasquez 1993, 1995; Vasquez and Henehan 2001) and we suggest that the same is true for internal conflict. The incompatibility over territory, in other words, cuts across the distinction between interstate and intra-state conflict.

The same applies to the second incompatibility, control over government. This refers to the command over the existing central government authority and the composition of the government. The most serious disputes in this category are those where an opposition challenges the existing authority and wants to have it removed, rather than just achieve a change in a particular policy. Repression by governments aims at keeping a particular group in power. Criticism of government policy may be interpreted as a challenge to its authority. Repression can set in at an early stage. In fact, a larger number of incumbent governments have come to power through non-democratic means. Coups, revolutions, civil wars and dynastic arrangements are still routes to power and they are as frequent as are democratic procedures. The struggle over governmental control is classic in politics and continues to be an important aspect of conflict. The state, as we have just seen, contains such attractive resources that many will find it worthwhile to fight to stay in power or take over power. Thus, it draws on a different dynamic from territorial issues, which focus on particular areas or regions, not the state as a whole. In internal affairs, this incompatibility makes sense.

Is this incompatibility also of value for the analysis of international conflicts? Yes, the Cold War demonstrated this convincingly. The interventions by the Soviet Union and the United States were not motivated in terms of territorial gains but with regard to government control. The ambitions of both sides were to promote particular types of regime, not change borders after the territorial realignments of the Second World War. The return of Soviet authority in Ukraine, Belarus and the Baltic states actually met strong armed resistance going on until the early 1950s and explains why these countries were the first to opt out from the Soviet Union in 1990–91. Elsewhere, Soviet policy was concerned with the installation of Soviet-style governments. There were, no doubt, military and strategic considerations, but the conflicts placed local communists loyal to the Soviet Union against non-communist members of the same society. The USA and the West were supporting or installing particular governments in Iran and other places in the Middle East, as well as in South America and Indochina, for instance, without the idea of changing their own borders. The hot wars that were part of the Cold War focused on the control over government: which type of regime should there be in a particular country? Some countries may have had a more crucial, geographical position in these global strategies (for instance, Cuba and Turkey). Nevertheless, it was the allegiance of the country as such that was disputed, not the idea of breaking up existing units.[2] The Cold War dualism is no longer present on the global level, but the issue of regime types remains important, both regionally (for instance, there are still communist regimes in East Asia) and in particular cases (not least Iraq in 2003, when the final stated goal by the USA was to change the regime). The West remains committed to promoting democracy, even with military means, and other actors pledge to resist this, or argue for the right to make counter-actions (even justifying terrorism). Thus, we can observe that both intra-state and interstate conflicts have similar incompatibilities when conflicts are armed and serious. It can be concluded that the distinction of territory and government as two separate incompatibilities is fruitful.

This gives us four categories of conflict to consider, but we will merge two into one, making three categories. This creates the trichotomy for conflict analysis. The first category consists of *the interstate conflicts around territory and government*. It is treated as one category, as this is an established group of conflicts, identified with criteria used in international law. Then there are *intra-state conflicts over government* and a third category containing *the intra-state conflict over territory*. It can be said that this trichotomy follows the distinction of international law, but develops it with respect to the intra-state conflicts. Interstate negotiations between sovereign states are similar no matter what the incompatibility concerns, but this, we will show, is not the case for intra-state conflicts. The trichotomy also makes sense as the number of interstate conflicts is limited, and much of today's conflict materials are of an intra-state nature. Furthermore, in the case of intra-state conflict resolution, there are likely to be different arrangements depending on the incompatibility.

It is interesting to note that this distinction for internal conflicts applied here is parallel to the one made by Zartman (1995a) between 'regional' and 'central' conflicts. However, there is no understanding here that conflict resolution, in Zartman's words, necessarily leads to the 'restoration of normal politics' (1995a: 24). The political realities after a serious conflict are likely to be dramatically different, depending on the incompatibility. The solution to a conflict over government may aim at achieving integration and thus some form of restoration and 'normalcy'. A negotiated settlement of a conflict over territory is not likely to have such an outcome. It is not going to be a return to the conditions that prevailed before 'the troubles', but rather involve different forms of separation, even to the point where new states are created. Relationships are changed in a fundamental way. There are, consequently, strong arguments for making the distinction between government and territory particularly important for internal conflicts.

Locating conflicts in the trichotomy

It is not necessarily simple to separate one category from another. Thus, the following questions can help to sort out the categorization of the conflicts. For finding a conflict of the first type, it is helpful to ask the following:

Does a particular conflict have a significant interstate component? This can be decided primarily by observing if there are troops from different states involved, meaning that the direct command goes to a particular decision-centre. If there are two regular armies fighting each other from two different states, the conflict is a classical interstate confrontation. Most important is if the troops of one or the other party are there as part of an alliance or have an internationally legitimate authorization (for instance, by the United Nations or an international regional organization). This shows an additional component of the interstate character of the conflict. The issue becomes more complicated if the 'foreign' troops are fighting on the territory of a country with the consent of the government. The problem is to decide whether this is a collective defence arrangement and, thus, a case of legitimate assistance, or whether it is a case of intervention, to which a particular government cannot but agree. An even more complex situation is if the external actor is supporting a non-state actor in the other country. Is this then to be regarded as intervention into an internal conflict between a non-state actor (the rebels) and the government? Or is this, in fact, an interstate conflict, where the external actor is only using the non-state actor as a Trojan horse, or an excuse for expansionism? Determining the true state of affairs is often easier than may first appear, if one applies strict criteria. By observing where the non-state actor gets training for its forces, how its finances are raised, how logistics are set up, how weapons reach the rebels and where political support is expressed, a picture emerges. Key questions are actually: who can stop the fighting, and who will sign an agreement that will be implemented? Two states in direct or indirect conflict are likely to prefer to settle the conflict between themselves and not allow space for others. Armed conflicts which meet these criteria are interstate conflicts, and their solution is discussed in Chapter 5.

The second type of conflict can be identified by asking: *Does a particular intra-state conflict have a significant component of being an incompatibility over government?* In this case, we are considering a conflict between a government and a non-state actor, and the conclusion is based not only on the military actions of the parties, but on the stated purposes of the parties. If the goal is keeping or taking power within the same country to which both sides claim allegiance, it is clear that we are talking about a conflict that traditionally has been identified as *civil war*. It is a struggle for power within a particular state, not only a fight for a change in the policies pursued by a government.

Recent developments indicate that non-state actors may not be primarily interested in taking state power as such, but may settle for control over particular areas or want to make external supporters withdraw so that internal change can be achieved. For instance, the peace agreement in Sierra Leone in July 1999 gave the non-state actor, RUF/SL, access to the mining resources in the country. The war was, however, fought on more general grounds and there were no stated intentions of breaking away a particular piece of territory from the country. On the contrary, the peace agreement reaffirmed the unity of the state. This conflict, therefore, is a part of new wars, where public welfare questions are no longer the primary driving forces. These are cases of *'warlordism'* (Duffield 1998; Reno 1998). In practice, they concern access to particular resources in a country, and aim to achieve this by forcibly removing the incumbent government from attractive areas. They challenge government control.

A second case in this category is *internationalized terrorism*, where the ultimate goal is change in particular societies but where the armed attacks are directed primarily against international supporters of the incumbent regimes. A typical case is the al-Qaida grouping attacking the USA on September 11, 2001 with the hope of achieving US withdrawal from the Middle East. This is in turn expected to lead to regime change in the region. In Chapter 6 the conflicts over state power will be analysed in more detail.

The third type of conflict can be found by asking: *Does a particular intra-state conflict have a significant territorial component?* In this case, the conflict posits a government versus a non-state actor, where the former demands the upholding of the integrity of the state. Its opponent, however, wants to break away a particular piece of territory from the existing state. This may come in different forms. It can include either demanding significant constitutional changes, achieving full sovereignty or attaining integration with the neighbouring state. These aspirations are here subsumed under one: the question of territorial control. More refined labels can be given, such as separatism, secessionism, liberation, irredentism, reunification, restoration, but all these labels have strong value connotations. Discussing them under the heading of territory as incompatibility makes possible a less charged analysis. These conflicts are labelled *conflicts over state formation*. From the government's point of view, it is a matter of keeping the present state form intact. To the non-state actor, it is a question of changing this very set-up in a profound way. These are the conflicts to which considerable attention will be devoted in Chapter 7.

4.4 Applying the Trichotomy of Conflict and Peace

Armed conflict since the Cold War

The three types of conflict identified in Section 4.3 are applied to the armed conflicts reported in the Uppsala Conflict Data Program since 1989. The result is seen in Table 4.1. It shows the empirical validity of merging inter-state conflicts into one category. There are few such conflicts in the period, in all only eight. This has been observed before and has often been regarded as a prime hallmark of the post-Cold War period. In fact, there have probably been few interstate conflicts for a long time. During the Cold War, however, internal conflicts were internationalized in such a way as to make the local issues subordinate to the global confrontation. It appeared that there were more interstate conflicts. In those days, furthermore, government issues were probably more important. Although the distinction government–territory is not systematically applied in Table 4.1, it does have a strong impact on the data. For instance, we can add that most interstate conflicts dealt with territorial issues, notably changes of borders (Ecuador–Peru, Eritrea–Ethiopia), more complex relationships focusing on particular territories (India–Pakistan) and the resurrection of an occupied state (the Gulf War over Kuwait in 1991). There were two interstate conflicts over government. One was the intervention by the United States in Panama in 1989. The other case was the 2003 Iraq War to remove the regime of Saddam Hussein. The Panama case may in fact have been the last of a typical Cold War pattern. The Cold War saw many interstate interventions to remove or support incumbent regimes (Hungary 1956, Dominican Republic 1965, Czechoslovakia 1968, and Afghanistan and Nicaragua in the 1980s are but a few examples). It has been argued that such unilateral interventionism by a major power may be something of the past. There was an international operation to remove the military regime in Haiti in 1994 in order to bring back the democratically elected government. It was a US-led activity, but under a mandate of the United Nations. The 2003 Iraq War would then have to be an exceptional event. The issue initially concerned the removal of any potential Iraqi capacity for weapons of mass destruction, but in the final round came to concern the regime itself. The war was not sanctioned by the UN, although it had a limited collective ring to it, being supported, for instance, by troops from the United Kingdom and Australia. As the formal occupation ended in 2004, the war in Iraq continued, but then it is recorded as an internationalized intra-state conflict over government. At that time it also had the support of the United Nations. Thus, this example may not signify a return to a pattern of unilateral interventionism.

Table 4.1 presents the armed conflicts during the 21 years since 1989 in three seven-year periods. We can see that the total number of armed conflicts actually is declining, period by period. The table also shows that

Table 4.1 Basic types of armed conflicts, 1989–2009 (absolute number of conflicts active per seven-year period)

	1989–95	1996–2002	2003–09	Total
Interstate	4	3	3	8
Intra-state over government	45	36	28	58
Intra-state over territory	49	33	32	64
Total	98	72	63	130

Note: The column 'Total' concerns conflicts active during the whole period 1989–2009 and does not constitute the sum of the three periods. The ambiguous case of Sudan is here treated as a conflict over government.

Source: Uppsala Conflict Data Program Conflict Encyclopedia, September 16, 2010, compiled by Rachel Miller.

the bulk of the conflicts deal with incompatibilities that are internal. At no moment in time did the interstate conflicts constitute more than 5 per cent of the total number of conflicts. Even among the wars of the period (that is, conflicts with more than 1,000 casualties in one year) only four were interstate (the 1991 Gulf War, the Ethiopia–Eritrea border war 1998–2000, India–Pakistan in 1999 and the 2003 Iraq War) of a total 47 wars in the period. There are borderline cases, notably Yugoslavia's involvement in Bosnia-Herzegovina, where regular forces took part in the first months of the war in 1992, and Armenia's commitment to Nagorno-Karabakh, but even if these were added, the total still would not rise above 10 per cent. Nevertheless, the interstate category is important. Such wars may have a stronger potential for escalation and diffusion. They may become more destructive and more unsettling for entire regions, in a shorter period of time, than intra-state conflicts.

The other two categories include the largest number of all conflicts and wars in the period. Many have become very protracted and the accumulated destruction is immense. It is likely that Afghanistan is the most serious case, with more than 1 million deaths. The war in Bosnia, as horrible as it was, still does not compare. The genocide in Rwanda stands out as the humanly most destructive of the events of the decade. The killings were directed at defenceless individuals. Shelters or churches were not spared. The genocide took place in a short period of time. In this case, the killings were not even part of the armed conflict, nor did they serve a strategic, military purpose. It was an attempt to wipe out an entire population (Prunier 1995). In the Uppsala Conflict Data Program, this is treated as a case of one-sided violence, in addition to the armed conflict. The protracted war in Sudan ceased with the peace agreement in 2005, and the long war in Sri Lanka ended with government victory in 2009. Both cases saw considerable cruelty against civilian populations, from deliberate starvation to suicide bombings.

Table 4.1 shows that the two categories of internal conflict that we have identified in Section 4.3 are of about equal size. This is also illustrated in the five cases just mentioned: two are clearly conflicts over government (Afghanistan and Rwanda) and two concern particular territories and the formation of the state (Bosnia and Sri Lanka). The fifth one, Sudan, is an interesting combination, where the leading movement, SPLA, demanded an autonomous state in the south, thus changing the territorial and constitutional basis of the country, but at the same time aspired to be part of the national government. This is also what the peace agreement stipulated. Thus the conflict is placed under the government heading in Table 4.1. In 2011, however, a referendum was held on a territorial division granting independence to South Sudan by July 2011. It is also noteworthy in Table 4.1 that these two categories of intra-state conflict gradually shift over time, but none clearly dominates the other. This suggests that the categories are stable and meaningful for purposes of analysis. As is the case with all three basic conflicts, there are likely to be interconnections, and to them we shall return in Part Three.

There are some distinct regional differences. Conflicts over territory are almost non-existent in South America. The conflict between Ecuador and Peru indicates that there are a number of unsettled interstate borders on the continent. Indeed, the Falklands/Malvinas conflict of the 1980s was an important reminder of that. There is, however, limited resort to separatism and autonomy, which is common in other parts of the world. Even the conflict in Chiapas, Mexico, which erupted violently in 1994, is more a question of central government policy than an issue of autonomy for a poverty-stricken region.

On the other end of the spectrum is Europe, where almost all conflicts are concerned with territorial issues. This is most marked for the wars, that have all been about territorial issues. This includes Northern Ireland. On the whole, conflicts are concentrated in the Balkan and Caucasus regions. During the Cold War, conflicts around government were central; thus, the promotion of democracy was focal in political and academic thinking, apart from the standard defence considerations. Also, the European integration project stemmed from a desire to denationalize European affairs, something which has been relatively successfully achieved in Western Europe. However, East, Central and Southeast Europe came out of the Cold War with a strong nationalistic fervour, as part of the popular mobilization against the communist regimes (for instance, Croatia), and where such regimes quickly took on a nationalistic rhetoric (notably, Serbia). However, the EU enlargement process, making the European Union into an association of 27 states in 2007, has been a check on such tendencies. By emphasizing democracy and human rights, countries aspiring to become members have adjusted their policies accordingly.

Other regions find themselves somewhere between the South American and European patterns. The Middle East and Asia have somewhat more conflicts dealing with territory. Africa, surprisingly, exhibits conflicts framed in terms of government. There is a political taboo against breaking up states in Africa, a shared policy that has been pursued on the continent by the African Union (AU, until 2003 known as the Organization for African Unity, OAU) since 1964. Even in the case of Rwanda, where much of the political mobilization and carnage largely followed the 'ethnic' lines of Tutsi and Hutu, no leader has asked for the breakup of the country.

The trichotomy used in this book is based on the incompatibility in the conflict and this is drawn from the parties' own descriptions of the conflicts. It means it does not treat 'ethnic', 'religious' or 'ideological' as separate categories. Such labels are analytically difficult to compare from one situation to another and not particularly useful from the viewpoint of conflict resolution. It is political demands for change that are crucial for the outcome of a conflict. 'Ethnic', 'religious' or other identity variables may cut across the categories and perhaps help to understand the intensity of demands, the mobilization of social groups, or interconnections. The resolution of the conflicts, however, has to depart from the specific demands made by the parties. These are captured by the trichotomy.

Peace agreements since the Cold War

The Uppsala Conflict Data Program contains systematic information on the outcomes of conflicts and on peace agreements. In Chapter 2, different outcomes were presented (Table 2.1), and an overview was given of the relative frequency of peace agreements. The trend data of Table 4.1 shows a gradual reduction in the total number of active armed conflicts, from 98 in the first period after the Cold War to 63 in the third one, a reduction of 36 per cent. One explanation given for this is an increased international commitment to peacemaking (*Human Security Report 2005*).

The peace agreements can now be related to the trichotomy of conflict. A first observation is that such an agreement may be concluded long after a particular conflict was active. The almost simultaneous ending of the war and the signing of a peace agreement in Bosnia-Herzegovina in the last months of 1995 is not typical. There were peace agreements concluded in the 1990s for conflicts that had not been armed for many years. There was a peace treaty in 1994 between Israel and Jordan. The most recent, severe military encounters between these parties were in 1967. Also, a peace agreement may be concluded one year, while the armed conflict is still not ended nor the agreements implemented until the following year, or even later. Thus, there is a discrepancy between peace agreements and armed conflicts. This makes it more reasonable to deal with longer periods rather than focusing on the annual shifts. Table 4.2 lists the peace agreements concluded for armed conflicts that have been active in the post-Cold War period.

Table 4.2 shows the tangible outcomes of considerable international, national and local efforts to deal with armed conflict. Many of the agreements are part of peace processes with mediators, facilitators, experts, civil society representation, public debate, as well as the politically responsible actors. These 178 agreements were often signed under solemn conditions and generated high hopes. Many actually fulfilled the expectations, others become part of further learning on the requirements for durable peace.

There are many difficulties in defining a peace agreement. The war between Iran and Iraq ended with the two sides accepting a resolution by the Security Council in 1987. There was no treaty signed between the two heads of state. Their support for the arrangement was a result of a decision by the Security Council. Still, it regulated important aspects of the contentious issues, adhered to by the two parties, and there was no further fighting between them. Neither side could be said to have won the war, but both could claim that they prevented the other from winning. The Security Council resolution was the main modality through which war termination was expressed.

The case of Kosovo is similar. It ended with official negotiations between the Western powers and the government in Yugoslavia through intermediaries. It was a document that both NATO and Yugoslavia could accept. It led to the cessation of air warfare and a withdrawal of Yugoslav forces from Kosovo. It left central issues unresolved. Most notable was the absence of a solution for the status of Kosovo, which was the focus of the conflict. It was agreed that the forces of Yugoslavia were to be replaced with an international

Table 4.2   Peace agreements in armed conflicts, 1989–2009
The number of agreements are shown in parentheses. The year marks the latest agreement.

Peace agreements in intra-state conflicts over government:	Peace agreements in intra-state conflicts over territory:
Afghanistan (3) 1996	Angola (Cabinda) (1) 2006
Angola (4) 2002	Bangladesh (Chittagong Hill Tracts) (1) 1997
Burundi (8) 2008	
Cambodia (1) 1991	Bosnia and Herzegovina (Croat) (1) 1994
Central African Republic (2) 2008	Bosnia and Herzegovina (Serb) (1) 1995
Chad (11) 2006	Comoros (Anjouan) (3) 2003
Colombia (4) 2002	Croatia (Serb) (1) 1995
Congo (1) 1999	Georgia (Abkhazia) (1) 1994
Côte d'Ivoire (9) 2008	India (Bodoloand) (1) 1993
Democratic Republic of Congo (6) 2009	India (Tripura) (1) 1993
Djibouti (3) 2001	Indonesia (Aech) (2) 2005
El Salvador (9) 1992	Israel (Palestine) (8) 2007
Guatemala (16) 1996	Mali (Azawad) (2) 1992
Guinea Bissau (1) 1998	Moldova (Dniestr) (1) 1997
Haiti (1) 1993	Niger (Air and Azawad) (2) 1995
Liberia (11) 2003	Papua New Guinea (Bougainville) (3) 2001
Macedonia (1) 2001	
Mexico (1) 1996	Philippines (Mindanao) (2) (2001)
Mozambique (5) 1992	Senegal (Casamance) (1) 2004
Nepal (1) 2006	UK (Northern Ireland) (1) 1998
Niger (1) 1993	Yugoslavia (Slovenia) (1) 1991
Philippines (1) 1995	Yugoslavia (Kosovo) (1) 1999
Rwanda (6) 1993[a]	
Sierra Leone (3) 2000	**Peace agreements in interstate conflicts:**
Somalia (5) 2008	
South Africa (5) 1993	
Sudan (8) 2006[b]	Cameroon–Nigeria (1) 2006
Tajikistan (5) 1997	Ecuador–Peru (1) 1998
Uganda (8) 2008	Eritrea–Ethiopia (1) 2000

[a]The two agreements on August 3, 1993, are treated as one.
[b]The three agreements on May 26, 2004, are treated as one.

Note: Peace agreements are defined as signed treaties which regulate (resolve or find a process for) the incompatibility, which are concluded between the warring parties and put an end to conflict behaviour. Cease-fire agreements are not included. Agreements signed up to 2009 are included.

Source: Uppsala Conflict Data Program Conflict Encyclopedia, September 23, 2010, compiled by Rachel Miller.

force (KFOR), and that the opposite side, Kosovo Albanian forces (UCK/KLA), were to be disbanded. It is a military arrangement, ending the combat between the different sides. It also regulates the situation for Kosovo for an unspecified period of time. It outlines a process for settlement. Thus, it is comparable to other peace agreements which also have this element and it is included as a peace agreement. The most noteworthy are the agreements between Israel and the PLO in 1993. In this case, a number of interim agreements had been concluded during the 1990s. During the Second Intifada and the Sharon government, there were no agreements. A restart of negotiations took place in November 2007 resulting in an agreement on a peace process and a new attempt was initiated by the Obama administration in September 2010.

An additional noteworthy case which is not included in Table 4.2 is the termination of the Gulf War. It ended through UN Security Council Resolution 687 (1991). It was an asymmetrical document. It specified the conditions to which Iraq had to adhere for international forces to withdraw and economic sanctions to be lifted. Iraq had virtually no input into the document, and was not expected to influence the process that followed. This included the disarmament of particular weapons systems, acceptance of a procedure for drawing the boundary between Iraq and Kuwait, and the payment of compensation. It is a document written by a victorious coalition. Thus, it cannot be regarded as a peace agreement. It makes clear who won the war. There was little ambiguity. The outcome of the Gulf War in 1991 was more a victory than the Kosovo conflict in 1999.

A further complication is that there may be many agreements in the same conflict. Agreements are overturned, reworked or extended. This is why notions such as spoilers and spoiler management became valid for the international community (Stedman 1997, 1998). In Table 4.2 there are 178 agreements for 52 armed conflicts, an average of more than three per conflict with a treaty. The highest number is found in the conflicts in Burundi, Sudan, Uganda and Israel (Palestine) with eight each, El Salvador and Côte d'Ivoire both with nine each, Chad and Liberia with 11 each and Guatemala's 16 testifying to considerable complexities, failures, mistrust and renewed efforts for a solution. In fact, these nine conflicts have a total of 88 peace agreements, that is half of all agreements. By 2010 only three of them had an ongoing minor armed conflict.

Table 4.3   Armed conflicts and peace agreements, 1989–2009

	No. of conflicts with peace agreements	No. of armed conflicts	Proportion of peace agreements to armed conflicts (%)
Interstate	3	8	38
Intra-state over government	29	58	50
Intra-state over territory	20	64	31
Total	52	130	40

Note: Armed conflicts with at least one peace agreement. Sudan is treated as a conflict over government.

Source: Uppsala Conflict Data Program Conflict Encyclopedia, September 30, 2010, compiled by Rachel Miller.

If we concentrate attention to the conflicts with agreements and relate this to the trichotomy, Table 4.3 emerges. It compares the frequencies of conflict resolution in the three categories of conflict.

Table 4.3 shows that there is considerable similarity in the ability to conclude peace agreements no matter what type of conflict. About one-third of all conflicts appear likely, sooner or later, to find a negotiated settlement, sometimes even more. There is a consistent pattern of such settlements being somewhat more common for intra-state conflicts over government, however. It is reasonably common that agreements will be reached to make this a most serious aspect in any analysis of war and peace. Also, the fact that the differences are not very strong among the categories in the trichotomy suggests that it is valid as a guide for conflict resolution.

Furthermore, studying the duration of peace agreements, armed conflict restarted within three years in 21 per cent of all internal armed conflicts over government, compared to 13 per cent in conflicts over territory, and 0 per cent of interstate conflicts, again pointing to significant differences between these categories (Table 2.1; UCDP Conflict Termination Dataset v 2010-1; Kreutz 2010).

Further Readings

Go to the *Understanding Conflict Resolution* web page at www.sagepub.co.uk for free access to journal articles listed.

Harbom, L., Högbladh, S. and Wallensteen, P. 2006. 'Armed Conflict and Peace Agreements', *Journal of Peace Research*, 43 (5): 617–31.
Stedman, S. J., Rothchild, D. and Cousens, E. M. (eds) 2002. *Ending Civil Wars: The Implementation of Peace Agreements*. Boulder, Colorado: Lynne Rienner.

Notes

1 In the early contacts between South and North Korea, the head of South Korean car manufacturer Hyundai was important. Also, Lonrho played a role in the negotiations ending the civil war in Mozambique.

2 This is a broad generalization. The four most glaring exceptions are Germany, China, Korea and Vietnam. It is noteworthy that none of these cases was seen by the Cold War superpowers as a question of separatism. The Western support for West Germany was built on the idea of a reunification in the future under a democratic, federal system, the East's support for East Germany emphasized a new legitimacy, not separation of an 'East German' identity. Similarly, the divisions of China, Korea and Vietnam follow such Cold War lines of legitimacy, not separation of identities. This can be seen also in the attitude to reunification. In Germany, it was the West that pressed for unification. In Vietnam, it was instead the communist side that favoured this option, as has also been the case for China in its relation to Taiwan, particularly when the latter was ruled by a pro-independence party.

PART TWO
BASICS OF CONFLICT
RESOLUTION

THE RESOLUTION OF CONFLICTS BETWEEN STATES 5

5.1 Armed Conflicts and Peace Accords between States

Are wars between states disappearing? They are fewer, but were such wars frequent during the Cold War? If they always were few, then the changes may not be so dramatic. Either way, finding solutions to interstate war remains important. In this chapter, wars and peace settlements among states will be analysed. Of particular interest is the way incompatibilities between states are handled. We will begin by recording the experiences of the last decades of the Cold War, then see what has happened since 1989, thus giving a basis for a discussion on how interstate conflicts can be solved.

The last decades of the Cold War

The global conflagration between East and West made any country or area an object of strategic consideration. Even highly local disputes acquired an interstate quality. Judging from incompatibilities, we find that many Cold War conflicts actually concerned the control over government *in* particular countries. This is true for the events in Nicaragua in the 1980s, in Chile in the 1970s, Czechoslovakia and the Dominican Republic in the 1960s, Hungary in the 1950s, etc. To major powers, these situations had relevance for strategic and nuclear calculations. Direct or indirect interventions were common. The logic was that if the 'other side' is involved 'so should we'. Still, there were classical interstate conflicts during the last two decades of the Cold War.

In the 1980s, some interstate wars received global attention. Among the most devastating was the Iran–Iraq War 1980–88, whereas most press coverage may have been extended to the more limited Falklands/Malvinas War between Argentina and the United Kingdom in 1982 and Israel's invasion and occupation of large parts of Lebanon 1982–85. There was a short war between Chad and Libya. There was also a US intervention in Grenada (1983), in the Caribbean, defined as a minor armed conflict. There were four interstate conflicts during the 1980s. In the 1970s there were more interstate wars, notably between Vietnam and Cambodia, Vietnam and China, Vietnam and the United States, as well as between India and Pakistan (over the creation of Bangladesh) and the October War between Egypt, Syria and Israel. Israel took control over a part of Lebanon at the end of the 1970s. In 1974 Turkey invaded the sovereign state of Cyprus, and still continues to hold almost 40 per cent of the island's territory. Indonesia occupied East Timor, a territory that formally was under Portugal, in 1975. There was also a war between Ethiopia and Somalia over the Ogaden area and an intervention by Tanzania into Uganda to remove the regime of Idi Amin. In this decade there were ten interstate wars. This clearly was more than we saw in the 1980s and 1990s.

The interstate conflicts in the 1970s and 1980s could not all be subsumed under the heading of the Cold War. Some of them involved major Cold War actors and became part of global politics. But the origins and the incompatibilities were often more specific, concerning territorial issues (islands in the South Atlantic, the status of East Pakistan and East Timor, relations between communities, border questions, etc.) or governance (who should rule in South Vietnam, Uganda, Cambodia, Grenada, etc.). There were strong local dynamics. Major powers may have involved themselves although the conflicts had different origins. Often this contributed to an escalation of conflict. The US engagement in Indochina is one such case. When a major power sends in troops, helps finance one party or in other ways interferes substantially, this is likely to become the main feature of the conflict. In many conflicts, however, the Cold War opponents refrained from provoking each other. Where one was strongly involved, the other might stay out (the Soviet Union was cautious in the Falkland/Malvinas conflict, for instance). There were instances of them supporting the same side (Iraq in the Iran–Iraq War is an example) and cases where both restrained themselves from too heavy involvement (India–Pakistan in 1971).

What does this entail for conflict resolution? It means lessons from these interstate conflicts are relevant also beyond the Cold War. Furthermore, the conventional wisdom is that it is easier to negotiate peace agreements among states. Thorny issues of recognition and legitimacy that plague parties in internal conflict are not as significant. Classical wars take place between states which are recognized at least by some members of the international system, if not directly by the warring parties themselves. Thus, contacts should be easier to establish. In addition, the UN Charter and other international instruments are available to handle such conflicts. What is the record from the last two decades of the Cold War?

Victory and defeat were the more frequent outcomes in the 14 interstate wars. Many resulted in the withdrawal of one party. Argentina evacuated the islands in the South Atlantic. China pulled out its troops from Vietnam. Pakistan left East Pakistan, ultimately recognizing the independence of the new country, Bangladesh. The PLO had to leave Lebanon and Somalia withdrew from the Ogaden desert. There were deals or agreements behind these moves, but they cannot be defined as peace agreements arrived at through symmetrical negotiations between equal parties. The developments on the battlefield made clear that one party had prevailed.

When victorious endings were not forthcoming, the conflicts resulted in protracted territorial occupation. Many lasted for several decades. Examples are Israel in South Lebanon (22 years), Sinai (15 years) and still continuing in the Golan Heights. Similarly, Turkey kept control in Cyprus, Indonesia in East Timor (ended in 1999 after 24 years) and Vietnam in Cambodia (11 years). In the case of Iran and Iraq, the parties controlled different parts of the opponent's territory as long as the war lasted. Territorial conflicts, in other words, were difficult to solve in a speedy fashion through negotiations, although the parties have been internationally recognized states.

In conflicts where the regime issue was central, the conflicts resulted in the defeat and removal of these regimes (Ugandan leader Idi Amin escaping to Saudi Arabia, Cambodian leader Pol Pot continuing resistance from the jungles on the Thai border). This, in a way, made the wars shorter. Once this was accomplished, the intervening state was often willing to withdraw its troops, or at least to take measures to mask its presence. This does not speak in favour of negotiated settlements. On the contrary: as the issue was the government, negotiations were ruled out. Often both sides regarded the other as an illegitimate actor who could not be dealt with through direct contacts. Thus, we find that interstate conflicts are not easily amenable to international diplomacy, although some objective conditions would speak in favour of that proposition.

Actually, among the 14 conflicts, there are only two with mutually developed peace agreements. The one receiving the most attention was the Camp David Accords between Israel and Egypt, negotiated in 1978 and 1979 and implemented in the following years. This agreement meets the criteria set out in Chapter 3 for a conflict resolution ending to a conflict. The same can be said for the arrangement to terminate the war between Chad and Libya. It took the form of a process that lasted into the 1990s. The deal between Ethiopia and Somalia in 1988 can be regarded as a settlement. It took place ten years after actual fighting had ended and the agreement confirmed the outcome of the war. The ending of the Iran–Iraq War, through the auspices of the United Nations, included a cease-fire, an exchange of prisoners of war, and an investigation of responsibility for the conflict. It is still difficult to classify as a peace treaty, as mentioned in Chapter 4. It is noteworthy, as it was done through the UN Security Council and the UN Secretary-General. This particular war has many lessons for conflict resolution and we will return to them later in this chapter.

Thus, the notion that states have fewer problems negotiating among themselves is not borne out, at least for the Cold War period. The 14 wars followed their own dynamics. In some cases, Cold War parties aligned with conflict actors, for strategic and other reasons, thus reinforcing tensions. The chances of peaceful settlements became intertwined with the overall relations between major powers. It is interesting to note that many of the conflicts are still not solved, two decades after the Cold War ended.

This underlines that their origin was different. From this test, it appears that conflicts in Indochina, after the US withdrawal in 1973, were closely related to major power dynamics between the Soviet Union and China. As this tension subsided, these conflicts found solutions. Many other conflicts remained on the agenda and peace initiatives stemmed from other dynamics: India–Pakistan continued to be a contentious relationship, with a short-lived peace process in early 2000s; the Cyprus question remained on the agenda, with a UN attempt failing in 2004, and later pursued directly between the Cypriotic actors; the East Timor conflict found a solution after the fall of the Suharto regime in Indonesia, not as a result of the end of the Cold War.

The post-Cold War period

It is important to note that the frequency of interstate armed conflicts is low and this is not a novel phenomenon. It remains, of course, true also for the period after 1989. Table 5.1 reports on interstate conflicts and peace agreements.

There were nine interstate armed conflicts since the end of the Cold War and by 2010 none was active as a typical interstate war. The US war on Iraq, however, had been transformed into an internationalized civil war. The status of some wars could be discussed. For instance, the Gulf War was not over as air strikes on Iraq by the United States and Britain continued throughout the period. The war of 2003, however, was not a simple escalation from this, but instead concerned the regime in Iraq itself. Four interstate conflicts rose to the level of war. It is fewer than in the previous periods, but not significantly so. It is difficult to judge if there is a long-term trend towards fewer interstate conflicts.

Three conflicts resulted in victory of one party over the other (USA–Panama, the Gulf War, USA–Iraq). One was taken to the International Court of Justice for settlement (Cameroon–Nigeria). One was settled through the mediation of a neighbouring country (Mauritania–Senegal) and two were concluded through a negotiated process resulting in a peace agreement, signed by the two sides (Ecuador–Peru, Eritrea–Ethiopia). India and Pakistan initiated a peace process in early 2004 and violence on the border diminished, but no solution was found and India became sceptical about Pakistan's possible knowledge of the terror attack on Mumbai in 2008. Similarly, there was no settlement between Djibouti and Eritrea, although

Table 5.1 Interstate armed conflicts, 1989–2010

Parties	Incompatibility	Outcome	Intensity
Panama v. USA	Regime in Panama	Victory	Minor
Mauritania v. Senegal	Border	Settlement	Minor
India v. Pakistan	Border, Kashmir	Peace process	War
The Gulf War	Kuwait's independence	Victory	War
Ecuador v. Peru	Border	Settlement	Minor
Cameroon v. Nigeria	Border	Settlement	Minor
Eritrea v. Ethiopia	Border	Settlement	War
Iraq v. USA, allies	Regime in Iraq	Victory, civil war	War
Djibouti v. Eritrea	Border	No settlement	Minor

Note: Chronological order, parties listed alphabetically in English, issues indicated, outcome or status by end of 2010 and highest intensity reached during this period.

Source: Uppsala Conflict Data Program Conflict Encyclopedia.

violence ceased. Of the nine conflicts, five ceased through a process of conflict resolution. It made negotiations a more frequent outcome of conflict than military victory. Also, military victory was the outcome only in conflicts that were very asymmetric. The USA was a party to all and its interventionary capacity was crucial to the result (Panama, the Gulf War, Iraq 2003). In Iraq, the USA and its allies, chiefly Britain, encountered unexpected and protracted resistance. Still, this period shows different ways of ending conflict compared to the preceding decades.

The incompatibilities in the armed conflicts were related to territorial issues, with the exception of the interventions in Panama and Iraq. In the Panama case, the USA captured the country's strong man, General Manuel Noriega, and brought him to an American court for violation of US drug laws. The political issue of who rules Panama was turned into a police issue. Objections to US actions were vetoed in the Security Council.[1] In the Iraq case, the leader, Saddam Hussein, was captured by the end of 2003, sentenced by a special Iraqi court and executed in 2006. The other conflicts concerned border questions and issues of territorial integrity of states. If it is correct, as reported, that the total number of land borders in the world is around 300, six border conflicts is a small number (Blake 1999: 150). As most of the armed conflicts have remained on a low level of intensity and also found solutions, there seem to be ways in which border conflicts can be handled. This means that those conflicts that were not managed, but turned into wars, need particular attention.

The four interstate conflicts that became wars point to the propensity of military escalation in interstate conflicts. This might distinguish them from other types of conflict. There might even be a tendency for earlier and less reluctant use of military capacities in such conflicts. The escalation of conflicts was rapid. Within a few weeks the resources amassed by the parties were immense. This is the more striking as one case involved two poor agricultural societies (Ethiopia and Eritrea). In the 1991 Gulf War, the swift deployment of US and Western military resources to the Middle East was used to apply pressure on the government in Iraq at the same time as it was part of war planning. A similar tactic was used in the months leading up to the Iraq War that was started in March 2003. Relations between India and Pakistan have been on the brink of war several times during the decade. Nuclear weapons tests by the two countries in 1998 increased tensions, and for some months in 1999 the countries were close to a major conflagration. In interstate conflicts, the parties have military organizations, which are trained for conflict options, at their disposal and, thus, the ability actually to use them is higher. Military options are more tempting, more credible and, thus, more likely to be applied.

The escalatory potential of interstate conflicts is well known and is particularly felt in the regions that are affected. This means that the early activities by neighbouring countries to contain conflicts are important. Such actions were taken in the Gulf War, without a solving formula being found. In the case of the 2003 Iraq War, the alleged presence of weapons of mass destruction or capacity to produce such weapons was an issue. An alternative route existed, supported by the UN Security Council from November 2002: weapons inspections by capable international experts. Thus, the Council was not willing or ready to authorize an attack on Iraq by March 2003. In the case of India and Pakistan, neighbours have been effectively barred from involving themselves, as India consistently has seen the problems as a bilateral or internal issue. The official peace attempts have been strictly bilateral. In the case of Djibouti v. Eritrea, the UN Security Council demanded that the troops of the parties withdraw to the status before the armed conflict. Djibouti did, Eritrea did not and was subsequently exposed to an arms embargo by December 2009.

The peace agreements during the post-Cold War period are listed in Table 5.2. Settlements take time. Table 5.2 also lists armed conflicts which saw little or no fighting in the 1990s. It means that peace processes have been protracted. By 1994, the conflict between Chad and Libya over the Aouzou strip was settled. The final issues were handled by a UN mission, following a decision by the International Court of Justice (ICJ) (Merrills 1999: 105–6; Shaw 1999: 51). By then there had been no armed conflict since the mid-1980s. Similarly, the border issues between Russia (succeeding the Soviet Union) and China found solutions through a series of agreements, the first one concluded in 1991 (Kotliar 1999; Su Wei 1999). The most severe confrontation between these countries took place in 1969, more than 20 years earlier. A peace agreement was signed between Israel and Jordan in 1994, but the countries had not been at war since 1967, more than a quarter-century earlier. Why was there a lack of concerted efforts to settle these conflicts earlier? A high level of tension between states is but one answer. Tension in the surrounding region is another. But the answer could also be found elsewhere. Although conflicts may have their own dynamics, their ending requires efforts by the

Table 5.2 Peace agreements in interstate armed conflicts, 1989–2010

Parties	Solution through the use of	Highest intensity 1989–2010 (or earlier)
Iran v. Iraq	UN Security Council	War
Chad v. Libya	ICJ, UN peacekeeping	War
Mauritania v. Senegal	Bilateral agreement	Minor
China v. Soviet Union/Russia	Bilateral agreement	(Minor)
Eritrea v. Yemen	ICJ	Dispute
Israel v. Jordan	Bilateral, US support	(War)
Ecuador v. Peru	Four guarantors	Minor (War)
Cameroon v. Nigeria	ICJ	Minor
Botswana v. Namibia	ICJ	Dispute
Eritrea v. Ethiopia	UN, OAU	War

Note: Peace agreements concluded by parties since 1989, where the parties have been in an armed conflict with one another at some point since 1946. The table also includes some disputes, that is, conflicts below the intensity of an armed conflict. Parentheses indicate that the highest intensity was recorded before 1989. The order of the two parties in each dispute is alphabetical in English and does not imply a statement on the initiator of hostilities.

Source: Uppsala Conflict Data Program Conflict Encyclopedia.

international community. When victory is preferred among leading states, there will be little interest in local settlements.

Some disputes, which did not result in severe casualties, found settlements since the end of the Cold War. Table 5.2 includes Eritrea v. Yemen, which had a dispute over the Hanish Islands and associated maritime boundaries in the Red Sea. Instead of letting the conflict escalate or linger, it was brought by the parties to the International Court of Justice. International arbitration was used for the conflict between Botswana and Namibia, again a dispute not qualifying as an armed conflict. In an earlier era, there may not have been the same swiftness in finding a solution.

This underlines that there is a stronger emphasis on peaceful settlement in the post-Cold War period than earlier. Whereas most conflicts in the last two decades were ended through victory/defeat outcomes, the most common ending since 1989 has been through settlement. This says something about a changed climate, perhaps also a shift in practice, at least for some types of conflict. It means that conflict resolution is higher on the agenda for interstate conflicts than earlier. The attempts by many states to use the UN as a way to resolve the Iraq situation prior to the beginning of the 2003 war also testifies to the willingness to find peaceful solutions. The fact that Iraq has been at war with the USA twice in this period also indicates the limits of such ambitions. This makes it most important to explore how negotiated settlements of conflict issues between states actually have been dealt with, in this era as well as previously.

Geopolitik, Realpolitik, Idealpolitik and *Kapitalpolitik*

The Cold War was a global power conflagration, entangling all major powers. It did not result in an armed conflict between the leading two. With the experiences of the First and Second World Wars in mind, a peaceful outcome of the Cold War could not be taken for granted. The polarization between East and West was a high-risk policy venture. Major power relations since then are different. There is now a frequency of summit meetings. The UN Security Council, as we will study later, has taken up a new position as a forum for managing some of these relations.

Indeed, also after the Cold War, there are complicated relations between major powers. Much attention has lately been given to China's relations with its neighbours and with the Western powers. This includes questions over the status of Taiwan and control in the South China Sea. Equally or more important for the East Asia region is the China–Japan relationship. Japan participated for the first time in a peacekeeping operation in 1992, sending personnel to Cambodia. It suggests that Japan is taking a larger role, particularly in its own region. Also, other major powers need to be considered. Russia continues to be significant, not least because it is an actor in several world regions. Germany, mostly working with the EU and NATO, for the first time sent ground troops outside alliance areas in 1999, when a German contingent was stationed in Kosovo. These developments notwithstanding, major powers have not had any direct territorial or other confrontations among themselves since the end of the Cold War.

The wars and armed conflicts since 1989 have involved regional or local issues. This has given rise to new questions. For instance, should major powers, or an international organization where major powers are crucial, act to contain or resolve a particular conflict between states? There is no definite answer: in interstate wars since the end of the Cold War – the Gulf War, the Eritrea–Ethiopia War, the India–Pakistan War in Kargil in 1999, and the 2003 Iraq War – the states not strategically involved pursued distinctly different courses of action. In the first case, the UN authorized an armed intervention, in the second, international mediation was preferred. In the third, there was little involvement at all. In the fourth, two major states were allied in the war (the USA and Britain), four others were against it, but did not act militarily on the issue (France, Germany, Russia and China). The answer is more varied today, in general giving settlement higher priority. In the face of a determined major power, this may not necessarily be an effective alternative. Nevertheless, let us see what the settlement response entails. The duty of the UN is to deal with interstate conflicts wherever they occur and this ambition is no longer frequently blocked by permanent member states in the Security Council. The existence of an internationally agreed framework also means that there are particular procedures for the settlement of interstate conflicts. Chapter VI of the UN Charter is devoted to this. Article 33 recommends member states to take a number of measures: 'negotiation, enquiry, mediation, conciliation, arbitration, judicial settlement, resort to regional agencies or arrangements, or other peaceful means of their own choice'. It is a mixed group of activities, where some more readily relate to certain types of interstate conflict. For instance, for boundary conflicts, arbitration is frequently used. In this case, the parties commit themselves in advance to accept the outcome of a court of arbitration. Arbitration may be difficult to apply to conflicts dealing with governmental power or a regional balance of power.

It is likely that the danger of conflicts spreading inadvertently is more immediately apparent in cases of interstate conflicts today. Earlier, conflicts were held in check by the global powers. Today, there are new patterns of arms trade, unsettling interruptions in civilian trade, and a less controlled flow of refugees. This means there are heavy pressures on neighbouring governments to take sides or to take their own defensively motivated actions, thus spreading the conflict. There are also neighbours being challenged by the warring actors or by groups linked to the ongoing war. Furthermore, interstate conflicts often involve challenges to principles of international law. This implies that a particular settlement may create precedents that affect active or potential conflicts in other member states.

The interstate security dilemma takes on a new meaning after the Cold War. Its original formulation assumed that sovereign states feared the attacks of other states whose intentions were difficult to read and, thus, they prepared to defend themselves. These very preparations created fear and induced the opposite side also to prepare for war. It could give an advantage to the one that would attack first, a first strike option that would be intended to pre-empt actions by the opponent. In a world dominated by superpower rivalry and global tensions, such dilemmas seemed to repeat themselves throughout the planet. However, in a world which instead sees conflict as an aberration, a peculiar exception, fears of attacks should diminish. With evidence that wars become protracted conflicts, rather than military victories, the incentive to strike first should reduce. With increasing difficulty of finding allies for war efforts, again fears may be reduced. With an emphasis by major international actors to find solutions, local actors may see fewer reasons to prepare for military attack.

However, September 11, 2001, has created a new security dilemma which clearly affects international relations. The insecurity of the leading state, the United States, induced insecurity throughout the planet. The 2003 Iraq War has been explained as part of the campaign on global terrorism. This intervention in itself, however, fuelled insecurities in Iraq, leading to a seemingly protracted internal war with heavy outside engagement. Such internal security dilemmas will be considered in the following chapters.

Although the interstate conflicts are few, their significance for the international system is very high. This means they have to be scrutinized in considerable detail. In so doing, it is also apparent that they exhibit different origins, incompatibilities, dynamics and solutions. The interstate conflicts are purposefully divided into four categories (Wallensteen 1981, 1994a, 2011b) to simplify comparability. The four categories are *Geopolitik, Realpolitik, Idealpolitik* and *Kapitalpolitik.*

First, there are *Geopolitik* conflicts, where particular types of territory are afforded such significance by one or more states as to give rise to war or serious armed conflict. The concept of *Geopolitik* goes back to classical thinking on international relations. Certain areas were seen as so important that control over them would also mean control over an entire continent or even the globe. Candidate territories have been certain areas on the Eurasian landmass, control over the High Seas, and today control over outer space. On the local level, states may regard particular border areas as rightfully theirs, for historical as well as strategic reasons.

Second, there is a category of *Realpolitik* thinking, where prime importance is attached to power and the power capabilities of the actors. Mostly, this refers to military instruments and the latest military technology, as well as the quantitative strength that can be mustered. This logic also has classical roots. *Realpolitik* has primarily been seen as a driving force for major powers. It may, however, be applied equally well to regional conflicts, where issues of balance of power may be as important. A goal of the fighting parties could be to gain the upper hand as regionally dominant.

These two notions are often closely related to each other, as power has implications for territorial control, and vice versa. Thus, we treat these aspects together in Section 5.2, although they will point to different solutions of conflicts.

Third, there is a category of *Idealpolitik*, meaning an emphasis on ideological and legitimacy issues. Two governments may dispute each other's rights due to the way in which they have been created or gained legitimacy. It is often maintained that there is a built-in tension between democracies and non-democracies. The appeal or fear of political thought on one side of the border may affect the politics on the other. There are often conflicts arising from revolutions in one country affecting neighbouring states. Indeed, revolutionary changes in one major power affects its relations to all the other major powers and is, thus, an event of significance for global affairs. The revolution in China (actually the military victory by the Communist Party in 1949) certainly had a global impact, as did the coming to power of Hitler in Germany in 1933 and the Bolsheviks in Russia in 1917, just to give some examples. The legitimacy issue needs to be dealt with, particularly in the light of the democracy–peace proposition, stating that interstate relations between democratic states are more peaceful than all other types of relations (Russett 1993).

Fourth, there is a category that is not given as much prominence as it probably deserves, and that is here called *Kapitalpolitik*. This means that economic issues are central, be they questions of oil prices, the drawing of pipelines, transportation routes, or relations between rich and poor, industrial and non-industrial producers. Some theorists see these as fundamental for the formation of conflict patterns, and with capitalism as the global guideline for economics, it is a pertinent issue to consider.

The *Idealpolitik* and *Kapitalpolitik* conflicts are dealt with together in Section 5.3. As is often the case, of course, a particular conflict may well contain strands of all four elements, and we will have to see how that impacts on conflict resolution possibilities.

5.2 Conflict Resolution: *Geopolitik* and *Realpolitik*

Geopolitik, as we have defined it, is concerned with territories of particular interest. In its original form, dealing with major powers, particular regions would gain pre-eminence in global strategies. This was also the situation during the Cold War, where locations strategic to the movement of fleets, troops or aircraft could readily be identified. In the post-Cold War era this is no longer as clear-cut, although arguments for its significance can be made (Cohen 1999). Indeed, areas which are close to major powers continue to be important in strategic considerations. There are some straits and islands which acquire such significance, but now probably more because of their role in the global economy than for their intrinsic military value. In the vocabulary introduced here they are *Kapitalpolitik* assets rather than *Geopolitik* ones. To these belong the Persian Gulf, the South China Sea, the Cape of Good Hope, perhaps the Suez Canal and the Gibraltar Strait. Also, locations along major pipelines take on significance. In the South Caucasus region, much of the politics is concerned with the routes through which oil from the Caspian Sea can reach the world market. Geopolitically interesting areas are possible to identify and would, in themselves, be a worthwhile subject for study. Certainly, such considerations will have an impact on the major powers and their attention to particular areas. In the last analysis, what matters are the lenses through which decision-makers view these territories. Territorial issues remain important as conflict issues (Diehl 1999; Starr and Thomas 2005; Vasquez 1993, 1995). The settlement of such disputes is important for shaping of future relations between the countries involved (Gibler 1999b).

In the 1990s, interstate war was associated less with grand strategies of *Geopolitik* and more with local territorial issues. Some of these, in fact, have little economic significance to the involved parties, but border questions have proved to be rallying points for action. As can be seen from Table 5.1, most of the recent interstate conflicts were border disputes. Some, such as Ecuador–Peru, had a previous history which influenced the prospects for their settlement. The ending of this dispute in 1998 was thus of historical significance (Einaudi 1999). Other conflicts that were new still turned out to be difficult to handle, as the parties grappled with their own positions, trying to locate historical evidence and contemporary precedents for their case. The repeated conflicts between the United States and Iraq, first over Kuwait 1990–91 and then the full-scale invasion in 2003, gave rise to global attention, illustrating some of the dimensions identified above: Iraq is found in a region that is a leading producer and exporter of oil.

Status Quo or *Status Quo Ante Bellum*?

The key question from the point of view of resolving such conflicts, once an armed conflict has occurred, is what is the point of departure for the settlement? Shall those interested in a settlement use the (new) *status quo* created by actions of one party or shall they demand a return to *status quo ante bellum* before negotiations can be considered? Accepting the newly created situation, *status quo*, is the more convenient, less demanding approach. It is a realistic position. It could be said that it would provide a speedy way of resolving a conflict and undo the effects of war, for instance, by allowing an immediate return of refugees. The demand for a return to the situation before the war started, *status quo ante bellum*, has many complications, but it rests on a normative imperative. It makes clear that international relations are not entirely ruled by raw might, but follow certain agreed rules. It can be argued that strict adherence to this principle contributes to deterring future conflicts of the same type. If we follow the wording of the UN Charter, we would expect this perspective to dominate. It is a matter of undoing aggression. The most obvious understanding of aggression is when one country without permission comes into a territory held by another state and claims that it intends to hold on to the area. The principled stand is attractive. However, the demand that territorial conquest is to be undone before any talks can be considered is not an easy proposition to maintain, in spite of its attraction. Realities may force conflict resolution promoters into more complicated strategies. Let us look at some situations among the wars we have recorded in Section 5.1 and in Table 5.1 as a guide to the experiences of the most recent three decades.

During these years, the *status quo* approach was applied in a series of situations, but often with some qualification. The UN Security Council resolution of 1967 demanded that Israel return occupied territories in exchange for a lasting peace with Egypt, Syria and Jordan. Thus, the Council took the more convenient approach, but not without conditions. There was an obvious difficulty: there were no international boundaries to return to, only armistice lines negotiated in 1949. It would not have been acceptable to either side to define these as international borders. Only in the case of Egypt have the intentions of the Security Council materialized, in a land-for-peace deal. There is also a peace agreement between Israel and Jordan, but it was simplified by Jordan's decision in 1988 to abandon its claim to the West Bank. Syria maintains that peace with Israel requires that Israel commit itself to returning to the exact previous lines, before negotiations can take place. Thus, although all agree that the conditions prior to the war should serve as a basis, 40 years have passed without the parties finding an agreement for the full implementation of this principle.

A second case is the one of Turkey versus Cyprus, where also a withdrawal is expected, but this is tied to a solution to the communal problems of Cyprus. The withdrawal of Turkish troops is one demand, but there are other security concerns (for the Turkish Cypriot community) as well as demands for freedom of movement, settlements and property (for the Greek Cypriot community). It leads us into the security concerns of the parties. In the cases of Cyprus and Palestine, the demand for withdrawal has been coupled to a settlement of the conflict as a whole, suggesting that the particular circumstances of each case have been attended to. It means, at the same time, that the militarily established *status quo* has been maintained for many decades. Thus, they turn into near-permanent situations and new generations adapt to their existence. It makes some comfortable, others highly frustrated.

An important test on the application of this approach is found in the war between Iraq and Iran. When the war broke out in 1980, the UN Security Council demanded a cease-fire and did not specify a force withdrawal to the international boundaries. This meant that the Council was satisfied with the less demanding position, but instead faced a situation where the authority of the Council was badly damaged in the eyes of one warring party, Iran. From an Iranian perspective, a cease-fire meant that Iraqi troops would remain on Iranian territory, and only withdraw through negotiations. Iran would have to make additional concessions to achieve this. Iran rejected this stance, and thus preferred to work only with the Secretary-General or the special representatives appointed by him (Pérez de Cuéllar 1997).

The demanding principle of *status quo ante bellum* was specifically raised and implemented, sometimes with superior military force, in some of the conflicts recorded in Section 5.1. Argentina was forced to withdraw from the Falklands/Malvinas Islands. Iraq left Kuwait after being militarily defeated. Vietnam removed its troops from Cambodia after ten years. Somalia pulled back from Ogaden. Israel withdrew unconditionally from Southern Lebanon in May 2000 when the government was led by Ehud Barak. Thus, the principle has general acceptance and its application is seen as the end point of a particular conflict. In none of the examples quoted, however, has it been an easy process. The role of force in achieving this has been obvious.

In the conflict between Ethiopia and Eritrea, the third parties, in particular the Organization for African Unity (OAU), worked from a normative framework on border changes. According to this, there has to be a return to the status that existed prior to the onset of the fighting in 1998. In the words of the OAU Framework Agreement presented to the parties: 'the armed forces ... should be redeployed to the positions they held before 6 May 1998 as a mark of goodwill and consideration for our continental Organization'. The OAU summit meeting in Cairo in 1964 took the fundamental decision to accept the borders that were inherited from colonial times. The record is that African states have avoided international border revisions by force. The OAU peace plan built on this consensus. The reference in the Framework Agreement to the organization itself appeals to this legacy, its continental significance and its ability to talk 'on behalf of Africa.' These elements were additional pressures on Eritrea and Ethiopia. However, the parties continued to raise questions on the Framework Agreement and later documents derived from it. As part of the process, a high-level delegation from the OAU concluded that the disputed territory around the town of Badme, where the conflict originated in 1998, was administered by Ethiopia at the time the fighting began. Thus, the demand was on Eritrea to withdraw. It is also 'understood that this redeployment will not prejudice the final status of the area concerned'. The choice of words was important: 'redeployment' not the same as 'withdrawal', or 'evacuation'. A later, legitimate decision could award the territory to Eritrea. This is also what happened. As part of the peace settlement a border commission was created and in 2002 awarded Badme to Eritrea. Since the end of the war, this territory had been held by Ethiopia, which showed no inclination of giving it up. Eritrea's frustration over this resulted in crisis at the end of 2005, and the UN peacekeeping mission was ended in 2006, without a settlement. In the Eritrea–Djibouti territorial conflict, Eritrea is accused of having occupied areas belonging to its neighbour. The UN Security Council in 2009 explicitly demanded a return of Eritrean forces to their *status quo ante* positions (UN Security Council Resolution 1907).

As this case illustrates, both the UN and the OAU (now African Union – AU) have enunciated clear principles against forceful change of borders. The same is true for many other international and regional organizations. Territorial integrity is built into the normative framework on which these organizations operate. By bringing a particular conflict to one of these organizations, the parties will know what principles will be applied. There is a common interest among most states in favour of keeping the present boundaries and, thus, to support peace processes on that basis.

The principles are only applicable if the cases are reasonably evident, which means they have to concern fairly sizeable territories and not appear to be merely border adjustments. The occupations by Israel in 1967, Turkey in 1974 and Iraq in 1990 had high visibility. This made it imperative for the international community, chiefly the UN Security Council, to take a marked position on the return to the previous dividing lines. Whether such decisions are followed by effective measures to change the situation on the ground apparently is a separate matter as the mixed record suggests. In cases where a *status quo* approach has been applied, explicitly or in practice, there is little international interest in bringing about a visible change in the disputed territories. This frustrated the Arab states in their conflict with Israel; Greek Cypriots in dealing with Turkey; and Iran in dealing with the Security Council. In contrast, the conflict between Ecuador and Peru, highly important to both countries, drew less international attention. The dispute concentrated on the treaty of 1942, with many complexities in interpretation. The fighting in 1995 was kept on a low scale, not least due to the efforts of neighbouring countries to contain the conflict. International peacemaking did not have to confront withdrawal issues as the cease-fire was instituted. Instead, diplomacy could concentrate on the incompatibilities.

Although there is an ambition to uphold the demanding principle of a return to the previous *status quo* before negotiations, the successes in achieving this have not come easily. The record shows that it is not enough with diplomatic persuasion. In the case of Argentina, the occupation resulted in war and the defeat of the Argentinean forces. The islands were returned to British control only a few months after being taken by Argentina. The war was a military and political victory for Britain and there was a return to *status quo ante bellum*. The costs for this were high. Furthermore, Argentina has not accepted the new (or restored) situation. The umbrella agreement of 1989 made possible the return to diplomatic and commercial relations without solving the incompatibility. In the case of Vietnam, a unilateral withdrawal was implemented in 1989, that is, ten years after the troops entered the neighbouring country. By that time, a new regime had been able to establish itself in Cambodia. It was evidently strong enough to maintain control on its own, as it remains in place more than 15 years after the withdrawal. Somalia held on to the territories it conquered in Ethiopia for about one year, but in the face of close cooperation between the United States and the Soviet Union it withdrew. Still, it took until 1988 for Ethiopia and Somalia to conclude an agreement on the basis of the restored *status quo*.

From these experiences, it can be concluded that the conflict resolution policy in the UN Charter – the demand for a restoration of the *status quo ante bellum* – in reality is subject to interpretation and evasion. It is obvious that other factors are also relevant. For instance, political proximity to the United States may appear to be an important factor for states to avoid being pressured to comply with the principle. For Israel, there are special arguments for its security, undoubtedly with considerable support in the Western world. With respect to Turkey, there has been a similar 'understanding', taking into account Turkey's strategic location even after the Cold War, and as a NATO member. It is not necessarily shared in parliamentary assemblies throughout Europe, however, where the debate on Turkey's human rights record has been lively. In the Iran–Iraq War, Iraq was the preferred party of the USA, but interestingly enough also for the Soviet Union. Thus, the UN resolutions were consistently biased, and Iran reacted to that with international legal arguments.

However, the correlation between strategic affinity to the USA and acceptance of the *status quo* is not always that simple. The United States opposed Argentina's actions in the Falklands/Malvinas but might have been expected to respond negatively to a forceful British reaction. The USA had a traditional record of objecting to extra-Hemispheric interventions in South America. After a period of mediation, however, the United States chose to support Britain. That the USA opposed Iraq's actions against

Kuwait may have come as a surprise to the Iraqi leader, Saddam Hussein, remembering the support he received in the war with Iran, which had just ended. The leaders in Iraq and Argentina may have thought of themselves as so close to the USA that no effective counter-actions would be forthcoming. It is less surprising that the USA opposed Somalia's actions in Ogaden (Somalia by that time was regarded as a Soviet client state) and Vietnam's war in Cambodia (Vietnam's alliance with the Soviet Union was opposed by China and the USA alike). Arguments on conflict resolution principles are evidently not the full story.

However, on issues of territorial change, there has often been a remarkable consensus among the major powers. There is a preference for such issues to be handled peacefully, and there is a record of such arrangements (Kacowicz 1994). Defending the territorial integrity of states is a cornerstone of the UN Charter, however, and thus states are likely to be resistant to forceful changes in principle, as they may also affect them. The *status quo ante bellum* principle is, consequently, the one most easily agreed to by the major powers and UN member states. In instances where this is not so, we can suspect that a member state has a particular interest in a given conflict. We would, on the whole, expect permanent members of the Security Council to support the more demanding position of a return to the pre-war lines, except in cases where it sees particular reasons for not doing so. It means that, for instance, the USA sometimes will use its veto in order to prevent the Security Council from taking unwanted action. For the United States there is a consistent pattern in issues involving Israel.

For interstate geopolitical conflicts questions of *status quo* and *status quo ante bellum* are highly relevant. There is a general preference for demanding a return to the situation before the outbreak of hostilities. In some cases, however, we find exceptions to this rule, weakening its consistent application and, thus, also reducing its deterrent effect. We have seen that this is connected to other forces in the global system.

Punitive or integrative solutions?

Realpolitik conflicts build on the power of the parties. In this analysis, power is what ultimately decides the outcome of conflicts. Such outcomes, furthermore, are formed in clear alternatives, preferably victory or defeat. If a conflict results in negotiations and compromises, this is because none of the parties is strong enough. Furthermore, the analysis emphasizes that the objectives of the parties involve power and domination. Power is both a means and an end.

When the British government decided to reconquer the Falkland Islands, this was not only a question of the islands and their status. It also involved regional and global influence. To regain control meant that Britain would continue to have a role in South America and that it retained value as a partner for others (most notably, the close connection to Chile, under General Augusto

Pinochet). Also, if successful, the operation would display that Britain was a power in the highest league. To project force across large distances is an indicator impressing other powers. Obviously, it would have been more difficult for Britain to react in a similar way had, for instance, Hong Kong been occupied by China. Guatemala, on the other hand, may have refrained from challenging British control in Belize, knowing that it would meet strong opposition. Argentina, when assessing Britain's likely response, may have had severe problems in actually predicting what would happen.

Territorial issues have power implications. Whether Iran or Iraq prevailed in their war in the 1980s was thought to affect influence in the Gulf region. Iran, during the reign of the Shah, had been the dominant actor in this sensitive locale and the Islamic revolutionary leadership preferred to maintain this position, albeit with a different ideological content, as we shall see in Section 5.3. Iraq, on the other hand, was likely to use a victorious outcome of the war to bolster the position of radical pan-Arabism. It might tilt the regional balance against Israel, for instance. This analysis leads to a cynical attitude, where a major power perspective would say that it is acceptable if the two regional actors weaken each other. This approach gives little incentive for major powers actively to bring a war to a speedy end. Would there ever be a *Realpolitik* interest in conflict resolution?

Yes, there are such concerns. Thought has been given to relations between major powers after a war. The logic also would be the same for other interstate conflicts. The key question is whether a losing side should be dealt with in a punitive or integrative way. What is the 'best' approach for terminating a war and avoiding a future repetition of this particular war? It is a discussion with roots in Machiavelli's writings and it continues to have validity. Kegley and Raymond have formulated this as an issue of whether one should prefer a punitive or lenient peace (1999: 33–6). This summarizes *Realpolitik* thinking in a coherent way. Let us look more closely at these two lines of thought.

In punitive, or harsh, peacemaking a firm distinction is made between winners and losers. The idea is to establish such a strong power asymmetry that the winners will rule for the foreseeable future and the losers, therefore, willingly accept their roles as subordinate members of the international system. It means that a war is likely to be waged until the complete capitulation of one side. The destruction is the price for a lasting peace after the war, it is argued. The winner has to keep up its superior military, economic and political position after the war. Peace requires heavy military expenditures for a long time to come. In *Realpolitik* understanding, there are always actors who are interested in challenging the stronger ones and who will try to locate its weakest spots. Thus, preponderance is the only solution.

There are critics of this line of thinking. There is a danger that even after a severe and humiliating loss, the loser will rise again, and now be more bitter and frustrated. Thus, there will be a new round of conflict, new attempts at revenge, new victories and new defeats. Such a cycle of events may be broken by the superiority of one party, a realist may argue, but, the critics will respond, this requires heavy armaments, invites arms races and prevents the development of civilian sectors of either of the societies.

The integrative approach, in contrast, argues that it is important to reintegrate the loser quickly into the new international or regional order. This means that, once the loser has met stated demands, normalization should follow, with rewards for good behaviour, an extension of respect and incentives for non-aggressive stances. There is an asymmetry also in this relationship, but it is less pronounced, and there is a willingness to contribute to reintegration. The perspective is long-term and reformist. The purpose is to change the asymmetric relationship into a mutually beneficial partnership, something which, it is assumed, is also in the interests of other parties. The hope is that in this way there will be fewer reasons for a resurgence of conflict. It could be objected that this strategy might be self-deceptive and wishful thinking. It is even dangerous if it leads to early disarmament, encouraging uncompromising elements on the other side. Opportunities are created for the defeated to strike back. Even a defeat with a human face is a defeat, and is going to be felt as such. War is likely to result anyway, a critic may argue. Neither argument is without its logic as well as plausible critique. This makes it interesting to study the historical record. An overview of the experiences of 200 years of major power relations shows how different strands of thought have dominated at different times (Wallensteen 1984). In periods of universalist or integrative thinking, the frequency of major wars has been reduced; in periods of more particularist thinking, major wars have been more numerous. This means that the overall approach major powers take to each other does have important effects on their international relations.

An account of the German–French relationships is instructive. The war between the two countries in 1870–71 ended in a humiliating way for France. Not only did Germany take control over two important provinces, Alsace-Lorraine (in German, Elsass-Lothringen), but it also proclaimed the new German Empire in the halls of Versailles, the French monarchical residence. These actions made it evident that the conflict would not go away. Any form of partnership and alliance was excluded. Instead, the conflict between Germany and France became the axis around which European international affairs operated for the following seven decades.

The First World War ended in a similarly humiliating way, but this time the outcome was reversed. Now, it was France that could dictate – in Versailles – the conditions for Germany's post-war situation. These involved not only the return of territory to France (Alsace-Lorraine), the acquisition of new territories (colonial areas), and the creation of new states in the territory formerly held by the losing powers (the new states in Central Europe emerging from German, Austrian and Hungarian territories). There was also a requirement of heavy financial compensation and restrictions on German military power. It was meant to be a punitive peace and, by any standard, it was. The treaty has been much debated. For instance, it has been noted that it had to be implemented by a newly created democratic regime in

Germany that had not been responsible for the war. Thus, it came to be seen as a treaty against all Germans, not just the elite that controlled the country in 1914. Hitler used this and, aided by the economic crisis, came to power on an agenda for undoing the Versailles Treaty. The Second World War followed.

The allies in the Second World War demanded unconditional surrender by Germany. There was never a peace agreement signed with Germany after the war. Instead the country was divided. This was only in part a strategy for dealing with Germany. The original plan among the allies was that Germany would be treated as one unit, although each of the victors would control certain parts for a period of time. Their disagreement precluded the unification and resulted instead in two German states, the Federal Republic in the West and the German Democratic Republic in the East. The *de facto* solution of two German states may have served a purpose, as it focused German attention not at the victors, but at ways of overcoming the cleavage. Unintentionally, the Cold War led to a more rapid integration of the two German states into the international system, albeit in opposite camps, than would otherwise have been the case. There were additional elements, which served to break the cycle of punitive peace. One was the Marshall Plan. Instead of demanding economic compensation from Germany, the allies resolved to rebuild West Germany as fast as possible. An economically strong Germany, connected with the other Western countries, was seen as a more promising arrangement. Again it was defined in terms of a struggle against communism and prevention of the spread of revolutionary ideas. The measures were also to prevent a return of neo-Nazism, drawing on the lessons learned from the economic crisis of the early 1930s. The Soviet leadership took a more punitive and less integrative attitude to 'its' Germany. Entire industries were dismantled to be used in the reconstruction of Russia after the war. The Soviet Union chose not to participate in the Marshall aid programme. If it had, Europe might have developed differently.

The emphasis on reconstructing democracy was an important element of the post-1945 policy towards West Germany. This meant learning some of the lessons from the First World War. The democratic system had become too weak, and was identified with the defeat. In the post-Second World War period the tribunals against Nazi war criminals made clear that some Germans were more responsible than others and, thus, a new political elite could act with fewer constraints. It included building a new Germany. The demilitarization of Germany was another important aspect of the changing relationship. Only in 1955 was a German armed force again set up. It was not on its own, however, but within the NATO alliance, and it contained some innovative democratic features. It was not until the conflict in Kosovo in 1999 that German soldiers were stationed outside the country. Since then German troops have also been used in Afghanistan, well outside the traditional NATO area of operation.

The integration of Germany into two major frameworks of international cooperation was also important. The creation of the European Coal and

Steel Community in 1950 was a first aspect of this, and Germany has since then been an active, powerful member of what is today the European Union (EU). In 1955, West Germany became a member of NATO. Ten years after the end of the Second World War it had gone from loser to allied partner. This again shows how differently the allies reacted after the two world wars and the consequences of this basic attitude for the future of relations. The attitude towards Germany shifted from a punitive to an integrative strategy, and it appears that the latter has produced more promising results for a future without war between the same parties. Remarkably, (West) Germany continued to pay the First World War reparations and could celebrate paying the last installment in October 2010.

The distinction of punitive and integrative endings of wars thus has empirical application. Is this framework relevant for interstate conflicts since the Cold War? Looking at the war endings we have mentioned, it is clear that the attitude has been more punitive than integrative. The Iran–Iraq War displays that fully. The Iranian side, feeling that it was victimized by Iraq and the world, initially demanded the elimination of the regime in Baghdad and compensation for the destruction it had inflicted on Iran. In the end, it had to accept the regime, but the hostility remained. On the Iraqi side, the ambition was to eliminate a regime built on the Shiite version of Islam. The majority of the Iraqi population is Shiite and was seen as a threat to Saddam Hussein's hold on power. The war did not have this result. Thus, two antagonistic parties had to accept each other. It was bitter to their leaders. It also meant that the war could have been concluded much earlier, had a realization of the likely outcome been predicted. The lasting, punitive attitudes are reflected in the parties' interpretation of the cease-fire arrangement, where both sides have been as strict as possible, for instance, in dealing with the exchange of prisoners of war. It is as if the war was continued in the implementation of the peace.

The Gulf War of 1991 ended in a similar way, with a cease-fire resolution by the Security Council. Its strict enforcement reflected the sceptical attitude of the parties. The UN was not going to reward Iraq for good behaviour, only punish it for bad actions. Iraq had no interest in being forthcoming to the UN, for instance, in the disarmament provisions. The ending of the war was punitive, and Iraq's interstate relations continued to be difficult, until the regime was overthrown in March 2003. The US action partly stemmed from an ambition to create new power relations in the region.

There are few examples of integrative thinking in wars between smaller, neighbouring countries, but one of the most daring initiatives is found in this category. The visit by Egypt's President Anwar Sadat to Jerusalem in 1977. It was a remarkable gesture, and the negotiations that followed were difficult. The Israeli government was not prepared to meet the Egyptian leadership on the generous level the visit initiated. Without the intervention of the Carter administration in the USA, the initiative may have failed. It did not, but came to be an important, though still controversial, breakthrough in Israeli–Arab relations (Carter 1992). It has resulted in a cold peace, rather than close integration, however. This might be attributable to the fact that other elements of the conflicts around Israel have not been settled. It is instructive to observe the important role of Egypt in promoting peace talks among other actors. Relations may take a different turn once there is a complete set of peace agreements on the Palestinian issues.

Conflicts defined in *Realpolitik* terms tend to be dealt with as matters of bilateral relationship. There are many examples of very difficult negotiations and careful implementation. The parties themselves seldom seem to view the solution to their common conflict as a way of establishing a novel relationship for a particular region. Consequently, the wars have not resulted in novel regional orders, only in temporary endings of one war in a series of wars. If this is true, it means that the parties expect a repetition and will do little to prevent this through innovative thinking. South Asia is a case in point, with repetitive conflicts between India and Pakistan over a 60-year period. There is a particular challenge to search for ways in which this can be changed. The peace process initiated in 2004 between these two countries signalled the potential of such a possibility. Integrative solutions may require a regional approach to conflicts in several conflict-prone regions, for instance, the Middle East, the Gulf region, South Asia, Indochina and the Horn of Africa. In some, there are embryonic organizations on which to build. The history of the French–German relationship suggests that changes are possible. There is, furthermore, little evidence that the punitive approach can bring a conflict to a lasting termination.

The seven mechanisms

Turning to the solutions to interstate wars, to what extent are the seven mechanisms identified in Section 3.5 relevant and useful? Let us look at them one by one and apply each to recent conflicts and settlements between states.

The first one concerns the *change of a basic position* by one or several parties. There are instances of demands being dropped. In the war termination which is closest to a peace agreement, the settlement between Iran and Iraq, both sides abandoned key demands, particularly those pertaining to the question of the legitimacy of the regime in the other country and to issues of compensation. Thus, the negotiations came to concentrate on the sequencing of issues, particularly whether a cease-fire should come first or not. In the end, the cease-fire, implemented in August 1988, was followed by the first direct meeting between officials of the two sides some days later. This meant that the two sides accepted the other as the party to talk to. The positions changed without a shift in the leadership. The key issues that remained concerned recognition, responsibility and compensation. They recognized each other, found a formula for determining responsibility and left the issue of compensation. Thus, a war ending was possible. No doubt, this can be attributed to war weariness. There was little prospect of any side winning and, thus, there was little point in continuing. But that had been obvious much earlier. It was told to the parties by the international mediators. It is also possible to attribute the final agreement to changes in the international environment. The West as well as the Soviet Union united in demanding an end to the war, whereas they previously, by individual calculation, had supported the same side against the other. This was manifested in the unity of the Security Council. In the face of this change, the warring parties could comply only by giving up the demands they learned were the least acceptable to the other side as well as to the international actors. In so doing, it also became clear which demands were the most significant in the conflict, as a political choice had to be made.

A second way of transcending the incompatibility is by *dividing the contested values*. In a conflict driven by *Geopolitik* considerations, this would mean dividing a particular territory between the contestants. Such outright territorial deals have been rare recently. They seem to belong to a previous era. In the Munich accord in 1938 and the Hitler–Stalin agreement in 1939 this was a prominent feature. Perhaps, popular considerations today make such agreements impossible. It would suggest, however, that they are doable in unpopulated areas, typically for maritime disputes. We also need to consider the possibility of dividing authority. In a major power perspective, this means creating geographical spheres of influence. Major powers have historically been uninhibited in dividing areas, openly or in secret, to reduce the frictions between themselves. The Cold War had such features. The USA was unwilling to challenge Soviet control behind the lines drawn at the Yalta and Potsdam conferences in 1945. Both sides kept their forces off these divisions, as both sides perceived a danger of escalation and nuclear war. There might be many such understandings in the world, but they are today seldom expressed in peace agreements. They can be detected by observing which states act and which ones refrain from acting in particular areas where they could have a reach. It has been noted that the United States lately has been more active in Africa, and that it has taken a role in peacemaking previously held by France, for instance, in Central Africa.

Horse-trading is identified as a third mechanism. Geopolitically, this would mean yielding control over one area in exchange for control in another. Sometimes this is what is done in delimitation and demarcation of new borderlines. It is seldom explicit, however, and may be observed only with a close scrutiny of the results. A problem in the Iran–Iraq War was the return to previous international borders. These were regulated in a 1975 accord which Iraq had unilaterally abrogated. Iraq was not willing to return to this document. The final outcome did not envisage a border change, however. Instead, it said that forces should be withdrawn to the internationally recognized borders, although these were technically not agreed. In fact, the borders from 1975 were used. It meant both sides had to leave some areas to gain access to others. The occupied territories, in a sense, were traded against each other.

Horse-trading may also involve the trading of one issue for another. A party can agree to drop a particular question, to be rewarded by receiving full support on another. As we have just seen, in the interstate conflicts there has been little of such give-and-take in the last three decades. It could well be that horse-trading requires better relations than these cases exemplify. We can observe that it is more likely to be taking place between major powers. Their vast interests make such actions more possible, as commitment to particular actors or issues vary in strength. The negotiations on major arms and nuclear weapons reductions do contain many such arrangements, where entire categories are exchanged. The deal of 1987 on intermediate nuclear forces (INF) is instructive. The USA promised to eliminate all of its new cruise missiles (Tomahawk) and ballistic missiles (Pershing II) in return for the Soviet Union eliminating its numerous SS-20 missiles. The weapons systems were seen to have similar functions and could thus be traded. Each side had publicly committed itself to the elimination of the other's weapons of this type. The INF included considerable verification measures. The USA was willing to yield on some of these in order to gain Soviet acceptance of the complete elimination of all missiles (Woodworth 1999: 188). As we observed in Section 2.4, this ability to deal with armaments far surpassed the willingness of the same parties to deal with ongoing conflicts.

A fourth way of transcending an incompatibility is by *creating shared rule*. Again, there is a difference in dynamics among conflicts between major powers and those among non-major powers. In the former cases, there is a history of creating shared organizations. The UN is, in itself, the outcome of such an effort. The key elements were agreed directly between the American and Soviet leaderships in the negotiations of 1944–45. The UN has, as we have indicated, set standards for resolution of *Geopolitik* conflicts (notably the inviolability of boundaries of states) which has had a profound impact on relations between states. In direct deliberation between major powers there are joint organizations, such as inspection teams for arms control agreements, for instance, in the INF agreement in December 1987. These were strictly bilateral arrangements; no third party was let in.[2] In conflicts between non-major powers, such arrangements appear difficult to create. Between India and Pakistan there are agreements pertaining to nuclear installations. Between Iran and Iraq no joint organization was set up between the two, for instance, for operating the important waters of Shatt-al-Arab. This would have been a reasonable way of handling a shared waterway, but was not part of the concluding negotiations. Thus, the issue of control over this international waterway remains unresolved. In the agreement between Israel and Egypt some shared organs were created. The same is true for the agreement between Israel and Jordan. In both cases, the agreements have run into difficulties. It is possible that their smooth functioning will depend on the ability to find solutions for the remaining aspects of the Palestinian equation and for the relations between Israel and Syria. Under such circumstances, the regional frameworks that were developed in the early 1990s (the Madrid conferences) may be seen in a different light.

If the parties cannot share control, a logical possibility is *to leave control to another party*; this is the fifth form indicated in Section 3.5. This is a frequently used form in interstate relations. From a major power perspective, this could mean neutralization or the creation of buffer zones. This is how it was possible for East and West to agree to the reintegration of Austria in 1955. Its neutralization was a solution that met concerns among the major powers. There are other examples of such measures, solving at the same time a *Geopolitik* and *Realpolitik* question. In the 1991 Paris accords on Cambodia, the country was defined as non-aligned. Thus, neither China nor Vietnam nor Thailand could count on the country as a potential ally. This was satisfactory to all parties. It meant, for Vietnam, that it would not face a two-front challenge from a Cambodia allied to China. The gain for Thailand was that it would not have Vietnamese forces close to its borders. For China, the advantage was that the influence of Vietnam was reduced or less visible. Furthermore, it was also preferable to most Khmers, as it ensured the independence of the country. The stationing of peacekeeping troops along exposed borders, as has been done in the Sinai and Lebanon, or the creation of demilitarized zones are examples of partial neutralization. The expectation is that they will be withdrawn when general peace exists. It can be a long-term commitment. In 1993, Sweden and Norway decided to dismantle their demilitarized zone, stretching along both sides of the border. It was part of the agreement on Norway's independence and had been in effect since 1905.

These are successful examples. However, one of the modern wars relates to a failed agreement: Cyprus. The agreement on independence in 1960 made Cyprus an independent and neutral state. It could not align with any of its neighbours. It was part of an arrangement whereby Greece and Turkey agreed that they would not forcefully incorporate Cyprus into their own territory (in whole or in part). This was a form of neutralization of the island, in spite of the majority population (Greek Cypriots) wanting to reunite with Greece (*enosis*) and the minority group (Turkish Cypriots) interested in uniting with Turkey by dividing the island (*taksim*). None of the actors achieved their main objectives. Instead, an independent state, Cyprus, not desired by any side as their first choice, was created. It had a constitution that balanced the various interests, and it also gave the right to the neighbours to interfere in the affairs of the independent state. The conflicts on the island escalated dramatically in 1963. UN forces were stationed there from 1964 onwards, but still an invasion took place by Turkey in 1974, *de facto* dividing the island. A proposed peace agreement in 2004, the Annan Plan, which would have created a federal state, was accepted by one community but resisted by the other in two separate referenda. The solution of having the inhabitants rule the island on their own was still not feasible due to continuing conflicting interests.

These examples illustrate that neutralization is a difficult course of action. It may function, particularly as long as the surrounding states support the arrangement and it can be upheld by strong local opinion. However, it can also mean that neighbours will anxiously watch what is happening and react rapidly if the agreed order is unravelling. Turkey in 1974 acted after the pro-Greece junta had taken over Cyprus. In its view, the island was about to be incorporated into Greece. Quick, pre-emptive action was seen as necessary. Rather than deterring action, the neutral status spurred action. Thus, leaving important territories outside the control of strongly interested parties may work, but it may also create new dangers. Could such measures be used to solve disputes around areas that are of a particularly high value? For instance, could Jerusalem be handled according to a formula involving internationalization? The 1947 UN plan passed by the General Assembly made Jerusalem an international territory, separated from the states in the region. It was not possible to get full support for this idea. Jerusalem is today regarded by the state of Israel as the country's capital. Similarly, Palestinians regard Jerusalem as their capital. There are few precedents for solving such disputes. Many peace plans have proposed that parts of the city would be international. The Oslo peace process has resulted in creative suggestions, but none has so far been accepted by the two negotiating parties. There is only one city which is the capital in two states: Rome. It is shared between the Republic of Italy and the Holy See (the Vatican). This case might provide a better model than the original UN plan. Such a solution has to assume that a part of Jerusalem is an autonomous unit, and there have to be arrangements for unhindered access to the holy places. Still, there is an issue of control and sovereignty that has to be handled in such a way as not to invite a division of the city. Lessons need to be drawn from the fate of neighbouring Cyprus, where even the capital, Nicosia, is divided.

A sixth form for transcending incompatibility is the resort to *conflict resolution mechanisms*. There are a number of such experiences. It may mean that conflicts are handed from a political to a legal level and, thus, are treated in accordance with precedence and the parties do not have to invent the solution themselves (Corell 1999: 33–4). There are also *ad hoc* mechanisms created for particular occasions, such as arbitration courts. The most central issue is whether a mechanism has legitimacy with the international system and the parties. In reality, actual solutions may integrate the first five mechanisms we have just recounted. The conflict resolution mechanism adds a procedural and argumentative level to the resolution, which helps to make the outcome more acceptable.

The legal means of conflict resolution are those that have been described most carefully. One of the most interesting is arbitration, where the parties commit themselves to accept the outcome, whatever it is, before the deliberations begin. Since 1945, Bilder claims, there have been 'at least several dozen significant arbitrations'. Here there are more cases from relationships among non-major powers. There are arbitrations handling some of the aspects of the conflicts listed in Tables 5.1 and 5.2, notably between India and Pakistan over the Rann of Kutch area in 1968 and Egypt and Israel over the Taba area in 1988 (Bilder 1997: 161). In none of these cases can we say that the mechanism dealt with the central, often political, aspect of the conflict. It was useful, however, in avoiding further tension around implementation. It is particularly applicable to issues that concern territory. The most recent case is worth a closer analysis.

In the Eritrea–Ethiopia peace agreement of December 2000, the border issue was handled through the creation of a special Commission (Article 4 of the peace treaty). In fact, 17 (out of a total of 47) paragraphs were devoted to this Commission in the final peace agreements. Its composition and mandate were crucial, as this was what the conflict was originally all about. In the text, the parties agreed, for instance, that this neutral Border Commission would consist of five members, with two appointed by each side. It was stated that neither of these 'shall be nationals or permanent residents of the party making the appointment'. These four members were then to agree on the fifth one, who would be the President of the Commission. If they could not agree, the UN Secretary-General was given the role of selecting the president, who would be 'neither a national nor permanent resident of either party'. The parties took special precautions to ensure that the members of the Commission would have no connection to either party. It was also specified that decisions by the Commission were to be made by a majority of the Commissioners. It suggests that the parties did not expect consensus and that, in severe cases, the President of the Commission might become the sole arbiter of the outcome. In 2002, the Commission nevertheless was able to deliver a unanimous decision on the border delimitations. Ethiopia chose not to abide by the decision by claiming procedural objections. Its position was weak, as it had agreed to the arrangement. By the end of 2010 the decision had still not been implemented and there was little pressure on Ethiopia to do so.

The solution to the conflict between Ecuador and Peru was made through a special procedure, which in essence was arbitration. The Guarantor countries to the 1942 treaty that was in dispute were asked to solve the remaining issues. They provided a package deal where the parties had already agreed to certain matters (navigation rights, border integration, confidence-building measures). The Guarantors resolved the outstanding territorial issues by giving parts to Peru, but one crucial square kilometre to Ecuador (as private property), thereby meeting a central Ecuadorian demand. Interestingly, the area surrounding this, a total of more than 50 square kilometres, was made an ecological reserve (Einaudi 1999: 425). Thus, the solution contained elements of a division of territory, but also relinquished control (the ecological reserve). Most important was that the final decision was left to others than the parties themselves, thus reducing domestic criticism of the governments. Importantly, both the Congress of Ecuador and the one of Peru had accepted this procedure in advance.

Arbitration may not solve matters of power directly, but can have an impact indirectly. Using such a mechanism might be the way to reduce the centrality of a particular issue. The border between Ecuador and Peru was a highly sensitive question in Ecuador, where it took on existential dimensions. It related to the self-perception of being a state of the Amazon basin. Thus, the solution was of vital importance to the standing of the country in the region. Similarly, Peru was not willing to yield, as it had a record of lost wars. Its regional position would be affected, at least in its own eyes, if territory were yielded once again. The conflict resolution mechanism thus solved an issue while maintaining the parties' self-respect and position in the regional context. It did not make any of the parties more or less powerful than before.

The UN and International Atomic Energy Agency (IAEA) missions on issues of weapons of mass destruction in Iraq were reactivated by the UN Security Council in November 2002. UNMOVIC was led by Dr Hans Blix and the IAEA team by Director Mohamed ElBaradei. This was seen, by many member states, as a mechanism for dealing with the contradictory facts of the case, and possibly as a way to avoid war. The US actions on Iraq in March 2003 effectively ended this route. Interestingly, US teams later reported on the issues, demonstrating that no such capacity existed in Iraq at the time of the war.[3]

Finally, we noted that there are ways in which issues can be *left to the future*, without the parties changing their views on a preferred outcome. This requires, of course, that the parties not commit themselves to a settlement by a certain date, thus preventing the easy resort to this mechanism. By leaving the question open, time is gained and options are maintained. To defer issues to commissions is a possibility. An example is the ending of the war between Iran and Iraq where Iran demanded that the responsibility for the war be determined. The agreed solution in 1988 was to appoint a group to document this. It presented its report, by December 1991, at a time when much had changed in the Gulf area. To many actors the findings had only historical interest. However, it showed that Iraq had committed the initial aggression and should be held responsible for damage inflicted on Iran. In short, it vindicated Iran's position. By that time, however, this had been overtaken by other events and the impact was not the one that Iran had expected.

Similarly, in the peace treaty for the Eritrea–Ethiopia War, it was agreed that an investigation into the origin of the conflict was to be carried out. Article 3.2 gave this assignment to an 'independent, impartial body appointed by the Secretary-General of the OAU, in consultation with the Secretary-General of the United Nations and the two parties'. The Commission reported in 2005, saying that Eritrea's attack on Ethiopia in May 1998 could not be justified as lawful self-defence and that the country, thus, should compensate Ethiopia.

These commissions proceeded at such a pace that the verdict would come later, and thus not raise obstacles in implementing other, more pressing provisions of the agreements. In the case of Eritrea–Ethiopia, however, the implementation of the border decision had not been completed. Nevertheless, in two of the most destructive recent wars, issues of responsibility for the initiation of hostilities have been central. They have even been so important that they were maintained by the parties to the very end of the negotiation process. It returns us to the issues of legitimacy and the right to initiate war. Undoubtedly, it has become increasingly difficult for states to be involved in wars, unless it can be clearly attributed to self-defence (as accepted in the UN Charter, Article 51). When convincing arguments cannot be made, and this can be determined by commissions, it opens the possibility of compensation as well as increases the obstacles to renewed war.

5.3 Conflict Resolution: *Idealpolitik* and *Kapitalpolitik*

Ideological matters and economics are often seen as driving forces in conflict. They require closer scrutiny. We need to see to what extent such factors have been important in the origins of conflicts, thus having implications for the issues with which peace agreements will have to grapple. Given the dynamic character of conflicts, however, issues may also arise as the war proceeds and generate new issues that have to be remedied. Let us look at the role of *Idealpolitik* and *Kapitalpolitik* in general in interstate conflicts, and then proceed to the use of the seven mechanisms for solving the issues.

In two of the interstate armed conflicts of the 1990s an incompatibility over government can be clearly identified (Table 5.1). Obviously, the US intervention in Panama aimed at removing a strong force behind the government. The purpose was to enhance the prospects of democracy in Panama. It was also thought to improve stability and secure the operations of the Panama Canal. The war on Iraq in 2003 also aimed at removing the incumbent regime, which was seen by the US government as a potential terrorist threat, as a negation of democracy as well as being a country with important oil resources. The interventions had several purposes, one of them dealing with *Idealpolitik* (furthering the ideals of democracy) and one with *Kapitalpolitik* (that is, safeguarding economic interests). This does not exhaust this dimension in interstate conflict, however.

We have also seen that *Idealpolitik* was an important consideration in the Iran–Iraq War. Both sides feared being overthrown by the other. A change of government in Iraq was also an explicit demand by Iran. It stalled negotiations. The same concerns were voiced in Eritrea and Ethiopia, each accusing the other of supporting designs on the government or planning to attack the capital of the other. The fact that both leaders were present in Algiers, Algeria, in December 2000, to sign the agreement also made clear that they accepted the other's hold on power. Similar concerns were an aspect of the Cold War confrontation in particular countries. A country might have a role in the global strategy of the two superpowers. Both had a record of attempting or actually overthrowing governments in other countries. The US intervention in Panama was the last one related to the Cold War. Its explicit motives pointed to a new era, where concerns were no longer with governments' alleged communist inclinations, but their ability to combat the drug trade or deal with terrorism. In this way, concern over government continues to be a valid dimension for interstate relations.

Idealpolitik and the settlement of conflicts

There are two major debates in international affairs on *Idealpolitik* issues. The first concerns the democracy–peace hypothesis. It maintains that democratic states rarely fight wars with each other. If this is so, as statistical evidence shows, does it mean that, if democracies nevertheless are involved in wars, these will be settled more easily? The second debate concerns the alleged clash of civilization, where the argument can be translated into saying that deep cultural or political differences are likely to generate more conflict and make settlements less likely. A less ambitious formulation is that ethnic divisions are central for interstate conflict. Let us build on these two forms of thinking and see what it brings for the possibility of ending conflicts.

The *democracy–peace hypothesis* is the one most easily handled with the available evidence (Russett 1993). Of the 14 wars identified during the last two decades of the Cold War and the four wars following it, democratic states were at least one party to ten. This means that they were involved in more than half of all armed conflicts that escalated to war. In nine conflicts the opposing sides were non-democratic states. This observation confirms that democracies are not peaceful under all circumstances. The point in the democracy–peace hypothesis is, however, that they are at peace in the relations among themselves. This is also borne out by the data presented here. There is only one case where it could be maintained that both sides were democratic societies: the Turkey–Cyprus War in 1974. Let us, consequently, investigate this conflict a little further.

The democratic systems were, in both Turkey and Cyprus, less well entrenched than the systems normally studied by the democratic peace writers. Clearly, both societies were exposed to considerable internal strain, from the military in one case, and from the conflict with the minority in the other. The Cyprus dispute, furthermore, had a long history. The country became independent from British rule in 1960. It was equipped with a special democratic constitution that gave most power to the majority population, the Greek Cypriots, which constituted four-fifths of the inhabitants. Within this framework, strong measures were instituted to protect the rights of the minority, the Turkish Cypriots. In July 1974, the democratic government of Cyprus under Greek Cypriot President Macharios was deposed in a coup masterminded by the military junta ruling in Greece. The coup leaders controlled the island for a short period of time. The situation was used by Turkey, led by an elected prime minister, to launch a military intervention. In two consecutive military moves, Turkey took control over 40 per cent of the island. Turkey's objective was not to restore democracy on the island, but to safeguard the interests of the Turkish Cypriots and meet strategic Turkish concerns. The government it faced was in disarray. It is difficult to define this as a conflict between two democracies of the type postulated by the democracy–peace hypothesis. It was more a question of state collapse in Cyprus and the grasping of a window of opportunity by an outside power. Thus, it does not challenge the basic proposition on the improbability of war between stable democracies.

The following developments are interesting, however. The intervention stimulated the downfall of the military regime in Greece. A stable period of democracy followed in Greece. Also, the elected government in Cyprus was returned to power. The case, thus, is important in a discussion on conflict resolution as all the parties to the conflict have now been open societies for more than a quarter of a century. The same is true for those particularly interested in a settlement: Britain, the USA and the EU. Still, the conflict remains unsettled. There is no war, but there is no peace either, among these democratic states, in spite of considerable international efforts. There are even arguments saying that the very openness of the societies prevents a solution, as each proposal immediately is available to everybody. Doctrinaire objections prohibit serious discussion. Thus, although democracies may not make war, they certainly have difficulties making peace.

There is an *Idealpolitik* divide among the parties in a number of the other wars in the three decades. Leaving Cyprus aside, there are cleavages along the democracy–dictatorship dimension in nine conflicts, a high share of all conflicts. In two more, an objective for one side was the removal of a dictatorial regime in the other (Tanzania aimed at overthrowing the government in Uganda; Vietnam had similar goals in Cambodia). Of the remaining conflicts, four belong to the Cold War divide (two strongly so: Vietnam–China, Somalia–Ethiopia; two more weakly connected: East Timor, Chad–Libya). Two have a strong dynamic of their own, Iran–Iraq and Eritrea–Ethiopia, not least as the government issue was present in both. Iran believed that Iraq wanted to undermine the new and not yet consolidated Islamic leadership in Tehran. Iraq feared that the new Iranian leadership was instigating an uprising among the large Shiite population in the country. Both sides may have entertained such ideas. Eritrea continued to worry that Ethiopia would not accept its newly won independence, while Ethiopia accused Eritrea of fomenting unrest among different ethnic groups in Ethiopia. In neither case was democracy a question, but there was definitely an issue of the government's political standing in society. This element can also be seen in the India–Pakistan War in 1999, which resulted in the later removal of the shaky, and only in a very formal sense democratic, government in Pakistan. However, many governments probably constantly worry about their standing. This does not mean that they would want to go to war, for instance, as this would rather serve to increase their vulnerability (Heldt 1996).

From this we need to conclude that *Idealpolitik* considerations are important in the origins and dynamics of conflict. The settlements have, however, seldom referred to these matters. As they are done between states, such matters are the internal affairs of each state. If one side raises them, it is likely that the other will reciprocate with similar issues. Thus, both sides are likely to avoid the matter, or ask for adherence to principles of non-interference in internal affairs. Sometimes it may go a bit further, as there are likely to be nationals on both sides of the border. This was an issue in the Eritrea–Ethiopia War and the agreement in December 2000 makes reference to it: 'The parties shall afford humane treatment to each other's nationals and persons of each other's national origin within their respective territories' (Article 3). This aims at protecting the rights of Eritreans in Ethiopia and vice versa. There are no mechanisms specifying the implementation of this agreement, but the statement still means that certain internal matters are of concern to the other side, and that this is acknowledged.

The record of imposing a new, democratic regime after a war is not impressive. In the wars where ruthless regimes were deposed (the regime under Pol Pot in Cambodia and Idi Amin in Uganda), the governments that followed were hardly democratic. The US interventions in Grenada and Panama have fared better, even suggesting to some that highly asymmetric military interventions may serve to promote democracy. The Iraq War of 2003 has been followed by a bloody and complicated internal conflict at the same time that a democracy-building effort was being pursued. In fact, the conflicts across the democracy–dictatorship divide involve only four democracies: the USA, the UK, India and Israel. Only in the Vietnam War did their war involvement result in a defeat. The United States led the wars in Vietnam, in the Gulf, and on Iraq in 2003, Britain was involved in the Falklands/Malvinas conflict, and Israel was a party to wars with Egypt, Syria and Lebanon. India's wars all stem from the conflict with Pakistan. India has for most of the period retained its democratic system. Pakistan sometimes experienced more open forms of government. The Vietnam War was waged in the name of democracy, but the US-supported regime in South Vietnam crumbled, partly due to its lack of national legitimacy. The Gulf War led to the restoration of the emirate in Kuwait, and only later did a more open society emerge. The complexities of Iraq are still unfolding, and in 2010 a second democratic election took place in spite of considerable domestic strife. The Falklands/ Malvinas conflict resulted in a new democracy, as the military junta in Argentina lost legitimacy and was replaced by a democratic regime. India's involvement in East Pakistan was in support of a popularly based independence movement, and led to a democratic constitution in the new country of Bangladesh. It was not until the 1990s that a more stable democracy took root. The record of democracies creating democracy by war, in other words, is not striking. Wars between democratic states and non-democratic regimes end at points which have military significance, not when they have led to new governments. The democracies may be successful in their war-fighting, but war is still different from the expansion of democracy. In 1991, US forces stopped the Gulf War well before entering Baghdad. The effects of the wars may unleash social forces contributing to democracy in some cases, but this is not always intended or likely. It may also strengthen regimes building on nationalist or authoritarian legitimacy. The regimes the USA confronted in Vietnam and Iraq, remained, the one in Iraq being removed by force 12 years after the first war. *Idealpolitik* considerations are important in ending wars but, even when democracies are on the one side, does it mean wars lead to the creation of new democracies. The post-war dynamics are difficult to predict.

An analysis of *civilizational dynamics* as a clash between 'the West and the rest' (Huntington 1996) largely becomes parallel to the one of democratic versus other forms of government. If it is defined to mean an Islamic challenge towards non-Islamic societies, it is more interesting. Among the 18 interstate wars during these three decades, societies with a predominantly Muslim population were party to 14. Three were between Muslim societies (Iran–Iraq, Chad–Libya and Iraq's invasion of Kuwait, as the first part of the Gulf War), and three involved Israel's relations with its neighbours. It means that in eight cases there was a Muslim/non-Muslim divide. If we look at societies at war which have Christian leadership, defined in an equally wide sense, the list becomes equally long, with ten cases where one was between two predominantly Christian states (UK–Argentina). Islam and Christianity, in other words, have long lists of war involvements. The civilizational clash, as a conflict between Christianity and Islam, is possibly relevant for the wars over Cyprus and East Timor, where the primary parties may be described as 'Christian' and 'Muslim', respectively. Even so, their self-descriptions would probably be more secular. The Muslim character of the Turkish Cypriot society has not been strong, and Islam in Indonesia was, for most of the period, moderate. Even so, international alliance patterns do not follow this divide. The USA did not side with the Greek Cypriots (Greek Orthodox Christians) and for a long time it supported the regime in Indonesia (although Muslim) against the East Timorese (largely Roman Catholic). Also, some of the more devastating wars were not part of this particular divide at all (Vietnam–China, the USA–Vietnam, Vietnam–Cambodia, Eritrea–Ethiopia). The Iraq War has sometimes been seen in this light, but the fact is that the majority in Iraq, being Shiite Muslims or Kurds, were the chief beneficiaries of the removal of Saddam Hussein, who for most of his rule, took a secularist approach. Furthermore, there were agreements terminating wars across these very divides, for instance, between Israel and Egypt, Ethiopia and Somalia. In none of these was religion or civilization important for ending the wars. Thus, this perspective neither captures the dynamics of conflicts, nor the ability of settling conflicts.

In a version of civilizational divides which emphasizes ethnic differences between actors, a theme that will be further elaborated in Chapter 7, the patterns are not striking either, even in the post-Cold War era. There were such elements in the conflicts between Mauritania and Senegal. They may also be found overlapping with the civilizational paradigm in the conflict between India and Pakistan. It is more interesting to observe that some conflicts strengthen ethnic differences or even create them. The conflict between Ecuador and Peru may have been important for the identity of these parties. It made people on both sides more aware of their own preferences. The same may be the long-term result of the war between Eritrea and Ethiopia. For peacemaking, the ethnic dimension introduces complicating elements. Seldom, however, has it been the origin of interstate conflict.

A more general pattern that can be observed when considering *Idealpolitik* dimensions is the importance of *domestic political change* for conflict dynamics and conflict resolution. Revolutionary regimes create regional repercussions that affect neighbouring countries and give rise to considerable tension, rearrangement of alliances and wars. The victory of the revolutionary Khmer Rouge in Cambodia in 1975 initiated such a series of events, ultimately resulting in the occupation of the country by Vietnam. The attempts to repress the results in the Pakistani elections in 1971 led to resistance in East Pakistan against rule from West Pakistan, an uprising, India's intervention, and the disintegration of the bifurcated country. The civil war in Lebanon affected the neighbouring countries and made them intervene, making the conflict into an interstate war. The coup in Cyprus led to the Turkish invasion. The coming to power of a new and revolutionary regime in Iran initiated a sequence of events that eventually led to war with Iraq. Ethiopia and Eritrea were both governed by victorious, revolutionary governments. Although this pattern is unable to capture all the conflicts, it points to dynamics which affect entire regions. As the new regimes are the ones that later will have to enter into the agreements, the internal dynamics of peacemaking have to be considered. It may be more difficult to convince revolutionaries of the need to settle scores with former enemies. Successful revolutionaries are likely to believe more strongly than others that they will prevail even under difficult circumstances. Thus, their resistance to negotiated agreements, short of victory, is likely to be solid. The difficulties in ending the Iran–Iraq, Eritrea–Ethiopia and Indochinese wars testify to this.

Thus, we find that the *Idealpolitik* component is important, particularly as it introduces the question of legitimacy and governance inside states. *Idealpolitik* considerations contribute to an understanding of the origins of conflict, not least the impact revolutionary changes have in regional settings. For interstate agreement-making, internal affairs have to be taken for granted. Increasingly, more democratic regimes are likely to have a long-term impact on interstate conflict, but ending wars will require having to deal with regimes of many different kinds.

Peacemaking and *Kapitalpolitik*

Much theorizing assumes that economic matters are decisive for human action. Indeed, very little happens without economic considerations. However, the exact linkages between economic factors, the onset of conflict and conflict resolution are not easy to disentangle. Even more problematic is to estimate their significance when there are other factors in the picture, such as those we have mentioned earlier in this chapter.

It is obvious that an armed conflict is a costly undertaking, and it involves high risks. It is unlikely that there will be a 'return on the investment' in the same way as is the case when building a factory, launching a new product or hiring new workers. From a strictly economic perspective, other opportunities are more predictable and, thus, preferable. There are, of course, certain industrial interests which have war as their particular 'niche': arms manufacturers, arms traders, armed forces, intelligence operations. During the Cold War many of these interests learned that most profit is actually not made from war, but from continuous rearmament and the *threat* of war. An arms race may be economically more lucrative than the actual use of weaponry in armed conflict. Wars, we have repeatedly argued, are waged on decisions made by political actors. Wars are explained and legitimized in ways which relate to political affairs. The issues of *Geo-*, *Real-* and *Idealpolitik* all belong to this sphere of 'legitimate' explanations. Economics do not. A slogan in the American opposition against the Gulf War in 1991 was 'no blood for oil', expressing exactly this. The same slogan returned after 2003. It is not possible, particularly in a democratic and open society, to argue for a military intervention based on the economic gains that it is likely to generate. Armed conflicts involve the death of people and the destruction of investments, and these cannot be publicly defended with economic calculations. Thus, little will be openly stated on economic considerations for particular courses of action. Does it mean that there are no economic considerations? Probably not, but it suggests that there are also other concerns.

Let us first look at the economic arguments in the wars presented in Section 5.1. The discussion concentrates on two economic assets: oil resources and transportation routes. Oil is such a significant aspect of the energy supply of industrial economies that it takes a special role. Reductions in oil supplies or strong increases in oil prices (or both, as the former would lead to the latter) will unsettle economies in most countries, particularly those which rely heavily on oil imports. This afflicts rich as well as poor countries. No other single commodity has such a global impact. Transportation routes are important, meaning that, for instance, the blocking of certain waterways would affect economies in many countries, as they are used not only for oil shipping but also for general trade. It is possible to mark resources and routes on a map. This means that *Kapitalpolitik* assets have a geopolitical component. They are not the same. There is a difference in time and pricing. New sources of oil are still discovered. Alternative energy technologies can be developed. New routes can be found. More rapid transportation can be created. With increasing prices for one source, incentives are created for development of alternatives. Thus, *Kapitalpolitik* concerns can adapt. All this takes time and it will gradually shift political considerations. However, an economy is a daily operation and it reacts to short-term prospects. Thus, in a short-term perspective, *Kapitalpolitik* concerns over resources and transportation can be close to traditional *Geopolitik* interests.

The presence of oil resources was evident in three of the wars in the last three decades: the Iran–Iraq War, the Gulf War and the 2003 Iraq War. Oil also figured in other wars. There were expectations of oil discoveries around the Falkland/Malvinas Islands, and drilling has taken place since the war. In the Vietnam–China relations, access to potential oil resources in the adjacent waters has been mentioned. Among the lower-level conflicts reported in

Table 5.1, the potential for oil discovery was an element in the Cameroon–Nigeria border dispute. Even so, most of the interstate conflicts have no relationship to oil production. If we include the issue of transportation routes, two more conflicts can be added: Israel–Egypt across the Suez Canal and the Panama–USA conflict, on the site of the Panama Canal. It is not obvious that the economic benefits of the canals were primary motives for decision-makers. Thus, among the interstate wars and armed conflicts of these three decades, there is no strong evidence in favour of a simple *Kapitalpolitik* hypothesis that such concerns always are present and even paramount. It gains significance in particular conflicts, not in the overall picture.

In the cases where economic motives are important, the question still remains: how? For instance, it is not theoretically clear whether economic growth or economic decline is the primary motive for why economic considerations move countries into conflict. The Iraqi experience is a good illustration. Iraq gained from the high oil prices in the 1970s. At the start of the war against Iran in 1980 it had considerable financial strength, a well-equipped army and a functioning administrative system. The war soon ended most of this and Iraq became a debtor state. It had to borrow from its wealthier neighbours, not least Kuwait and Saudi Arabia. When the war finally ended, these countries asked for repayment. Iraq responded that this was unfair, as it had been fighting, as it were, for the entire 'Arab Nation' against external 'Persian aggression'. Besides, Iraq argued, to repay its debts the international oil prices had to increase. This was the central aspect of Iraq's dispute with Kuwait in 1990. Neither Kuwait nor Saudi Arabia was willing to increase the price by lowering its own production, thus giving more room on the market for Iraqi oil sales. By mid-July, the Iraqi leadership raised issues of the border with Kuwait and accused Kuwait of stealing Iraqi oil by drilling holes from the Kuwaiti side of the border. On August 2, 1990, Iraq invaded and occupied its neighbour. Thus, on top of the economic issue was placed a question of *Geopolitik*. This is instructive and shows how economics can enter into the decisions that lead to interstate military conflict. The key observation is this: in 1980 the Iraqi economy was in good shape, in 1990 it was in crisis. In both these years the same leadership decided to launch the country into an unpredictable war. There is no straight line between economic performance (or lack thereof) and the onset of war. We have to conclude that economic questions need to be seen in a larger perspective, not just as economic matters in their own right.

This appears to be a promising way to understand the *Kapitalpolitik* element in armed conflicts. It enters in combination with other concerns. As long as economic issues are handled in isolation, they are likely to find solutions. After all, economic aspects of social life are those that are most easy to divide. That is the point in having economic values translated into currencies, such as dollars and cents. It is when combining economics with any of the other three types of issues that it becomes deadly. This is what happened in 1990 when Saddam Hussein began to invoke territorial issues. This was a clear warning signal, not picked up by leaders around the world.

They continued to see the dispute with Kuwait as bargaining over oil prices and oil production. The impending escalation was missed.

Thus, economic issues, taken by themselves, are more readily solvable than any other issue. This suggests a negotiation strategy for interstate conflict resolution, where economic questions are separated from other issues, improving the chances of agreement in at least one sphere of incompatibility. In the negotiations between Ecuador and Peru, agreements on navigation rights and development projects were the first to come, while the border issue remained to the very end. Still, these agreements may be important to clarify that a final deal has many components, and that there are economic benefits to the peace arrangement. Economics can help forge larger package deals, but these are not complete unless they also solve the other matters. After all, the purpose is not to make lucrative trade arrangements, but to solve important incompatibilities between nations.

An informative example relates to the process ending the Cold War, the Helsinki process. It aimed at reducing tension between East and West during the Cold War and was agreed on in Helsinki, Finland, in 1975. In this case, different 'baskets' and fora were created for the four types of issues that we have identified here. One basket was concerned with border issues, a second one with economic cooperation, and a third one with human rights. A separate forum was created for reduction in troop strengths. Agreement was first reached in the second basket. The *Geopolitik* questions of borders were handled in a deal that also involved the *Idealpolitik* questions of human rights. By accepting Soviet demands on the *status quo* of borders in Europe, the West achieved an agreement from the Soviet Union on human rights. In the West, the treaty became known as a treaty for human rights, and Helsinki human rights groups continue to be important. This is also the way it was read by dissidents in Eastern Europe. In the official circles at the time, however, it was hailed as a way of consolidating Soviet control in Eastern Europe. Fifteen years later, it was clear that they were wrong.

Thus, economic matters can be important elements in peace agreements, and oftentimes there are compatible interests in such arrangements. Since the Cold War there has been a contentious matter, as a result of war: the issue of compensation. This has been an age-old problem in peacemaking. The winner has often demanded resources from the loser, in order to cover losses, or even to make war profitable. It has been less common in the twentieth century. It was an important element in the Versailles Treaty ending the First World War. Germany was subjected to reparations. They were part of the punitive approach described in Section 5.2. It has been argued that this prevented the recovery of the German economy. It was exploited by Hitler and other critics of the agreement. Thus, compensation issues did not become important after the Second World War in how the West treated Germany. The Soviet Union, however, demanded reparations from its defeated enemies. For Finland, for instance, this was a heavy burden, which actually was turned into an asset, as it gave Finland access to a

Soviet market that no others had. In many of the wars during the following decades, economic compensation was not of central concern.

The Paris treaty ending US involvement in Vietnam in 1973 actually included such provisions, but they were not implemented by the USA. Following the Gulf War, a special institution was created for recovering the losses Kuwait had suffered under Iraqi occupation. In this case, compensation could be paid from funds maintained by the UN as it was controlling the income from Iraqi oil sales. A version of this formula has been agreed in the peace agreement between Eritrea and Ethiopia. A Claims Commission was created, seated in the Hague, Netherlands. The parties, that is, the governments, submitted their claims to the Commission, which considered them. In its final award the Commission found that Eritrea and Eritrean individuals should be compensated by US$163 million, whereas the corresponding award for Ethiopia was US$174 million. As the Commission said in its press release on August 17, 2009, this was 'probably much less than each Party believes it is due'.

Kapitalpolitik considerations play a role in origins of interstate conflict, primarily with respect to certain commodities. In many conflicts, such concerns have not figured prominently, however. In the wars on the Horn of Africa or in Kashmir they had no direct role. In peacemaking, other concerns are likely to step forward and become the object of negotiations. However, we find that matters of compensation are significant in the processes that end wars. Even though the *Kapitalpolitik* dimension is seldom directly confronted in peacemaking, it is important to keep in mind.

The seven mechanisms

The seven mechanisms have different implications for *Idealpolitik* and *Kapitalpolitik* issues, as the following systematic overview shows.

The first mechanism deals with *changes of priority*. In the case of *Idealpolitik,* it might be that the parties go from a rigid to a more flexible interpretation of what their demands are. All ideological systems contain the possibility of making 'hard' or 'soft' interpretations. A hard interpretation means that the thought-system is regarded as entirely correct and exclusive, and cannot entertain alternative ideas. This is likely to be a position associated with conflict. In a soft version, an open, searching and more tolerant approach is preferred, including an ability to accommodate other views. The positions maintained by the parties will be crucial for conflict resolution. The ability to accommodate debate is key for reaching understanding and respect. It may even result in a change among the parties on *Idealpolitik* issues. An interstate negotiation process is unlikely to come that far. The development of alternative positions is important in a long-term perspective. It suggests that peace agreements would need to include the possibilities of changes, opening the possibilities of dialogue and meetings on levels other than the strictly political one. This has rarely been an element in interstate peace agreements. As observed above, it may be a side-effect of a war ending. It is important for long-term relations, even if such discussions are shared only among a small group. It becomes a way of broadening the spectrum of options in a society.

The ending of the Cold War is closely associated with the ability of developing new perspectives on communist ideology and finding its compatibility with democracy (what was termed 'Euro-Communism', *glasnost* and *perestroika*). It led to the demise of an empire and a party, but also to the rise of new organizations, specifically combining a communist agenda with a democratic society. Softer interpretations mean that a party accommodates changes. They are often described as 'moderate' positions. Such developments are important, particularly in societies which have long experience of hard ideological systems. A 'nationalist' does not need to be a 'chauvinist', for instance, but retaining a national identity can still be important for conflict resolution and for its acceptability in society.

In the *Kapitalpolitik* field, the first mechanism might point to the need for a deliberate decoupling of economic issues from those that are more immediately political, for instance, building on the realization that economic issues are more manageable. It is also easier to shift position if it is based on an economic calculation. When the benefits of agreement outweigh the benefits from confrontation, deals can be made.

Dividing the values, the second mechanism, appears difficult to apply to secular and religious ideologies. It is interesting to ask, however, what actually goes on in a debate. It is a give and take. Positions may be found that are halfway between the parties. It is notable, for instance, that new forms of thinking emerge where thought-systems clash geographically. It might not be a coincidence that the four most influential monotheist religions all developed in the area stretching from the Mediterranean to the Indus River (Judaism, Christianity, Islam, Sikhism, all probably drawing on ancient Zoroastrian thinking). Also, *horse-trading* may be seen to take place between these thoughts, reformulating ideas into entirely new combinations that transcend some of the previous dichotomies. Such rethinking is not arrived at quickly, however, and rests on a societal ability for open discussion.

These two forms, division and horse-trading, are easily handled in *Kapitalpolitik* conflicts through a process of bargaining, and using economic values as a baseline. It becomes a matter of fixing the price of the commodities in question, and then working out an arrangement that is mutually acceptable. None of the other issues has a similar scale of values that all sides agree to and that can be used in negotiations.

The fourth mechanism concerns *sharing of assets*. By pointing to shared values, *Idealpolitik* considerations may be able to develop unexpected links with an opposite side. History has seen many surprising alliances. Even in the Cold War, there were some shared values between East and West. For instance, both sides looked negatively on fascism in Spain and Portugal. There was a shared understanding in favour of decolonization and against

Apartheid South Africa. This was not based on power considerations, but stemmed from the same *Idealpolitik* positions that made the two sides allies during the Second World War. Sharing some values can lead to joint action. Initially, both sides were supportive of the creation of Israel; only later did they become separated on questions of peace in the Middle East. The opening of the Soviet system in the late 1980s built on giving a new priority to environmental concerns, matters that also stretched beyond the borders of the Soviet bloc. In the peace agreements since the Cold War, there are few references to such shared values. However, in the case of the Ecuador–Peru peace, the instituting of ecological reserves in the disputed area obviously was something the parties could agree to.

In the *Kapitalpolitik* field, this is less problematic. It is simply a question of creating a joint company, through which profits can be reaped and shared according to a formula set up at the founding of the company. Many disputes over oil resources could probably be handled this way, if other issues did not enter into the considerations.

The fifth mechanism, of *turning control over contested values over to other parties*, is perfectly well designed for *Kapitalpolitik* issues. This is sometimes seen as privatization. This has rarely been used in peace agreements, but the Ecuador–Peru accord includes the solution of making a key territory private property. *Idealpolitik* issues are not resolvable in this way. Ideas live their own lives and are only replaced with other ideas, as has happened partly with the democracy–dictatorship divide. However, environmental issues have brought in concerns which create new challenges to governance and legitimacy.

Similar reflections can be made on the sixth form of transcending conflicts, the *use of courts and other conflict resolution mechanisms* outside the parties. On ideological issues, it would mean that there is a legitimate authority to decide the 'correct' interpretation of particular thoughts. In countries with a sizable Catholic population, the Pope's ruling on different issues will be a possible way of transcending internal debates. As a matter of fact, this authority of the Vatican has been used for settling *Geopolitik* disputes, for instance, between Argentina and Chile. In the Islamic world, the Al Azar University, in Cairo, Egypt, plays a similar role (particularly for the Sunni branch of Islam). Its statement of the compatibility between Islamic teaching and the Camp David agreements between Egypt and Israel was important for the peace process. It made clear that unspecified 'temporary peace' is possible between Muslims and non-believers. In *Kapitalpolitik*, the resort to conflict resolution mechanisms is very important and common. The World Trade Organization (WTO) contains clauses for arbitration. For the five years of 2006–10, 82 cases were brought to the WTO, while the International Court of Justice, largely dealing with non-economic issues, added 15 new contentious cases for the same period (according to the websites of these institutions).

Finally, the issues can be left to *oblivion*. This is probably what happens to a considerable number of *Idealpolitik* issues. Confrontations that seemed important fade away or diminish in significance. In that sense, *Idealpolitik* concerns do not have the same permanence as those of *Geopolitik* or *Realpolitik*. As a class of phenomena, they remain, but their influence changes. Ideas of fascism, Nazism and communism are not central in debate on government legitimacy in much of the world, but they still have appeal to some groups, also in the Western world. Fascist and neo-Nazi groups constitute a problem in Europe. Chauvinism that was part of the European experience in the early twentieth century unexpectedly came back as the Cold War was waning. Communist parties still rule in parts of East Asia, and less reformed communist parties are still significant in Eastern Europe. Thus, ideas do not disappear, they change in relevance. Globally, democracy has gained in significance as a legitimate value. In a way, it has sharpened the dichotomy between democracy and non-democracy. It can be seen in the discussions on humanitarian intervention. The rights of states to intervene in another state to protect human lives threatened by their own governments is given increased salience. It rests on the value of human survival, but also on the strength of democratic thinking and democratic powers. There is a transformation of *Idealpolitik* concerns. *Idealpolitik* as such is not disappearing.

In *Kapitalpolitik* matters, economy has a prosaic quality. It is not an issue which easily translates into conflict and war, and for which it is worth risking life, at least not on the public level. Various mafia-like structures exist, and their violence may be more directly connected to economic interests. For international relations, however, this is seldom the case. Economic matters are often regulated, and renegotiations are possible at agreed intervals and levels of government. Thus, economic matters become routine and part of daily life in ways which are not open for *Geo-*, *Real-* and *Idealpolitik* concerns. For much of the 1990s, large-scale economic negotiations were pursued without much public debate. These issues appeared forgotten and technical. However, towards the end of the decade, they came back in full force, in a widespread critique of the globalization pursued by the World Trade Organization and the International Monetary Fund (IMF). Thus, they remain important in shaping actors and agendas. What we find is that *Kapitalpolitik* matters are not strong forces behind the interstate wars we have seen lately and, consequently, do not appear in the peace agreements, except for matters relating to particular resources (oil) and to compensation.

5.4 Conclusions for Interstate Conflict Resolution

Interstate conflicts continue to be a problem for international affairs and international organizations, although it has not been as large an issue since the Cold War ended as it was 20 years earlier. There have been fewer interstate wars and the global confrontation between East and West has disappeared. However, interstate conflicts are still occurring, and there is no reason to expect them to cease entirely. Although the spread of democracy and integration may ultimately result in an international system which is less warprone, as implied by the research on the democracy–peace hypothesis (Russett 1993; Russett and Oneal 2001; Weart 1998), this is far from a linear process. There have still been wars involving non-democracies and democracies. Forcefully removing a dictatorial regime, in the name of democracy, still does not make a democracy, and may lead to severe internal conflicts. We have even noted a complex situation, the one over Cyprus, involving only democratic states. More important for the future is probably the potential rise of major power conflict, involving Western actors, China, Russia and India. Interstate conflicts still need to be attended to with great severity. The analysis and resolution indicated in this chapter remain important for the foreseeable future.

We have seen that there are four matters that are continuously pointed to in studies of the risk of interstate war. *Geopolitik* concerns over borders and other territory, *Realpolitik* interest in power and armaments to maintain power, *Idealpolitik* considerations of legitimacy and governance, and *Kapitalpolitik* interest in particular resources and other economic assets. As this chapter has made clear, issues of territory and power remain the most frequent ones. Questions of ideology and economy gain significance, particularly as causes of conflict combine with these factors. Thus, peace agreements have to find ways of dealing primarily with territorial and power considerations.

There is, however, a lesson also in this. Economic conflicts, if dealt with in isolation, are likely to find a solution. The seven mechanisms are applicable to all forms of *Kapitalpolitik* conflict. In this area, parties are able to change positions, find ways of dividing or horse-trading, sharing or handing over matters to others, including conflict mechanisms. The simplicity of the measurements (dollars, cents and corresponding measures) make this easier. The moral obstacles for fighting wars over money contribute as well. In this, *Kapitalpolitik* contrasts in particular to *Idealpolitik,* which has a higher potential to inflame populations and spur humans into action. It is more correct to die in the fight for a higher value (be it the Nation, God or Democracy, for instance). Thus, *Idealpolitik* has a higher mobilizing ability than any of the other categories. Nevertheless, *Geopolitik* and *Realpolitik* seem to be at the core of much interstate conflict. This is where the parties have the largest difficulties in finding agreements, and these are the issue areas where agreements are the most likely to break down.

It is encouraging to find that agreements have been made also in these more cumbersome areas. We have shown that the international community is equipped with some principles for handling *Geopolitik* issues. There is a strong preference for negotiations to depart from the *status quo ante bellum* position. Territorial gains in a war are to be undone, either prior to or as part of a settlement. The UN Charter emphasizes territorial integrity as a fundamental principle for international peace and security. This means that there is a customary demand that the parties revert to the territorial dividing lines that existed prior to the war. However, we have also seen cases where this has not been applied as strictly as could be expected. The principle still appears stronger and is probably also the one that gives rise to more durable settlements.

The seven mechanisms of conflict resolution are all relevant for the settlement of *Geopolitik* disputes. Parties do change their positions, although simple deals of dividing or horse-trading territory today appear less common. There is also a resort to conflict resolution mechanisms even for handling highly sensitive matters (as seen in the settlement between Ecuador and Peru in 1998, and Eritrea and Ethiopia in 2000). The creation of neutral states, that is, situations where none of the major contestants gets their way, has both positive (Cambodia) and negative (Cyprus) recent experiences. Buffer zones, controlled by outsiders, may be a more promising venue, but require long-term commitment from the parties and outsiders (Sinai is an example). Although border disputes may be old, they are often kept alive and become part of the national conscience. Under these circumstances, they are not likely to be forgotten. They require a peace process. Ecuador and Peru could finally reach a settlement in 1998 using some of the seven mechanisms we have mentioned.

Realpolitik issues are seldom properly addressed in peace agreements. The closest we come is the regulation of armaments. These can be measures directly dealt with by the parties in special arms control deals. The Cold War saw many of these. Since then there have been fewer such arrangements in the field of nuclear weapons. The ending of interstate conflict has involved relatively few measures of disarmament. A general impression is, however, that weapons issues are manageable through agreements. Weapons can be counted and weighed. There are often agreements among military experts on what different weapons systems can accomplish. Thus, parties can change position, divide and horse-trade in armament negotiations. They can also agree to bilateral and multilateral inspections. Indeed, weapons become obsolete, which means that older systems may no longer be relevant. However, the rapid transfer of arms technology generates renewed dangers and instabilities. The range of possible solutions is more limited.

The most important lesson may instead be another. How are the parties dealing with one another after a war? It is tied to issues of responsibility for the war. Is there accountability for the destructive events in a war between states? In several agreements this issue has been raised and prevented early deals (Iran–Iraq, Eritrea–Ethiopia). The compensation arrangement in the Gulf War also built on the assumption that one side was more responsible. It is less likely to be something the parties agree to in interstate negotiations. Responsibility is related to the need for court procedures and international criminal legislation. This has developed in the 1990s, culminating with the convention on the International Criminal Court in 1998. Now ratified and in operation, this Court might have an impact on interstate peacemaking, but its primary focus so far has been on intra-state situations.

Further Readings

Go to the *Understanding Conflict Resolution* web page at www.sagepub.co.uk for free access to journal articles listed.

Buzan, B. 1991. *People, States and Fear* (second edition). Boulder, Colorado: Lynne Rienner.

Geller, D. and Singer, J. D. 1998. *Nations at War: A Scientific Study of International Conflict*. Cambridge: Cambridge University Press.

Holsti, K. J. 1991. *Peace and War: Armed Conflicts and International Order 1648–1989*. Cambridge: Cambridge University Press.

Jervis, R. 1976. *Perception and Misperception in International Politics*. Princeton, NJ: Princeton University Press.

Russett, B. M. 1993. *Grasping the Democratic Peace: Principles for a Post-Cold War World*. Princeton, New Jersey: Princeton University Press.

Russett, B. M. and Oneal, J. R. 2001. *Triangulating Peace: Democracy, Interdependence, and International Organizations*. New York: W.W. Norton.

Tilly, C. 1992. *Coercion, Capital and the European States, AD 1990–1992*. Oxford: Blackwell.

Vasquez, J. A. (ed.) 2000. *What Do We Know about War?* Lanham, Maryland: Rowman & Littlefield.

Wallensteen, P. 1981. 'Incompatibility, Confrontation and War: Four Models and Three Historical Systems, 1816–1976', *Journal of Peace Research*, 18 (1): 57–90.

Wallensteen, P. 1984. 'Universalism vs. Particularism. On the Limits of Major Power Order', *Journal of Peace Research*, 21 (3): 243–57.

Wallensteen, P. 2011. *Peace Research: Theory and Practice*. London: Routledge. pp 23–92.

Notes

1   By the International Committee of the Red Cross (ICRC), Manuel Noriega was regarded as a prisoner of war. After his prison term expired he was extradited to France in 2010.

2   The USA was so eager to have inspections at a particular production plant in the Urals that it agreed to establish a comparable monitoring machinery in Utah, 'not because the Soviet Union had serious concerns about … violations … but rather in order to meet Soviet demands for equal treatment' (Woodworth 1999: 188)

3   The argument for intervention has later shifted to include what the Iraqi regime might have done in the future (Blair 2010).

CONFLICT RESOLUTION IN CIVIL WARS 6

6.1 Armed Conflicts and Peace Accords within States

Civil war, or more specifically intra-state conflict concerning the control over government, has been a constant feature in the global conflict picture. It has received particular attention in its own right since the end of the Cold War.[1] It consists of many different phenomena, only one of which is the narrowly defined armed conflict. There are also military coups which sometimes are swift and result in limited violence, attempted coups, short-lived rebellions, actions by militias, armed gangs, bands, freedom movements and terrorist organizations. There is also government action as an important component and often in a close relationship to the actions of opponents. There are forms of repression, police measures, legal instruments such as preventive detention, human rights violations and arrests. Indeed, there is a close relation between police brutality and violent riots. This is a pattern that can be observed in rich and poor countries alike. A considerable share of all violence in the world can be attributed to conflicts dealing with control over governmental power in particular states. It is an old issue to which much political analysis has been devoted. The events of September 11, 2001, demonstrated the international implications of such dynamics. An organization primarily concerned with change in particular countries (Saudi Arabia, Egypt) chose to attack the main external supporter of the incumbent regimes. Global terrorism mostly has its roots in internal conflicts, some of which deal with government control, some with territorial issues. Let us now examine the situation of internal conflict during and after the Cold War.

Civil wars during and after the Cold War

Civil war is sometimes described as the most important feature of the period after the Cold War. This is not entirely correct, however. As we have noted in Section 5.1, many of the Cold War conflicts dealt with intra-state conditions and control over the government apparatus. The contention centred on whether a particular state was controlled by the 'left' or the 'right', by pro-Soviet or pro-Western groups. The conflicts were perceived to be part of the Cold War. Thus, they became of international concern. Various forms of intervention took place, internationalizing the civil war. Actions included the dispatching of troops from a bloc leader. Some examples are the US interventions in Guatemala in 1954, in the Dominican Republic in 1965, in Grenada in 1983 and in Panama in 1989, and Soviet troops were used to change governments in Hungary in 1956, in Czechoslovakia in 1968 and in Afghanistan in 1979. Sometimes these interventions also had the participation of allied countries (East German troops participated in the Soviet invasion of Czechoslovakia, for instance). There were other, clandestine forms of intervention, as well as support to particular governments or groups doing the actual combat in internal conflicts. Intervention in internal conflicts was a marked feature of the Cold War. Some of its most severe confrontations grew out of such situations, for instance, the conflicts around Cuba (with a US-sponsored intervention in 1961) and the war in Vietnam (particularly following a US-supported coup in Saigon in 1963).

Although the UN Charter specifies that issues which are 'essentially within the domestic jurisdiction' of a state (Article 2.7) should not be of concern to the UN, and thus not be internationalized, they were. The Charter provision was often only barring the UN itself from involvement where a host of other actors were heavily engaged. Article 2.7 was principally used by the Soviet Union to obstruct international actions in situations among members of its bloc. Even obvious Soviet interventions, such as those in Hungary, Czechoslovakia and Afghanistan, were excused as being done on the invitation of a legitimate government. The West was barred from intervening by the fear of a crisis escalating into a nuclear confrontation. Similarly, US interventions were kept from the UN agenda by Western dominance in the Security Council and by referring situations to regional organizations controlled by the USA (for instance, in the case of Guatemala). The strict interpretation of Article 2.7 was also used by military regimes to minimize external and internal criticism and fend off interference into their brutal rule. Newly independent states in Africa and Asia used it as a legal defence of their independence against former colonial powers. Thus, the UN and other international actors met severe constraints in entering into internal conflicts.

Since the Cold War, the picture has changed. In the early 1990s, the UN and other international agencies were authorized to enter into a series of intra-state conflicts and peace processes, notably in Central America, Indochina, Africa and Southeast Europe. Many of these situations would, during the Cold War, have been defined as outside the parameters of international action, with reference to Article 2.7. This may explain today's conventional wisdom that there are more internal conflicts than ever before. It is more accurate to say that there are now more internal conflicts in which international organizations are involved.

Internal conflicts are often seen as particularly difficult to handle. A civil war means the breaking up of existing social relationships. Families may be divided, friendships are destroyed, and local communities are shattered. Thus, socially and psychologically, they are more devastating than many interstate wars. This is true for situations where the interstate conflicts take place between states that have long been separated. In cases of states being neighbours or when states are newly created, there may, however, exist similar networks across borders as there are inside states. The distinguishing features of civil wars and other internal conflicts is primarily not the brutality or the social impact. All armed conflicts have such effects, which makes war a shared phenomenon across cultures and continents.

The mark of the internal conflict is instead found in the incompatibility and in the primary parties. Civil wars are a matter of keeping or taking control over a particular government and its state machinery. Furthermore, the primary parties are rooted within the same state. Thus, initial conflict dynamics tend to build on internal grievances, such as the ones indicated in Section 3.3. Many of these relate to power relations, economic interactions and the internal social fabric. To a larger degree than is the case in interstate conflicts, the actor will have a longer shared history of conflict and cooperation prior to the war experience. This is one element in the perception of internal conflicts as more socially devastating than other conflicts. The lines drawn between people are ideological, economic or social. Civil wars may also be 'ethnic' or 'racial'. The civil strife in South Africa and the genocide in Rwanda concerned the control of state power in these countries. The actors were largely, but not entirely, formed along lines of historically ascribed identities.[2] Thus, the conflicts were 'ethnic' but did not include ambitions of territorially dividing the state.

This means that internal conflicts raise two particularly sharp and interlinked questions for conflict resolution and a durable peace settlement. First, there is the problem of how to construct a social and political system which gives reasonable social and political space to all groups in a society. This is necessary as civil wars concern the distribution of power in society. Answers will have to deal with *participation* and influence in a society. This points to the question of democracy as a solution, theoretically and empirically. The second problem is the one of *security*. The experience of a civil war raises a pointed internal security dilemma, which the actors may put in the following form: 'If I win, you lose', and thus as a consequence: 'As you may act against me, I had better act before you do.' This is the logic of repression and terror prior to war. It is the reasoning of armed action. Thus, ending violence in a way which removes this security dilemma has to be part of any settlement. Without the parties being secure, subjectively and objectively, a peace agreement is unlikely to be sustained. This involves control over government, as government resources can be used to maintain the security dilemma or to transcend it. Indeed, we may locate the phenomenon of corruption in the same insecurity. It will pay for leaders to accumulate personal wealth, as this is a way to bribe others, whether contenders or loyalists. To put money abroad is providing for an alternative exit in case of challenges. Kleptocracy, in other words, finds its roots in the internal security dilemma. Solutions to the dilemma might improve the chances for honest government.

Peace agreements in civil wars

Before proceeding we need to approach the experiences since the Cold War in ending civil wars through peace processes. Table 6.1 lists all such peace agreements entered into from 1989 to 2009.

Table 6.1 lists 29 countries with armed conflicts that were ended, at least for a period, through a peace agreement. Most of them are in Africa, some in Central Asia and South America. There are different dates given in cases where agreements were later abandoned or a new one added. Some failed completely, meaning that fighting soon broke out again. Even in such cases, however, the parties may revert to the original agreement, as happened for instance in Cambodia. In Chad, changes of government resulted in new agreements, and in Liberia the agreement in 2003 is the most recent in a long series of agreement experiences. It should also be noted that some agreements concerned only some of the parties in the internal conflict.

One of the chief lessons since the end of the Cold War is the extraordinary complexity of peacemaking. This is further illustrated in Table 6.1, in the many cases with repeated agreements. Some of these attempt at solving the problem stated by the parties (for example, dealing directly with an issue, such as finding a power-sharing formula) and others indicate a process for how the parties are going to continue peacefully (such as an electoral process). There is also often an interaction between the two, as can be seen from a number of cases mentioned in Table 6.1. By the end of 2009, there were functioning peace agreements in most of the conflicts with an agreement. Agreements have been lasting, suggesting that the parties mostly are serious when signing a treaty. This, however, did not necessarily include all conflicts in a particular country (in Colombia, for example, there was a durable agreement between some parties in 1991, but failed peace processes among others in 2001–02).

It is interesting to observe that many cases show a continuous process of new, more elaborate agreements. The notion of a 'peace process' accurately describes what many peace agreements are all about. The original idea of conflict resolution efforts was to reach an agreement that would regulate conclusively all the aspects of a conflict. The experience since the end of the Cold War has made clear that such comprehensive and final settlements often are unlikely. There are nine cases in Table 6.1 with only one agreement. Most

Table 6.1   Peace agreements in civil wars since the Cold War

Conflict location	Year of agreement	Number of agreements
Afghanistan	1993, 1996	3
Angola	1989, 1991, 1994, 2002	4
Burundi	2000, 2002, 2003, 2006, 2008	8
Cambodia	1991	1
Central African Republic	2008	2
Chad	1991, 1992, 1993, 1994, 1995, 1997, 1998, 1999, 2002, 2005, 2006	11
Colombia	1991, 1999, 2001, 2002	4
Congo, Republic	1999	1
Cote d'Ivoire	2003, 2004, 2005, 2007, 2008	9
Dem. Rep. Congo	1999, 2001, 2002, 2003, 2009	6
Djibouti	1994, 2000, 2001	3
El Salvador	1990, 1991, 1992	9
Guatemala	1990, 1991, 1994, 1995, 1996	16
Guinea Bissau	1998	1
Haiti	1993	1
Liberia	1990, 1991, 1993, 1994, 1995, 1996, 2003	11
Macedonia	2001	1
Mexico[a]	1996	1
Mozambique	1991, 1992	5
Nepal	2006	1
Niger	1993	1
Philippines	1995	1
Rwanda	1991, 1992, 1993	6
Sierra Leone	1996, 1999, 2000	3
Somalia	1993, 1994, 1997, 2008	5
South Africa[b]	1990, 1991, 1992, 1993	5
Sudan	2002, 2003, 2004, 2005, 2006	8
Tajikistan	1995, 1996, 1997	5
Uganda	2002, 2007, 2008	8

[a]The agreement was not implemented, but fighting did not resume.
[b]Strictly seen, this case should not be included as the armed conflict between ANC and the apartheid regime took place prior to 1989.

Note: Peace agreements in armed conflicts concerning the control over government, active in the period 1989–2009. The table includes treaties that have been signed, that regulate (resolve or find a process for the solution of) the incompatibility, and have been concluded between the warring parties, and have ended armed conflict behaviour. Cease-fire agreements are not included. The parties are listed in English alphabetical order.

Source: Uppsala Conflict Data Program Conflict Encyclopedia; Table 4.2 in this volume; Högbladh 2006.

of them were later overturned, without being replaced with a new arrangement. However, the agreements on Macedonia and Nepal were still in place by 2010. It might be true that the longer a conflict has continued, the greater the need for a durable process for restoring peaceful conditions. This might even be more pronounced for internal conflicts. Furthermore, the longer the peace process the more dangers there will be of a relapse into war, due to activities of 'spoilers', effects of unmet expectations or external intervention. Peace processes are fragile routes to peace.

The total number of civil wars for the period 1989–2009 is 58 (see Table 4.1). Comparing this to the lasting peace agreements in the same period, it means that half of all internal armed conflicts saw an agreement (see Table 4.3). This is higher than other researchers report from civil wars in previous periods. The definitions of 'civil war' are not the same as applied here, as they often include state formation conflicts as well. Also, 'agreement' or 'negotiated ending' is determined slightly differently. Still, there are some interesting long-term patterns. For instance, Mason and Fett (1996) report that there were 13 peace agreements for the period 1945–92 in a total of 56 civil wars, that is, 23 per cent of the cases. Licklider gives an even lower number, finding that for the period 1945–93 there were 14 conflicts which ended through negotiations out of a total of 84, that is, 17 per cent.[3] Stedman finds that for the period 1900–89 there were solutions through negotiations in 15 per cent of the civil wars in this century (Licklider 1995: 684; Mason and Fett 1996; Stedman 1991: 8).[4] The negotiated agreements have been few, and even fewer in cases which have concerned the civil war category as here defined. It suggests that peace agreements are more common as ways of ending such wars today than previously. Given that the time span for the cases reported in Table 6.1 is much shorter, it definitely means that peacemaking in civil wars is now a higher priority. For the periods covered by the three studies, a peace agreement was concluded every third to eighth year. Table 6.1 shows that there was an average of more than six peace agreements reached every year in the post-Cold War period. Terminating civil wars through negotiations has become very important.

This notwithstanding, a number of internal conflicts ended in the elimination or capitulation of one party, that is, victory. The share of such endings is somewhat lower than previously. For the post-Cold War period this outcome is evenly distributed between victories for the opposition (for instance, in Panama, Paraguay and Romania in 1989, in Ethiopia in 1991, in Zaire in 1997) and for the government (for instance, Sri Lanka in the non-Tamil conflict in 1991, Venezuela in 1992, Russia and Georgia in 1993). In two cases, peace agreements were never implemented, instead resulting in victory (in both cases by the opposition): Haiti (the Governor's Island Agreement) and Rwanda (the Arusha Peace Accord), both completed in 1993. In the first case, it nearly resulted in an intervention by a multinational force; in the second case, the world was standing idle when an unprecedented genocide followed. It was directed against the Tutsi minority and stopped only when forces composed largely of Tutsi rebels took over the capital. In a more recent internal conflict there was no room for negotiations: Afghanistan 2001. In this case, victory could be declared as the incumbent government was deposed, the capital taken by the forces of the other side (the 'Northern Alliance' with US support) and a new regime was recognized. A peace agreement of sorts was signed, the Bonn Agreement of 2001, with broad Afghan participation but without representatives of the deposed Taliban. The agreement has been basic for subsequent events in Afghanistan, but Taliban resistance has continued. These examples notwithstanding, we can conclude that clear-cut victory for one or the other side is not as common as are peace agreements.

However, many internal conflicts have 'other outcomes', meaning that the fighting recedes to levels which are below the Uppsala Conflict Data Program inclusion threshold of more than 25 killed in battle per year. In reality, this means that governments remained in power. The conflicts may have ended in *de facto* victories for the *status quo*, the government side, without this being clearly acknowledged by the losing side. For either side, perhaps more for the weaker one, a peace agreement may actually provide a greater chance for survival and, thus, there might be an incentive for a peaceful solution. In an interstate conflict, the sides can withdraw behind an internationally recognized boundary and the survival of that side is not directly threatened.

These observations are further underscored by the fact that many intra-state conflicts continued at the end of the recording period. This means that some civil wars have persisted for a considerable period of time. Situations which have received ample international attention at times, but without a sustained programme of international action, are, for instance, Algeria, Burma/Myanmar, Peru, the Philippines (the conflict involving the Communist Party, NPA), Rwanda, Somalia, and Uganda. These internal conflicts are more than five years old. Many have been going on for decades. There are some newer conflicts which may have the potential to become equally entrenched if no solutions are found (for instance, the Maoist rebellion in Nepal). Some protracted conflicts have, at times, drawn much interest, notably Somalia in 1992–94, Colombia, particularly since 1999, and in the early 2000s also Afghanistan, Burundi and Sudan. A conclusion is that if the parties in an intra-state conflict cannot solve their incompatibilities, it is more likely that a conflict will become protracted than end in victory.

It should be noted that most of the intra-state conflicts concerning government are taking place in classical Third World countries, many of which are poor, overpopulated or marked by stark contrasts between rich and poor. This is also where regimes have turned into kleptocracy. The resources of the state have been used to corrupt leaderships and opponents alike. There are armed conflicts in some oil-rich or industrialized states but, interestingly, many have been of a shorter duration (Venezuela, Azerbaijan and Russia) except when connected to religious or racial dimensions (Algeria,

South Africa). In predominantly agricultural economies, control over the state may be a particularly valuable asset, as there are fewer alternative sources of income. Some studies also point to environmental degradation as a source of internal conflict, particularly if connected to other factors (Hauge and Ellingsen 1998; Wantechekon 1999).

There is one striking change in internal conflict and that is the reduction in military coups. Military regimes and transition to democratic institutions were an important topic throughout the 1980s. The problem has not lost its relevance, although the patterns have changed. South and Central America, which used to be central in the discussions, now have few such military governments. There is even considerable popular resistance to them. The coups that have taken place during the 1990s include the one in Haiti in 1991, the President's actions in Peru in 1992, Guatemala in 1993 and the failed coup in Venezuela in 1992. By 1994 these coups were undone. The coup leaders were forced to leave power in Haiti. President Fujimori in Peru retreated, won a second period in office but his third victory in 2000 was highly fraudulent and he had to resign and leave the country. He later returned only to be put in prison. The chief plotter in Venezuela, Hugo Chávez, was brought to court, later freed to embark on a political career, and took power in 1999 by democratic means. He survived a short-lived coup attempt in 2002. There is now reluctance – nationally, regionally and internationally – to accept military intrusion into political life. This was clear when facing the coup in Honduras in 2009. Latin American opinion was overwhelmingly negative.

The same trend can be seen in the Middle East, where there were 21 coups in the period 1950–69 and six in 1970–89.[5] In early 2011, an unprecedented wave of peaceful, democratic protests swept through the Middle East, the Arab Spring. The protests unseated the regimes in Tunisia and Egypt. They were strongly repressed in Bahrain and Syria, and led to armed conflicts in Yemen and Libya. Particularly in the case of Libya it resulted in UN and NATO action to protect civilians, based on the new principle of the international responsibility to protect exposed populations.

Another coup-prone region has been Africa, but it has seen fewer military takeover attempts in recent years. In Sudan in 1989, a military junta based on a stricter interpretation of Islam took power from a civilian government. A new brand of leaders emerged through revolutionary wars in Uganda, Ethiopia, Eritrea, Rwanda and Zaire. Established one-party states were replaced through democratic elections (for instance, in Zambia and Malawi). Although the plotters in Burundi in 1993 failed in taking control over the government, their actions unsettled domestic relations not only in Burundi, but also in Rwanda. A new coup took place in 1996. A coup in Lesotho in 1994 was rejected by its neighbours, the previous regime was reinstated and peacekeeping troops from the region were posted in the country in 1998. A military regime yielded to democratic procedures in Nigeria in 1999. There was an unsettling coup in the Cote d'Ivoire in December 1999, followed by an armed conflict in 2002. The peace agreements included new registrations of voters and new elections. The elections in 2010 clearly gave the opposition the majority of the votes, but the incumbent, Laurent Gbagbo, refused to step down. After a short, internationally supported war in March and April 2011 he capitulated, accepted the election-winner Alassane Ouattara as president and now faces a trial in the country. A coup in Togo in 2005 was rejected by African states and led to demonstrations, forcing an election. The phenomenon has not been eliminated, but the frequency is clearly lower. In 1960–69, forced removal accounted for close to three-quarters of all regime changes in Africa; in the first five years of the 2000s the share was down to one-sixth (Southall, et al. 2005). Unconstitutional removal of leaders remains a problem and the African Union (AU) has instituted a sanctions policy against such events (Eriksson 2010).

There were some coups and attempted coups in Southeast Asia. The military takeover in Thailand in 1991 led to a successful, popular uprising and democratization in 1992 and a military attempt against the democratic regime in the Philippines in 1989 failed. The Asian economic crisis in 1997 hastened the downfall of oligarchs in South Korea as well as in Indonesia, at the same time as it strengthened democratic tendencies in Thailand, Taiwan and the Philippines. The trend towards democratization has been pronounced in much of Asia. The only typical military intervention in a South Asian country occurred in Pakistan in October 1999, when General Pervez Musharraf took control of the country in a bloodless coup, but then staged another coup in 2007 when the High Court annulled his victory in the elections. He was forced out by popular uprisings in 2008. Such movements have repeatedly affected the governments in Thailand. In 2010 the so-called Red Shirts were violently repressed by a government that came into power due to a similar movement by other segments of the population.

As this overview suggests, the coup phenomenon has become more rare in a world of democratization. Political leadership changes, in many parts of the world, have taken more constitutional forms in the post-Cold War era than before. Also, authoritarian regimes have been challenged by mass-movements which have been able to defy police repression by turning out in huge numbers. Mobilization through the Internet in general, and through social media in particular, is a new feature in politics, as seen in Iran in 2009 and in Arab countries in 2011. It is interesting because there is a debate over whether, for instance, Islam is intrinsically incompatible with democracy. Certainly, the democratization of Indonesia – the country with the largest Muslim population in the world – the democratic transitions from one party to another in Bangladesh during the 1990s, and the rise to power of an Islamic party in Turkey in 2004, qualify such notions. The spring of 2011 saw wide pro-democracy movements in a series of Arab countries, further confirming that demands for democracy transcend such cultural differences.

The decline of the military coup does not mean it is a phenomenon of the past, or that military influence over political life has disappeared. Instead, military establishments are finding novel ways of influencing democratic policies. In some countries, the military remains, according to its own view, the sole guarantor of the 'order' of the day. Thus, the Turkish armed forces act to ensure a secular, Europe-oriented state in a country with a predominantly Muslim population. The armed forces in Thailand safeguard the monarchical system of the state, although they have taken direct control over the government more frequently than in Turkey, for instance. The failure of military leaderships to maintain open political control in the early 1990s suggests that times are changing. A less visible, more retracted, but still effective role may be what military establishments hope for in South Korea, Taiwan, Indonesia, the Philippines, Bangladesh, and perhaps also in Russia. For the outside observers, it means that the analytical tools have to be sharpened to discern the influence of the armed forces on politics.

There are many ways in which military leaders can adjust to democratization, and they do not necessarily have to be hostile to it. The democratic system assumes civilian control over the military, but also that a workable arrangement can be found between a professionally defined military establishment and democratic authorities. Normally this means that the tasks of the military are separated as clearly as possible from civilian responsibilities. This appears to be a global tendency.[6] The ability of the civilian state to control the military will depend on the competence and strength of the state. Some argue that economic and technological globalization might undermine the state and weaken its hold over the legitimate use of force (Desch 1999: 128–30). Ultimately, the strength of the democratic system will rest on its support from the population. This requires that state structures are strong and autonomous enough to set the agenda for a society. The weakening of state institutions in the 1990s has implications for the performance of peace agreements as well as for managing the civil–military relationship. The notion of state failure has implications for conflict resolution.

At the same time, overly strong states become repressive and create new conditions for revolt. The terrorism seen in recent times stems from both ends of this spectrum. Closed political systems (such as in Saudi Arabia and Egypt) stimulate opposition, which in turn may draw energy from unsolved regional issues (the Palestinian issue, for example) and find allies in states in turmoil (such as Afghanistan and Pakistan) where it might be possible to establish bases for dramatic actions (such as those on September 11, 2001, and other suicide attacks). Some roots of terrorism, in other words, come from ongoing conflicts and prevalent political conditions. The solution is neither a very weak state nor an overpowering one.

In this chapter we are dealing with democracy as a solution to internal war, theoretically in Section 6.2 and empirically in Section 6.3. The question of internal security dilemmas and state failure are approached in Sections 6.4 and 6.5. Newly created democracies have to rest on considerable popular support to manage the balancing act with the military, at the same time sustaining transitions from internal war to peaceful conditions. The role of civil society, in other words, is crucial for the survival of democracy. We shall return to this problem in Section 6.6.

6.2 Dealing with Incompatibilities over State Power

Most peace agreements listed in Table 6.1 include democratization as a central element in the settlement. It is logical as these wars involve a struggle for power and influence in society. This is a way to handle the *participation of parties* in a society after a war: to give space to a host of actors who have previously been suppressed or excluded from influence. A solution may encompass procedures for transferring the struggle into constitutional and non-violent forms. This typically means a system of political parties, with freedom of association, safeguards for human rights, access to media, security for election campaigns, independent election commissions, fair elections and the free forming of new governments on the basis of election outcome. In other words, democratization is not a quick fix, but a multidimensional process. It is not only a matter of arranging an election. It also relates to an underlying balance of forces in a society, where parties realize that they cannot monopolize power. They have to adjust their demands in accordance with their electoral strength. It means that the incumbent government may lose power, due to the outcome of a previously agreed upon process (as happened, for instance, in Nicaragua, Cambodia and Iraq). This contributes to making a new system of governance credible and improves its attraction to political forces. This notwithstanding, newly created democracies are likely to remain fragile. We need to analyse how a democratic system, once established, can handle disputes that are likely to arise over the distribution of power in a society.

This aspect is particularly important in connection with the second problem indicated in Section 6.1, the one of *the security of the parties*. Can the democratic system simultaneously solve a basic incompatibility and move a society away from the sharp internal security dilemma where 'If A wins, B perishes – if B wins, A perishes'? There is no doubt that in conflicts with a clear-cut victory/defeat outcome, this is the logic that will apply: Nicolae Ceauşescu, leader in Romania, was executed, almost on television, in 1989. Mengistu Haile Mariam, the losing leader in Ethiopia, fled to Zimbabwe in 1991 to avoid being captured. Mobutu Sese Seko, the deposed leader in Zaire, escaped with his family and died in Morocco in 1997. Charles Taylor was 'persuaded' to leave Liberia in 2003, residing for a while under government control in Nigeria and was extradited to the court for Sierra Leone in 2006. Sometimes, the loser is in mortal danger, but there are other examples. The coup leader in Venezuela was jailed, but later made a new political career. The losers in armed conflict in Moscow in 1993 disappeared from politics but remained alive as ordinary citizens. There is a reality of an absolute internal security dilemma, but it can be modified. We may ask whether it takes a resource-rich or diversified social system for accepting another outcome (as was the case in Venezuela and Russia) and thus make the conflict shorter. An answer is that if the shift in power goes in the direction of democratization, the security dilemma is mitigated. In such cases, other outcomes are reported, notably in Thailand, South Korea and Indonesia, where the leaders could stay in the country, sometimes being convicted for crimes or corruption, but having their lives, families and dependents protected by the new system.

The question of human rights has entered into the settlement in a new way since the Cold War. It affects particularly the issue of what happens to the parties after a settlement and after a loss of power. The emphasis on accountability introduces higher criteria for what is an acceptable peace agreement. This was brought out strongly by the peace agreement for Sierra Leone in 1999. It provided amnesty for perpetrators of some of the worst violations of human rights and dignity. It served to end the war, for a time, but it was also unacceptable to the international community. In a reworked peace agreement, the conditions were changed and after some time a tribunal was created specifically for Sierra Leone.

Still, the democratic system appears to be a social system with possibilities of handling political losers and the changing fortunes of political forces. The human rights criteria help to draw a line between those who can participate in the democratic system and those who are to be brought to trial. Let us see how, in principle, a democratic system works.

The seven ways of conflict resolution we have identified in Section 3.5 are typical of the way a democratic system operates. The first form concerns *changes of priorities*. In a democratic system, the electoral outcome gives party leaders the chance to change their goals. They can claim that they have insufficient votes or seats in order to carry out the promises made. Such excuses are not available to the leaders of authoritarian regimes. Instead, the credibility of an absolute ruler hinges on the notion that he/she knows what should be done and is capable of delivering results. The fact that in authoritarian regimes there will also be (hidden) power struggles is not part of the image. The democratic system, furthermore, has the advantage of actually giving the loser a second or third chance. New elections are an agreed, regulated, intrinsic element, and this gives a defeated actor another chance. In fact, the best indicator of a functioning democratic system is the second or third election, not the first one. Alternative political systems neither give nor protect such a second opportunity. The possibility of a comeback can be regarded as the single most important instrument for breaking out of the internal security dilemma. It is a strong point for a democratic system.

The second solution, *dividing the values* in conflict, as well as the third one, *horse-trading*, are integral parts of any parliamentary system. Compromises, trade-off deals, and multi-issue packages are continuously the substance of politics. A struggle for power can be solved through ingenious divisions of power (over years, over functions), trade-off arrangements (according to the logic 'I support you on issue A, you support me on issue B') or combinations of the two. A society does in fact contain many attractive positions that can be part of a deal of power distribution. Some ministerial posts are customarily regarded as more important than others (for instance, portfolios as prime minister, or foreign, defence, interior or finance ministries). There are also posts such as speaker of parliament, head of particular committees, control of particular functions in society, governor positions, etc. In a one-party system, these are all available, but the difference is that they are only distributed to loyal party members to prevent them from becoming the basis for critics or attacks on the government. In the democratic system, however, they may equally likely go to opponents and to generally competent person-alities. They also give a position of power to opponents, and thus serve to protect their security.

The fourth solution, *ruling together*, is represented by coalition govern-ments, which are necessarily formed in a democracy in a multidimensional state and where proportional representation is the formula. A special aspect of this is the power-sharing arrangement, to which we shall return shortly.

The fifth solution, of *leaving control* to a minority or third force, is also a common feature in any established democratic system. Minority govern-ments may in fact be the most common form of governance, particularly if minority is defined as representation of the general population. For exam-ple, if 80 per cent of the population votes in an election and those getting the majority, say 55 per cent of the votes, take control of the government, this still does not represent more than 45 per cent of the electorate. The key lies in the way the minority government is formed. An open process pro-vides assurances to the population as well as to competing political leaders.

The sixth solution, bringing issues to a *conflict resolution mechanism*, is also available to the democratic system. It can be done, for instance, in the form of a referendum on a particular issue or new elections to break a political stalemate. Some systems do not have this possibility, which means there is more pressure on using the five other mechanisms.

Finally, there is the seventh way: *postponing issues*, by referring them to commissions. This is more difficult in a direct power struggle, but such struggles can be contained if the main contenders agree to let a minority run the government, that is, using the fifth way as a temporary measure. Leaving constitutional issues to commissions for later proposals can be a way of handling transition questions. The expectation is that once a com-mission presents its findings, the struggle has lost some of its intensity.

These examples illustrate that the incompatibility over government can be handled in ways which serve to remedy the internal security dilemma. More theoretically, we may ask, what is it actually that the democratic sys-tem does? The answer is easier said than translated into practice: it enlarges the number of options to the conflicting parties. There is no longer only a choice between (1) winning and (2) perishing. The democratic system pro-vides intermediate options such as (1.2) winning, but not gaining complete dominance, (1.4) being strong enough to play a role, (1.6) having some strength which can be enough to prevent undesirable developments, or (1.8) losing, but still keeping a position in society. Democracy expands the political alternatives in society. The actors have more real choices, which is to the benefit of the society as a whole. Still, the system is capable of making decisions. It may be slower, but decisions are more likely to be more durable.

For this to function, however, three conditions must be met. The winner must be committed to respecting the rights of the loser to be a loser, even to have a chance to make a comeback. This might be in the enlightened self-interest of the winner, if the winner realizes he/she could be the loser at a later stage. Furthermore, the loser must feel secure enough to accept defeat and not risk annihilation at that moment of conceding defeat. In an intra-state war, these are two conditions not easily met in a credible way. In a democratic society, respect and guarantees are customarily extended and the control of weaponry is restricted. The period immediately after a civil war is uncertain for all actors. There are plenty of weapons around. There may be anger and frustration. Economic conditions are often chaotic. This is why a reasonably strong and efficient international peacekeeping force can be important for a peace process in a civil war. It provides a neutral power resource which can extend guarantees to all sides.

Behind these two conditions there is a more deep-rooted notion, a third condition. It is that the state is not seen to 'belong' to any of the parties. Even a given government is only a temporary custodian of the state machinery. State resources are not at the unlimited disposal of the government or the winner. This is the essential meaning of the expression 'the rule of law'. The uses of state resources are limited by rules: there are safeguards, watchdogs and ombudsmen that protect the citizens. If generally accepted, the principles of the rule of law will make the state apparatus less attractive as a resource in society. It means that the significance of the state is deliberately restricted. In this way, the democratic system creates its own guarantees. For instance, the loser, if it is the former government repositioned as the opposition, is as important for the continuation of the rules of society as is the winner, who moves in to assume government control. The limit of what the state can do is what provides guarantees for the survival of the system. The struggle for state power, however, often stems from an ambition to gain control of an unlimited resource. To accept the principles of such limits is not easy for any contender.

How can such a transformation take place in a situation where the actors are entrenched in a deadly conflict over the state? How did it take place in the countries that today have democratically stable systems? The solution may be found in a special balance of strength where neither side completely wins or loses all its resources in a society. This means there is a balance among contending forces, giving them a chance to formulate the rules of the game. This is normally done in a constitutional reform with assemblies that bring together influential strands of a society. The agreed rules create a way of life which affects and helps to maintain the underlying societal balance. Some of the peace agreements in Table 6.1 are such formative documents, which become frameworks as the political system evolves. The fate of such peace agreements also gives insight into how democracy can be established under extreme conditions. Few, if any, of today's entrenched democracies in Western Europe and North America evolved directly from such strong internal conflicts as several of the countries in Table 6.1 face today.

Clearly, it is a process that is little understood. The following could be suggested. After the parties have signed a peace agreement they face the difficult phase of implementation. The former warring parties are still the paramount actors and they will attempt to control the developments. As they are the signatories to the agreement, their interpretation is difficult to challenge, as long as they agree on the process. Their disagreement can imperil the whole arrangement. Thus, this is a period requiring considerable trust and confidence. Also for this reason, an international presence may be conducive for the continuation of the process. It should be clear, however, that the primary actors themselves are responsible for the progress of implementation. It is a learning period, where the parties discover new traits about each other as well as how different building peace is from waging war.

After this comes a period where the previous conflict may no longer seem significant, but where the new conditions in themselves create tensions. This is when the peace treaty is consolidated, but also exposed to unforeseen tests. There may be topics that were neglected or not understood at the time of the peace accord (Stedman et al. 2002). There may be problems which arise as a result of the agreement, for instance, the problem of how to handle the former military forces. As we are interested in peace agreements after war, the latter aspect is particularly pertinent. Is it possible for the parties that were fighting a war among each other to integrate into the same societal framework again? The fact that there are more peace agreements in the post-Cold War period than previously means that there is little historical precedent on which to build. This, furthermore, is probably more true for civil wars than any other category. Thus, the questions of physical security and ability to cooperate are put at particular strains. Seen in this way, the fact that so many peace agreements actually survive is an achievement.

The physical security of the fighting parties is of particular concern in the settlement of internal conflicts. Such settlements do not normally establish dividing lines within a country behind which the parties can withdraw, as is the case in interstate conflicts. There is a limit to dissociative solutions. Sooner or later the accord assumes that the parties reintegrate or relate closely to each other. Thus, transition requires special measures to provide sufficient security for leaders and to familiarize the general public to their presence in public life. Their freedom becomes a symbol of a new reality of peaceful cooperation. Let us proceed by looking at the experiences since the Cold War in this light.

6.3 Democracy and the Settlement of Civil Wars

The peace agreements in Table 6.1 were concluded in societies with important differences in political institutions on which to build democratic solutions. First, there were cases of conflicts going on in countries which already had limited forms of popular participation in politics. For instance, elections, party competition and media independence were accepted principles. Thus, the question became largely one of reforming this system so as to accommodate the demands arising from the civil wars. The peace arrangements in Colombia, El Salvador, Guatemala, and South Africa could all use existing legal structures. The peace agreements meant fundamental changes in these constitutions so as to allow for a broader participation, as well as the dismantling of structures that were antithetical to the new democratic system (more specifically, the military institutions and all apartheid institutions, respectively). Although basic changes took place, institutions could remain and transcend themselves into the new realities. Particularly in South Africa, the changes in power in all central institutions meant considerable social change. Accountability for repression and war crimes were issues raised in the peace processes and resulted in a path-setting institution in South Africa (the Truth and Reconciliation Commission). In all three cases, public security concerns were high following the ending of the armed conflicts. El Salvador faced a test in 2009 when a leader of the former rebel movement who was not a commander, Mauricio Funes, was elected president on a moderate platform of change.

Second, there were civil wars in societies which had had elections and appropriate institutions, but where one-party rule had been the dominant feature for a considerable period of time. To these cases belong, for instance, Nicaragua, Angola, Mozambique and Macedonia. As part of the peace initiatives, constitutions were amended to allow for multiparty politics. The agreements could build on existing structures, but also had to consider that these institutions were likely to be biased. The credibility of an open multiparty system was questioned. In the cases mentioned, the conflict was also strongly polarized into opposing camps. In Nicaragua, polarization has remained. The Sandinista leader Daniel Ortega, who lost elections in 1990, was elected President in 2006 and there have been concerns about his adherence to democracy since then. In Mozambique, polarization from the war appears to have defused. In Angola, new wars started ending only in 2002, and in Macedonia an ethnic divide remained. The long-term ability of eliminating the war divides through democracy may be limited, but the likelihood of renewed violence might be reduced.

Third, there was a category of states where the agreements entailed more or less a complete reconstruction of state institutions, including the training of electoral staff, supervision of new institutions, etc. The peace agreements on Lebanon, Cambodia, Chad, the Democratic Republic of Congo,

Liberia, Sierra Leone and Tajikistan had such elements. While the agenda for implementation of agreements, needless to say, becomes more extensive, the less there is for institutions to build on. For instance, the application of principles of accountability and war crimes has met difficulties.

It is probably correct to say that the countries in the first category, today, are functioning more democratically. Thus, it is less likely that there will be a return to the previous wars. Three examples (El Salvador, South Africa, Guatemala) are post-war societies which have found themselves engulfed by considerable violence, often criminal in character and with some roots in the civil war itself. Many social inequities that originally motivated the war linger and may give rise to new parties with new sharp demands. There are seeds of possible revolt, but along different lines than before. In Colombia, settling one dispute has not spilled over to settling the other conflicts in the country.

The second category includes some successes, but also a repeated failure (Angola). Nicaragua has seen several shifts in government; Mozambique has yet to experience such a test of the strength of its reformed institutions.

The most difficult processes can be expected in the third category. It is also a group of societies which will depend most on external support for success. Cambodia was the object of a largely successful UN peace operation in 1992–93 (Hampson 1996: 200–4), but low-scale wars and coup behaviour have been part of the experiences since then. In Haiti, the international commitment was high in the mid-1990s, then waned and the country relapsed into conflict in 2004. Not until the devastating earthquakes of January 2010 was there significant attention, however. This is to suggest that democratization following a civil war is more likely to succeed if there is a previous legal system building at least on some principles of rule of law. Also, sustained international support is likely to be required for countries such as Liberia and Sierra Leone.

The seven forms of conflict resolution help us to illustrate the process of change more closely. First, there is the gradual acceptance by the governments of, as it were, new principles for ruling society. This means that new priorities are made. The National Party in South Africa had to accommodate to a new situation. What mattered to the party was no longer to keep power for itself, but to maintain the social positions of the white minority. In the words of Zartman, the party had to make 'a trade-off of power for position'. Similar moves of accommodation had to be made by other parties. For the ANC, there was a choice between demanding a pact with power-sharing or taking full control by itself (Zartman 1995a: 149, 162), where the ANC, in the end preferred the former. The agreements were predicated on such shifts in position by the parties. This meant that one party agreed on the legality of other parties and, thus, opponents were able to enter into negotiations. It also implied that the view of the outcome changed. The possibility of losing power or not achieving complete state control was part of the understanding, thus making it important for a dominant actor to appreciate the need of safeguards for the losers.

For all the peace agreements, it is obvious that the negotiations leading to settlement involved considerable compromise, including locating middle points and horse-trading deals, that is, the second and third forms of transcending the incompatibility. This could, for instance, concern issues of the length of transition periods, timetables for demilitarization, changes in institutions with hostile mandates, introduction of human rights provisions, etc. In some cases, it also involved agreements on dividing cabinet posts according to particular preferences.

Most interesting is the use of the fourth and fifth forms for solving incompatibilities: power-sharing or leaving control to another actor. Obviously, rebel groups are suspicious of the government and fear its potential power in, for instance, manipulating upcoming elections. In some of the agreements, innovative arrangements were made. In the case of South Africa, a multiparty Transitional Executive Council was instituted to oversee the government's activities for a period of about five months, up to the elections held in April 1994. In the case of Cambodia, a Supreme National Council was created with representation from all four leading groups as well as a strong UN presence supervising five of the key ministries in the central government (Hampson 1996: 178–88). Thus, forms of power-sharing were instituted before the elections, and there were expectations of coalitions or national unity governments after the elections. Such inclusive arrangements may have contributed to the durability of these peace agreements. It is interesting that in some conflicts, the opposition did not demand a share in the government, but preferred to be able to participate securely in the political process. This was the position of the FMLN in El Salvador (not winning Presidential power until 2009). Instead, a National Commission for the Consolidation of Peace (in Spanish, COPAZ) was agreed (Hampson 1996: 140; Pérez de Cuéllar 1997: 419–20, 434). In the 1991 Angolan agreement, both sides expected to win the elections, and only a weak joint commission was instituted. The next agreement contained more cooperative arrangements, but without leading to a full implementation of the peace agreement (Ohlson 1998: 74–82). It took until 2008, six years after the war ended, for the government to arrange parliamentary elections.

In civil war agreements, there is little resort to formal conflict resolution mechanisms, apart from giving room for negotiations or referenda. This is understandable. Such mechanisms are often legal, and the legal institutions are often part of the dispute. Their roles have frequently been tarnished by the incumbent regime or its predecessors. There is considerable use of international mediation, however, and the involvement of the UN in the Nicaraguan settlement was a breakthrough for UN actions in internal conflicts. The supervision of Nicaragua's elections in February 1990 was the first time the UN monitored elections in a sovereign state (Pérez de Cuéllar 1997: 405–16). It has, since then, become an important practice. It is remarkable, however, that there are few international institutions to turn to for settlement of internal conflicts.

Postponing issues, the seventh model, is also a frequent approach, in order to reach an agreement on other topics. In the case of El Salvador, the armed opposition coalition, the FMLN, agreed not to push the land reform issue at this stage (Cañas and Dada 1999; Hampson 1996: 141), although it had been a key demand for its entire political and military campaign. It was partly a matter of giving priority to reforms of the military institutions and gaining access to political institutions. The party remained free to return to the problems. The issue remains contentious in El Salvador. In the case of Cambodia, the incumbent government, known as SOC (State of Cambodia), gradually reduced its demands to insert words on 'genocide' in the concluding document. The question of possible trials on human rights grounds against leaders of the Khmer Rouge regime in Cambodia did not subside, however, and later a combined international and national court was set up.

These examples illustrate that the democratic framework is helpful in handling conflicts over power in society. It is also noteworthy that the transitions have been made possible by temporary power-sharing arrangements. These may well have contributed to introducing parties, previously excluded from decision-making, into the real financial, administrative and international constraints under which governments have to operate. Power-sharing has an educational effect. It is noteworthy that the agreements that have failed have not had such elements. In Angola, the first peace agreement was a 'winner-take-all' arrangement, whereas the second accord allowed for power-sharing. It was never implemented in full, mostly because of actions by UNITA, the armed opposition party (Ohlson 1998: 152). The use of power-sharing for democratization involves a conversion of views. It 'moves towards success when it shifts elections from being a mechanism to award victory denied on the battlefield to being the means to admit all parties to legitimate and ongoing participation in the future political system' (Zartman 1995a: 339). As a transition from civil war to civil peace, power-sharing may be a useful device, but if instituted for too long a period, it may have stifling effects.

What this overview shows is that the central provisions in peace agreements have dealt with procedural issues and government institutions. Particular ways of sharing power have been important. Underlying issues, such as land reform questions, poverty and other questions of economic and social justice, and economic policies, which many would deem as important, have seldom been solved through peace agreements. Human rights issues have not always been important. It seems that the opposing sides have had a similar belief that with access to government power, they will be able to deal with substantive matters according to their goals. The democratic systems that follow, however, do not only represent the voices of change, but also the voices of the *status quo*. The reverse is also true: democratic systems do not necessarily protect the *status quo*, but provide opportunities for social change. Either way, societies change, perhaps more slowly than many would expect, more quickly than others would want.

Decisive for the fate of the agreement are the priorities of the carriers of the peace, the parties that signed and committed themselves to its implementation. Their attention to the procedural aspects and the substantive matters will mix with the new realities following the ending of the war. These actors will have to make a choice among the many elements that any peace agreement entails. For instance, the peace agreement for Guatemala included 13 separate agreements. To implement them all, at the same time, is clearly impossible. Some matters get more attention and more support, others meet more resistance. Furthermore, the direction of society may turn out to be very different from what any of the warring parties had expected. The more open a society, the more will voices other than those of the warring parties make themselves heard. For instance, the issue of justice and human rights is one of the concerns that often gets more attention than the warring sides may prefer. Their primary interest is often with their own security under peace-time conditions.

6.4 Dealing with the Internal Security Dilemma

A major issue for the origin of civil wars, we have said, stems from the intra-state security dilemma. To the parties, this is a major concern. What will be their future following the end of the war and the accompanying demobilization of soldiers, closing of bases and other measures that are necessary for the reconstruction of peace and the formation of an integrated society? The parties that sign the agreements are likely to be highly suspicious of each other. They have good reasons. In their agitation, they have often emphasized that the other side is criminal, illegitimate, corrupt and/or untrustworthy. To negotiate, conclude agreements and, perhaps, even share power, with such an actor is a difficult transition. Thus, the conclusion by Ohlson in his analysis of the peace agreements in Southern Africa is to the point. Agreements are more likely not to fail if the 'physical and organizational security concerns of the primary parties are addressed to their satisfaction' (1998: 186). There are likely to be some security guarantees for the parties to sign the accords.

Such guarantees and reintegration among the parties might work better if leaders on both sides come from the same social class or share a normative system. This is not often the case. Many civil wars have revolutionary origins, meaning that they pit an established regime against an organization of previously marginalized persons and groups. For the regime, it means fighting people who come from unknown circumstances and are understood only to have ambitions to wrest their power. To make deals and even yield power is frightening and likely to encounter criticism in the regime's camp. For the opposition, the war means getting closer to power and a chance to change society. Not to win might be perceived as failure. If leaders have difficulties in adjusting to a compromise agreement, it is probably even more frustrating for the followers on the opposite sides. To them, it may appear that leaders are betraying the causes for which the lower echelons have risked their lives. For many, victory will be the only acceptable outcome. The leaders, in other words, have a major educational task in explaining their strategy and why a peace agreement will suffice. They may be aided by war fatigue, economic deterioration, death tolls and rampant destruction, which make the general public responsive to peace. The soldiers, officers and leaders, however, may not necessarily share the perspective of the public at large. The educational task, in other words, has to deal with the internal dynamics of an actor, rather than the general public.

The need to make the rank-and-file follow the leadership into a peace agreement adds strains to the negotiations. The settlement has to include sufficient security guarantees, as well as benefits, to make peace acceptable to the party's internal sceptics. The negotiations need not only to solve the problem with the opponent, they must also address the inner concerns of the party itself. This is where the outside world may have a particular role, as it can commit resources to smooth transitions.

Studying the peace agreements since the Cold War, we find that they attempt to manage the security dilemmas of the transition from war to peace with the help of five different measures. These are: (a) a general demilitarization and creation of a unified army; (b) specific guarantees for leaders; (c) international presence, for instance, peacekeeping forces; (d) transitory power-sharing; and (e) amnesty to leaders, officers and agents. These measures are used, whether the agreement is one of depriving a military regime of its power or giving power to a successful guerrilla movement. In the case of victory, these five measures are likely to be used in a one-sided manner. Demilitarization will be only for the opponents, privileges only for the winners, international presence only for legitimization of the new *status quo*, power-sharing only for those who cooperate and amnesty only for the supporters. In the peace agreements of Table 6.1, there are many examples of these five measures being used, but in a less biased manner. The five measures do not exclude one another. There is so far little evidence to suggest that some are more successful than others, or that certain combinations are more optimal. An exemplification will suffice.

Demilitarization deals directly with the ability of one side to threaten the security of the other. A rapid reduction in armed forces and firepower is necessary in order to reduce insecurity among the parties. In many peace negotiations, these are issues which are agreed at a late stage. This indicates that the more obvious 'political' elements are central and that the military force is there to back up the parties' position on these issues. By delaying the security issues, some leverage is kept on the other side. It means also that a cease-fire may be late in coming (as was the case in El Salvador). Alternatively, if there is an early cease-fire, the parties may retain the option of restarting the war (a more common approach). Either way, the timing suggests that the security issues are among the most difficult to deal with. For instance, demilitarization means removing troops from positions conquered in deadly battle, or giving up hard-earned and strategic weaponry. To some military leaders this may appear close to defeat, not victory or peace. Political gains must be considerable to convince the military side to make such concessions.

From an analytical point of view, demilitarization is almost a definitional necessity for ending a civil war. Without it, there will be the threat of a resumption of war. The military forces have to be part of a new setup. Particularly important in civil war endings is the idea of combining the fighting forces into one large, new unit. The definition of a state is the existence of *one* military force under one central command, the government. However, simply combining the two sides into one unit would create an unbearably large army. If integration is successful, this force might become an overwhelmingly powerful factor, potentially to be used against the new political order. It might even become threatening towards neighbours.[7] Demilitarization and the creation of a new army is a logical outcome of these concerns and of the peace process. It has the additional advantage of making it possible to screen the new military forces so as to include only officers willing to cooperate with the new conditions and integrate with the former opponents. Involvement in war crimes is another obvious criterion for exclusion.

However, the experiences from Southern Africa do not suggest that there has always been complete demobilization (Ohlson 1998: 181). Most important may well be the possibility of reducing the threat to the other side. The formation of a unified army may be a protracted process. In some agreements, such as the one in El Salvador, an important FMLN demand was the elimination of certain officers or certain units in the regular army (in El Salvador this was called 'purification'). Also in this case, three police services were disbanded and a new force created (Cañas and Dada 1999). This integration process proceeded surprisingly well. The more difficult problem has been what to do with the decommissioned officers and soldiers. When turning in their weapons they have sometimes been paid (which risks starting a local arms trade) or been given implements to start a new life (land, seeds and fertilizers, for instance, plus assistance in reintegrating into villages or towns of their origin). These approaches were used in Mozambique and El Salvador. Counter-reactions by decommissioned soldiers who have kept their weapons have become a problem in the aftermath of some peace agreements. The former soldiers have demanded jobs and payments or joined underground groups. It turns out, however, that this is a dilemma also in cases of victory. It is not only something facing a losing army, but also the victorious military force has to be reduced once the fighting is over. The problem of decommissioned soldiers reflects the availability of weapons, the breakdown in social fabric and the disturbed economy that any protracted war is likely to produce. Lately, donor attention has focused on these issues, termed DDR (disarmament, demobilization and reintegration of ex-combatants). Recent studies point to the importance of the networks among former combatants for their ability to become engaged in military action again (A. Nilsson 2008). A particular aspect is the fate of former child soldiers.

Security guarantees for leaders are a particular problem, arising as an important factor in the peace agreements in Southern Africa (Ohlson 1998). The leaders entering the accords find themselves in exposed situations. Those who see the outcome as betrayal may turn against their leaders, who thus are vulnerable not only to revenge by their enemies, but also to assassination attempts by their (former) supporters. There are examples of leaders being killed during the peace process. This gives incentives for some leaders not to pursue demilitarization in full. There is a temptation to hide weapons or 'civilianize' units which, in practice, have para-military functions. A distinction between different types of weaponry probably would help sort out this problem. If larger, offensive and provocative weapons are banned and handed in, smaller and defensive ones might be allowed during a transition period, for a smaller unit geared to the protection of particularly controversial leaders. This, however, has to be a transitory phenomenon; otherwise, it becomes a privilege with a negative effect on popular acceptance of the agreement. Seen in this light, many of the peace agreements in civil wars have turned out to be more manageable than expected. They have seldom resulted in mass killings, contrary to some reports for earlier periods (Licklider 1995). The return of refugees is an indicator of this. There may be a larger problem in cases of clear-cut victories, where losers are in immediate physical danger and have little political future.

International military presence, in the form of a new generation of peacekeeping operations, can contribute both to demilitarization and leader security. The prime motive for peacekeeping, however, is a different one: to provide a measure of security to the process as such. It gives time for adjustment and for building confidence. The international presence leads to international attention which may assist in reducing the insecurities. Obviously, peacekeeping operations have more specific functions in the implementation of elements in the peace agreements, but that is a separate matter. In the peace agreements reported here, peacekeeping has typically been part of the transition from war to peace and then it has been withdrawn. This is logical, and also in line with the commitment that the international community makes. The goal is to return the primary parties to a 'normal' situation, where they have to work out their relations among themselves. Some agreements had no international troop presence at all (most obviously in South Africa).

There is a debate, however, as to the ability of the international peacekeepers to achieve their task. The mandates, for instance for UN troops, are often very limited and the priority is often to protect the security of the force itself, rather than the peace process it is there to guard and promote. The mandates are set by the UN Security Council and it may have other concerns in mind than a particular crisis, notably the well-being of the national forces that are committed to the international force. There have also been complaints about the quality of the military training of some troops. Much of the credibility of the international presence rests on the ability of the peacekeepers to act effectively and quickly. Also, they are there to indicate the possibilities for additional support from the international community, that is, to be a tripwire for further international support if necessary. In several instances since the end of the Cold War, this support has not been forthcoming. When challenged, the forces have instead been withdrawn. This was illustrated in Somalia in 1993, when the United States withdrew its force after 18 US Army Rangers had been killed, something which affected peacekeeping for the rest of the decade.

Most of the peace agreements contain some element of *power-sharing* or influence on the process, either before, during or after the implementation of the agreement. This aspect is primarily there to transcend some of the incompatibilities in the conflict, as we observed above. Power-sharing also contains a degree of physical protection for the leaders, as they are included in official institutions and, thus, are to be protected by them. In such capacities, the leaders will find ways of protecting their followers. This is, from a security perspective, preferable to the suggestions that leaders keep their own security force. Its usefulness hinges on the normalization of society after the war. There is a risk that one part of the government apparatus will become controlled by one of the former fighting parties. A change in the composition of the cabinet would then have security implications for certain actors, for instance. It could lead to resistance and state institutions would turn into resources in a potential renewal of the civil war. Such a scenario unfolded in the civil war in Lebanon from 1975 to 1989.

Finally, several agreements have wrestled with the issue of *amnesty*. Are those leaders, officers and soldiers who are responsible for atrocities during the war to be brought to trial or not? In civil wars which end as victories, the victor may use the legal system to prosecute the losers. This is a factor which may make losers reluctant to accept an agreement. The security dilemma in this legal form may be a powerful incentive for a leader to fight on. In the end, capitulation may include some form of amnesty as the loser's last demand. It means that there is a high likelihood that a peace agreement will include protective clauses, often for all sides. It makes it possible for the fighting parties to conclude an agreement. For instance, in the peace plan for Central America that Costa Rica's President Oscar Arias proposed in 1987, and which was essential for ending the wars in this region, amnesty was among the conditions given (Pérez de Cuéllar 1997: 402). This was immediately accepted at the time. It was complemented, however, with ideas of national dialogue and reconciliation.

Ten years later, the issue of amnesty in civil wars is more complicated. As was mentioned in Section 6.2, in the peace treaty for Sierra Leone of July 1999, some of the perpetrators of war crimes during the civil war were granted amnesty. It was a condition for them signing. But there was no longer international acceptance of this and the counter-reaction was overwhelming. The war crime tribunals for former Yugoslavia and Rwanda have made impunity less acceptable. The convention on an international permanent court on war crimes was concluded in Rome in 1998 and the court is now operational. For the fighting parties, amnesty may no longer be a convenient way out. Even if agreements are signed by the parties, international law may eventually overtake them. In 2005, key members of the Lord's Resistance Army in northern Uganda became the first to be indicted by the International Criminal Court (ICC). Previous negotiations have held out the chance of amnesty. As mediation did not end the war, the ICC issued its indictments, asking for international support in capturing the indicted. The conflict, however, continued unabated.

Since the end of the Cold War there have been a number of innovative ways of dealing with the issue of human rights in the conditions of war, severe conflict and military government. This has important implications for the prevention of renewed war. It affects the security concerns of the fighting parties, and points to the emergence of new norms which make impunity less acceptable. The creation of truth commissions is one of these. There is experience with such commissions from many different conflicts (Heyner 2000; International Center for Transitional Justice 2005). Most of these relate to conflicts over power in society, that is, civil wars and repressive governments. They are important elements in forging a society after a devastating experience. For the society to function, a process of healing and reconciliation is necessary. It runs counter to the demands of particular leaders. Interestingly, such commissions are rare in peace agreements for interstate wars as well as for state formation conflicts.

It is important to note that many peace agreements in civil wars have provisions for human rights commissions, investigations into brutalities and war crimes. Such provisions may appear as a threat to some leaders, but in particular it gives a role to the civil society that exists beyond the fighting parties. These are instruments that can be used. There are examples of governments making unilateral amnesty decisions, thus pre-empting later legal procedures. This difficult issue has led to innovative solutions. One of the most celebrated ones was actually a political compromise, the Truth and Reconciliation Commission in South Africa. It has been heralded as a new model. It does provide amnesty for those who agree to have their cases processed through the Commission. The Commission was only a temporary measure, which meant that the process started immediately, not waiting for the new political situation to consolidate. Other forms, such as the Commission for Truth in El Salvador, have a broader mandate, but have also led to political counter-measures, where some persons were protected from prosecution by the government. This was only the first in a series of measures that prevented the implementation of recommendations on justice (Cañas and Dada 1999; Hampson 1996: 157).

The international war crimes tribunals now give particular emphasis to this issue. It is applicable to all three forms of armed conflict with which we are dealing in this book. The longest functioning tribunal for a civil war is the one on the genocide in Rwanda. It is based in Arusha, Tanzania. The present Rwandan government is simultaneously pursuing its own legal processes and a process of local reconciliation, the gacaca. For former leaders, there may be a preference to go to Arusha, as the international tribunal does not hand out capital punishment. The tribunal is restricted to the events of one year, 1994, which means that only one part of the Rwandan conflict dynamic is captured, basically the genocide of that year (Johnson 1999: 193). There was a civil war before this tragedy and there remains a complex regional situation with huge numbers of refugees outside the borders of Rwanda. The impact of the gacaca can be debated. Psychologically, it means a retraumatization that may impede reconciliation (Brounéus 2008). The most prudent solution is a generally applicable, permanent international court for war crimes, the ICC.

These are five ways, reflected in peace agreements, of mitigating the immediate internal security dilemma. Thus, it was possible to enter into the agreements. But the agenda was often broader than this. As the agreements are recent, it is difficult to draw long-term conclusions. The hope was to transcend the classical security dilemma. We cannot say what the societies will look like 10 or 20 years after the peace agreements. In some countries there has been a rise in public insecurity, with criminal violence more widespread than before (South Africa). There have also been political assassinations, often directed at former guerrillas (El Salvador) and against independent voices (Guatemala). This points to the dangerous period that follows an accord. It certainly is not the same as the war breaking out again, but it is also far from the peaceful conditions and expectations of development that sustained the peace processes.

A key question for the internal security dilemma in the long run is what happens to the armed services. The peace agreements expected that constitutional authority would grow by, for instance, enhancing the role of parliament. It would make the armed forces (police, military) subordinate to civilian authority. To restructure a military force would be necessary, but not easily done. A new armed force would need considerable training, find new ways for recruitment, implant a new understanding of the role of the armed forces in society and integrate human rights in the self-definition of these forces and in society as a whole. Such restructuring was initiated in El Salvador, Guatemala and South Africa. It means that the military forces are to be separated from police functions. The rule of civilian leadership is taught to new generations. It is made clear that army, air force and navy are to be used for external defence only. In the end, a professional army with a different ethos will be established. Part of this is, of course, that the armed forces are to operate professionally, and thus refuse to be involved in political projects of particular, unauthorized leaders. In short, the propensity for military coups should be reduced. In fact, there have been few coups after the peace agreements listed in Table 6.1.

It is interesting to note that reforms of the military institutions could be part of an international preventive strategy. In development cooperation, security sector reform (SSR) has become a novel undertaking, unusual for foreign aid donors who have previously deliberately preferred to be civilian in their approach. By infusing professional values into the military establishments worldwide, the likelihood of military coups may gradually recede. Today it appears that such programmes are undertaken, notably in the Philippines (learning from a long experience of martial law) and in some of the newly independent states in Central and Eastern Europe (as part of a Westernization of the military forces). Such programmes may meet more resistance in countries where the armed forces are strongly entrenched, and may be seen by many as the guarantors of the existing order and the cohesion of the state (Indonesia, Thailand and Turkey).

The solutions to incompatibilities indicated in this section are those that the parties have agreed on in serious negotiations and where implementation is under way. Thus, they are measures deemed by the parties to be necessary for ending a war. The agreements may have been difficult to reach and that could be a good sign that they are taken seriously. This has also been understood as an indication of their willingness to implement what is agreed. This cannot, however, always be taken for granted. In reality, there is a difficult period from the conclusion of an accord to its full implementation. This period is crucial for the creation of goodwill among the parties. Several agreements failed as the parties were not willing to carry out what they had solemnly agreed. This was most apparent in an agreement not listed in Table 6.1, the series of accords agreed in Rwanda in 1992–93 to end the civil war. These agreements contained many of the provisions shown above. However, the key stipulation of a broad-based transitional government was resisted by many groups in the Hutu majority population. It even led to violence between different Hutu factions. When the president of the republic was killed in April 1994, after he had been pressured by neighbouring state leaders to begin the implementation, it was the signal for one of the worst genocides. It illustrated the significance, but also the difficulty, of making peace processes all-inclusive. It gave rise to the notion of spoiler and spoiler management (Prunier 1995; Stedman 1997, 1998). There are parties who see their interest threatened by a peace agreement, and who are willing to pursue their own agenda, even at very high cost.

6.5 State Failure, State Reconstruction and Non-state Terrorism

In extreme but not infrequent cases, civil wars have resulted in the collapse of state institutions. In such a case, the legal system has broken down, extortion and murder have taken place with impunity, normal operations in society have ceased to function (from garbage collection to tax collection). This is a case of state failure. As was observed in Section 6.3, peace agreements will then face entirely different challenges. Peacemaking will have to include state building or state reconstruction. Some such cases since the Cold War are Angola, Lebanon, Cambodia, Chad, Liberia, Sierra Leone, Tajikistan and the Democratic Republic of Congo. There are also cases where no such reconstruction took place, Somalia being the most notable case, but others include Afghanistan and Burundi. Rwanda may suggest an alternative route to state recreation after war: the victory of one faction then creating its own state machinery. The State Failure Project has noted: 'No more than a dozen complete collapses of state authority have occurred during the last 40 years, too few for meaningful generalization.' In this case, state failure is defined as a state which has considerable experience of civil, revolutionary and ethnic wars (Esty et al. 1998). With this definition, the short period after the Cold War has witnessed close to half of all state failures in the second half of the twentieth century.

The definition is somewhat close to the one of war, however. If we depart from the political science definition of the state as the sole authoritative user of physical violence (see Section 4.2), it might be reasonable to conclude that a state which cannot keep order throughout its territory, for all practical purposes, is a failed or, more diplomatically, a fragile state.[8] Theoretically and practically, state failure, then, is separate from the phenomenon of civil war. It can take place without civil war, and there can be a civil war without a state failure. It is a matter of the relations between state and society (Migdal 1988). As we are concerned with situations after civil wars, state failure is one such possible outcome. It may not be the most frequent one, but one that is among the most difficult to repair. We have already concluded that if legal systems and institutions are intact, rehabilitation after war is more likely to succeed. This means there is a special challenge to peacemaking if state institutions are no longer in place. Some lessons have been learned on the possibilities of recovery from state failure after civil war.

For a long time, Lebanon was seen as the archetype of a state failure. It is normally attributed to the onset of the civil war in 1975. In a rapid series of events, central state institutions ceased to function, the armed forces and the territory of the country were divided along the lines of the contestants. Prior to this, Lebanon had been held together through a delicate political balancing act. It was a permanent power-sharing arrangement. When this began to unravel, the constituent parts started to operate as separate actors. The integration was limited among the parties carrying the state. Add to this family ties, old alliances and enmities, ideological convictions and the involvement of actors with other agendas, for instance, Palestinian liberation organizations, Cold War intelligence agencies, Egypt, Syria, Israel, Iran, and the completeness of the fragmentation can be understood. What followed was a series of changing alliances, local power struggles, *de facto* self-ruling areas, and a proliferation of warlords. Lebanon became an arena for vicious bombings and for capturing, keeping and trading Western hostages. What was once a prosperous financial and entertainment centre turned into ruins. After 15 years of wars, a peace process gained momentum. The full extent of state failure can be understood from the fact that in the peace negotiations in Taif, Saudi Arabia, there were no representatives of the government as such. It was not a 'distinct actor' in the negotiations (Deeb and Deeb 1995: 126). Lebanon was recreated, through the passage of the peace treaty reforms in 1990. The state was again a functioning entity, but under heavy Syrian tutelage. After a decade, the state was once more performing basic internal functions, but was hardly an independent international actor. It has taken Lebanon 15 years to reach a peace from which recovery could be initiated. In 2005, former Prime Minister Rafik Hariri was killed in a bomb blast together with 20 other persons. The action was initially linked to Syria. Large demonstrations and UN Security Council action followed, Syrian military forces were withdrawn and the elections resulted in a new government, more critical of Syria. Some form of an independent, democratic state had a chance to emerge. However, in 2010, the special inquiry into the assassination appeared to point to Hezbollah, the strong Shiite organization in Lebanon, as responsible. Objecting to this, the government was brought down, and the concerns of Lebanon's future were again rising. The difficulties of combining democracy, stable governance and independent crime investigations with sustained economic recovery were underscored.

A slightly older case that has been seen as a success in recovery is Uganda. Its predicament rose from internal mismanagement. The regime of Idi Amin has to take the blame for the state's deteriorating conditions. Amin took power in a military coup in 1971, forced the entrepreneurial Asian population out of the country in the following year, and the country subsequently saw the economy sharply decline. He involved the country in a war with Tanzania (1978–79), only to find himself chased out of his own country by Tanzanian forces. The ensuing regime, under Milton Obote, did not improve matters. Inter-ethnic conflicts arose, and the state gradually lost all legitimacy. From this crisis emerged an entirely new leader and a new movement: Yoweri Museveni and his movement for reconstruction. In 1986 his troops conquered Kampala, the capital. However, it was a victory where the new government took some unexpected measures. An important element was the generous attitude of the victor. Museveni initiated a process of reintegrating opponents and competing movements into society. The first government was a broad-based coalition. With this there was political predictability. Economic recovery followed. The state failure lasted for about 15 years. The reconstruction has gone on for an equally long time. The situation has improved, but remains fragile, particularly at election time. In 2006 Museveni was elected – in a debatable electoral campaign – for a third term as President and a fourth one in 2011. This indicates a reluctance to give up control. Democracy is still not entrenched.

This time frame for reconstruction in Uganda is parallel to the one of Lebanon. The political management used for recovery is also similar. It is a version of a power-sharing scheme to include many factions of the society. The two experiences indicate the need for at least one strong actor interested in recovery. It could be either an external, neighbouring power (Syria), or a victorious movement not tainted by the previous rivalries (Museveni). However, at some time there has to be a role for the rest of society, as events demonstrated in Lebanon in 2005, and as was difficult in Uganda in 2006.

These lessons are applicable to other cases, but also suggest the difficulties. Afghanistan had a chance of recovery after a protracted war, but its disunited leadership failed to grasp it. The withdrawal of the Soviet troops by February 15, 1989 did not result in the fall of the Soviet-supported communist regime, as anticipated. The internationally supported Afghan coalition could not take power until 1992. The coalition, furthermore, remained divided. In 1996, a new force, the Taliban, supported by Pakistan, entered the scene and captured the capital, Kabul. Although it had, by 1999, taken control over most of the territory of Afghanistan, it was not internationally recognized as the Afghan government. In 1999, UN sanctions were instituted on Afghanistan for its support of terrorism as the country had become a refuge for Osama bin Laden and his al-Qaida network. It was accused by US authorities of responsibility for the attacks on the American embassies in Dar-es-Salaam, Tanzania and Nairobi, Kenya, in 1998. American air strikes were directed against Afghanistan in 1998. The Taliban faction was not recognized as a government, as a result of its policies on human and religious rights, women's issues, and its support for terrorist actions aimed both at the West and at Russia. Its refusal to hand over Osama bin Laden and his followers after the September 11, 2001 attacks on the United States mainland made the country a target for further sanctions and war. The war resulted in the removal of the regime by the end of 2001, a broader government was installed, freer elections were carried out, but security rested on NATO, the USA and local warlords.

The role of the international community appears significant. It was willing to accept the interference of an external, neighbouring power (Syria). It was also supportive of an untainted revolutionary movement to bring some order (Uganda). In both cases, the international community refrained from intervening in the basic political arrangement. As investment and trade followed the increased stability, this can also be seen as reward and support for the present setup. From the point of view of the international actors, there is probably a greater interest in supporting a movement of locals to take power. This is particularly true if these are local movements that have basic support in the society, and are not associated with the previous regime, the downfall of which led to the state failure. The advantage for a supportive state to find such a solution is that it avoids direct interference, but may still get a friendly government or at least reduced chaos. Initially, the Taliban in Afghanistan corresponded to such a notion: it had support from a neighbour concerned about the stability of the country, and it was not tainted by the previous rivalries. After the removal of the Taliban, the new government was headed by Hamid Karzai, who spent much of his career outside the country. It was hoped that he could perform the bridging role necessary for Afghanistan's state reconstruction. The presidential elections of 2009 left many questions unanswered. Clearly, Afghanistan's reconstruction was slow.

Civil wars resulting in state failure are clearly more difficult to handle through the usual mechanisms of conflict resolution. There have to be actors who are willing to break the cycle of violence. Too often it is likely that surrounding states will engage themselves in a particular civil war to pursue their own goals, and thus soon find themselves in new conflicts, rather than in solutions. However, non-interference may not be an option either. Thus, the focus is turned to new groups, emerging from the local society, that can provide a chance for a break in the reproduction of conflict dynamics. We also can see that a recovery will not be possible unless the new social forces are able to include and incorporate elements of the old system. There is an intricate balance that has to be made between being revolutionary and maintaining continuity.

Not only neighbouring states but also non-state actors have taken advantage of the turmoil that is created by state fragility. This has been typical for the way organized crime has acted historically. In the post-Cold War period also, non-state actors using terrorist tactics have seen this possibility. Al-Qaida found its base in Afghanistan and later in Pakistan. The protracted civil war in Iraq has provided conditions that are close to state failure and, thus, further new terrorist acts. This confirms the thesis that the breakdown in the state machinery may provide opportunities for rebellious groups using terror tactics. In the examples given, this has had unsettling conditions beyond the state.

There is still no global consensus on a definition of terrorism, but the one provided by the High-Level Panel on UN reform may suffice: 'any action ... that is intended to cause death or serious bodily harm to civilians or non-combatants, when the purpose of such act ... is to intimidate a population, or compel a Government or an international organization to do or to abstain from doing any act' (High-Level Panel 2004: para. 164). An objection to this definition has been whether it applies under occupation and, thus, possibly, defines some forms of resistance as terrorism. Still, there is consensus on the illegality of targeting civilians or non-combatants in most circumstances. The suggested definition would apply equally to actions by states and non-state actors.

Let us conclude that civil war may result in state failure, which at the same time requires sustained efforts for recovery and can generate conditions for new armed conflicts and terrorism that will have an effect beyond the borders of that state. In other words, the peaceful solution to civil war is an international interest. This has gradually been understood since 1989, and increasingly so since 2001.

6.6 Civil Society in Internal Conflict Resolution

The endings of civil wars, military regimes and state failures have some common traits. They all require the reconstruction of societies on principles which are inclusive, provide some broader participation in state affairs, and offer a sense of security to leaders and citizens alike. The political arrangements are necessary also for solving the problem of refugees that all civil wars, military repression and state failures produce. They lay a foundation for economic recovery. They can be used to provide the rise of a new kleptocracy. From the point of view of future conflicts, most important is the opening they may provide for an active civil society.

Many peace agreements have clauses stipulating the unimpeded return of refugees. There is a record of people moving back to their countries and areas. Also, in cases of victory, refugees begin to re-enter their country of origin. However, the outcome of the war may make it difficult for many to return. They may fear for their own safety, or they may be blocked from returning by groups who believe their return would hamper a particular cause. In the Cambodian conflict, refugees were stranded on the borders of Thailand for more than a decade. Only with the peace agreement in Paris in 1991 and with international assistance was it possible for them to return. On their return they became part of the new political system, not only with the right to vote, but also to organize themselves as pressure groups. In the aftermath of the genocide in Rwanda in 1994, the Tutsi army took control of the country. Fearing revenge, huge numbers of Hutus fled across the borders to Zaire (now the Democratic Republic of Congo) and Tanzania. Particularly in Zaire, they ended up in camps controlled by Hutu militias. When a war erupted in eastern Zaire, these militias withdrew further west. Refugees, freed from militia control, could return in large numbers to Rwanda 30 months after they left. The fears of revenge were less than the plight of the camps. Reports show that they rapidly reintegrated into society and the economy. Their role in the political life was minimal, however (Sollenberg and van Dassen 1998). Thus, the two examples illustrate the different positions of refugees. In the first example, the peace agreement allowed for their return as well as for an open political system. Measures were instituted to ensure this and they were integrated into the society, although they had been outside the country for a considerable period of time. In the second case, there was no peace deal, only a victory by one of the parties. The refugees could return, but on the conditions set by the victors. To return was still preferable for most.

The issue of the return of refugees is important, as this signifies, more than many other actions, that the extreme conditions that gave rise to their flight have been remedied to some extent. As most of the cross-border refugees in the world stem from conflict situations, peace is also important for handling the world's refugee problem. Stipulations in peace agreements or the conditions offered by victorious parties are important, and deserve closer scrutiny. As the civil wars end with a reconstruction of the same political unit, the return of the refugees needs to be as unrestricted as possible. This separates the refugee situation in civil wars from those in state formation wars (which are dealt with in Chapter 7), where the purpose often is to remove some people from a particular area in favour of others. Unlike civil wars, when refugees are regarded as legitimate citizens of the society, state formation conflicts sometimes distinguish between those with a right to the territory and those who will not be given such a right.

The conditions created by peace agreements are also significant for economic recovery. Without the predictability that peace accords and democratization provide, large-scale investments are not likely to come. It will instead risk making societies dependent on international assistance. The agreements since the Cold War are still too recent for making observations on their ability to actually change the economic conditions. The experience from democratization in South America in the 1980s suggests that economic development became positive. These experiences also point in the direction of the significance of a more participatory democratic society, for the stability of the society. An active civil society, that is, the existence of numerous independent (non-governmental), civilian-based organizations non-violently and freely pursuing civilian values on issues of societal significance, is important for sustaining democratic society (Putnam has termed this 'social capital', 1993). Thus, voluntary organizations, professional associations, student movements, trade unions, religious groupings, clans, tribes, women's movements, environmental groups, etc., would be part of such an independent civil society. It can be debated whether political parties, military-based associations, exclusivist groupings and sects are to be included as part of 'civil' society. In sum, it may all be important for democratic life, and it is definitely a part of the picture of what makes established democracies vibrant. Civil society in this form has been instrumental in bringing down autocratic regimes, as witnessed in Thailand in 1992, in Indonesia in 1998, in the Philippines and Yugoslavia in 2000, in Georgia in 2003, in Ukraine in 2004, Pakistan in 2008, and Tunisia and Egypt in 2011.

This is to suggest that a strong civil society can be a barrier to military control in society. It probably assumes that the civil state is seen, by the civil society, as a protector of civil values. It has been remarked that there was no public support for the government in the wake of the military takeover in Pakistan in October 1999. There were no celebrations of the coup either. The indifference of the population was remarkable. The ten-year experience of democratic rule in Pakistan did not seem to entrench institutions and did not result in general support for them. Instead, it appears that these institutions were identified with the political parties of the day and thus were part of a societal polarization. The disputes between leading civilian politicians were detached from the needs of the population. They were perceived as ways for leaders to gain access to governmental resources. The democratic system generated kleptocracy, not popular participation. In 2008 the military government met the same critique and was brought down, being replaced by a democratic regime that soon was exposed to the same concerns. Legitimate democracy requires social forces to improve honesty and accountability.

The implementation of peace agreements gives a special role to civil society. As we saw in Section 6.3, human rights provisions have been important ingredients in the peace accords since 1989. Their implementation directly depends on the existence of a civil society. Governments may institute investigatory commissions and ombudsmen. However, it has to be the civil society that takes up violations and brings them to the attention of the institutions. For this to happen, the environment must be sufficiently secure. The stronger the civil society, the more such security is created. The government may, by its actions, reduce security and thus act to curtail the civil society. In the implementation period after a peace agreement, there may often be a preference for not taking up human rights issues. The consolidation of the peace is given priority. This attitude is strengthened if some of the chief culprits escape from responsibility by the granting of amnesty or pardon. As we have seen, this has been part of some agreements.

However, few peace agreements prohibit the publication of material on what has happened. Human rights commissions often have the mandate of describing violations that have taken place. Such documentations are crucial, as are their publication and dissemination. As peace is consolidated, there may emerge various ways in which court cases can be pursued. The arrest of the former Chilean dictator General Augusto Pinochet in London in 1998, as a court in Spain demanded his extradition, is suggestive. There may be ways in which cases can be brought without jeopardizing the particular peace agreement. The international arena provides such a possibility. Also, after the consolidation of peace, peace agreements may be reworked or made obsolete. As observed, with the international criminal court, it provides the possibility of trials outside the country, making it possible to manage peace and justice at the same time. It is more likely that a civil society will pursue matters of justice. Governments may find excuses and other interests may impinge on their ability to act. There is, however, also a point in holding such trials inside the state where crimes have been committed. It can make the proceedings more accessible and credible to the local community. Since 1989, the options for war crime prosecution have been dramatically enlarged.

The international connections are increasingly important. The civil society of one country is often linked to those of other countries. The emerging international civil society provides new ways in which peace agreements, civilian control and state institutions can be sustained? First, it provides a network for early warning, if matters threaten to go in the wrong direction. The possibilities of instant communication mean that information can be transferred quickly. Thus, it may be difficult for actors to say that they 'did not know'. Second, it provides opportunities for quick action. There may be official visits which can be affected or used to raise particular civil concerns. There may be contracts which are about to be signed, and which can be blocked or postponed. Thus, it might be difficult for decision-makers to say that there 'was nothing that could be done'. International diplomatic conferences and meetings, to which issues can be brought, are constantly being held. These are only some examples of how the international civil society is increasingly able to affect the internal affairs of countries, in a direction that is favourable to peace, civilian control and functioning state institutions.

Recent experiences demonstrate the impact of the Internet and social media on the flow of information as well as the ability to mobilize a population.

Together with strong local organizations, this gives civil society a possibility of effecting change that opens up society and at the same time may improve the quality of peacemaking. A defender of the 1999 coup in Pakistan asked: 'Is democracy an end in itself or a means to an end? What do you do when democracy leads ineluctably to chaos?'(quoted by Safire 1997) The answer is that democracy is a way in which a society can be governed so that all competing interests are given a chance. It is not an end in itself, but a way in which inevitably arising conflicts can be steered in constructive directions. For many parties, it took a protracted war, a long period of military rule or the experience of state failure to realize this.

Further Readings

Go to the *Understanding Conflict Resolution* web page at www.sagepub.co.uk for free access to journal articles listed.

Diamond, L. J. 2005. 'Lessons from Iraq', *Journal of Democracy,* 16 (1): 9–23.
Mani, R. 1999. 'Promoting the Rule of Law in Post-conflict Societies', in L. Wohlgemuth et al. (eds), *Common Security and Civil Society in Africa.* Uppsala: Nordic Africa Institute. pp. 145–62.
Walter, B. F. 1997. 'The Critical Barrier to Civil War Settlement', *International Organization,* 51 (3): 335–64.
Walter, B. F. 2004. 'Does Conflict Beget Conflict. Explaining Recurring Civil War', *Journal of Peace Research* 41 (3): 371–88.

Notes

1 A note on the term 'civil war': In the United States it is a common label for the war of 1861–65. However, that was not directly a war about control over the central government. Instead, it was a conflict over state formation, where the right to secede was central. In some parts of the USA it is still referred to as the 'War between the States'.

2 In South Africa, democratization was the central issue, thus uniting organizations with interracial or non-racial composition with those representing a black majority. In Rwanda, the genocide was directed also against moderate Hutus, not only Tutsis. It is noteworthy that the powerholders, in both cases, were 'ethnically' more homogeneous than the opposition.

3 Licklider reports seven conflicts that ended too close to the cut-off date, of which four were terminated through negotiations. Adding them would make 18 negotiated endings out of 91 civil wars, that is, close to 20 per cent (Licklider 1995: 684). This confirms that peaceful endings are more common since the end of the Cold War.

4 Clearly there is a disagreement as to which endings are to be included as 'negotiated'. Stedman reports 11 cases for a longer period than the one for which Mason and Fett find 13 and Licklider 14.

5 For instance, there were smooth dynastic transitions in Jordan and Morocco in 1999. In effect, this is also what happened in Syria in 2000. The regime changes in Iraq in 2003, Tunisia and Egypt in 2011 are different stories.
6 The Chávez regime in Venezuela pursues a different course, however, giving the military new, civilian-style functions (Rohter 1999).
7 There are no examples of such threats to neighbours arising from peace agreements, however. In the cases of victories, there is evidence of such fear in neighbouring countries (meaning an interstate security dilemma is created as an result of an intra-state victory). In the 1990s this happened, for instance, in the case of Ethiopia and Eritrea, and following the victory of Kabila's forces in Zaire in 1997, which affected civil wars in Congo-Brazzaville and Angola.
8 This is the definition given by Snow: 'The failed states are those in which governance has broken down and virtual anarchy … has persisted across time' (Snow 1996: 100).

CONFLICT RESOLUTION IN STATE FORMATION CONFLICTS 7

7.1 State Formation Conflicts

State formation conflicts put a government against an identity-based, territorially focused opposition, where the key issue is the security of a particular group. Often such conflicts are tied to a geographical region of an existing state, but they may also involve questions of discrimination in the society at large. These conflicts are linked to some form of nationalism, and thus relate to European history of the nineteenth century, when nationalist ideologies were first presented. During the 1920s and the 1930s the League of Nations sought to find strategies for handling nationalistically defined conflicts. The formulation of the principle of national self-determination by US President Woodrow Wilson during the First World War was one such measure favouring nationalist aspirations. At the same time, there was a need to consolidate newly created states and avoid further fragmentation. Territorial integrity of existing states was the counter-principle. The tension between these two concepts coloured much of the twentieth century.

Nazi Germany included a racial project of uniting all Germans into one state, thus breaking up other states. It also wanted to develop hegemony based on German power and lineage. It resulted in the Second World War, the largest war ever fought on this planet. It also led to the Holocaust, primarily aimed at Jews wherever they were. This was the largest, most systematic killing of innocent people in history. Suffering and destruction were enormous. The lessons still have to be learned.

One conclusion was to make issues of ethnic homogeneity contentious. Exclusive nationalism was discredited. When international relations were reconstructed after the Second World War, it could be seen, for instance in the UN Charter, that territorial integrity was given a stronger role than self-determination. Expansionist intervention for nationalist reasons was not to be allowed and, thus, fewer state formation conflicts were to be expected. At the same time, democracy and human rights were given a stronger position in international relations, manifested, for instance, in the Universal Declaration of Human Rights in 1948. It was meant to counter authoritarian regimes, but some nationalist aspirations had a popular following. Let us review the record of state formation conflicts during the Cold War, then proceed to the present era.

State formation conflicts during the Cold War

For four decades, from 1948 to 1989, the territorial dividing lines that were in place after the Second World War remained unchanged. The last changes seemed to be the internationally agreed or accepted divisions of India and Palestine into two states, both decided on in 1947. Following this no new states which required the adjustment of borders were recognized. The demands for border revisions for national self-determination reasons that had plagued Europe and East Asia in the period between the world wars were no longer common, and certainly not legitimate. Still, a number of new states became independent. This took place through the agreed process of decolonization. It was a dramatic change in international relations, most clearly indicated in the change in membership of the United Nations. It went from around 50 members during its first years of existence to 170 as the Cold War ended. It was done almost entirely without border changes. A key aspect was that independence was granted within the borders drawn by the colonial powers. Even the creation of Bangladesh from Pakistan in 1971 took place within the lines of 1947. A remarkable stability was maintained at the same time as it allowed for change. This requires a closer analysis.

The arguments for maintaining territorial integrity and political sovereignty of the existing states, as written into the UN Charter, Article 2.4, were supported by an unusual international consensus on the preservation of existing territorial units. It was a result of the lessons drawn from the actions of Nazi Germany, Fascist Italy and militaristic Japan. All major powers had been victims of actions of one or several of these states. Furthermore, none of the five permanent members of the Security Council saw a benefit in supporting separatist movements in other countries. It could only complicate matters or even hit back at the major powers themselves.

The strongest supporter of non-interference and territorial integrity was the Soviet Union. It was also the country that had made the largest territorial gains as a result of the Second World War. This included the annexation of the Baltic states, the incorporation of territory which formerly was part of Eastern Poland and Germany, and taking over Bessarabia from Romania. The return of Soviet control often met severe resistance, notably in the Ukraine and Lithuania. The Soviet Union became a strong defender of a territorial *status quo*. Soviet concern led to constant actions to secure borders and political influence in Europe. The anti-colonial movements provided a potential dilemma and challenge as they argued in terms of self-determination. At the same time, these movements were anti-Western and anti-capitalist, thus being potential allies of the Soviet side in the Cold War. It made it necessary for the Soviet Union to support self-determination. Soviet support for this, however, applied only to colonial situations. A distinction had to be introduced between state formation conflicts in Europe, which were not to be allowed, and those in other parts of the world. Other major powers were also interested in such a distinction.

The consensus among the major powers was to describe anti-colonial conflicts as a particular category of conflict. The goal in the decolonization process was the creation of new states from the territories legally and militarily held by colonial powers. Thus, the issue was control over territory within what was, formally speaking, one state. Some colonial territories were highly integrated into the colonial 'motherland', even with representation in the National Assembly. This was true for Algeria and other French possessions in Africa, and it was the way the United Kingdom regarded Ireland, India and the dominions, for instance. Mostly, however, the legal status of colonial possessions made clear their subordinate position. The degree of integration was not comparable to those of territories closer to the centres. It was not too difficult to distinguish between what was a significant 'colony' and what was not. It also made it possible to distinguish between countries that did not have colonies and those that did. The United States and the Soviet Union put themselves in the first category; a host of European larger or smaller states were in the other. The USA actually could define itself as the first country to rebel against European colonialism; the Soviet Union argued that it was the first to break out of European capitalism through its Socialist revolution in 1917. Either way, the two dominant states of the time supported the decolonization process.

Decolonization conflicts constituted a sizable fraction of all conflicts during the Cold War period. They were located in the Middle East, South and Southeast Asia in the 1940s and 1950s, in North Africa in the 1950s, in sub-Saharan Africa in the 1960s and 1970s, in Pacific and Caribbean waters in the 1970s and 1980s. The momentum was strong and rolled irresistibly across the southern continents. There was also an important element of solidarity between the anti-colonial movements. With increasing success in achieving independence, they turned into a distinct and united force in international affairs. This was the origin of the Third World, a group which was independent and not aligned to either side in the Cold War. In particular, it became a strong coalition in international organizations building on the one state–one vote principle. Thus, decolonization profoundly changed international affairs.

It is important to observe that the nationalist movements for decolonization were often heterogeneous coalitions of ethnic groups, educated urban dwellers and visionary intellectuals. The focus was not on the rights of one particular ethnic group, but on the collectivity, united in a struggle against a dominant, mostly distant, white colonial power. Self-determination was a matter of removing one form of control, more than taking control by a particular, determined ethnic group that expected to replace colonial domination with its own power. The liberation movements that pursued anti-colonial struggles were fronts and coalitions. They built on an ability to unite different interests into one cause. Thus, this form of nationalism was different from the exclusive and chauvinistic version seen in the 1920s and 1930s. Furthermore, once the cause was achieved, the fronts often turned into one-party systems building legitimacy on the anti-colonial struggle. In matters of territorial change, they became highly conservative adherents to the principle of territorial integrity of the state. Thus, they did not challenge the established territorial consensus, but instead joined it (Kacowicz 1994: 67). One of the few states that pursued a traditional nationalist agenda was Somalia, aiming at the creation of one state for all Somalis. The merger between the former Italian and British possessions was achieved in 1960, but the continuation of the programme involved the country in war with Ethiopia and conflict with Kenya, for instance.

The decolonization era was seen as finished after the southern continents had been liberated from colonial domination. This verdict, of course, depends on the definition of colonialism. The one used to separate 'colonialism' from traditional occupation, annexation and conquest contains several elements. The distinguishing feature is that a metropolis exerts control over a territory populated by people of a different ethnic background, located at a considerable distance and geographically separated from the metropolis. Some settlement of the centre's population in the colony may also have taken place, creating an interest of a settler community. The most obvious differentiation between colonialism and traditional conquest, it has been said, is the saltwater between the metropolis and the periphery. With this definition, the colonization by Western and Southern European powers of the Americas, Africa, the Middle East and Asia, is a distinct phenomenon. Furthermore, it arose at a particular historical moment, often associated with victorious capitalism. These elements distinguish colonialism from traditional military conquest of a neighbouring territory. However, only with such a definition is decolonization a finished process. If another form of colonization, such as traditional conquest, is included, it is not. Also, if other elements are included, such as economic dependence, colonialism and neocolonialism, it is still an important feature. Furthermore, the notion of self-determination was always wider than its application only to colonial situations. In the 1920s it was applied to adjacent territories in Central Europe. Thus, the colonial era may not have been finished as easily as is often argued.

There are, in fact, a number of definitional questions that make this a matter of general interest. For instance, was the issue of British control over Ireland to be seen as colonialism or traditional conquest? It certainly took place before the phenomenon of colonialism was defined, but the different elements in the definition would apply, including colonial-type settlements. The Irish revolt and the creation of the Republic of Ireland preceded the international movement of decolonization, and was seldom seen to be part of it, but in essence aimed at the same goal.

Another case is the Soviet annexation of the three independent Baltic countries in 1940. The centre of Moscow was distant, control was ethnically separate and there were deliberate settlements of Russians in the areas. There was no saltwater between the metropolis and these areas, but would that change many of the consequences? Certainly, the Soviet Union voted in favour of the famous decolonization resolution in the Fifteenth UN General Assembly in 1960 (Resolution No. 1514) in the belief that it did not apply to its own situation. It could argue that the annexation had taken place after colonialism, was done under a banner of socialism and that the Baltic states became 'sovereign' units within one functioning union. During the Cold War, the charge of colonialism against the Soviet Union seldom received significant support.

A similar challenge could be made to the United States where, for instance, Hawaii and Alaska became states with equal rights only the year before the UN resolution was passed. The two territories were defined not as colonial possessions, but as integral parts of the United States of America. They had freely entered into this association. Certainly, their accession to the union was done democratically. But in that case, it meant that democratic procedures could have more weight than decolonization. Actually, the second UN General Assembly resolution on this issue (Resolution 1541) did suggest forms of decolonization other than independence. During the Cold War, however, independence was seen as the basic form of decolonization and the experiences of Hawaii and Alaska were seldom part of the debate. It was, of course, feared that such arguments could be used by settler communities to block decolonization.

Challenges to the definition of colonialism are many and not only theoretical. The discussion may seem obsolete today, but some conflicts have their roots in how decolonization was handled also among the newly independent countries in the Third World. An early challenge was posed by Biafra, in the southeastern part of Nigeria, dominated by the Igbo community. It declared independence in 1967, following massacres of ethnic kin in other parts of Nigeria. It led to one of the most destructive wars in Africa. Some African states recognized Biafra on humanitarian grounds (for instance, Tanzania). Others feared that their own states could meet similar threats and supported the central government. Biafra was defeated in 1970. In the same year, East Pakistani leaders objected to the control of the country from the distant centres of West Pakistan. Military repression followed, a war resulted, India intervened and by 1971 Bangladesh was created as a new state. West Pakistan acquiesced. After this, international recognition followed. This outcome said that if the metropolis accepts independence, so will the international community.

In the Helsinki Final Act of 1975, signed by all states directly party to or neutral in the Cold War, only peacefully agreed changes of territory in Europe were accepted. The story of East Pakistan was not to repeat itself in Europe, or anywhere else. This was strongly encountered by the Eritrean liberation movements which demanded independence from Ethiopia. They argued that their country was also a victim of colonialism, first under Italian rule, then under Ethiopia. This was accepted neither by other African states nor by the larger international community of the time. The established view of colonialism made that clear. To other states, such wars threatened to invite fragmentation and weakened state authority. They were dangerous precedents. The consensus on the abolition of 'saltwater colonialism' did not extend to questioning established borders. Eritrea did not gain its independence until after the Cold War.

State formation conflicts after the Cold War

State formation conflicts after the Cold War have some features in common with those witnessed in the earlier era. They are often seen as justified anti-colonial and/or historical struggles for self-determination (the rebel perspective) or fights to preserve territorial integrity of a state for the benefit of all inhabitants (the government's view). However, they have less simple solutions. The cutting of a formal link across distant waters is no longer an available option. The centres in today's states are not easily allowing dissolution of their territories, as the colonial metropolises were willing and able to do after the Second World War. One reason is that the territorial cutting points are difficult to locate and that people are interspersed throughout the entire territory. Sometimes these are recent and deliberately created settler communities, such as the Jewish settlers in the West Bank (and until 2005 also in Gaza); sometimes they go further back in history, as has been the case with Serbs in different parts of former Yugoslavia. Still, the number of new states has continued to increase. In 20 years, the UN membership increased to 192 (by 2010), that is adding more than 20 states since 1989. It is a rate of state creation that is comparable to the Cold War era. A new aspect is that new states are mostly found in Europe. This is the continent which already had the highest incidence of states in relation to its territory. The opposite effect of state formation, (re)unification of states, has also taken place (Germany, Yemen), but the net effect is still an increase in the number of states. In addition, there are today (2011) about a dozen unrecognized *de facto* states (such as Northern Cyprus, Somaliland, Abkhazia and South Ossetia) as well as Taiwan, Western Sahara, Palestine and Kosovo, to which a larger number of countries have extended diplomatic recognition.

Still these trends in state formation have been remarkably peaceful. Three-quarters of the new, recognized states were created without a major war, as was also true for the decolonization process. Neither the ending of the Soviet Union nor Czechoslovakia required a major armed conflict. This, of course, was not the experience of the dissolution of socialist Yugoslavia. It is interesting to ask why the processes were so different.

The main reason can be found in the attitude of the centre of the state being dissolved. When Boris Yeltsin took over leadership in August 1991, it was on a platform of Russian independence from the Soviet Union. The centre, in other words, was in favour of dismantling its own empire.

In Yeltsin's view, the Soviet state had deliberately discriminated against Russia in order to have the cooperation of the other republics. It was claimed that Soviet authorities had invested more in the non-Russian areas. Russia's independence would be beneficial to Russia itself. Thus, there was no reason for Russia to object. Russian populations outside Russia would be in less danger if the demands for self-determination were met. In fact, Russia had an interest in speeding up the process. By the end of 1991, the Soviet Union ceased to exist. In a similar way, the largely Czech leadership of Czechoslovakia did not object to Slovakia leaving the shared federation, and a peaceful separation was in effect from 1993. Although there were no water divides, the breakup could follow what used to be internal administrative lines.

In Yugoslavia, the story was different. The Serb leadership objected to the dissolution of the state and acted militarily to prevent it. It feared the consequences for a dispersed Serb population, but it was also a matter of self-interest. Following the demise of Soviet-style socialism, the regime built on exclusive nationalism to keep itself in power. The resulting inability to find an agreed formula for dissolution involved the area in four armed conflicts in less than ten years (in Slovenia in 1991, in Croatia in 1991–92 and 1995, in Bosnia-Herzegovina in 1992–95 and in Kosovo in 1998–99). The consequences of the wars for the Serb population were uniformly disastrous. The results were the creation of new states, a separated region turning into a state (Kosovo), a reconfiguration of the state into a federation between Serbia and Montenegro, and eventually also its dissolution (in 2006). The borderlines sometimes could follow previous administrative divides and sometimes (as in Bosnia) were new creations. Major population movements resulted, and the chances for people to return to their homes were low, affecting also the Serb populations.

The conclusion from these experiences is that a leadership that favours or accepts the dissolution of a state can accomplish a peaceful transfer of authority. It requires that it sees this to be in its own interest. Often, however, the self-interest is different. Thus, a leadership that is against such a policy, while meeting an equally determined opposition, is likely to face a protracted conflict. Both government and opposition should have an interest in finding better solutions.

The post-Cold War period shows that there have been more than 50 armed state formation conflicts. These have put an incumbent government against a regionally based, armed opposition demanding a radically different status for a particular territory. The demands concern autonomy, federalism, independence or joining a neighbouring state. Often they followed a weakening of state authority, with groups demanding further autonomy (Chechen groups in Russia) or a return to centralization (the Sunni-based rebellions in post-Saddam Hussein Iraq demanding a stronger centre, while Kurdish groups and many Shia Arabs wanted more power to the constituent parts). The armed phase of some of these conflicts predate the end of the Cold War. This is the case, for instance, for Northern Ireland, the Basque provinces, the Kurdish disputes and the Palestinian conflict. The same can be said of conflicts over Namibia in Southern Africa, and several of the conflicts in India, Sri Lanka and Burma. Also in Southeast Asia there are protracted conflicts, such as those over Mindanao (the Philippines) and East Timor (Indonesia). The examples show that most regions of the world have some experience of state formation conflicts. They also indicate that the conflicts may become long and drawn out. The ferocity of some conflicts has been extraordinary. The conflicts were previously regarded as marginal, belonging to an earlier era, and thus not important to attend to. They were neglected and did not fit the established paradigm of state formation conflicts. They also had some features which made them different from anti-colonialism.

The actors appeared to be driven by sentiments of self-determination and anti-colonialism that were sharper than in many decolonization struggles during the Cold War. In particular, the close connection between political demands and certain ethnic identities was striking. The new political fronts and constellations were pursuing the causes for one ethnic group within a nationalist umbrella, rather than cutting across many identities in a multi-ethnic nationalist formation. They played on sentiments that were largely avoided in the anti-colonial struggles. It appeared that the new conflicts were neither new in terms of their history, nor accepted the conclusions on the dangers of nationalist war that had governed Cold War thinking. The notion of 'ethnic conflict' came to be associated with this type of conflict. This notion, furthermore, became synonymous with separatism and the quest for ethnically homogeneous states. All this appeared to throw the world back to the pre-1939 era.

It is necessary to reiterate that most of the new state formation conflicts were located in Europe. It strongly affected a European self-understanding of having successfully left a dark time of chauvinist nationalism. Europe was not prepared to deal with this new reality. Africa, which often is understood as a continent of ethnic conflict, actually had fewer such conflicts.[1] In Africa, opponents seldom directly challenged established state units. Differences in regional, historical or cultural identities resulted in struggles over government rather than in the breakup of states. The same was true of the Middle East, where the Kurdish striving for independence was the only one following historically and linguistically given lines. The Palestinian situation is, for instance, not a quest for the breakup of an existing Arab state, but has features of an anti-colonial struggle. Thus, it is possible for Arab countries to support the Palestinian cause for self-determination and statehood at the same time as they oppose Kurdish desires for similar goals.

The state formation conflicts of the post-Cold War era often involved neighbour states. This was novel, as states previously avoided entangling themselves, at least openly, in state formation conflicts in neighbouring countries. There used to be little official sympathy for separatist movements. In the post-Cold War period, such inhibitions have declined and neighbours have been heavily engaged in what goes on beyond their borders. Furthermore, in the Cold War era, there was a measure of solidarity across regions and even continents, between different liberation movements. The anti-colonial ambition united them. In the present epoch, this is not the case. Each struggle is separate from others. Each nationalist struggle sees itself as, in principle, unique and only a few generalizations are made, for instance, if the same ethnic group is involved in several different struggles, or if the opponent is the same. The search for international allies builds on allegiances that can be exploited, rather than on a sentiment of being part of the same global cause. For instance, there are reportedly connections between Taliban leaders in Afghanistan and Chechen groups building on Muslim identity, and Christian support in the West for Christian groups in Southern Sudan.

Thus, the state formation conflicts confronting the international community after the Cold War have some features which are different from the colonial experience. This has had an impact on their solution. Decolonization struggles ended in the withdrawal of the metropolis. This ending has not been available in conflicts without obvious geographical features that separate the opponents. Other dividing lines have been resorted to, with mixed success. Often, solutions have to be found within the confines of a shared territory. This may seem difficult. Still, a most remarkable phenomenon is that such conflicts have found solutions through negotiations. Let us turn to these.

Peace agreements in the post-Cold War era

There are 17 countries that have seen peace agreements on territorial issues after the Cold War, all agreed by the parties and with some lasting impact. They are listed in Table 7.1 overleaf.

The settlements of Table 7.1 are testimony to the possibility of finding solutions to conflicts which have a long history, and where the understanding of that history seldom is shared among the parties. Different, if not contradictory, historical narratives are integral to the conflicts. Thus, the peace agreements are part of a shift in historical relationships. That is also often the way they are understood by the parties themselves. This historical dimension is something that sets state formation conflicts apart. They often concern peoples that live close to each other. They are aware and informed of each other. In most of the conflicts there is evidence of close neighbourly cooperation. There are also accounts of intimidation and repression. These are narratives passed from one generation to the next, thus solidifying themselves as stereotypes of the other side. The ambivalence of neighbourly cooperation and tension may be a factor that makes these conflicts particularly volatile. It is easier to mobilize action along these dimensions than

Table 7.1   Peace agreements in state formation conflicts since the Cold War

Conflict location	Years of agreement	Number of agreements
Angola (Cabinda)	2006	1
Bangladesh (Chittagong Hill Tracts)	1997	1
Bosnia-Herzegovina (Croat)	1994	1
Bosnia-Herzegovina (Serb Republic)	1995	1
Comoros (Anjuan)	2000, 2001, 2003	3
Croatia (Serb)	1995	1
Georgia (Abkhazia)	1994	1
India (Bodoland)	1993	1
India (Tripura)	1993	1
Indonesia (Aceh)	2002, 2005	2
Indonesia (East Timor)[a]	1999	1
Israel (Palestine)	1993, 1994, 1995 1997, 1998, 1999, 2007	8
Mali (Azawad)	1991, 1992	2
Moldova (Dniestr)	1997	1
Niger (Air, Azawad)	1993, 1994, 1995	3
PNG (Bougainville)	1991, 1994, 2001	3
Philippines (Mindanao)	1996	1
Senegal (Casamance)	2004	1
UK (Northern Ireland)	1998	1
Yugoslavia (Kosovo)[b]	1999	1
Yugoslavia (Slovenia)	1991	1

Note: Peace agreements in armed conflicts concerning the control over territory in a state, active in the period 1989–2009. The table includes treaties that have been signed, that regulate (resolve or find a process for the solution of) the incompatibility, and have been concluded between the warring parties, and ends armed conflict behaviour. Cease-fire agreements are not included. The parties are listed in English alphabetical order. Sudan is included in Table 6.1
[a]This agreement was concluded by other actors, implemented by warring parties.
[b]Different agreements signed by different parties, conflict terminated 1999.

Source: Uppsala Conflict Data Program Conflict Encyclopedia; Table 4.2 in this book, and Högbladh 2006.

others. This has given rise to the notion of an 'ethnic security dilemma', as a conflict-driving force (Kaufman 1996; Kaufmann 1996; Melander 1999). On the local level, minority groups will be insecure *vis-à-vis* a dominant group, and from this tension, militant action can begin, sometimes quickly accelerating conflict dynamics. For instance, if violence takes place against members of one group, this can (correctly or not) be attributed to the other group as a whole. That group in turn will take action to prepare its own defence, which then – to the first group – confirms expected hostile intentions and justifies pre-emptive action. Such dynamics have been reported from some, but not all, conflicts in Bosnia-Herzegovina (Melander 1999).

The ethnic security dilemma operates on a local level, making it exploitable by leaders. This is parallel to the internal security dilemma described in Sections 6.2 and 6.4, as well as the interstate situation for which it was originally developed (Chapter 5). Peacemaking in state formation conflicts faces problems which are manifestly different from those encountered in other types of conflict. To these problems belong the return of refugees to their original homes, from which they may have been forced out and replaced by others. Comparing Tables 6.1 and 7.1 we can also note that the agreements on state formation conflicts more frequently appear to solve the problem, rather than leading to a process of renewed conflict and settlement. These agreements are fewer, less frequently challenged and thus not reworked. This illustrates some of the differences between internal conflict over government and territory. The former deal with constitutions and political arrangements that are likely to change, also under 'normal' circumstances. Solutions to territorial issues, however, are more permanent: a border is drawn, a federal structure is created, thus changing the conditions for future politics in a way that is more difficult to change once again. There is irreversibility to such agreements. The agreements, in other words, may be fewer, more difficult to reach, but also involve more lasting changes that are even visible on a geographical map. The only 'true' settlement process is the one over Palestine, with an unmatched set of consecutive agreements.

The record of peace agreements means that close to one-third of the conflicts of this type have reached an agreed settlement or an agreement on a process to such a settlement, comparing Tables 4.1 and 7.1. This is of particular interest, as victories are less common. For the same period, there are only a handful of situations where one side has clearly defeated the other, forcing, for instance, its withdrawal, capitulation or surrendering of demands on the disputed territory. Among the victories are, in effect, Slovenia's and Croatia's exits from Yugoslavia, although involving negotiations and agreements as well (1991, 1992), Eritrea winning Ethiopia's acceptance of its independence (agreed in 1993), India's subjugation of the Khalistan independence movements in Punjab (by 1993), Yemen's victory over South Yemen's attempt at secession (in 1994) and Sri Lanka's victory over the Tamil Tigers (LTTE) (in 2009). The few examples show that victory is not easily achieved. The commitments are strong on the opposite sides of the divides. Some of the victories include mass-eviction of the members of the losing side (most notably the eviction of Serbs from Krajina, Croatia, in 1995).

Several of the peace agreements in Table 7.1 are linked to the decolonization process and, as a consequence, to the United Nations: Palestine and East Timor. Before 1989, there were also such agreements for Namibia and Western Sahara. With the exception of Israel/Palestine, the security dilemma has stemmed from distant control, not from the direct influence of locals over locals. This is true for Namibia's independence as well as for the agreement on Western Sahara. The Palestinian struggle has been seen in that light, as has the East Timor conflict. The internationalized disputes over the status of some of these territories emanated from them being mandates by the League of Nations (Namibia, then known as Southwest Africa, a former German colony; and Palestine), and thus legally a concern for the UN as the successor. South Africa and Britain held these mandates. Western Sahara was a colonial territory under Spain; East Timor was under Portugal. Both colonial powers gave up control in 1975. Morocco then took control over Western Sahara, its neighbour to the South, and Indonesia occupied East Timor, as it already held West Timor. These actions were resisted by local movements and gave rise to considerable international opposition. Through the deliberate settlement of people, local ethnic security dilemmas were created. This has been most obvious in the case of Palestine, with an eviction of the former inhabitants, a massive settlement of Jewish immigrants and, following the outcome of the war in 1967, Jewish settlements also in the West Bank and Gaza (until Israel's unilateral withdrawal in 2005). In these areas, particularly strong escalation could be observed during the First Intifada (1987–93) and even more so during the Second Intifada (approximately 2000–06), two major uprisings of Palestinians. These issues continue to be of international concern.

The UN played an important role in the search for solutions for Namibia, Western Sahara and East Timor. The conflict over Namibia was the first to come to a generally accepted ending. Western Sahara is to have a referendum, but the composition of the electorate has not yet been determined. East Timor became an independent country, Timor Leste, in 2002. This was the will expressed by the overwhelming majority in the referendum of August 1999, leading to carnage by Indonesia-supported militias, but also to a UN peacekeeping operation, first by Australia, to protect the agreed outcome. In the Palestinian issue, the UN has mostly been on the sidelines. Particularly since the Camp David agreements in 1978–79 between Egypt and Israel, the United States has been the leading outside actor for a settlement. However, we can still conclude that in conflicts relating to decolonization, as defined in the Cold War era, the UN is likely to have a particular role.

UN involvement has a peculiar effect. Leading actors were not party to certain agreements. This is the case when the conflicts are built on decolonization frameworks. This means that the actors were sufficiently informed and accepted what was agreed, but nevertheless they did not sign documents. This is true for Namibia, where SWAPO, the leading liberation movement for Namibia, was not a signatory, and for East Timor, where the agreement was concluded between Indonesia and Portugal, as the former colonial power. In both cases, the UN was party to negotiations and implementation. It is not likely to be of great consequence, as these very actors were heavily involved in the following implementations, and were treated as legitimate parties.

It is also important to note that several settlements were reached without the input of the international community (Mali, Niger, Mindanao, and Chittagong Hill Tracts). The issues were seen by the governments as internal affairs. This view was accepted internationally. For a long time,

Britain resisted international participation in the settlement of the conflict in Northern Ireland, but eventually an arrangement was found involving the Republic of Ireland as well as the United States. It still is managed outside any international or regional organization. Similarly, Indonesia did not want to see Aceh as a parallel to East Timor, and thus did not involve the UN as a third party. Instead, a group led by the former President of Finland, Martti Ahtisaari, brokered a deal in Helsinki and its implementation was supervised by EU observers. The great tsunami disaster of December 26, 2004, leading to the demise of almost a quarter of a million people on Sumatra, contributed to galvanize an interest in a settlement. For the conflict in Chechnya, for which a cease-fire agreement was found in 1996, to be overturned by 1999, Russia has refused to have any international participation. It is likely to be difficult for international organizations to get involved if it is resisted by a major power that also happens to be party to the conflict. As we can see, however, small or weak states also may prefer to deal on their own with their state formation conflicts and they may succeed in finding agreement.

In contrast, the conflicts over Yugoslavia and the settlements agreed to in 1994 and 1995 all became highly internationalized. The same is true for the war in Kosovo in 1999 where there was considerable negotiation in the events leading to the unilateral declaration of independence in 2008. The European Union, the Organization for Security and Cooperation in Europe (OSCE), the UN, NATO and a number of NGOs were heavily engaged in the search for solutions. Although it is generally true that solutions to state formation conflicts have considerable international interest, this does not automatically lead to international involvement in the settlement process. In the Balkan conflicts, governments and oppositions alike appealed for international support and, thus, succeeded in internationalizing the conflicts. It led to isolation of one party, Yugoslavia under Slobodan Milosevic. Only after his resignation in 2000 was isolation ended. Still there is no agreement by Serbia to Kosovo's independence, although the *de facto* situation is acknowledged.

These outcomes do not suggest that there is now international consensus in support of national self-determination for state sovereignty as a way of solving the ethnic security dilemma. The international actors were unwilling to endorse this principle for the settlement of the conflict in Kosovo. However, there may no longer be as firm a consensus on the ways of settling state formation conflicts. The decolonization principle is still applied in some instances. The notion of prior recognition by the previous centre can be used in others. The democratic principle – that is, to accept what the majority of the population in a particular territory favours – has been applied in some instances. But there are contradictions. Bosnia-Herzegovina was recognized as a sovereign state although there was no prior recognition from the previous unit, Yugoslavia. East Timor, Western Sahara and South Sudan in 2011 were given the right to vote on independence, but why would this not apply to Kosovo or to Chechnya?

In Section 7.2 we discuss the possibility of finding solutions to identity conflicts which do not directly involve a territorial issue. In Section 7.3 the different forms of territorial divisions within existing states are presented, particularly autonomy and federalism. Section 7.4 discusses possible solutions in conjunction with international integration, and Section 7.5 reflects on state formation conflicts and democracy.

7.2 Identity Discrimination and Conflict Resolution

It is often assumed that, at the heart of intra-state conflicts over territory, the experience of discrimination is found. Groups and peoples who will not have their rights respected by the governmental authorities, according to their own understanding of what such rights should include, are likely to become dissatisfied and this gives rise to action. This way of understanding ethnic conflicts is an application of the social frustration model presented in Section 3.3. A fuller explanation would rest on all the models given in Chapter 3. The argument would then be reformulated in the following way. There are certain basic needs that are not met. These may not necessarily be material, but also immaterial, for instance, cultural. Often, in reality, there is a close connection between these two. For instance, if a person cannot use his or her own language to pursue a particular grievance with official authorities, this person is at a distinct disadvantage against those who command it, and thus the person is more likely not to receive a fair share of, say, social services or business deals. Repeated experiences of such differentiated treatment may lead some in the identity group to mobilize for action. Thus, a leadership emerges and the options are calculated according to the rationality of the resulting movement. Actions are initiated, conflict escalates and after a while a state finds itself in an increasingly complicated conflict situation.

What are the needs that could give rise to such dramatic escalation? They are not obvious from the outset. There are some 6,700 languages in the world. Many are rapidly disappearing. Some argue that only with a state is it possible to protect languages and, thus, linguistic nationalism has become a feature in analysis. People's identity is sometimes strongly connected to language. The linguistic differences may be small, as is the case between Croatian, Serbian and Bosnian, but they may be sufficient for locating a significant element in an identity profile. However, it should be clear from the outset that language is not the typical factor that makes one state different from another. There are a great number of states that share the same language, although differently spoken. English is the official language of a number of states, as is the case with French, Spanish, Portuguese, Russian, Arabic and Chinese. A number of languages are strongly related, making it possible to understand spoken idioms across borders. This is the case among the Nordic countries and between India and Pakistan (Hindi/Urdu). Also, there are states that manage well with two (Finland), four (Switzerland) or more than 20 official languages (India). The close connection between state and language is, thus, not as strong as might first be thought. Although nationalism often invokes history and language, conflict formation and the quest for a state probably has more complicated origins. Societies clearly are able to accommodate considerable language diversity, and states can survive with other states using the same language.

There are other identity carriers that might result in violence-prone discrimination. Among those are access to education, right of worship, discrimination built on race, gender, sexual orientation, legal discrimination, economic discrimination, oppression by police or military forces dominated by other groups, lack of access to public administration, lack of political representation and human rights, difficulty to cross borders, etc. In short, many of the matters mentioned in the Universal Declaration of Human Rights from 1948 and the Convention on Human Rights from 1966 are potential elements in the escalation of conflict. Most likely, none of these, alone, would give a full explanation. In a given state, there may be groups discriminated against for different reasons which find sufficiently common cause to combine in support of a particular movement, whether this movement is in power or a challenger. Any society is likely to react early and search for appropriate measures. This means that escalation is not necessarily driven by the movements pressing the anti-discriminatory demands, but by the government's reactions to these demands. If the reactions go in the predicted direction, that is, repressive, dismissive or intolerant, it is likely that an opposition movement gains strength. If that attitude, furthermore, is one of using violent repression, legal harassment and special sanctions, the chance of escalation is likely to increase. Thus, the most appropriate early-warning indicators would be the government response to identity-based demands.

There are many options for governments, and only some result in an escalation of conflict. Early action for accommodation would have the greatest chance of channelling such demands into constructive societal development. A responsive government has to consider demands from many groups and, in a resource-scarce society, this dilemma will be more difficult to handle. Table 7.2 presents some ways in which such demands are dealt with in responsive societies. These solutions can be reached with the help of the seven ways of conflict resolution given in Section 3.5. They particularly aim at finding compromises and horse-trading between competing demands arising from discrimination.

To remove discrimination for one group may affect rights of other groups; simply replacing the rights of one group with the rights of another is no solution. It perpetuates discrimination. Thus, measures have to transcend discrimination in ways where the reconciliation of opposing demands are seen to be of interest to all groups as well as to the general concern of the state. Legitimate principles have to be found. There has to

Table 7.2 Solutions to non-territorial, identity-driven conflicts

Incompatibility	Solution
Acceptance of language	Several official and administrative languages Shared 'superlanguage', a lingua franca
Access to educational system	Several parallel systems of equal quality Recruitment quota for unified system
Application of religion, morals	Freedom of religion Secular state, separated from religion
Legal system	Shared legal system, with certain allowances Separate legal system for defined groups
Economic inferiority	Positive action for specified period of time Earmarked resources for regions or sectors
Access to natural resources (land, water, subsurface)	National law with specified conditions Local administration of natural resources
Population movements (migration, refugees)	Protection for indigenous settlement Rights of return Significance of documentation
Access to police, armed forces	Recruitment quota for unified system High admission requirements Training in human rights Transparent procedures for redressing issues Disbanding of questionable forces
Access to administration	Recruitment quota for unified system High admission requirements
Oversight of implementation	Independent ombudsmen International review
Political representation	Minority rights, minimum representation Electoral system with equal access
Constitution	Human and minority rights Guarantee against rapid constitutional change
Human rights	Human rights for all, positive action for some
International transparency	Review of implementation International access accepted

be a commitment to review the actions after a time with a chance of revision. The procedures for instituting solutions are important. Imposition, even of reasonable propositions, will not do. Imposition may, sooner or later, be seen as violation in itself.

Practical applications of the solutions in Table 7.2 can be found all over the world. They are attempts to handle difficult conflicts. Issues can be resolved in ways which are satisfactory to the involved parties. On the whole, there are two basic strategies used. One is inclusive and integrative, trying to make all groups work within the same unified system. It requires particular care so that all concerns are met, the approach is understood by all involved and it finds a practical application that functions in daily life. Another approach is more exclusive and decentralized. Special arrangements are made for particular groups. The overall framework remains the same, but some individuals are treated positively differently from others in order to remedy past grievances and create an equal platform for the future. Each of these strategies can be evaluated, with respect to its short- and long-term impact on society.

The solutions have not often been instituted as preventive measures in order to avoid future conflict. Rather, they are the result of considerable thought and struggle, particularly by the groups that have a strong grievance against the way society functions at a particular moment in time. Issues of discrimination have given rise to considerable internal conflict the world over. Much conflict action has been non-armed and has affected government policies, without resulting in civil wars. A model-forming experience was the civil rights movement in the United States in the 1960s. The demands by the African-American population changed politics locally and nationally. It also changed the reality for all segments of the population. It was pursued largely with non-violent means. The Nobel Peace Prize was given to a prominent leader, Martin Luther King, Jr. The creativity of this movement led to an interest in non-violent methods. The systematization of such methods made the experiences useful in other contexts, injecting new thinking for other struggles (Sharp 1973).

However, violence was also part of the picture. Sometimes it was spontaneous and badly organized, but nevertheless highly destructive, as in the riots that followed the assassination of Dr King in 1968. At other times it was more deliberate, and regarded as a necessary defence, as advocated by the Black Panther Party. This resulted in gunfights with police units as well as between members of the movement. It was seen as a necessary, revolutionary, way for changing society. It increased the pressure on the government and threatened to turn the issue into a civil war. Severe discrimination, in other words, could lead to the types of conflict we discussed in Chapter 6. In the US case, however, it seldom translated into a demand for secession. This is worth exploring one step further.

It takes two to conflict. Thus, we have to observe that discrimination in a society affects most groups in a particular state. Some are favoured and others are discriminated against. Thus, there are vested interests in discriminatory practices, which makes it possible to maintain such policies over a long period of time. Regimes desiring to keep power may exploit ethnic divides for their own advantage, as was witnessed in the Milosevic reign in Yugoslavia (1987–2000). Such regimes are likely to be repressive and manipulative in order for a leading group to retain advantages. They may be ruthless when meeting resistance. They can play different groups against each other. Some can be invited to join the government, others can be severely harassed. Thus, opposition will be diluted and divided. It is difficult

to organize opposition under such circumstances. It requires strategies that
focus on particular matters and an ability to pursue them with vigour and
creativity. Only then is it likely that governments become interested in solutions. Sometimes they implement reforms which are genuine; many times
they remain window dressing. Achieving an end to discrimination requires
an understanding of how power is exerted in a society, and whether that
power structure is affected by measures such as those listed in Table 7.2.
Ending discrimination, in other words, is not only a matter of possessing the
right instruments, but also in applying them in the right ways.

Matters may develop differently if there is a significant, regional concentration of a particular group. It may provide a closer-knit experience of discrimination. It makes resistance easier. It may also invite more repression,
as the incumbent power realizes this potential. This, furthermore, makes
the fate of the area more important for those who are outside this territory.
Regional concentration of discriminated groups may provide for escalation. If, in that region, there are also members of other groups, which in fact
benefit from the policies, an additional element is added. The conflict over
Kosovo illustrates this.

In the Kosovo conflict, a key Albanian demand was access to education
in the Albanian language. The actions instituted by the Serb authorities in
1989–90 in Kosovo meant a reduced, public role for Albanians. Instead,
the Serb language gained in significance, even to the point where street
signs were changed. Instead of Albanian street names on the top, Serb
names were given that position (Magnusson 1999: 64–5). This signified
a loss of control for Albanians in running their own affairs in Kosovo, at
the same time as they could see the Serb inhabitants getting better access.
Street signs were daily reminders of a new society. From the Serb point
of view, however, this was simply redressing the previous situation, when
Albanians had dominated. Thus, the educational issue became a symbol of
what the conflict was all about: self-rule, but for whom?

The Albanians were the majority in the province, Serbs argued that
Kosovo was part of the Republic of Serbia (the largest unit in the Federal
Republic of Yugoslavia, as the country was called at the time) and, thus,
Serbs were in the majority. After Kosovo lost its autonomy, the Kosovo
Albanian leadership refused to cooperate with Serb and Yugoslav authorities, as this would imply the recognition of their legitimacy. The non-
violent methods were supported, but in late 1997 armed groups began to
appear. By 1999 there was full-fledged war in the country, including NATO
bombardments all over Yugoslavia. This resulted in an international administration, the armed groups were reconstituted as a force under civilian control, but relations between the remaining Serbs and the Albanian majority
remained tense. Kosovo's independence in 2008 has not yet changed this.

From this history, we can conclude that the issues of discrimination can be
closely linked to political and territorial control. Tight connections between
issues, such as those listed in Table 7.2, are likely to escalate a situation into
a state formation conflict. This, furthermore, would be particularly strong if

some of the issues concern territorial control. The discriminatory experience provides the frustration, the territorial concentration, the shared community, the boundaries, the majority–minority relationship and, if the territory is close to an international border, it provides for access to weapons, finances and international assistance (Cornell 2002).

These arguments find support in the work by Ted R. Gurr (1993), which shows that the removal of autonomy has been strongly associated with the onset of a higher level of armed conflict within a decade. Probably, the loss of control is in itself the most distinguishing experience a political unit can suffer, if it is done without the consent of the governed. In the Kosovo case, there was no consultation and it was done with intentions that were threatening to the majority population in the area. That questions of discrimination were important in the conflicts can be seen from a cursory review of the peace agreements in Table 7.1. It is possible to find strong identity groups as governmental and, particularly, as opposition actors. All these cases concerned areas where the population had a shared experience of losing territorial control, recently or in historical times. This provides an element of self-righteousness that can sustain a political battle. The forms of discrimination may vary. It can be based on race, as in the case of Namibia. Negative memories went back to German colonization. It can be based on religion, as in the case of Mindanao, an area with a large Muslim population finding itself subject to discrimination from a Christian majority of the Philippines. Again, this dates back to Spanish colonial conquest. It can be based on economic opportunities, as was the way the civil rights movement began in the late 1960s in Northern Ireland (housing was a first key issue).

Also, in the cases of state formation conflicts resulting in victories, we find similar experiences. Eritrea was initially defined as an equal partner in union with Ethiopia, but was relegated to a province by the Ethiopian government in 1962. Tamils continue to point to their exclusion from political life in Sri Lanka, perhaps made even more severe after the defeat of the Tamil Tigers (LTTE) in 2009. In this, as in many other cases, there are alternative movements, something to be dealt with in Section 7.5. Since the fall of Saddam Hussein the Iraqi Shiite population has reasserted itself, pointing to its experience of religious discrimination as well as political exclusion, but largely hoping for constitutional changes to generate conditions of majority rule. In this case, instead, violent opposition has stemmed from the previous powerholders, secular or Sunni Arabs fearing discrimination in the future.

Discrimination issues have importance in their own right. They can be addressed in political life, either as challenges to the existing state (state formation conflicts) or against government policies (making them into conflicts over government, that is, intra-state conflicts). When connected to territorial dimensions and loss of control, they are likely to be more entrenched and difficult to settle. In other words, not all questions of discrimination lead to armed conflict and challenges to the state. Those that do, however, will require particular efforts to identity solutions. Thus, we are moved to study the ways in which solutions can be found to the territorial security dilemmas of the state formation conflicts. This we will do in the following sections.

7.3 Autonomy and Federalism: Territorial Solutions within a State

Discrimination was an essential motive for the opposition in the conflicts listed in Table 7.1. It is given as a cause for action. Of course, there can be other motives and, indeed, whether such a grievance results in armed conflict depends on a host of other conditions. There is no straight line between the depth of a grievance and the onset or continuation of an armed conflict. Still, the reasoning in Section 7.2 leads to the conclusion that the territorial control question is essential. The ethnic security dilemma takes on a territorial dimension that needs to be handled. A state with more than one identity group formed on the basis of a territorial dimension will have to give thought to possible solutions. The following overview exemplifies remedies, using the seven mechanisms of conflict resolution identified in Section 3.5.

The first way points to the possibility of *reducing the significance of the territorial dimension*. This means that the parties, and particularly the opposition, will find that it would benefit from regarding the conflict as one purely of discrimination, equal opportunity, improved legislation, etc. This would mean reverting the conflict to the questions dealt with in Section 7.2. As we can assume that this already has been on the minds of the leaders – indeed even been an earlier phase of the conflict – this shift is less probable. Once a territorial demand has been raised, it is difficult to remove it from the agenda. Even if the original instigator gives it up, others may well follow. If it has come to a sustained armed conflict, this is even more unlikely. It is more possible that the demands for independence can be scaled back and that autonomy, for instance, can be acceptable as a final or interim solution. Nevertheless, there are interesting examples of policy shifts. One is the redefinition of the aims of PKK for the Kurdish cause in Turkey. In a statement to his followers while imprisoned, the leader of the organization, Abduallah Öcalan, argued that the struggle was no longer about a separate Kurdistan. Violent rebellion was, thus, to end (Kinzer 1999). The new approach was supposed to transform the struggle from a territorial issue to one of participation in the existing Turkish state. Not all PKK followers accepted this, but returned to arms. The armed conflict has continued and it has not led to negotiations between PKK and the Turkish authorities. The Kurdish issue as a non-territorial issue has been taken up through Turkey's EU accession process.

A second form that was mentioned is to find *ways in which territory can be divided* within the state's present confines. To some, this is seen as partition. An important issue is the impenetrability of the borders. Another is whether it leads to further division. This is where autonomy and federalism come in. Table 7.3 suggests all forms of internal and international partition to provide as complete a picture as possible. The basic idea is that an area – and its inhabitants – are given a degree of self-rule of their own affairs. It means that it affects not only the territory, but also the functions that this entity is going to handle. There can be various ways in which such functions can be divided as well.

The first five solutions in Table 7.3 are located within the existing state; the last three assume sovereignty and international recognition of the outcome. Also an autonomy arrangement can be internationalized if there are strong international guarantees. Federalism, furthermore, can provide the right to secede to the constituent units, giving them powerful levers against the central government. Independence can be restricted and conditional, as is the case with two of the options in Table 7.3. The agreement on independence may include the right for guaranteeing powers to intervene or even keep forces in an independent country. It may actually be asked if an autonomy arrangement sometimes gives more self-rule than a sovereign state would have, if particular restrictions were applied. Notions such as

Table 7.3 Territorial solutions to state formation conflicts (with examples from cases mentioned in the text and in Table 7.1)

Status of unit	Characteristics of self-rule	Examples
Self-administration	Devolution of powers from the centre to local, communal or provincial levels	Niger, Mali
Autonomy	Given from the centre and subject to policy changes of the centre; exists in weaker or stronger forms	Mindanao
Autonomy	Given or guaranteed by outside actors, thus not subject only to the policy of the centre, but to international developments	Åland, South Tyrol, Northern Ireland
Federalism	Created for many units, uniform constitution, central government composed of the constituent units	India, Switzerland
Federalism	Created for a few units, with equal rights	Bosnia-Herzegovina (two forms)
Independence	Created with international guarantees, close monitoring	Cyprus, 1960–63
Independence	Done without formal guarantees, but with integration in a regional framework	Within the EU?
Independence	No restrictions except adherence to regular international conventions	Eritrea

Note: The distinctions in this table concern territorial control. Each form could contain a range of self-rule authority over particular issues, for instance, taxation, policing, international representation, external security, etc.

'confederalism' are diffuse and find themselves somewhere between federalism and independence. In reality, the authority provided for the constituent units is decisive, not the labels.

Among the agreements in Table 7.1, decentralization was a chief element in two solutions (Niger, Mali). Various forms of autonomy were instituted, temporarily or permanently, in a number of cases (Palestine, as an interim arrangement, Chittagong Hill Tracts, Aceh and Mindanao as more permanent institutions, although a review is to take place in the latter case and fighting has continued). In some instances, the population has been given a choice between 'independence' and 'integration'. In Western Sahara, this is to be the subject of a referendum that is still being awaited due to disagreement on who should be in the electorate. East Timor in August 1999 had such a choice and the population overwhelmingly voted for independence. In Bougainville, such a vote is promised in the near future. In elections in 2010 the non-separatist candidate won. South Sudan had a referendum on independence in January 2011. The outcome was in favour of creating a new state.

It is noteworthy that there is only one case of a federal solution after a war. This is the status given to Bosnia-Herzegovina in the Dayton agreement of 1995. The new State of Bosnia-Herzegovina has a presidency (three presidents, one from each community), a two-unit federation, where one actually is another federation (the Federation of Bosnia-Herzegovina and the Serb Republic), and where the units were maintaining separate armies. The statewide federal level has been difficult to implement. So has the unit-level federation, concluded between the Bosniak (Bosnian Muslims) and Croat leaderships a year before the Dayton agreement.

For post-Saddam Hussein Iraq, federalism has been seen as the only viable solution. This is resented by the groups benefiting from the previous order and expecting to lose in such a new order (that is, not having access to oil resources: Sunni Arabs). For the Kurdish and Shiites, this instead provides an opportunity to guarantee their identities. The disputes also have a territorial dimension: which areas should be part of which federated unit, for instance, and where should the multi-ethnic and oil-rich Kirkuk be placed?

The solution to Northern Ireland, found in the Belfast agreement signed on Good Friday 1998, can be seen in this light. It gives considerable autonomy to the province, and it maintains the territory in the United Kingdom for the time being. It is a unique solution as it provides a functioning autonomous unit, which actually can switch its allegiance to the Republic of Ireland, while retaining its self-rule arrangement. The agreement also makes a connection between the North and the South of Ireland, and institutes a new regional council for the British Isles. There is a federal-like order developing for the United Kingdom as a whole, but the Belfast solution is more complex, as it combines different elements in Table 7.3 in a creative way.

There are objections to such territorial solutions. It has been argued that autonomy may in fact result in an area being ruled by illegal and criminal groups. This charge has been levied in Russia against the solution for Chechnya in 1996. The bombings of apartment buildings in Moscow in

1999 were explained in this way, and thus it undermined the credibility of the arrangement in the eyes of the centre. Instead of instituting democracy and working for economic development, it is possible that various armed groups could take control, exploiting the fact that there would be no interference of a legitimate superior authority. There has also been the opposite charge, that the autonomies often become too dependent on policies of the centre. The centre may choose to abolish the special status of a particular territory. This would serve to undermine the credibility of the solution in that particular area. For instance, Eritrean movements claimed that an autonomous status within Ethiopia was no longer acceptable as Ethiopia had abolished the self-rule the area had in the 1950s.

A third way is the issue of *horse-trading*. In this context, it would refer to the possibility of agreements on exchanges. Such exchanges, only some of which can be part of a treaty, may occur in state formation conflicts through a process where a people changes identity, there are population exchanges across internal borders and exchanges of territories. None of these is attractive following the experiences of the Second World War. In the post-Cold War era, however, they have returned as possible options, although their legitimacy is low, as they run counter to principles of human rights and conflict resolution. The three forms can be illustrated in the following way.

The first refers to a process of integration into the society of previously marginalized groups. This is assimilation, meaning that these groups take on the traits of the dominant side. It is possible, as a long-term result, but it is difficult to see assimilation resulting from an agreement. In reality, assimilation is the strategy a victor prefers to use towards the conquered. In a less harsh form, however, there could be stipulations in an agreement as to the rights of the populations on opposite sides of internal frontiers.

The exchange of populations has sometimes been agreed in international treaties, thus being part of a state creation process. Between Turkey and Greece, there are examples of agreed population exchanges. In the 1920s a total of more than half a million people were forcibly moved, either from Greece to Turkey (more than 350,000) or from Turkey to Greece (more than 190,000) (Ekstrand 1944). Some see this as an achievement and as a contribution to a reduction in hostility. However, tensions have remained between the peoples and the states. The experiences of being forced to move (by the other side, under international supervision, notably) served to fuel the conflict, not dampen it. There are writers who regard such population transfer, humanely done, as a way of solving the problem of minorities on one side of a border being loyal to a majority living on the other side (Bell-Fialkoff 1996).

The third approach would mean that one side holds a territory the other one wants, for instance, as a result of a recent war. It would be returned in exchange for concessions on other issues. Such horse-trading is today probably not legitimate, except in the immediate aftermath of a war, and then relating to military arrangements rather than population resettlements. It would today appear more like hostage-taking.

The fourth and fifth mechanisms for solving territorial conflicts within states point to the possibilities of *providing access to government*. This can take place on the local or national level. It means that solutions may be found, without resorting to territorial divisions. Examples are power-sharing arrangements and coalition governments (Jarstad 2001; Sisk 1996). The Belfast agreement created a government for Northern Ireland composed according to the strength of the parties in elections. The minority was assured its seats. Sinn Fein, seen to be close to the Provisional IRA, was thus seated and has, since then, exerted influence on the developments of the area. Similarly, the Dayton agreement includes an ethnically defined composition of leading bodies in Bosnia-Herzegovina. In federal arrangements it is customary that one of two chambers in a federal parliament provides over-representation for certain areas. A federal arrangement gives more influence on state affairs to a particular group through such representation than does autonomy. This suggests the need for a national government for the period of transition.

The sixth model for conflict resolution would mean that a territorial issue is settled through the resort to *conflict resolution mechanisms*. Some such decisions have been made, but only with respect to territorially limited disputes. The status of the town of Brcko was decided through a process of arbitration (making the city a unit directly under the State of Bosnia-Herzegovina, not belonging to either the Federation or the Republic), as the last remaining issue in the Dayton negotiations on peace in Bosnia-Herzegovina in 1995.

On the seventh way, *postponing issues or the creation of timetables*, we can note that, although territorial issues are at the heart of state formation disputes, there are certain issues that tend to come last. As just mentioned, this was the case with Brcko. It was known in advance that this would be a strategically important decision. By keeping it as the last agenda item, negotiators may have believed that it would recede in importance. Then a solution could be found, particularly as the alternative would be to jeopardize the entire agreement. As it turned out, the parties were close to doing just that. The resort to arbitration became the last possibility. As a form of brinkmanship it is a high-risk game that could easily go wrong.

A central question in the Israeli–Palestinian negotiations concerns the status of Jerusalem, which both Israel and Palestine are committed to as the capital in their state. It was left to last in previous negotiations, for instance, in Camp David in 1978. In the Oslo process, it was again defined to belong to the final status issues. There was a limit to how long this issue could be postponed, however, and when a solution was presented, in July 2000, it may have been too late. It involved elements of what we have suggested above on the division of functional influence, sovereignty and guarantees. It was still not enough. Too many other matters have not worked out according to expectation, leaving little confidence for settling this issue. Leaving important matters to last, it turns out, may be counter-productive. But so is the opposite strategy, of solving the most difficult issues first. Difficult questions have to be tackled when confidence and momentum are at their highest.

Judging from the record since the Cold War, autonomy solutions have been of increasing interest. From Table 7.1, it can be surmised that it is one element – under different names – in at least ten agreements. It has also been an important proposal in the search for solutions in some other cases, for instance, for Nagorno-Karabakh within Azerbaijan, Jafna and adjacent areas in Sri Lanka, and Basque areas in Spain. It was proposed for Corsica in France. The strength of the autonomy solution is its ability to provide a tailor-made solution for a particular problem. It meets simultaneously the interests of self-determination of a people and the interest of the centre to keep the state together, thus upholding its territorial integrity. From the point of view of the centre, this is important as it perceives a danger of other units also demanding self-rule. In its worst-case scenario, there is a threat of breakup of the entire state. Thus, a special arrangement can be defended as a particular measure which does not set a precedent for others. The history of the conflict may assist to provide such arguments. For the territorial unit itself, autonomy creates a direct link to the centre of state authority, thus according it a status no other unit has. Furthermore, if this linkage is sufficiently strong, it may provide the guarantees of self-rule and security that the inhabitants of the unit require (Nordquist 1998). However, mistrust is likely to be high. After all, there has been a war. There are often pertinent questions of the return of people of other identities to which the centre will give priority. Thus, solutions may not always be found only between the centre and the region. It may involve international actors, acting as guarantors. Regional arrangements, the UN or particular states can take this role, although there are not many examples in this period.

The interest in autonomy solutions may have other origins as well. For the opposition, it may be the first step to independence. This is the way East Timor resistance movements saw autonomy, for instance. It would be a way of building up an administration, shaping a functioning economy and forming a police system of its own. It would make the option between autonomy and independence a real choice. This plan was pre-empted by the Indonesian authorities, however, who in January 1999 gave the same choice to the East Timorese, without first acquainting the population to the practical experiences of self-rule. As it appeared to be a final offer and the only chance, the choice was easy for these movements. They had to take the chance for independence. The outcome of the internationally observed referendum in August 1999 was predictable. The violence that followed showed that the Indonesian government might not have fully understood the local political situation. It also underestimated the will of the international community to intervene after it saw the overwhelming support for independence.

The experience of East Timor may make central authorities in multiethnic societies less inclined to vie for autonomy solutions. In the 2005 solution to the conflict in Aceh, the independence option was also ruled out by the liberation movement, GAM, no doubt under the impact of the tsunami disaster. This made an agreement possible. This is underscored by the Kosovo crisis of 1999, where international action created a *de facto* independent unit, but for nine years maintained that it was part of Serbia. However, by declaring independence, Kosovo ended this fiction. Similarly, the self-government afforded to Palestinian-ruled areas of the West Bank and Gaza is seen as a prelude to independence. It means that an independent administration now has been created by Palestinian Prime Minister Salam Fayyad. The many crises in the Oslo peace process may have strengthened the desire for independence for the Palestinian population. An autonomy which allows the central authority, Israel, vast rights of interference loses its credibility.[2]

Under such circumstances, autonomy becomes a first step to independence, not a final settlement. However, this is not true for all the solutions. There is no expectation that Northern Ireland will become independent, but it could very well become an autonomous part of the Republic of Ireland. Independence is not likely to come to Mindanao and Chittagong Hill Tracts. In the agreements in Sudan and Papua New Guinea, a vote will determine the fate of provinces in South Sudan and of Bougainville. This will give the central authorities an incentive to please these regions so as to keep them inside the present state. It remains to be understood what separates the self-rule situations from those where autonomy is but a stepping stone. Most of the functioning autonomies have not seen ethnic cleansing on their territories or considerable refugee flows, as was the case with Palestine, Bosnia, Chechnya, East Timor and Kosovo. It is also interesting to ask if autonomy is more likely to gain local support under a stable democratic centre. This is true for each of the first four cases mentioned, whereas the last four have been exposed to semi-democratic or dictatorial regimes (former Yugoslavia, Russia, Indonesia, and post-1995 Yugoslavia). This might suggest that Sudan will become another case of secession, while Papua New Guinea might not. Democratic government provides for more transparency and predictability. With such experiences, less extreme measures may be sought. This argument would, interestingly enough, apply also to the Palestinian case. Nobody can refute the democratic strength of Israel. It is, however, an exclusive democracy, not willing to accommodate a large Palestinian population. In this case, a separate-state solution is the only viable one.

The federal solutions are theoretically attractive but obviously not frequent in the settlement of state formation conflicts. Bednar (2009) lists 26 federations for the period 1990–2000 and, at most, two can be seen as solutions to conflicts between parties that became units of the federation. Tanzania was formed to integrate Tanganyika and Zanzibar in 1974 in a peculiar coup episode. This leaves the Bosnia-Herzegovina federation as an exceptional case and its future is still in question. The Dayton accords from 1995, ending the three years of war in Bosnia, included an elaborate constitutional structure, with one central government and a federation parallel to an autonomous republic (the Bosnian Serb Republic). It builds on legal symmetry, in which each unit is on the same organizational level. It was argued in the Dayton negotiations that constituent units of the United States, for instance, use terms such as 'Commonwealth' and 'Republic', but still legally are on the same level (Holbrooke 1999: 131). This might not be the chief obstacle for the functioning of the solution, however.

Federal solutions involve a division of territory. In a federation with a strong central structure, such lines are less important, but the weaker the centre, and thus the stronger the constituent units, the more important are the territorial arrangements. According to accounts from the Dayton negotiations, considerable time and energy were expended at drawing boundaries. It is remarkable as they were supposed to be internal lines in a central state. The significance of the border issue suggests that the parties were not really contemplating the creation of a strong unitary state. The formula agreed to beforehand of a territorial division of 51 per cent for the Federation (that is, the Bosniak and Croat areas) and 49 per cent for the Republic (the Serb areas) was guiding the procedure. The maps were continuously adapted so as to arrive at this formula. Matters of constitutions and elections were dealt with more easily than the one of territory. It is illustrative that the final agreement, concluded in the morning of the last day of negotiations, was on a territorial question, the Brcko district (Holbrooke 1999: 302–9). Clearly, the negotiators expected the borderlines to be as important as between separate states. The borders were going to be 'hard', not 'soft' as inside a state, where the same sovereignty extends on both sides of the border. The implementation has had to face this problem, trying to 'soften' the borders by finding agreements on border crossings, common institutions and a common currency. The survival of the state may depend on the success of such measures. What was created at Dayton was not a 'normal' federal state.

Thus, it is not surprising that the Bosnia-Herzegovina federation is marred with problems. But they not only stem from the sharp boundary cutting across the country, or even the existence of hostile armies. The main problem is that the solution has little foundation in the minds of the population, even among the leaders. The Bosnian Serb population would still prefer to be united with Serbia, something explicitly excluded in the Dayton accords. Croats would still prefer to be with Croatia. The carriers of the State of Bosnia-Herzegovina are the Bosniaks, and they are not the majority. The international support the central government receives is crucial for the federation. It means that independence is severely circumscribed with respect to international relations and as to what state leaders can do inside their state. The commander of the international peacekeeping operations and the Office of High Representative (OHR), appointed by the international community, are the sources of real authority.

Federal solutions may still be of interest, but more as preventive measures than solutions after a war. This form of solution requires an arrangement for the full state, as its idea is that there are many units balancing each other, but also reflecting diversity in the country. Thus, a two-unit federation is at the bare minimum and may in fact lose a significant element of its contribution to conflict resolution, or actually become a *de facto* autonomy solution (Zanzibar is highly separated from Tanzania). Although there are only four languages in Switzerland, the units in the federation are many times this number. Also, territorial conflicts may not be of concern to all areas in a given state. It is problematic to extend federal rights to areas which have not asked for them, but get them as part of a solution to a problem in another part of that state. In the case of Bosnia-Herzegovina, the Dayton accords were drawing a constitution for a new country. In post-Saddam Hussein Iraq a federal state is being constructed by two of the largest communities, together representing a dominant majority – the Kurds and the Shiites. The opposition is coming from Sunni Arabs and worries are expressed by some smaller ethnic communities, in all around one-fifth of the population. This is a risky experiment that is being carried out as a constitutional process in the midst of a terrorist civil war. Federalism may appear intellectually and technically feasible. However, a common result of studies of the durability of federations is that they require a 'federal consensus' (Bednar 2009: 216; Duchacek 1977: 13). A war rarely creates such a consensus and, indeed, federal solutions have not normally emerged as solutions between the opposing sides in a state formation war.[3]

Thus far, the territorial solutions negotiated since the end of the Cold War using autonomy or federation have not failed. Some are still in an early phase of implementation (Bosnia-Herzegovina, Northern Ireland), others are in place but under review (Mindanao, Chittagong Hill Tracts), still others are seen as first steps (Palestine) and, thus, only to be judged with respect to that. We have also observed some of the difficulties, for instance, it seems hard to find a balancing point that can uphold autonomy. It is a compromise between independence and integration. It has strong intellectual appeal, but may be difficult to manage in situations of stark conflict. It might function under conditions where peoples of different identities live intermingled, where there is no experience of ethnic cleansing and where the centre is democratic. Also, we can observe that federal solutions are few and face severe difficulties in recreating an identity-divided state. The Dayton accords attempt to do this, and so far have been upheld through the Bosniak community and a strong international presence.

7.4 Independence with or without Integration

When parties are involved in war the original goal is to win or prevent the opponent from winning. In conflicts over territory within one state, the end result should be obvious. Either the existing state wins, order is restored and no changes of international borders are made, or the existing state loses, new states are born and borders are changed. There are victories that also fit into these two outcomes since the Cold War. Slovenia, Croatia and Eritrea all attribute their independence to military victories; the movement for an independent Khalistan for Sikhs was routed by Indian forces targeting the leadership. Coercion is not necessarily the only way to independence, however. It is noteworthy that negotiated solutions do not rule out the possibility of independence, as can be understood from Table 7.1. Independence would solve the ethnic security dilemma by creating borders between the opposing parties, thus alleviating the tensions of being in the same state and ending competition for the same recourses. As independence is an option, we need to ask what the experiences are in achieving independence in an armed conflict without victory.

Independence was an alternative for Namibia, as agreed before 1989, as well as East Timor. That is also what the majority chose. It remains a likely option for Western Sahara and for Palestine. The way the Bosnian conflict is defined in Table 7.1 assumes that Bosnia-Herzegovina was an independent country from 1992. However, as the Federal Republic of Yugoslavia did not extend recognition with diplomatic relations, there remained an uncertainty in the minds of the Bosnian leadership. The Dayton accords reaffirmed the independence of the country. A different outcome to the war may have resulted in a division of Bosnia between Serb and Croat forces with linkages to Belgrade and Zagreb. Diplomatic and military actions blocked such outcomes. Bosnia's independence was secured through a military stalemate. These examples show that independence can also be achieved in armed conflicts without a complete military victory.

For the many stalemated and ongoing armed conflicts this may be an important lesson. It means that governments may not necessarily fear to enter into talks. It does not necessarily lead only to secession. The opposition may not fear that talks will automatically rule out independence, if that is its preferred alternative. Are there situations in which independence may be the preferred alternative for both sides in a conflict? This can be answered by asking how it was possible for a centre to agree to the dissolution of 'its' state. There are three possible answers. The first is whether there is a solution that reduces the impact of granting independence by finding a regional framework of integration. The second is that this depends on the self-understanding of the centre, something that was mentioned in Section 7.1. A third response is that it depends on the demographic geography, particularly the size and significance of populations ending up on the 'wrong' side of new borders. Let us look at these three factors in some depth.

First, granting independence to a territory is more acceptable to the centre government if it takes place within a context of regional cooperation. It means that the interstate boundaries remain 'soft', allowing the movement of people as well as goods and capital. This all makes sense, for instance, if we discuss autonomy solutions. If the protagonists are members of the European Union, this may make agreements on self-rule less threatening to opponents and centres alike. It may well have been a factor for the agreement on Northern Ireland. The dissolution of the Soviet Union was followed by the quick formation of the Commonwealth of Independent States (CIS). It showed that ideas of regional cooperation were uppermost in the minds of leaders in the former Soviet states. CIS and other links would serve to undo some of the feared negative consequences of the new situation. The peaceful dissolution of Czechoslovakia may also have been helped by the hopes, on both sides, for closer cooperation with the EU and Western Europe. Violence would have reduced the chances of admission.

The possibility of future integration may convince the centre in accepting the ending of a union. The perspective on the seceding side may be different. Whether won through victory or negotiated process, independence still may be seen as the result of a conflict strategy. Thus, the will to cooperate and integrate with the old centre is likely to be modest on the part of the new state. Its first needs are for internal reconstruction, the creation of its own institutions and the development of its own economic and military capacity. The new unit, furthermore, will be busy extending new international contacts. The residual effects of war and separation are pressing concerns for the leadership on both sides. This scenario gains more support from the record since the Cold War than the hope for integration after a conflict. There was little incentive among the newly independent states from former Yugoslavia to work out new cooperative arrangements among themselves. They had gained independence from one tightly-knit union, and were looking for different integration projects. Slovenia and Croatia hoped to be early candidates for EU membership. Others were concerned about their international and internal security. Macedonia, for instance, had a conflict with Greece over its name, at the same time as it was exposed to the pressures of state failure in Albania, and increasing war in Kosovo. Thus, regional cooperation was given low priority. If it were to come, it would have to be induced by other actors. For the Balkans, this was left for the EU, which also launched a special cooperative initiative in 1999. The hope of joining EU in the future may also be what makes Serbia willing to accept Kosovo's independence, at least in practice.

The prospects of regional cooperation may be different if there is also a change in the former centre. This has been the case in South Africa. Southern African cooperation received considerable input from the peace agreements for Namibia, South Africa and Mozambique. It has also been strong enough to handle disputes among member states. The political changes that took place in the first part of the 1990s gave regional cooperation a chance, and the countries in the region were willing to use the opportunity. A similar chance was created in the Horn of Africa, with the 1991 defeat of the old regimes in Ethiopia (Mengistu) and Somalia (Barre). Within one year, however, a process of regional fragmentation unfolded, ending in the collapse of Somalia, the rise of ethnically based violence in Ethiopia and, by the end of the decade, a protracted war between Ethiopia and Eritrea. The regional organization, IGAD, did not have the opportunity it would have needed. In a short period, the Horn of Africa experienced all types of war: civil wars with state failure, state formation and interstate wars. In addition, it has had a recent history of authoritarian regimes, coups and economic mismanagement. Regional integration may follow a war, but only under particular circumstances. At best, regional reconstruction may be a protracted process, no matter what the outcome of the war. Rather, we may be able to identify 'failed regions', as we can discuss failed states.

It is worth noting that in two cases of independence (Slovenia and Namibia) there was considerable economic progress. Slovenia and Namibia belong to the countries that were the least economically affected by the war. In the first case, the armed conflict lasted only ten days; in the latter case, most of the fighting took place in neighbouring Angola, where the armed liberation movement, SWAPO, had its bases. Two other independent countries (Eritrea, Timor-Leste, that is, former East Timor) have experienced wars that have gone on for 20 or 30 years, meaning that vast resources have been destroyed and opportunities lost: young people have died or been crippled, infrastructure wasted and resources plundered. They have expectations of international assistance. In none of these cases is the new state turning to the former centre for support or even compensation. The hopes for regional integration may be important in the minds of the leaders of the centres. It may well underestimate the dynamics behind a struggle for independence. Sometimes regional cooperation can be achieved, but it may be a preferable strategy before a conflict rather than after it.

This brings us to the second aspect. The centre may accept independence of particular territories if this does not damage its self-understanding. It was easier for the Indonesian Parliament in October 1999 to accept the independence vote in East Timor as this did not threaten an Indonesian self-image. In this view, East Timor was a special case. It was not part of the original Indonesian state that was created from the Dutch colonial empire in 1945. West Irian was joined with Indonesia in 1963, but it had also been under Dutch rule. Thus, Indonesia's core self-definition was based on the former Dutch East Indies. The addition of East Timor, a former Portuguese holding, was alien and associated with the deposed military regime under General Suharto. Giving self-government to East Timor was compatible with Indonesia's regime before Suharto. It also made it possible to argue that no other areas were to leave the country. A coherent ideological position could be found. Thus, a settlement on Aceh required a solution within present-day Indonesia, and the same may be implied for West Papua (West Irian).

Similarly, Czech self-understanding made it possible to accept Slovakia's separation. To keep an empire has not been a Czech obsession. We have already observed the Russian self-understanding promoted by Boris Yeltsin while in opposition. Also, Russia had suffered from the Soviet Union, it was claimed, and thus there was a demand for leaving this union. The new rulers in Ethiopia in 1991, EPRDF, had a programme which allowed for Eritrea's separation. They gained power in close cooperation with the Eritrean People's Liberation Front (EPLF). The official view of Ethiopia no longer made control over Eritrea vital for the country's role domestically or internationally.

There are many such changes in self-definition in history. Sweden accepted the secession of Norway after an agreed referendum had been conducted and a demilitarized zone between the two countries had been created. This dissolved a union according to the demands of Norway. The union had been created by force but ended peacefully after lasting 90 years, 1814–1905. Its ending did not affect an emerging Swedish self-understanding, leaving regional power politics in favour of building a modern society of industry, democracy and welfare.

Also, the decolonization process was related to changed self-understanding among many colonial powers. There was a realization that their own economic growth was no longer benefiting from the colonial empires – the costs were increasing. There was a redefinition of their roles in the world. Improving the well-being of the population in the centre became more important than projecting power in distant territories. Some lessons, however, had to be learned the hard way. France lost two wars, in Indochina (1947–54) and in Algeria (1954–62). Britain lost to an ingenious and persistent non-violence campaign in India (led by Mahatma Gandhi, ending in independence for India and Pakistan in 1947) and in the Gold Coast in West Africa (ending in the creation of Ghana in 1957). Together, France and Britain lost trying to wrestle back control over the Suez Canal from Egypt in 1956. They encountered united opposition from the United States and the Soviet Union. The Netherlands fought Indonesian anti-colonial forces under Sukarno in the late 1940s before realizing the futility in the effort. The last stand of colonialism was by Portugal, where the so-called Carnation Revolution in 1974 ended its colonial ambition. Instead, Portugal gave priority to domestic development and economic integration with Europe, becoming an EU member in 1986.

Changes in self-understanding seem to be important for a more peaceful ending to conflicts over state formation. They may come about as a result of the efforts of the opposition in the controlled areas, but it may also relate to new internal priorities for state and society. Thus, we would argue that a similar self-understanding did not develop in the cases where the conflicts became violent and where independence was only reluctantly accepted. This, furthermore, might also be where regional cooperation has been the most difficult to accomplish. Certainly, South Africa's self-image today is entirely different from the one that existed at the end of the Cold War. This affects relations all over the region.

Third, the human costs may affect the centre's willingness to accept independence solutions. It seems generally true that drawing new international borders is likely to create new problems, not just solve old ones. The state dissolutions we have seen have used previously existing administrative divisions, where such have been applicable. The colonial borders were used for decolonization. There were few Czechs in Slovakia and vice versa, and the same is true with Swedes in Norway. This was not the case in all the situations. Particularly, the new borders among the former Yugoslav republics had the effect of creating Serb minorities in the new states. The notion of ethnic cleansing – by different sides – became the historical imprint of these wars. Serb authorities evicted peoples from their areas of control and, at other instances, Serbs were evicted from non-Yugoslav controlled areas. The rapid escalation of the conflicts in 1991 and 1992 removed any possibility of looking into alternative arrangements. There might have been ways of managing these minority problems, as has so far been possible for Russians outside the Russian Federation, and previously for Hungarians outside Hungary.

Together these three factors may explain why independence solutions are sometimes peaceful, sometimes not. A central aspect is the dominant unit's understanding of its role. A peaceful dissolution may be more easily achieved if it is done under an expectation of regional cooperation, where the centre has a non-offensive understanding of its role, and where the new borders can be managed so that new minorities, on either side of the border, are given sufficient security. These conditions are not easy to meet, but they have been present at some important occasions.

This means that independence, in order not to create future conflicts, will require accompanying measures, particularly relating to new borders. In general, it appears impossible to draw boundaries which will divide all inhabitants in a humane way. The interconnections between people are many and close, particularly if they are living in an interspersed pattern, as assumed by the idea of the ethnic security dilemma. Also, sources of income are likely to create such patterns. In a somewhat free economy, people of all backgrounds are converging on places of economic growth and new opportunity. Thus, simply drawing thick lines on the basis of population statistics will create unfair and unequal treatment.

Furthermore, one may ask how such a division can be decided in a democratic way. Is a majority decision sufficient or shall the minority be entitled to a veto? How can a referendum without harassment be conducted, particularly if there already is an armed conflict? An examination of the experience of the agreed partitions of former British India and Palestine cannot be avoided. There is a debate on these lessons (Bell-Fialkoff 1996; Schaeffer 1990).

The problem with the boundary divisions is that people have to move permanently and, thus, all their investments, memories and roots are affected. It is not likely to be something about which people are enthusiastic. The blame, furthermore, is going to be directed against the other group, and thus the hatred stemming from a war may become even more deep-seated. There have been two state divisions decided deliberately through legitimate fora. One was by responsible leaders in the case of India, the other by the UN General Assembly in the case of Palestine. Both were implemented more than 60 years ago. Both resulted in wars. The effects have yet to be overcome. The relationship between India and Pakistan has reached a stage of a nuclear arms race. Also Israel is known to possess nuclear weapons capacity. The issue of how to secure the rights of the dispossessed Palestinians remains unresolved. In other words, these are experiences where the solution to an internal ethnic security dilemma actually led to interstate security dilemmas of the type we have discussed in Chapter 5. One solution was bought at the price of a new problem.

The fate of refugee populations is likely to be central in any state division. Some of the settlements since the Cold War have allowed for the return of refugees, but in many cases such a prospect has been bleak. The Dayton accords stipulated the return of refugees, and many have done so. In this case, there is not only the insecurity of being a minority in surroundings dominated by other ethnic groups, but also the challenge of finding income. As the economies are not developing, it is difficult to return and, thus, the security that a multi-ethnic environment would provide will not emerge.

We see that independence, once achieved and recognized, has provided a measure of stability to a particular conflict. In some cases there is also an experience of economic growth. But the hope of dramatically changing the situation in a region is not borne out. Regional cooperation has become more difficult and the costs to independence higher than anticipated. A new state remains in an area where its old foes also are. New conflicts may follow, as seen in the Horn of Africa. The driving force behind the quest for independence has often been to escape an intolerable situation of dominance. Independence may achieve a change in relations. Whether the result is a less conflict-ridden and more tolerant society or region can be questioned. The record is positive in some cases, negative in others. It is important to observe alternative developments where combinations can be found and have been put in place without armed conflict.

7.5 State Formation Conflicts and Democracy

The solutions to state formation conflicts, which we discussed in Sections 7.3 and 7.4, have concerned territorial divisions between the contending groups, whether their conflict has dealt with decolonization or ethnically-based identity issues. The solutions to the ethnic security dilemma have been to create separate units, which provide protection for the different groups. This is in line with much thinking on self-determination. It is likely, however, that this is applicable only to some identity-based conflicts. Most can probably be handled equally well, or even better, through the existing units. Section 7.2 and Table 7.2 suggested some such possibilities. It is only under special circumstances that the ethnic security dilemma will be fully developed and necessitate more radical solutions, such as the creation of new units.

Territorial solutions mean drawing softer or harder lines between peoples in order to create security on each side. A particular ethnic group may feel more secure if it is shielded by a new border. However, some people will be on the 'wrong' side, from the point of view of the new state units. Thus, there are additional security concerns and they are not necessarily solved by the boundaries. Demilitarization and democratization will improve the situation for such groups. The softer the borders the more security will be provided to the new minorities. At the same time, the security demands of the new dominant group make it prefer impenetrable, hard borders. Some tension might be remedied by credible measures for minority rights, for instance, as complements to the independence solutions. The measures in Table 7.2 will be relevant. Also, with harder borders, it will be more difficult for refugees to return. This issue seems more difficult to deal with in the case of state formation conflicts than in civil wars. The restoration of refugee rights in state formation conflicts is more closely associated with security and economic chances for the returnees. For instance, their land and houses may be taken over by others, as part of a deliberate government policy to force them out. The right of return may not be accepted by the new authorities. This risks making the refugee population a permanent issue. Conflict resolution is prevented.

These dilemmas make it necessary to raise the question of whether there are still other possible solutions of state formation conflicts. We would then look for integrative solutions, which give different groups equal rights in the society. For democracies, in particular, this opens new possibilities. A related issue is that conflict situations do not only contain armed actors, who are often part of the final agreements, but a surrounding society of non-armed actors. Some may pursue the same goals as the armed actors, others may have dissenting views. Either way, they are part of the society and their roles need to be considered.

First, there is a possibility of sharing government, or even giving influence to minorities. The example of Finland is instructive. The Åland Islands have been mentioned as a functioning autonomy arrangement. Swedish-speaking inhabitants predominantly populate these islands. In an arrangement achieved through the League of Nations in 1921 and confirmed by the UN in 1950, this autonomy was created to preserve the Swedish language and culture on the islands. In this way, a dispute between Sweden and Finland about the sovereignty over these islands was solved. However, the Ålanders are only a fraction of all Swedish-speaking inhabitants in Finland. Their preference for a separate unit was not shared by others. This is where the story becomes interesting. Let us follow this.

Other Swedish speakers were not interested in autonomy arrangements, or were even sceptical of it, as it could reduce their influence in the society as a whole. They resolved the issue in favour of full participation in the political life of Finland. To them, it was more important that Swedish was recognized and respected as a national language. A political party pursuing Swedish and liberal interests was created and Swedish-speaking politicians emerged in other political parties. Thus, although being no more than 5 per cent of the total population, the Swedish-speaking group managed to exert considerable influence on national politics. At the same time, it could act to protect specific Swedish interests, which largely were questions of culture and language.

This experience suggests an integrative way of handling identity-based conflicts. It is a demanding strategy for a minority, but it also makes it a creative contributor to the society as a whole. It means that the minority is not primarily defining itself as a minority but as a legitimate participant in the affairs of the country as a whole. It escapes the danger of becoming a group concerned only with its own affairs. It avoids a potential danger in autonomy solutions of isolation, ghetto-like conditions and marginalization from the main currents of the state. This is the essence of an integrative strategy. This experience suggests interesting options, where combinations are possible. It could be that the integrative solution gains strength from the simultaneous existence of the autonomy, which in turn also benefits from the minority's participation in national affairs.

It is possible that such solutions are open only to stable democratic societies. It, of course, builds on an important premise: the rights of the minority are accepted in the society, socially as well as legally. Some democratic or open societies have encountered problems on this score. There are examples of minorities with elected representatives who encounter strong resistance when pursuing the interests of the minority. This has been a repeated experience in Turkey for parliamentary representatives of Kurdish origin, for instance. There are similar problems in the state of Israel, where Israeli Arab voters tend to vote for special Arab tickets and, although having their seats in the Knesset, still are not seen among the Israeli general public as a legitimate support-base for a governing majority.

A parallel history is found in the experience of Tamil political representation in the parliament in Sri Lanka. A Tamil party was the leading opposition party in 1977 and initially the government's measures included, for instance, the improvement of the status of the Tamil language. However, the government remained more concerned about its standing in the Singhalese majority community, and negotiations on a solution became increasingly sterile. Following the anti-Tamil riots in Colombo in 1983, the government passed an amendment forcing all members of parliament to take an oath to defend the unitary Constitution. The Tamil members resigned their seats. The negotiations for solutions that had preceded these events had dealt with the possibility of devolution (Wriggins 1995). We have also referred to the experience of Cyprus, also a society working under a democratic framework. Thus, as these experiences suggest, leaders of the majority have at times preferred to marginalize minority representatives, despite their democratic mandates. This is not likely to consolidate democratic procedures in the groups affected.

These examples concern cases where the majority is overwhelming and often able to govern without the support of the identity minority. In Finland, the Swedish party skilfully positioned itself in the middle of the political spectrum. It was party to coalitions with Left, Centre and Right. Its votes have been important for a government's majority. That was also the role earlier performed by Tamils in the parliament in Sri Lanka. In some other democratic societies, such arrangements have been undermined. In

Northern Ireland, the Catholic minority was excluded from local political influence, through a *de facto* one-party system. In Cyprus, the power-sharing arrangement was not allowed to accumulate experience. The dilemma for a democratic system is that democratic policies can either integrate or marginalize groups. As we see in these cases, policies have been pursued so as to keep a minority from influence during longer periods of time. This is done without breaking constitutional rules. The long-term consequences can be negative for the democratic system and for the viability of the state, as can be seen in Cyprus, Northern Ireland, Sri Lanka and Turkey. The societies have found themselves in state formation conflicts from which they have had severe difficulty extracting themselves.

In other instances, where the majority–minority relationship is less clear-cut, the possibility of semi-permanent, broad-based coalitions bridging ethnic divides may be larger. This is part of the formula for the central authority in the state of Bosnia-Herzegovina. In this case, a veto is given to each of the communities. A similar arrangement was made in the constitution for Cyprus (Jarstad 2001) as well as through the Annan Plan in 2004, and both failed to create a necessary atmosphere of cooperation. Functioning examples of such coalitions are found in more authoritarian states. An example is Malaysia, where the National Front, Barisan Nasional, has been ruling the country for 38 years. It is composed of parties representing different ethnic communities. As there are opposition parties, the system is more open than might be expected. It means, however, that the society builds on elite consensus, and that basic decisions are made through closed deals between the parties in the National Front. This is in line with the idea of consensual politics for ethnically divided society (Lijphart also calls this consociational, 1975, 1984). The Malaysian society has functioned remarkably well over a long period of time. The performance in economic growth has been exceptional. At the same time, it has resulted in an ethnicization of politics and society. All parties in the parliament now mobilize support along ethnic lines. The overriding shared interest is to maintain stability which enhances economic growth. In times of economic crises, this could expose the society to severe strain, as was seen in the late 1980s and in the Asian economic crisis of 1997–98 (Case 2001).

This discussion suggests that there are integrative solutions for state formation conflicts. The prerequisite seems to be that they are instituted early, at a time when ethnic polarization is not developed or entrenched. A tradition of national cooperation can be created. Even at a later stage, it is probably important that the democratic practices are given a real chance for a minority to have an impact on the overall policies of the state. The logic that influence leads to responsibility, commitment and identification is compelling: it is only then that the minority will see the state as 'its' own in much the same way as the majority. Without this, however, integrative solutions in democratic societies are likely to be difficult to maintain. There is a danger of marginalization of groups even under democracy. The bigger such excluded groups are, the more troublesome the future for the democratic framework. This is significant to recall in post-Saddam Hussein Iraq, where the Sunni Arab group is a community large enough to sustain armed resistance.

This leads us to the second issue, the role of non-armed groups in the creation and maintenance of solutions. We referred to this in Chapter 3. As was the case in the settlement of civil war disputes, the incorporation of the larger society has been a feature only in some of the solutions. As we noted, there are solutions where leading actors were not actually signatories to agreements (Namibia, East Timor) with even less involvement of other groups. The fact that these conflicts straddle the dichotomy of interstate and internal conflict means that their management is less consistent. Also, a broader participation requires a democratic system, and several of the settlements concerned countries which were fairly closed. Only a few of the agreements have given rise to a vigorous debate during the peace process. The typical examples are Palestine and Northern Ireland, where options have been discussed while the process was still under way. It is likely that, in both cases, the debate made clear to the negotiating parties the range of opinion and what was acceptable. In some of the ongoing armed conflicts (Sri Lanka, Turkey, Russia) as well as in Cyprus, there are democratic conditions that would be conducive for a broader discussion, but it seems to be difficult to initiate.

Still, the importance of non-armed groups as well as popular participation in the peace process should not be underestimated. The unarmed and largest party on the Irish Nationalist side in Northern Ireland, the SDLP led by John Hume, was instrumental in the furthering of peace. Its informal contacts with Sinn Fein, regarded to be close to the Provisional IRA, made it possible to broaden Nationalist participation in the peace process. There were also groups and parties bridging the gap between the two major communities in Northern Ireland. The main actors on the Unionist side were all, officially, unarmed actors, some no doubt still with links to para-military groups. The non-armed groups were essential in making contacts. At the same time, they also constituted alternative ways of pursuing basically the same demands. It was, for instance, the parties with a clear non-armed agenda that received most of the votes in the elections during the times of armed conflict.

It is likely that non-armed groups can play similar roles in other conflicts, but that makes a cease-fire a necessity – the earlier, the better. Without that, contacts initiated by non-armed groups can be seen as threatening to the solidarity of a particular side, and thus the groups become targets for terrorist attacks. This has been the fate of several early emissaries, for instance, in the Israeli–Palestinian conflict. A cease-fire is not only something that benefits the fighting parties at a certain moment or reduces the strain on the population as a whole, it also gives a chance for a more vibrant society to have an impact on the course of peace. In a study that has explored this issue quantitatively, Desirée Nilsson (2008) found that in a peace agreement which included civil society actors, the peace was more likely to endure.

For states and oppositions alike, there are no simple solutions to state formation conflicts. This chapter has illustrated some of the possibilities that have been agreed between the fighting parties. It has also showed that victory does take place in surprisingly few cases. State formation conflicts tend to be protracted. This suggests that they require early action for a settlement before they become too entrenched, or solutions in which states allow for constitutional variation, perhaps coupled to regional and international involvement.

Further Readings

Go to the *Understanding Conflict Resolution* web page at www.sagepub.co.uk for free access to journal articles listed.

Anderson, B. 1991. *Imagined Communities. Reflections on the Origin and Spread of Nationalism*. London: Verso.

Bednar, J. 2009. *The Robust Federation: Principles of Design*. Cambridge: Cambridge University Press.

Cornell, S. E. 2002. 'Autonomy as a Source of Conflict: Caucasian Conflicts in Theoretical Perspective', *World Politics*, 54 (2): 245–76.

Daalder, I. H. and Froman, M. B. G. 1999. 'Dayton's Incomplete Peace', *Foreign Affairs*, 78 (6): 106–13.

Fearon, J. D. and Laitin, D. D. 2003. 'Ethnicity, Insurgency and Civil War', *American Political Science Review*, 97 (1): 75–90.

Gurr, T. R. 2000. *Peoples versus States*. Washington, DC: USIP Press.

Gurr, T. R. 2000. 'Ethnic Warfare on the Wane', *Foreign Affairs*, 79 (3): 52–64.

Kaldor, M. 2006. *New and Old Wars* (2nd edn). Cambridge: Polity Press.

Makovsky, D. 1996. *Making Peace with the PLO. The Rabin Government's Road to the Oslo Accord*. Boulder, CO: Westview Press.

Suksi, M. (ed.) 1998. *Autonomy: Applications and Implications*. The Hague: Kluwer.

Notes

1   If we include the UCDP category of non-state conflicts, the picture is different. Africa has about three-quarters of these conflicts (Pettersson 2010).

2   A challenging new idea is the one of two parallel states on the same territory (Mossberg 2010).

3   United States of America was created by the victors in the war against the British, as a solution to their needs, building on an original confederation that was in effect a defence pact (Bednar 2009: 64–6). After the Civil War, the losing side was simply reintegrated into the existing structure. The Federal Republic of Germany was created by the victors in the Second World War, again their solution to the post-war needs. Both these cases have worked remarkably well and the federations are today profoundly entrenched in the two populations. The same is true for Switzerland, but again it originated as a shared defence pact against outsiders, not as a solution for intra-Swiss conflicts.

PART THREE
COMPLEXITIES IN
CONFLICT RESOLUTION

CONFLICT COMPLEXES AND CONFLICT RESOLUTION 8

8.1 Identifying Regional Conflict Complexes

The three basic types of conflict that we have been scrutinizing in Chapters 5, 6 and 7 have to be solved with different instruments intrinsic to each type. This is especially true as long as we can treat them as bilateral relationships between two dominant actors confronting each other. From a solution perspective these are the smallest possible elements into which a conflict can be dissected. However, conflicts are neither this simple nor stable. A particular conflict is rarely left alone to be the concern of only the original parties. Conflicts attract attention, some of which may be benign – outsiders will offer their services to help to solve the conflict; others may be more malicious – there are actors who search for ways of using a situation for their own, highly particular purposes. Still others are involved because they simply want to protect themselves, their economy or their extended interests. This may bring them into a conflict, siding with a party or making them into new parties. The linkages are many and the motives varied. This will have many effects: it may prolong the conflict; it may increase destruction; it may also do the reverse. Of particular concern here is how this affects the resolution process. The more parties with stakes in the outcome, the more difficult it will be to arrive at settlements through negotiations, mediation or other forms of intervention.

To capture these interconnections, the term *conflict complex* is useful. It is a way of describing how conflicts are connected to one another. At a given moment in time, we may observe conflicts going on in two different areas but in the same geographical region. Although they may appear separate, closer scrutiny is likely to establish interconnections (Buzan 1991; Buzan and Waever 2003). These are *regional conflict complexes*, where primary and secondary parties are engaged in the same region. In a study using the Uppsala Conflict Data Program, 16 such regional conflict complexes, or regional conflicts for short, could be established since the end of the Cold War. They are listed in Table 8.1. They include a large share of all armed conflicts. It means that the solution to a particular conflict cannot concentrate solely on finding ways of transcending the incompatibilities isolated in Chapters 5, 6 and 7. A follow-up study showed that three-quarters

Table 8.1 Regional conflict complexes with armed conflicts since the Cold War

Regional conflict complex	Examples of armed conflict
Southeast Europe	*Yugoslavia (Kosovo)*, Croatia, *Bosnia*, Slovenia, *East Slavonia*, Albania, *Macedonia*
Caucasus	Azerbaijan, Georgia, Chechnya, Dagestan
Palestine	Israel–Palestine, *Lebanon*, Israel–Syria, *Israel–Jordan*, *Israel-Egypt*, Iraq, Iran
Gulf region	Iraq–Kuwait, USA and allies; Iran–Iraq, Iraq, USA–Iraq, Iran, Saudi Arabia
Kurdish complex	Iraq, Iran, Turkey, Syria
Central Africa, West (Great Lakes Region)	Zaire, *Democratic Republic of Congo (Kinshasa)*, Angola, *Congo (Brazzaville)*, Rwanda, *Burundi*, Uganda
Central Africa, East	Uganda, *Sudan*, Kenya, Ethiopia, Eritrea, *Eritrea–Ethiopia*
Horn of Africa	Ethiopia, Eritrea, *Eritrea–Ethiopia*, Sudan, Somalia, *Djibouti*
Southern Africa	*South Africa*, Lesotho, *Mozambique, Namibia*, *Namibia–Botswana*, Angola
West Africa	*Liberia*, Guinea, *Sierra Leone*, *Guinea-Bissau*, *Senegal*
Sahel	*Mali, Niger, Libya–Chad, Chad*
Indochina	*Vietnam–Cambodia, Cambodia*, Thailand, Laos
South Asia, West	India, Pakistan, India–Pakistan, Afghanistan
South Asia, East	India, *Bangladesh*, Burma/Myanmar
Central Asia	Afghanistan, *Tajikistan*, Uzbekistan
Central America	*Nicaragua, El Salvador, Guatemala*

Note: Conflicts which saw a lasting peace agreement are in *italics*. This overview includes some armed conflicts that do not meet the thresholds for inclusion in the Uppsala Conflict Data Program, such as Botswana–Namibia, the peace agreements between Israel and Jordan (where fighting last occurred in 1967) and with Egypt (last fighting 1973). Also, the table makes no reference to maritime regions, where there might be contentious issues, notably the Bay of Aden, the South China Sea and polar areas.

Source: Adapted from Wallensteen and Sollenberg 1998

of all internal armed conflict had an outside actor involved – mostly neighbours – and is further testimony to the significance of the regional dimension (Harbom and Wallensteen 2005).

To this we may add the possibility of a *global conflict complex* of actual or potential rivalry between major powers. By way of their involvement, conflicts may become connected when this would not otherwise have been the case. The most instructive example is the Cold War, connecting distant areas into the same political and strategic thinking. After 2001, the global 'war' on terrorism had a similar effect, most specifically for areas with large Muslim populations. The major power dynamics will be dealt with in Sections 8.3 and 8.4.

Regional conflicts since the Cold War

The 16 regional conflict complexes include approximately half of all armed conflicts since the end of the Cold War. Their share of the most serious conflicts is even higher: more than two-thirds of the wars are in this group (Wallensteen and Sollenberg 1998). Thus, it is important to analyse conflicts in a regional context. Some conflicts have connection to several complexes, and the outer borders of complexes can be discussed. For instance, it is possible to argue that there is a chain of mutual, consecutive connections among conflicts stretching across Africa from Angola to Eritrea, that is, from the Atlantic to the Red Sea. The conflict material in this region, which is highly populated and resource-rich, has the potential to fuel conflict, if nothing is done, for many years to come. The three complexes identified in the Middle East may also be quite interrelated, as distances are short and the technological capacities of some actors in the region are considerable. However, it still makes sense, analytically and politically, to separate them. Each displays sufficiently independent dynamics to justify this.

It is interesting to note that these regional conflict complexes also include about half of all lasting peace agreements identified in Chapters 5, 6 and 7. Some are shown in italics in Table 8.1. Conflicts within regional conflict complexes are possible to solve. However, the fragility of some of the solutions has to do with the contentious political contexts in which they find themselves. In some regions, peace agreements have supported each other. This is true for Central America, which developed into a model of a regionally-driven peace process. Politically initiated by Costa Rica's President Oscar Arias in 1987, it resulted, within ten years, in peace agreements in all protracted internal conflicts in the region. It was based on a shared understanding of the leaders of five countries. They agreed to pursue similar policies of national conciliation and non-interference in neighbouring conflicts. By strengthening democratic institutions and human rights in all countries, the armed conflicts were brought to an end, one by one, beginning with Nicaragua.

The Sahel region in West Africa has witnessed something similar, although less coordinated. Conflicts, often connected to Libya, gradually have subsided and found solutions. A first case was the Libya–Chad conflict, which was brought to the International Court of Justice, followed by the settlement of Chad's civil war and a creative handling of conflicts in Niger and Mali. The 'Flamme de la Paix' ceremony in Timbuktu, Mali, in 1996 (a big fire consisting of thousands of arms turned in by former fighters) became a symbol for attempts to end conflict by eliminating trade in small arms. Conflicts in Southern Africa have all but ceased, partly through negotiated settlements. An example is the verdict by the International Arbitration Court on the Kasikili-Sedudu Island conflict between Namibia and Botswana (1999). The war in Angola connected this region to the complexes of Central Africa but, after the death of UNITA leader Jonas Savimbi in 2002, the parties quickly resorted to previous agreements. This also had a beneficial effect on the peace efforts in the Central African complexes.

The fact that the actors realize they are part of a larger regional framework makes learning possible. There are many examples of this (Ohlson 1998). In Southern Africa, the earlier failure in Angola had an impact on the settlement in Mozambique in 1992. Renamo, the armed opposition, learned from UNITA's fate in the transition in Angola that it was important to limit the choices of the government side as much as possible. Another element cited was the emphasis in the Mozambique settlement of a sizeable UN presence and early demilitarization, something lacking in Angola's 1991 agreement (Chan and Venancio 1998: 44–5, 63, 66).

Wars ending in victories also lead to important lessons. Again, the interconnectedness can have the effect of reducing the chance of a decisive outcome. A victory in one conflict can be undermined by the continuation of war in another. Also, a regional conflict complex is likely to be attractive for arms trading. It is most noteworthy that some regions have no examples of war endings other than victory. This is still true for the Gulf region, largely also for other parts of the Middle East and the Horn of Africa, and used to be the case for Central Africa. This is in sharp contrast to Central America. As a consequence, the security dilemmas described in the preceding chapters are particularly acute. If there is no practical experience of peaceful endings of armed conflicts, the parties may have very little reason to believe in the realism and relevance of such solutions. War termination through conflict resolution is not likely to be a credible alternative. At the same time, it might suffice to have one case of a successfully implemented peace agreement to change such perceptions. There was, of course, no previous experience of peace agreements in Central America. The Nicaraguan settlement may well have showed the possibility of such a route. The same is true for the accord on Namibia in Southern Africa. The chances of an agreement surviving in an unreceptive milieu of many security dilemmas are not the best, but at the same time it is likely to be necessary to change regional conflict dynamics.

It is interesting to note that the solutions to regional conflict complexes that have been successful have originated in the region itself. The

Esquipulas II process in Central America – named after the second summit meeting among Central American heads of state in Esquipulas, Guatemala – built on previous South American initiatives, the Contadora process. The Esquipulas initiatives were undertaken by the Central American countries themselves. It meant that if united, they could resist diplomatic and other interventions from the United States, the Soviet Union or other states. It turned the established agenda of peacemaking around, and set the region's own needs first. Outside powers had to make adjustments (Spalding 1999).

Approaching regional conflicts

Disentangling regional conflict complexes typically involves two contrasting approaches to a peace process. A gradual way is to approach a regional conflict complex *conflict by conflict*. This assumes that those conflicts which are open to solution are brought to an ending as speedily as is possible. This is done in the hope that continued conflict in neighbouring countries will not affect the implementation of the accords. By removing one conflict in one country from the agenda, the region has a shared experience which can generate energy to go on to the next conflict. A regional momentum for peace is created as tensions also decline in other relationships. The Sahel complex seems to have been handled in this way. The first agreement needs to be successful and have considerable support, both inside and outside the region. In this way it can create a new regional reality.

This approach is often the one preferred by stronger regional actors. It gives them a central role. For instance, India does not want to deal with its conflicts in other than bilateral negotiations. Similarly, Israel's preference has been for peacemaking with each of the Arab states and actors one by one. In the Israeli–Palestinian process, furthermore, the resolution was sought through a step-by-step approach, where the negotiations aimed at a gradual creation of a functioning Palestinian state next to Israel.

One danger with the conflict-by-conflict approach is that the interconnections in the region might be so strong that it will be difficult to implement an isolated agreement. Despite much effort, it was difficult to find an isolated settlement for Burundi in the midst of all the other conflicts in Central Africa. As can be understood from Table 8.1, this region has seen failed agreements (such as the one in Rwanda in 1993) and postponed agreements (such as the ones over the Democratic Republic of Congo in 1999, between Uganda and Sudan in 1999 and Burundi in 2000). Some of these have still resulted in later arrangements with a reasonable potential for the future (the Democratic Republic of Congo, with lingering uncertainty and Burundi, now with a record of two democratic elections). The danger is that the first step solving one of the regional conflicts will also be the last. This, certainly, has marred the negotiations between Israel and Palestine, where the latter constantly worried whether the goal, a viable

Palestinian state, would ever materialize. At the same time, this danger may spur other parties to be more insistent in finding a settlement.

Often, the first steps taken by the parties have been the establishment of a truce of some sort. It makes sense, as it is difficult to pursue negotiations at the same time as violence is continuing among the parties. Nevertheless, there are many negotiations that do not include cease-fire as a first step. Cease-fires often appeal more to a strong party and to regional actors. For the latter in particular, it will reduce acute tensions in the region and make it possible for governments to deal with other matters. It may, however, result in a gradual acceptance of a *status quo* that will be built on an unsolved conflict. This seems to have happened in the Southern Caucasus, where the much-needed cease-fire in 1994 still has not generated a solution to the conflict over Nagorno-Karabakh. Palestinian frustrations with the gradual peace process led the leadership to demand a quicker move to a final settlement. This move failed. A new, popular uprising – the Second Intifada – began at the end of September 2000, resulting in renewed polarization, violence (even through organized suicide deeds and targeted assassinations) and a complete standstill in negotiations. A credible step-by-step approach assumes a consistent and coherent leadership as well as extra-regional commitment.

There is also a bolder approach, which takes on *the most difficult conflict first*, thus hoping to remove the entire regional conflict complex in a short span of time. This means that the most crucial conflicts are identified and solved, even though they may initially seem to be the ones most difficult to manage. If this succeeds, the rest is expected to fall into place. This is bolder, as it requires a shared analysis of what the central issues are and highly concerted actions to tackle them. Sometimes the issues can be easily identified. The processes that dissolved the conflict complex of Southern Africa provide examples. South Africa had long been identified as a crucial actor by the international system. There were international sanctions on the Apartheid regime and considerable attention to its links to wars in the region. Following the settlement of the Namibia conflict in 1988, the apartheid system in South Africa began to open up. As South Africa was central in many conflicts, this had effects on all the surrounding states. Parallel to the democratization process in South Africa, the wars in Angola and Mozambique could find negotiated endings. For a while, this momentum stopped. The peace process in Angola repeatedly was brought to a halt. After the death of the UNITA leader, Savimbi, however, the region saw a negotiated ending to its last armed conflict. Thus, Southern Africa provides a partial example of the successful application of the bolder approach. After the release of Nelson Mandela in 1990 the dynamics of the region changed dramatically, and there was a momentum to build on. It did not immediately, however, carry all the way. Developments in Zimbabwe have resulted in one-sided violence and dangers of escalation.

Another case is Indochina, where Cambodia was seen as the core issue in the regional conflict complex. When relations between China and Vietnam improved, Vietnamese troops were pulled back from Cambodia, regional actors approached the different sides and a momentum could be generated.

It focused on finding an agreeable status for Cambodia, as well as issues of democratization, the return of refugees, protection of human rights, and demilitarization. The Paris Accord of 1991 had these provisions. The coup attempt in 1997 and the contentious elections in 1998 did not increase regional tensions. The inclusion of both Vietnam and Cambodia in the Association of South East Asian Nations (ASEAN), the regional cooperation organization for Southeast Asia, has served to maintain the stability for more than a decade. Lately, developments in Thailand have caused increasing concern, but without fears of regional repercussions.

Identifying such central regional issues, however, may not always be easy. For instance, there are at least two different ways to understand the post-Milosevic situation in Southeastern Europe. Many would argue that the most crucial issue in this complex is the government in Serbia. With democratization and a less nationalist and autocratic rule, many issues in the region have become easier to deal with. Serbia was a key actor in all conflicts in former Yugoslav republics, partly because of the presence of a Serb population, partly due to economic links and military considerations. After the fall of the Milosevic regime in October 2000, there was an expectation of changes in regional dynamics. Largely, this is also what happened. There have been no more wars in the region. Conflict issues have been handled through negotiations. The gradual dissolution of the Yugoslavia that remained, first into Serbia and Montenegro (in 2003) and then independence for Montenegro following a referendum (in 2006), was an entirely peaceful process. Kosovo's unilateral declaration of independence in 2008 resulted in tensions but no armed conflict, and by 2010 Serbia was prepared to *de facto* (but not *de jure*) accept the new situation. Important was the prospect of ultimately joining the European Union.

There is an alternative view, arguing that the Albanian predicament is the central conflict formation in the region. For instance, the Albanians are still the population group most divided among existing states. From this, it follows that finding ways to satisfy Albanian aspirations would be the primary target for a regional process. Certainly, the signs of conflicts in southern Serbia and Macedonia in early 2001 provided evidence for such an analysis. Measures have to be taken within a number of countries to prevent further tension and possible new conflicts. The Ohrid agreement on Macedonia in 2001 provided reforms and contributed to a reduction in violence. Kosovo had to wait for independence and remained under international control for nine years before independence was accepted by a significant part of the international community (Western Europe, North America and some neighbours). A peaceful future requires regional cooperation, perhaps even the formation of interstate connections. For a long time, the attitude in the region was one of promoting separation, self-determination and state formation. However, from an Albanian perspective as well as a Serb one, the possibilities of integration into Europe now hold a larger prospect, rather than developing a cooperative project only for Western Balkans.

The bolder settlement approach may be more difficult to implement. It means that it will often have to build on the interest of regional or international powers to pursue such a strategy. It is a strategy that is more often likely to find application against smaller or weaker actors. If a regional power is at the same time identified as central to the solution, its preferences are likely to be difficult to circumvent. However desirable a bolder strategy may be, it may not be universally applicable. Oftentimes, strategic peace thinking is pushed into the more tactical conflict-by-conflict approach, treating the problems as they emerge or become solvable. As observed, this approach may also appeal to regionally powerful states as it can give them a chance of pursuing a divide-and-rule strategy.

The gradual approach of dealing with conflicts has a practical attraction. It will be politically easier to agree that something needs to be done when a situation appears more acute. It becomes a crisis management strategy. The bolder approach means that there is a long-term strategy for regional peacebuilding for states, regional interests and relevant international organizations. It would point to the potential benefit from closer cooperation in other fields than the exclusively conflict-related ones. It will give room for confidence-building and regional learning. Let us see how the two strategies affect broader regional security and the building of regional organizations.

8.2 Regional Conflict and the Organizing of Regions

The two approaches to regional conflict complexes generate very different results for regional security when solving conflicts. The conflict-by-conflict approach is likely to result in a strengthening of the different actors in a region as each solution will be closely fitted to the particular needs of each conflict. It may, if at all, give rise to weak regional institutions. It would find solutions to particular grievances, but not necessarily shift regional relations to a new level of mutual cooperation. They are likely to result in tailor-made arrangements that can be adapted to the particular circumstances. Their longevity is difficult to predict. It will depend on their ability to adapt to new circumstances. Once they have served their function, they may even be disbanded.

Bolder approaches, on the other hand, will have the additional function of creating a security system with rules, guidelines and norms, not only for contemporary conflicts but also for future problems. These could be frameworks for cooperation not only based on the settlement of conflict, but on broader needs. Satisfying such needs is expected to contribute to cooperative relations. Experiences from the peace processes since the end of the Cold War may generate some insights into the effects of these different approaches in regional conflict resolution.

Regional frameworks

This means that there is a connection between regional conflict complexes and regional security systems. Theoretically, there are a number of such systems, for instance, regional security communities, concerts of cooperation among leading states, as well as regional balances of power (Kolodziej 1998). Many of these have come from conflict experiences and sometimes resulted in regional institutions. Regional security systems point to the importance of the distribution of power in particular regions. This should be kept in mind when we pursue the two approaches to regional conflict complexes. Let us clarify these distinctions with some examples and then evaluate the effects of different regional approaches.

Tailor-made frameworks

These are meetings, fora or other arrangements that are significant parts to solutions of regional conflicts, often originating in regional efforts. Their purpose is to bridge an existing conflict and to provide a venue for discussion and dialogue. Once the framework is established, the parties may find additional shared interests. The presence of extra-regional and supportive actors will be useful for the process. An example is from the Central American peace process. It was a new regional approach. It also gave a role to the United Nations, for instance, in El Salvador (Hampson 1996: 137–44; Pérez de Cuéllar 1997: 402–4) and later in Guatemala (Whitfield 1999). There were previous experiences of regional economic and university cooperation. The wars of the 1980s brought institutional and economic exchanges to a halt. Still, a shared understanding remained of a Central American identity. The process had wider ambitions than only conflict resolution, but settlement of the wars was its primary motive. The composition of the participating states was tailored to fit a regional concept, which included the five states most often cooperating but not, for instance, Panama. The framework did not result in grand organizational schemes or organization-building, following the endings of the wars. There were, however, initiatives for regional demilitarization.

For the conflicts in Southeastern Europe, a tailor-made attempt was tried with the International Conference on Former Yugoslavia (ICFY), as a forum of UN–EU cooperation. It was convened in 1992 and consisted of 31 countries. It was supplemented with a special Contact Group, consisting of France, Germany, Russia, the UK and the USA (Owen 1995). None of these frameworks spilled over into a regional order for former Yugoslavia after the war. Only in 1999 did an EU initiative for the entire region of Southeastern Europe take shape. By 2005, the EU had an elaborate policy of using the possibility of membership as an incentive for the countries in the Balkans to reform and negotiate solutions. It appears to have gained attraction, particularly after the inclusion of Bulgaria and Romania in 2007, making credible the promise of an extension also into the Western Balkans.

The Madrid conference in 1991, attempting to find a regional solution to the Arab–Israeli conflict, was a breakthrough. For the first time it brought together Arab states and Israel. The United States and the Soviet Union served as hosts. However, it soon ceased to function. Some argued that it was too strongly embraced by a visionary proponent, Shimon Peres, whose perspective of future cooperation made Arab leaders apprehensive (Peres 1993; Rabinovich 1999). More concretely, it foundered on Egypt's insistence that a nuclear weapons free zone be established.

It is interesting to note that a tailor-made framework, which today is used in a number of conflicts, is the Organization for Security and Cooperation in Europe (OSCE). It originated in the Cold War and was formed by that global conflict complex. Thus, we will return to it later in the chapter. After the Cold War it was recreated as an international organization and became important in several regional conflict complexes, notably in Southeast Europe and the Caucasus.

The tailor-made frameworks we have reviewed were not easy to create. They have been the results of serious efforts on the highest level of policy-making. Still, their success rate is low.

Needs-based frameworks

The second approach to regional conflict resolution takes its point of departure in shared interests which are not necessarily directly related to the war experience. There are normally many such issues, which can possibly be handled without the interference of ongoing conflicts. It may be beneficial if such a framework exists before serious conflicts are initiated. Issues include, for instance, providing assistance in times of drought, dealing with shared rivers, managing transportation routes, promoting industrial development cooperation and working out trading arrangements. The origin of the European Union is an example. It built on cooperation in the fields of coal and steel production, followed by atomic energy, agriculture, internal markets, and only slowly approaching the notion of shared foreign policy. The ambition was to tie the two former combatants, France and Germany, as closely to each other as was possible for independent states.

Africa, too, has considerable experience in needs-based frameworks, which have become useful in the settlement of conflict. The Economic Community for West African States (ECOWAS) has taken on a role as peacekeeper and peacemaker in the conflicts in Liberia, Sierra Leone, Côte d'Ivoire and Guinea. As the name suggests, its mandate was not primarily security but economic development.

The conflicts in the complex of Central Africa (West) – the Great Lakes Region – have been handled through a regional process, without a formal organizational framework. It resulted in a series of peace agreements where the ones of 2002 and 2003 may be lasting. For instance, the presidential elections in 2006 were conducted in an acceptable manner and Congo had its first elected leader since the 1960s. Conflicts in the Kivu regions followed, however, with a renewed agreement in 2009. For a period, members of the Southern African Development Community (SADC) were particularly active; later, however, they were supplanted by the African Union, the UN and then by the actions of neighbouring countries. SADC was created for purposes of economic development in the region, but had something of a mediating role and also kept its own peacekeeping troops in Lesotho in 1998–99, contributing to the management of the tensions in the country. It was not, however, able to deal with the civil tensions of Zimbabwe.

The limits of regional organizations can be understood when looking at the conflicts in the Horn of Africa. They were not dealt with by its regional needs-based organization, IGAD (Inter-Governmental Agency for Development). The two leading member states, Ethiopia and Eritrea, were at war with one another, thus preventing the organization from taking a role in the conflict. However, it has played a role in conflicts in Sudan.

The first initiatives to solve the conflict in Cambodia were regional in character. Indonesia was a prime mover. It gave a role to the Association of South East Asian Nations (ASEAN). This organization was formed to meet the needs for economic cooperation among Southeast Asian states. Initially it was a regional coalition against Vietnam and communist control in Indochina. During the late 1980s it took a new role and became acceptable to all the states of the region. It was used as a bridge-builder. Following the end of the conflict in Cambodia, it accepted Vietnam as a member (in 1995). By the end of the decade, the remainder of Indochina and Myanmar/Burma had become members. ASEAN attempted to initiate a dialogue with the regime in Burma/Myanmar on democratization, but with no result.

There are other organizations that have been formed on the basis of particular security needs and turned into operations of relevance for conflict resolution. The Organization of American States (OAS) is one case. It was, for instance, useful for the demobilization, following the end of the war in Nicaragua, and played a role in the conflict in Honduras in 2009 by refusing to seat the unconstitutional government. Still, previous history may make organizations with such backgrounds less useful in conflict resolution. Some of them have been created as alliances against other states in the same region and, thus, they cannot bridge conflicts. They may, however, be important in the aftermath of the conflicts, when agendas are formed (Glaser 1997).

One example is NATO, the chief vehicle for Western defence against the Soviet Union during the Cold War in Europe. NATO was used as a military instrument in the conflicts in former Yugoslavia, both in the war in Bosnia and in Kosovo. After the wars, it maintained troops in both places. In September 2001, NATO was invoked in defence against terrorism. A major engagement became ISAF, the international security assistance force, placed in Afghanistan under a UN mandate of December 2001. In 2011, NATO took charge of the UN proclaimed no-fly zone over Libya in order to protect the civillian population from attacks by the Gadaffi regime.

Another example is the Commonwealth of Independent States (CIS), which was created immediately after the dissolution of the Soviet Union. It is generally seen to adhere closely to Russia's foreign policy. Other organizations with similar problems are the League of Arab States and the Gulf Cooperation Council (GCC), bringing together different constellations of Arab states. The League of Arab States consists of the governments of Arab states, and thus represents one side in several of the conflicts in the Middle East. It has backed the PLO against Israel, Iraq against Iran, and Kuwait against Iraq. It has been unreceptive to Kurdish demands. It does have a record of mediating in some conflicts between Arab states. Remarkably in 2011 it supported the UN no-fly zone over Libya. The GCC was reluctant to take sides in the Gulf War, and did not play a role in bridging the conflict.

The Pacific Islands Forum (PIF) has lately become engaged in conflicts of the South Pacific, particularly taking an interest in preventive measures. It endorsed the Australian police mission to the Solomon Islands in 2003 (RAMSI; Henderson and Watson 2005) and has condemned coups in Fiji in 2006 and 2009, when it suspended Fiji's membership.

Transregional organizations such as the Non-Aligned Movement (NAM) and the Organization for Islamic Cooperation (OIC) are also relevant. NAM has been important in pursuing the collective needs of the developing world as a whole, thus spanning some contradictory demands. It has not, however, been an actor in managing armed conflicts among member states since the end of the Cold War. The same could be said of the OIC. Both organizations sent emissaries in connection with various conflicts, notably the Gulf War and the Kosovo conflict.

Also when studying the record of regional organizations built to serve particular needs, be they material or security-related, we find that their participation and success in conflict resolution have been limited. This requires further discussion.

The limits of intra-regional frameworks

Given the pervasive phenomenon of regional conflict complexes, the utility of a regional framework run by the regional members in creating peace is surprisingly limited. Whether tailor-made or needs-based, such intra-regional approaches have not been at the forefront in conflict resolution, globally speaking. In fact, many efforts have been driven by extra-regional actors, rather than being intra-regionally engineered, as was the case in the Central America model. We may ask why it has been so difficult to develop successful regional approaches.

One factor, mentioned in the literature, is that the aspect of power and dominance might be even more important in a regional context than in a global approach. A regional plan may be perceived to favour one party more than others, which appears to be the way Arab countries reacted to many of the schemes at the Madrid conference. The military might and economic strength of Israel may make many hesitant to choose a regional framework. We have also noted that regional initiatives are difficult to make, as a dominant actor in the region may be central to the ongoing conflict and have other ideas about solutions. The organization for South Asia, the South Asian Association for Regional Cooperation (SAARC), cannot serve to mitigate India's overwhelming power in the region. Yugoslavia's size, military strength and strategic location make regional initiatives difficult or meaningless if it is not joining. However, during the Milosevic era the country was politically isolated from the rest of the region. In such situations, countries are likely to develop support from states outside the region. This has been a pattern in Southeastern Europe. The same can be seen in South Asia, with Pakistan strongly linked to China and to the United States. Either way, it means that there is a limit to what regional initiatives can achieve.

There might also be strong rivalries between regional contenders, thus paralysing the efficiency of regional bodies. This certainly has been important for the League of Arab States, which, due to such disagreements, was unable to convene a summit meeting until more than ten years after the Gulf War. IGAD could not be used for the conflict in the Horn of Africa and SADC has been hampered by rivalry between the two strongest members, South Africa and Zimbabwe. In cases where members of the regional grouping are directly involved in the conflict, the regional setting is hard to use. If the strong state is not a direct participant in ongoing conflicts, the situation may be different. A case is West Africa, where Nigeria could take the lead with the support of other countries in the region.

Nevertheless, we can see that power considerations create a barrier for the utility of intra-regional approaches to regional conflicts. If a regionally strong state is part of the problem, a regional framework is unlikely to be used for peace processes or, alternatively, will be used by this actor to further its own goals.

Thus, it is logical that many regional conflict complexes instead are dealt with by actors outside the complex itself. This gives a role to continent-wide organizations, as seen in the case of the African Union (having replaced the Organization for African Unity (OAU)) in conflicts in Africa, or informal arrangements. Let us turn to these frameworks.

Extra-regional approaches to regional conflicts

Intra-regional frameworks have some distinct disadvantages in managing regional conflict complexes. However, the alternative, extra-regional approaches, may turn out to be geographically too wide for smooth operations. The membership of continent-wide organizations is likely to perceive particular conflicts in their own prism. Positions in conflicts may be taken through votes in large assemblies. Thus, there is a danger that too wide a forum will provide arenas for the same regional rivalries that we observed earlier, as well as for attempts to put forward unrelated agendas. The need to take sides will only sometimes be conducive for conflict resolution. This is a problem that afflicted, for instance, the OAU in dealing with the conflict in Western Sahara, or prevented it from taking up internal conflicts in member states. The African Union (AU) constitutes a new departure, however. Since 2004 it has been involved with a peace operation in the Darfur region in Sudan and since 2007 in Somalia.

This is an argument for more informal approaches, that is, approaches that only include some, often neighbouring, countries, together with outsiders. During the 1990s there emerged a number of such specific frameworks. The Contact Group for the conflict in Yugoslavia is one (including the USA, the UK, France, Germany, Russia and later also Italy). Four of these were permanent members of the Security Council, meaning it was a group excluding China, five were members of NATO, thus being able to include one NATO critic (Russia), with important links to the actors in the conflict.

There are precedents to such special groups even during the Cold War. For finding a solution to the Angola and Namibia conflicts, there was a 'Western Contact Group' in the 1970s. It consisted of the Western countries that originally were in the Security Council together (the USA, the UK, France, Germany and Canada) (Hampson 1996: 55). For the conflict in Sudan, IGAD played a peace-promoting role that was augmented with a constellation called 'Friends of IGAD', including the USA and Norway, for instance. In the conflicts in the Horn of Africa, the parties resorted to the OAU and the UN as well as to the USA. It meant creating new relations between two international organizations. The Guatemalan peace process saw its group of 'friends' as well. It also suggested a more informal way of dealing with such conflicts. In fact, forming special coalitions of concerned countries appears to be a most effective way in which regional conflicts can be approached.

It is instructive to note that the UN has found a role in such regional peace processes. The creation of special envoys, either as Special Representatives or Personal Representatives of the UN Secretary-General, has been one such instrument. More novel has been the convening of informal coalitions, sometimes dubbed 'Friends of the Secretary-General', for particular conflicts. It remains to be seen if the new UN Mediation Support Unit will be able to take up such a broader approach.

This approach has some strength in terms of diplomacy and its ability to mobilize actors with resources. Thus, it may contribute both to finding solutions and financing the post-war period. It is highly efficient. They are frameworks as tailor-made as one can get for handling regional conflicts. It has the disadvantage of being very temporary. Groups are formed on particular needs, thus not necessarily furthering learning from one achievement to the next. Nor are they easily transformed into organizations that can sustain peace after the end of the conflict. At that moment, established organizations will have to be brought in. It may create a problem of transferring the understandings. Also, it will be a less transparent process. The agreements may not necessarily be known to all parties, nor will the process by which they were reached. It may, furthermore, give a strong role to more powerful members of the international community, in particular, the five permanent members of the Security Council.

This overview shows that it is hard to find an ideal and generally applicable way of organizing peacemaking in regional conflict resolution. The most important lesson is that there are a variety of ways and, thus, each conflict complex may have to find its proper form.

Regional security after war

Finally, we ask whether the ending of the conflicts in a regional conflict complex also contributes to self-sustaining regional security. Obviously, few of these complexes, listed in Table 8.1, have been entirely resolved. There are four candidates: Central America, the Sahel region (or rather, parts of this vast area), Southern Africa and Indochina. We can note that the ending of these conflicts has not been followed by vigorous intra-regional integration. Rather, the international dependencies that existed previously seem to be intact or even reinforced. For the countries in Indochina, the incorporation into ASEAN may have given additional benefits and new opportunities. Only in a few cases has the war ending been followed by economic growth. Vietnam is one example; Cambodia also may have experienced a 'peace dividend'. Such a pattern may also be found elsewhere. Botswana and Namibia in Southern Africa have had consistent economic growth. Both are rich in minerals. The war effects were limited in both places. However, the stalemated situation in Zimbabwe has affected the possibilities of creating a stronger regional community based on shared democratic values.

The regional systems that can be observed in the post-war period are perhaps closer to a security community model than one of regional integration. The security community builds on the idea that conditions have been created which reduce the expectations that violence will be used to solve conflicts among the members of the community (Deutsch et al. 1957). Openness among the members, for instance in the form of democracy, would enhance this. That would also be the case with economic cooperation, reduced military spending and more experience in solving conflicts among the members. With these criteria in mind, we can note that there is no expectation of new wars among the members in these four regions. South Africa is unlikely to repeat the interventionist practices of the Apartheid regime. Vietnam is reluctant to involve itself again militarily in Cambodia. In a sense, these were the necessary conditions for making the peace agreements in the first place. Those conditions still remain.

Also, important external threats have declined. The conflicts in Central America and Indochina were associated with the Cold War. The post-war societies in Central America and Southern Africa have become more transparent, which contributes to reassurance within the region. Experiences in solving conflicts are increasing as regional issues are dealt with, without provoking new conflicts. The economic interactions, however, are limited. There are also new threats developing. For Central America, these are associated with the drug trade, and increasing concern in the USA to pursue trafficking in a regional framework. For Indochina and ASEAN, the relationship to China is always important and is watched with great care. These examples are testimony to the length of time and the amount of effort it takes to create peaceful conditions after protracted war.

Thus, we cannot say that these four regions have found new forms of cooperation. But they are not under the dominance of any particular actor either. There is a wider spread of regional power and a reluctance to engage in war. Thus, these four regions qualify as candidates for regional security communities. A peaceful democratization of Zimbabwe would enhance such a development. The organizational forms that were used for settling these particular conflicts may be less important for the future. Instead, they show that chances for peace can be taken and that entire regions may retract themselves from regional conflict.

8.3 Major Powers and Conflict Complexes

The period after the Cold War is dramatically different from almost all previous decades in the last 100 years. It has been without classical major power confrontation and world rivalry. Only the 1920s are comparable, as major powers focused on implementing the Versailles Treaty and rebuilding ties. It was, however, a period which was devoted to managing economic crisis and economic reconstruction after the First World War. After the Cold War there followed instead a period of rapid economic growth, not only pertaining to North America and Europe, but also to Southeast Asia, China, India and other parts of the world. In this book, it has repeatedly been noted that there are more peace agreements than in previous comparable periods. Conflict resolution is high on the political and scholarly agendas in major powers. New concepts have gained ground, commanding the attention of decision-makers in leading states: humanitarian intervention, preventive diplomacy, war crimes, bans for land mines and small arms, the international responsibility to protect exposed populations, and human security, to name a few. Concepts and issues that dominated Cold War thinking, such as balance of power, deterrence, escalation, pre-emption, strategic and tactical nuclear weapons, and first and second strike capability, have been marginalized. They have not, however, completely lost their relevance, and have not been thrown on the scrap heap of history. They are still important for arms control measures among major states and for regional affairs, for instance, in South Asia. In the efforts to counter internationalized

terrorism, matters of nuclear non-proliferation have again drawn attention. The significance of intelligence operations has increased.

The new focus means that the major powers are concerned with the settlement of armed conflicts. Let us explore this by first observing the role of
the major powers in the regional conflict complexes that we presented in
Table 8.1. A strong presence of one or several major powers makes a conflict part of a larger, global dynamic. In fact, it might turn a regional conflict complex into a global one, for instance, if it involves conflict between
major powers or their allies. This has implications for conflict resolution.
Then we must note that major powers have their own internal conflicts to
deal with, and we ask for their record in conflict resolution. Finally, we proceed to study the relationship between the major powers themselves, what
legitimately can be regarded as *the* global conflict complexes, as major
powers have a reach beyond their own regions. They all have the capacity
to impact on other regions. This also involves the question of major power
rivalries as well as counter-terrorism policies.

Major powers in regional conflicts

Most of the regional conflicts of Table 8.1 have had major powers engaged
with their own troops or through close allies since 1989. This is true for
more than three-quarters of the 16 cases. This might come as a surprise, as
it is often observed that the era of intervention is over. It was often attributed to the Cold War, with some justification. But the heavy involvement of
major powers in so many regional conflicts makes it important to include
this aspect in the analysis. The focus has to be on six major powers, that is
the five permanent members of the Security Council, plus India because of
its military capability, combined economy, intellectual power and international influence.

In some instances, several major powers have been involved in the same
conflict. Most notable are the conflicts in Southeast Europe, where there
were significant tensions between these powers, while many at the same
time had troops in the region. In the Gulf region, the three Western states
initially acted in concert and with the understanding of other major powers.
In most other instances, only one major power has been involved militarily.
This was the case with Russia in the Caucasus and Central Asia, Britain in
Sierra Leone in West Africa, France in Central Africa, China in the waters
of the South China Sea and India in South Asia. The pattern is classical and
in line with *Geopolitik* thinking. There are certain areas of concern to major
powers, and there is a traditional willingness to respect such areas. The attitude since the end of the Cold War has been just that: to avoid sharp polarization between the major powers. It has meant that the West has avoided
interfering in areas of particular concern to Russia (Caucasus including
Chechnya), while Russia has acted cautiously in areas of special interest
to the West and the USA in particular (the Gulf region, West South Asia,
for example, Afghanistan). The war on Iraq in 2003 displayed considerable

major power disagreement on the American and British actions, but not to the point of military reactions.

Thus, also after the Cold War, there are historically known traits. Major power relations correspond to a pattern of universalism that can be seen in recent history (Schahczenski 1991; Wallensteen 1984, 2011b). There have been such periods in which major powers have acted carefully against each other and been willing to 'understand' the interests of others. The post-Cold War period has traits of such historical periods as those which followed the Napoleonic Wars (1816–48), the Franco-Prussian War (1871–95), the period after the First World War (1919–33) and in *détente* periods of the Cold War (mid-1950s, parts of the 1960s, much of the 1970s). These contrast with more particularistic periods, where the major powers have instead pursued their own particular interests, even at the expense of other major powers, thus resulting in confrontations and major wars. In the Cold War, this was typical for the late 1940s, early 1950s, early 1960s and first part of the 1980s.

During the Cold War major powers were prepared to act early for specific strategic reasons when a crisis emerged, and when it was, in their understanding, related to the major power conflict. It oftentimes led to sharp confrontations. The period since then has seen a change in this dynamic. With respect to some of the regional conflict complexes, major powers appear to enter into conflicts at a later stage. The motives are also different, not least a concern for humanitarian considerations. It is true, for instance, that many of the conflicts that receive considerable attention also have large refugee flows. However, there are situations with an equal amount of refugees and still the attention is low. There has to be additional concern for conflicts to trigger resource-demanding actions. These may still not be strategic, but could have to do with domestic reactions to conflicts, thus prompting governments to act. This means that the type of action is different. There has been a surge in international peacekeeping operations. They now include troops from major powers. This was not conceivable before.

Most concern is likely to be given to conflicts which are closer to major powers, giving them a particular urgency. If there is considerable population movement, this is also likely to trigger action. Thus, it is not surprising to find the Western countries engaging with troops in Southeast Europe, or to find Russian troops throughout the former Soviet empire. In contrast, India and China have seldom sent their troops on unilateral missions outside their immediate region. India most recently had troops in Sri Lanka, China has had naval confrontations and sent missiles into the waters around Taiwan. However, India has a long record of participation in international peacekeeping missions, a pattern China now seems set to emulate.

The conflicts that are likely to receive most attention are those where there is a danger of major power confrontation. This was a constant concern during the crises in former Yugoslavia. Different historical connections complicated the efforts of the major European countries in dealing with these crises. In the final agreement on Bosnia-Herzegovina, these powers were all represented. There was support for the arrangement, and all participated with peacekeeping troops to maintain the solution.

The Kosovo War in 1999 made matters even more complicated. The Western strategy led to an aerial bombardment of Yugoslavia that lasted for more than two months. An American missile destroyed the embassy of another permanent member, China, causing further complications. In the end, the Yugoslav forces agreed to leave Kosovo and peacekeepers from the major powers were to take up positions. An indicative episode was when Russian troops unexpectedly and ahead of the Western contingents appeared in Kosovo's capital, Pristina, in June 1999. The Western powers reacted cautiously and refrained from escalating the situation. This restraint was costly to NATO, but a confrontation would have defeated the purpose of having both NATO and Russian forces on the ground in Kosovo. Different national contingents served to reassure different populations in the region. Something had been learned. The Cold War had many such incidents and they were early indicators of a potential breakdown of relations. This has not happened over the Kosovo issue. In post-war Southeast Europe, four permanent members of the UN Security Council and one aspiring member (Germany) are present with their own military forces. It requires them to have daily cooperation. This also means that events in Yugoslavia cannot be analysed as only a regional conflict complex. Changes in the region are likely to have immediate consequences for major power relations, and vice versa. Southeast Europe is a conflict complex that has global consequences.

This level of complexity is not found in any of the other regional conflicts. In the Caucasus, only Russia has forces. In the Palestinian and Gulf complexes, only the United States is strongly present diplomatically and militarily, particularly since 2003, with a sizeable force based in Iraq for an indefinite period of time. The fact that Britain also had forces in Iraq until 2009 does not challenge the pre-eminence of the United States. No other major power has a comparable presence in the region. In the Libya crisis of 2011, however, USA chose to work with NATO, thus giving more responsibility to its European allies.

In Central Asia complexity may increase. Both Russia and the USA have forces in Tajikistan, for instance. Although there are tens of thousands of Western European troops on the ground in Afghanistan, politically the United States is the leader. The Obama administration has taken a more regional approach to this conflict, emphasizing the connection between Pakistan and Afghanistan, thus also seeing the connections to India, the country about which Pakistan is most concerned. Peace in Afghanistan, in other words, has to involve a regional approach, where neighbours Iran and China also play a role, and a future US withdrawal will have regional repercussions.

The different complexes in Africa, however, have seen very little military involvement from major powers. France sent troops to Rwanda in 1994 in a controversial intervention. French forces have also been stationed in Côte d'Ivoire, following the outbreak of war in the country. Britain sent troops to

Sierra Leone in 2000. The European Union sent a force to the Democratic Republic of Congo in 2003 and again in 2006. The US interest in Somalia waned quickly after US soldiers were killed in 1993, only to resurface again when Somalia was seen as a safe haven for anti-US terrorists (the USA conducted air strikes in 2007, for instance). As far as the major powers are concerned, the military dimensions of regional conflict in Africa have been left to Africa. However, the pattern is not entirely the same with respect to peace processes. The USA has taken a leading role among the major powers in several of the settlements. This has been particularly true for conflicts in the Horn of Africa (ending the state formation war in 1991 as well as the interstate war in 1998–2000), Southern Africa (conflicts over Namibia and Angola) and the peace agreement in Sudan in 2005.

In fact, among the major powers, none has such a record of engagement in peace processes since the 1990s as the United States. Its representatives were involved in all the agreements in Southeastern Europe, the Middle East, many settlements in Africa as well as in the Central American processes. The results have been holding up reasonably well. It could be asked if this US commitment was because of particular factors (such as President Bill Clinton's own priorities) or if it was something necessitated by the new role in which the USA finds itself, as the sole superpower. The post-2001 focus on fighting terrorism is associated with a reduced interest in negotiations and peacemaking, particularly in conflicts that can be connected to terrorism.

Armed conflicts in major powers

The major powers have their own conflicts as well. Such conflicts are observed carefully as they are most revealing about the military, political and economic capacities of leading states. These conflicts are strongly defined as 'internal' matters by involved major powers. In some instances, a major power has its territory as part of a regional conflict complex. This is, for instance, the case with conflicts in the Caucasus, which also link to territory of the Russian Federation. In addition, there was a minor civil conflict in the capital of Moscow itself (1993). The outcome of this power struggle was of great interest to other major powers and the international community. Similarly, the Northern Ireland problem has not been seen as part of a regional conflict complex, although it does involve relations between Britain and the Republic of Ireland. India's many internal conflicts tend to attract little international attention, but clearly are a major problem for Indian states and for the Indian Union as a whole. Several of these are part of a regional conflict complex in the east of the subcontinent. China has conflicts in Tibet and Xinjiang (Uighur) which have some international connection, but so far not on the level of a regional conflict complex.

This suggests that major powers are often able to contain conflicts and will act strongly to prevent others from becoming involved. A case in point is the series of conflicts in Chechnya, where Russia's strategy has been criticized in the West but little else has happened. Major powers are often strong enough to fend off 'outside' involvement. It is also part of their strategy to prevent them from being connected to other issues. The conflicts are not only internal matters; they are also 'special' issues, not comparable to others. This, of course, is an attitude that is not exclusive to major powers. It is, however, forcefully maintained only by states that are internally cohesive and have considerable armed capacity. These are states that often would want to define themselves as 'strong' states.

This does not exclude international contributions to peacemaking, as indicated by the example of Northern Ireland. The list is not very long, however. More typical is that such conflicts either are subdued with considerable force (or 'excessive' force as the EU has described some actions) or become particularly protracted. An example is India's way of dealing with the uprising in Punjab, which was protracted but ended with much force. China's actions in Tibet have been very forceful. Major powers or strong states may be among those actors most unwilling to compromise in internal conflicts. To some, it might be a challenge to the very notion of being a major 'power' and a 'strong' state. Thus, their record as contributors to new ways of solving conflicts can seldom be built on their experience in their own internal conflicts.

Major powers and global conflict

There are also the direct relationships between major powers. These are sometimes described as global rivalry and are built into the international system. This is in line with *Realpolitik* thinking, for instance. We have already observed, however, that they are exposed to important swings, captured by the terms of particularism and universalism. It would mean that the relationships are formed by conflict complexes, where major power conflicts become interconnected, in the same way as we have seen in particular regions. Thus, we ask: are there major power conflict complexes, rivalries, other than those associated with the regional complexes? How are such relationships handled? Are there, for instance, rivalries that have ended? As the latter can be answered as a clear 'yes', it means there is also a 'yes' to the former question.

Whatever description one prefers, the Cold War was such a period of global conflict, and it was ended. It is difficult to agree on when the Cold War started. It could have begun in 1948 with the communist takeover of power in Prague, Czechoslovakia. It could have started with the disagreements in the Potsdam and Yalta conferences in 1945 over the composition of the new government in Poland. The Anglo-American agreement in 1941 to start the Manhattan Project on nuclear weapons without informing its Soviet ally may have fuelled suspicion on the Soviet side, once it understood what was going on. It could also be dated to the Bolshevik revolution in Russia in October 1917. It is most common to date the Cold War to events during the Second World War and immediately after. The term 'Cold War' was coined in 1947 by the American analyst Walter Lippman.

When did it end? It has become customary to see the ending as the fall of the Berlin Wall on November 9, 1989. It is a symbolic date for human rights and democracy, no doubt. But if the Cold War was about Poland, it ended with the accession of the Solidarity movement to power in March 1989, breaking the Communist Party monopoly of power. If it was about Czechoslovakia, the 'Velvet Revolution' in Czechoslovakia later in November 1989 may be more appropriate. If, however, the rivalry was over the defeated Germany and its division, the reunification of Germany in October 1990 would be the turning point. Still another possibility is the first complete nuclear disarmament treaty, eliminating whole classes of intermediate-range nuclear weapons, concluded in December 1987, as the effective ending of the rivalry. If, finally, the Cold War was about the creation of the Soviet Union, the dissolution of that union in 1991 would be the end point.

The Cold War may have begun somewhere between 1941 and 1945, and it may have ended somewhere between 1987 and 1991. The selection of an exact date partially reflects an understanding of what the conflict was all about. There is, interestingly enough, a treaty to point to as its ending. In Paris in October 1990 the Charter for Europe was agreed, for the first time emphasizing democracy as a leading principle for relations among European states. It is a treaty that also tied communist regimes to the new order. The rivalry between East and West was, over some years, transformed from competition, military posturing and propaganda to one of cooperation, with difficulty at times, non-provocative military positions and mutual gains as key marks.

This is not the first time that major power rivalries have been brought to an end, but it may be the most complete such change without a major power war. The USA established contacts with the People's Republic of China in 1972, followed by diplomatic relations in 1978. It was an end to rivalry, but tensions remained. There was, for instance, no *Idealpolitik* transformation following the *Realpolitik* and *Kapitalpolitik* changes. *Geopolitical* disagreements remained, for instance, over Taiwan. In the early twenty-first century the relations between China and the USA took on a new dimension of potential rivalry, but also for possible cooperation in a configuration of G2, the 'group' of two economically dominating powers. We have also taken note of the changes in Franco-German relations since 1945, although they were heavily influenced by the outcome of the Second World War.

If we go further back in history there are additional examples. The American–British relationship, which started with a state formation conflict (1770–83) and included an interstate war (1812–14), was turned into a close alliance for most of the twentieth century. Similarly, German–Austrian rivalry in the first part of the nineteenth century became a close alliance in the second part of that century. French and British competition, for instance in Africa, led to a severe crisis in Fashoda, in present-day Sudan (1898). This event was creatively turned into a partnership that has lasted for more than a century. Even Britain and Russia were serious rivals, for instance in Central Asia, ending this with an agreement on Persia in 1907. Oddly enough, these two countries were allies in the two world wars of the twentieth century. Obviously, major powers are not necessarily and always in conflict with one another. Rivals may become allies.

Such transformation requires closer analysis. It is most interesting to study the period immediately before the present. The ending of the Cold War suggests ways in which conflict complexes can be changed. It draws on similar logic that has been found in regional conflicts. It refers, however, to a level where the stakes are even higher. It is interesting to see that it was not only a process of shifts and changes in major power attitudes to one another, following the particularistic and universalist swings that we have identified. It also included a conscious construction of a framework for dealing with the particular conflict. Thus, we need to examine this more closely.

The ending of the Cold War included, first of all, direct relations between the major powers and their leaders. A feature of much major power rivalry is that the leaders have only met sporadically. One meeting can often lead to misunderstandings and misjudgements. Two such failures are widely reported in the history of the twentieth century. One is the meeting in Munich in 1938 between the Western leaders and Germany's Hitler. The understandings reached by Neville Chamberlain lacked depth and insight into the personality of the opponent. The agreement was quickly undermined by the German leader. The Cold War had a similar encounter, between the newly elected US President John F. Kennedy and Soviet leader Nikita Khrushchev in Vienna in 1961. It was followed by a Soviet-driven escalation of the conflict over Germany and resulted in the construction of the Berlin Wall. Thus, bilateral relations should not be entrusted to particular meetings but to regular contacts. The understanding reached at one meeting needs to be followed up with direct contacts immediately afterwards. This is the way political leaders act in internal affairs and international relations are not dramatically different.

The ending of the Cold War is closely associated with the personal and consistent diplomacy of Soviet leader Mikhail Gorbachev. His ability to communicate with his Western counterparts of the time, in particular US President Ronald Reagan and British Prime Minister Margaret Thatcher, changed the customary image of Soviet leadership and its intentions. There was a series of meetings between 1985 and 1990 that were important in bringing the Cold War to an end. It was accomplished in a peaceful manner, but also in a way in which the stronger party, the West, was not pushing the Soviet side into concessions. Rather, changes were brought about by internal forces, and the changes were accepted by the Soviet leadership.

The armament questions are likely to be central to major power relations. In Chapter 5 it turned out that matters within the *Realpolitik* paradigm were of particular importance. In bilateral dealings between the major powers during the Cold War, we have previously noted a surprisingly long record of agreement on such matters. We saw that there were more such arrangements than solutions to ongoing armed conflicts. For the major powers, strategic concerns are linked to the weaponry held by the potential opponent and the ways in which these can be counter-balanced or neutralized. The ending of the Cold War is closely associated with finding ways to stop the continued nuclear arms race. In particular, the newly developed intermediate-range nuclear weapons, which were stationed in Europe and largely targeted the different parts of Europe, were seen to create instability. They shortened the reaction time for each of the major nuclear weapons powers and thus increased the danger of nuclear war. One of the first accords between the two nuclear superpowers was the decision in 1987 to abolish this entire category of nuclear weapons. With the fear of being a victim to a first-strike attack from the other side removed, other changes also became possible.

A third important notion was the ability to act together in particular conflict areas. The *détente* between the major powers set in motion some of the peace processes we have observed earlier. To these belong the ending of the Iran–Iraq War (agreed in 1987, accepted in 1988). Another example was the withdrawal of the Soviet Union from Afghanistan (agreed in 1988, finished by 1989). There were the settlements for Angola and Namibia (agreed in 1988, implemented in 1989). Most important was also the normalization between Russia and China (begun in 1989, leading to solutions to border conflicts and a peace process for Indochina). Thus, a major power understanding was not only restricted to matters of their direct concern, but also affected their engagement in other parts of the world. It showed that the new policies, primarily in the Soviet Union, were not just cosmetic, but were transformed into concrete action.

A fourth element was the creation of a forum that involved the other participants in the conflict. The bilateral meetings and the nuclear arms reduction talks centred on the USA and the Soviet Union. These were also the actors in some of the peace agreements. However, the European states also had stakes in the Cold War. A tailor-made framework was created, that today is the Organization for Security and Cooperation in Europe (OSCE). Its history is instructive. It began as a discussion on principles of mutual relations, economic cooperation and human rights among the countries that were allies, opponents and neutrals in the Cold War, particularly in Europe. This was possible during a first period of *détente* between the two blocs, early in the 1970s. A founding document was the Final Act, signed in Helsinki in 1975. For 15 years, there were regular meetings on the governmental level in very public, often propagandistic, discussions. It proved successful in the sense that no side wanted to be responsible for a breakdown of the forum, but the meetings were also highly contentious. An important notion stemming from this, and which directly contributed to the reduction of tension in the Cold War, was the idea of confidence-building measures for conventional armed forces. They are actions that at the same time maintain military security and reduce the danger of unintended armed conflict. Such measures were part of the Helsinki Final Act in 1975 and were later elaborated in close detail in Stockholm, Sweden, in 1986, as the very first concrete measure agreed between the Soviet Union under Gorbachev and the Western countries. It was an issue of common concern for all the participating states and governments.

An important aspect of the ending of the Cold War was popular involvement. The Helsinki Final Act contained clear human rights provisions. The document was widely circulated throughout Central Europe, as agreed. It constituted the basis for the legitimacy of actions taken by dissident groups in Czechoslovakia, Poland and, most crucially, in East Germany. The breakup of the Soviet bloc had already begun in the late 1970s. Only through more repressive measures, such as the imposition of martial law in Poland in 1981, could the leadership keep the bloc together for a longer period of time. With increasing *détente* after 1986, it was again possible to advance issues of democracy and human rights. The acceptance of the Polish opposition as a coalition partner in 1989 signalled the end of the Communist Party monopoly on political life. The fall of the Berlin Wall in November 1989 was primarily a result of internal pressure on the leadership in East Germany. The non-violent domestic opposition made an opening up of society necessary. The same happened shortly thereafter in Czechoslovakia.

Thus, the ending of the Cold War was brought about through a remarkable confluence of factors, all highly related to *détente*, arms control, peacemaking, confidence-building, human rights and democratization. These notions helped to change major power relations, but also created a new period in international affairs. The organization, tailored for this conflict, was in 1994 converted into an international body, the OSCE. It now has 56 members, extending east from Vancouver to Vladivostok, that is, incorporating much of the Northern Hemisphere. With this example of the ending of major power confrontation we have also shown that it is a matter of making many levels of society move in a concerted effort. All conflicts are filled with suspicion. In the case of major powers, there are additional reasons for worry and fear. Their global stature may be at stake. Thus, proposed changes have to be convincingly demonstrated to become credible. The actions on one level have to conform to the actions on another level in order to generate the trust and confidence that is necessary. This has happened throughout history. The ending of the Cold War demonstrates that it is possible even in these times.

8.4 Global Dimensions of Conflict Resolution

As we have seen, many conflicts are connected to developments on regional and global levels. To solve regional conflict complexes it is necessary to bring together many or most parties in a region. If this is done under conditions of intense major power rivalry, the chances of success are limited. Global concerns may make major powers interested in block-ing such moves, or embracing them as they serve their purposes. Either way, they are not likely to address primarily the concerns of particular parties. Global conditions affect regional initiatives and local settlements. Distinguishing between universalist and particularist periods of major power relations seems to make sense as a way of capturing important traits. We would expect conflict resolution to be enhanced by universalist con-ditions. There is some historical evidence suggesting this (Schahczenski 1991; Wallensteen 1984, 2011b). It means, in particular, that the many set-tlements the world has witnessed since the end of the Cold War have to be attributed partly to the change in climate created by the ending of that confrontation. Let us explore some of the changes in major power actions in conflict resolution since the end of the Cold War.

First, the very way the Cold War ended may have pointed to new pos-sibilities. There was a resort to procedures that involved negotiations, talks, dialogue, non-violent change, rewards and promises of economic assistance. There were no military threats by one major party against the other. There was an expectation of peaceful change and the furthering of domestic reform. It could be contrasted with a more sinister approach to ending such a conflict, through uncompromising demands, stiff condi-tions, violent incursions, economic blockades and military threats. Such an ending, if it would have meant one, would leave behind it a legacy of intimidation and humiliation. It would not have ushered in an era of con-tinued peacemaking. The process, in other words, is important for ending any conflict, be it between major powers, in regional complexes or more isolated conflicts.

The cooperation among the major powers that was established during the ending of the Cold War also carried into the new era. The actions in the Gulf War in 1991 are testimony to that. Also later, such cooperation, explicit or tacit, has been a feature in regional conflicts where they have had opposing interests. Competing interests may, however, have stalled initiatives or made actions less effective. The inability of the major pow-ers to act in a concerted way in the Balkan conflicts may have served to prolong these conflicts. At the same time, however, such interest clashes are part of life, and reflect perspectives that also need to be incorporated in actual settlements. We may note, however, that the smooth international cooperation in other conflicts may be due to the fact that major powers have accepted each other's geographical areas of specific concern. The armed conflicts since the end of the Cold War have seldom been located, for instance, at the borders of a major power. In cases where they have, caution rather than confrontation has been the prevalent attitude among major powers. There has been reluctance for one major power to encour-age rebellion within another major power. This again can be attributed to the universalist attitude. It also means that some struggles, for instance, for human rights and self-determination, will not get support in some capitals where it might be expected.

There is one area of armed conflict where the major powers have established a new norm of action during the 1990s: the battle of what has been defined as terrorism. Fighting terrorism has been the argument used by Russia to combat rebel groups in Chechnya, and it builds on a strong national consensus created by the bombings of civilian apartment complexes in Russia in 1999. The United States has found itself a repeated target of terrorism: the destruction of a federal building in Oklahoma City in 1995, the attempt to blow up the World Trade Center in New York in 1993 are but two examples. There were also targets outside the USA. In 1996, 19 American soldiers were killed in the bombing of Khobar Towers in Saudi Arabia. The suicide bombings and explosions in Israel and Palestinian territories, including the assassination of Prime Minister Yitzhak Rabin in 1995, contributed to combine peacemaking efforts with anti-terrorist actions. A major international summit was convened in Sharm-el-Sheik in Egypt in 1996 to solicit support for this. After bombs destroyed the US embassies in Dar-es-Salaam, Tanzania, and Nairobi, Kenya, in 1998, the US administration specifically mentioned an organization and a culprit: the Saudi national Osama bin Laden was said to have engineered the bombings. In response, cruise missiles were targeted against a pharmaceutical factory in Khartoum, Sudan, and at bin Laden's hideout in Afghanistan. In 1999, the UN Security Council imposed targeted sanctions against Afghanistan as the country refused to hand over bin Laden. Sources argued that bin Laden also supported groups in Chechnya. The international unity behind the sanctions against Afghanistan on this score was complete.

On September 11, 2001, a coordinated terrorist attack on targets in the USA marked something entirely new. Four commercial airliners were hijacked by persons with some pilot training and ready for suicide. The planes were turned into flying bombs. Two crashed into the twin towers of the World Trade Center in New York, one went into the Pentagon, the Department of Defense headquarters building in Washington, DC. The fourth plane, with an unclear target in the Washington area, went into the ground in Pennsylvania, after civilian passengers managed to prevent the plane from reaching its goal. In all, close to 3,000 people, mostly civilians, perished in this unprecedented act of terror. Among the dead were citizens of more than 60 nations.

It was an attack with great consequences for the leading power, the United States, but also with effects for the global community as a whole. Temporarily, international air traffic was reduced, the world stock markets went down and oil prices increased. This event further strengthened the international unity against terrorism, expressed through a unanimous vote in the UN Security Council on September 12. In a speech to a joint session of the US Congress on September 20, US President George W. Bush declared that the al-Qaida network headed by Osama bin Laden was responsible for the attack. Training camps existed in Taliban-ruled Afghanistan. In six sharply formulated demands, he asked the Taliban to deliver to American authorities the al-Qaida leaders, to close the camps and to allow the US access to inspect the result.

Although Afghanistan was specifically singled out, Bush also made clear that 'our war on terror begins with al-Qaida but it does not end there. It will not end until every terrorist group of global reach has been found, stopped and defeated'. Thus, September 11 marked a new American commitment to global involvement. Bush underlined that '[e]very nation in every region now has a decision to make: Either you are with us, or you are with the terrorists'. All countries in the world were asked to join in, but to the American audience he also said that this was to be a 'lengthy campaign, unlike any other we have ever seen'.

The global shock and shared fear of becoming a target of terrorism brought the EU, NATO and the other major powers on to the same side. Russia and China were supportive of action. A military buildup followed in Central Asia, in agreement with Russia. Naval units and military aircraft were brought into the Gulf region. Former Taliban-supporter Pakistan conveyed the American demands to the leadership in Kabul. The American President could act with unusual political consensus both domestically and internationally.

The phenomenon of terrorism since the Cold War is different from such actions in earlier decades. Previously, hijacking of airplanes, taking of hostages and assassinations were ways for organizations to make themselves known, have their programmes published and, thus, in their own eyes, contribute to the advancement of their particular goals. In the 1990s, this has often not been the case. No organizations have taken responsibility for bombings against US targets or the bombs in apartment buildings in Moscow. The lack of public explanation has made the actions more difficult to understand politically and the official interpretations made by the targeted governments have seldom been disputed.

With the Security Council resolutions a remarkable consensus was demonstrated against terrorism. The international message was clearer than had been the case a decade earlier. Then, the three permanent Western members were more determined than other members of the Security Council in invoking sanctions on Libya. The occasion was the blowing up of an international passenger aircraft above Lockerbie, Scotland, in 1988. The experiences of the 1990s seemed to have forged a more entrenched agreement against such deeds, particularly as they could no longer be tied to a cause which was more widely shared. Some actions were directed against processes, such as the peace process in the Middle East, which were widely supported by the major powers, thus further reducing the international support for terrorist measures.

The 2001 war in Afghanistan resulted in the removal of the Taliban regime and the consensus on reconstruction of Afghanistan persisted. This remains true for the campaign against terrorism as well. New deeds, such as those in

Bali (Indonesia) in 2002, Moscow and Baghdad in 2003, Madrid and Beslan (Russia) in 2004, London in 2005, and Mumbai (India) in 2008 or repeated suicide bombings in Afghanistan, Pakistan and Iraq have received the same world-wide condemnation. However, the US administration's attempt to link the regime of Saddam Hussein in Iraq to international terrorism, the danger of nuclear weapons proliferation and threats to US security was not generally understood. The UN Security Council was sharply divided and no authorization for a war on Iraq was issued. The war still took place in 2003, the regime was removed, to be followed by a protracted internal war and US-led efforts to create a more democratic system. This war complicated international relations and resulted in increasing divisions in America itself. The election of Barack Obama as US President in 2008 followed such sentiment. In August 2010 Obama declared an end to the US combat mission in Iraq, but instead emphasized the increasingly intensified war in Afghanistan. There was strong international support for this effort from the UN Security Council and from Western European and other countries. On May 2, 2011 president Obama announced that USA had conducted an operation that killed Osama bin Laden in Pakistan, and added that this marked 'the most significant achievement to date' in US effort to defeat al-Qaida. It confirmed that there was little explicit interest in finding solutions beyond the military battlefield.

Still, there seems to be more consensus on how optimally to deal with terrorism. The handling of the Lockerbie case was a relevant precedent. The use of the court system would seem the natural way. The court in The Hague for war crimes in former Yugoslavia issued indictments demanding that particular individuals be brought to the court. The international community had committed itself to act accordingly. That seemed the most logical procedure to follow. This was also the gist of the Security Council resolution on September 12, 2001, when it urged 'all States to work together urgently to bring to justice' the perpetrators of terrorism. Among the available options, the resort to legal procedures probably has the largest support. The use of sanctions targeting particular individuals, their personal resources and their economic basis was a novel development which became part of the counter-terrorism measures but also a means for bringing about change in war-torn societies. The UN found new ways of acting. Still, nobody accused of international terrorism has been brought to an international court. Even national jurisdiction has faced difficulties in dealing with terrorism in a legally civilized way. There have been several court cases, however, notably in Indonesia, Spain and Britain.

Major power cooperation has emerged also in some other fields, such as in the fight against Somali pirates in the Indian Ocean. The pirate activity threatens the international shipping lanes and has resulted in an unprecedented international flotilla, including ships from, for instance, the EU, the USA, India, Russia, Japan and China.

Further Readings

Go to the *Understanding Conflict Resolution* web page at www.sagepub.co.uk for free access to journal articles listed.

Buzan, B. and Weaver. O. 2003. *Regions and Powers. The Structure of International Society*. Cambridge: Cambridge University Press.

Deutsch, K. W. et al. 1957. *Political Community and the North Atlantic Area*. Princeton, New Jersey: Princeton University Press.

Hammarström, M. 1994. 'The Diffusion of Military Conflict: Central and South-East Europe in 1919–20 and 1991–92', *Journal of Peace Research*, 31 (3): 263–80.

Wallensteen, P. and Sollenberg, M. 1998. 'Armed Conflict and Regional Conflict Complexes, 1989–1997', *Journal of Peace Research*, 35 (5): 593–606.

THE UNITED NATIONS IN CONFLICT RESOLUTION 9

9.1 The UN in Peace Agreements

The UN is the primary international body for peace and security. It has many different roles in peace processes, which can be seen from its record in conflict resolution since the end of the Cold War. A fuller understanding of the United Nations also requires a look at its special legal standing and the concept of collective security. We can then proceed to discuss how issues reach the UN agenda and what measures the world organization uses.

The durable peace agreements that we have presented in Table 4.2 have a high degree of UN involvement. If we define that involvement as decisions pertaining to the particular conflict and its resolution made by the UN Security Council, the General Assembly and the Secretary-General, there is a UN contribution in a majority of all conflicts, at one stage or another. The variation among the three types of conflict is not striking. There might be somewhat more involvement in civil wars than in state formation conflicts, with the interstate conflicts between. It is also important to observe that there are peace processes which have taken place almost entirely outside the purview of the UN. To these belong the settlement between Ecuador and Peru, the agreements on Guinea-Bissau, several of the Sahel conflicts, Mindanao and Northern Ireland. Either way, it means that the UN and its leading organs for international security are involved, but also that the commitments vary. Furthermore, the UN is seldom the only outside actor dealing with a particular peace process.

Some conflicts have actually ended through a decision in the Security Council. This is rare, but it was the way the Iran–Iraq War was terminated. The parties abided by a resolution from the Council. The settlement over Namibia followed a similar form, although there were considerable negotiations around the central Security Council resolution taken much earlier.

In other circumstances, the office of the Secretary-General has been the forum for working out the agreement. This was the case with East Timor, where the parties met under UN auspices in New York and signed the final agreement with the Secretary-General as a witness.

In other situations the UN has been involved in the negotiations through Special Representatives. It has also meant that the Secretary-General has been highly engaged. In some such cases, the main forum for talk has been through the UN. This happened, for instance, in peace processes in El Salvador, Angola, Mozambique, Liberia, Central African Republic, Tajikistan, Western Sahara and Sudan. Through such means, the UN continues to be engaged in conflicts which have not been settled as of yet, notably Cyprus and Georgia.

There were also situations which can be described as failures for the UN. It was central to peacemaking in Rwanda in 1993–94. The UN was not able to achieve a cease-fire or the implementation of the peace agreement. It did not have the will or the resources to prevent the genocide. It provided important lessons, clearly stated in the report of the Independent Inquiry. In Bosnia-Herzegovina the UN led the efforts, together with the European countries. It was party to the failure to protect the 'safe areas' that had been identified by the Security Council. The fall of Srebrenica in July 1995 hurt the credibility of the UN peacekeeping operation. The initiative for peacemaking was taken over by the United States. These two failures affected the standing of the UN in Western public opinion. It recovered through a thorough and open scrutiny of these experiences (*Independent Inquiry...* 1999; United Nations 1999). The perceived lack of determined action on Darfur in Sudan has drawn similar criticism.

The UN has been important in the implementation of many agreements. Finding their form in the middle of the 1950s, peacekeeping operations were changed after the Cold War. A generation of more comprehensive peacekeeping operations was developed, now including matters concerning elections, the return of refugees, educational components and human rights. The number and range of peacekeeping operations under UN auspices have been unprecedented. This has been important for making some of the agreements durable, notably in Mozambique and Cambodia, and for building a civilian administration in Kosovo and East Timor.

The UN has also authorized action, but left implementation to others. This was the case with the Gulf War, the primary example of peace enforcement. Security Council Resolution 678 of 1990 in essence gave the United States the right to use all necessary means to end the occupation of Kuwait. The war, furthermore, ended through a resolution in the Council, outlining the conditions on the losing side – Iraq – on such matters as compensation, border demarcation and weaponry. The implementation of this resolution led to further crises, continued sanctions and repeated air strikes during the following years. In the climate created by the events of September 11, 2001, the USA also targeted Iraq. The activation of the UN mission for inspection of the military capabilities of Iraq (UNMOVIC) was, after a while, determined to be unsatisfactory by the USA, the UK and some other countries. Without the authorization of the UN, this coalition invaded Iraq in 2003. Following the removal of the regime in Iraq, the UN was again asked to be involved in the reconstruction of the country. UN involvement, however, has remained limited.

Finally, the UN has been on the sidelines of several peace processes, although it has taken actions which have been important for conflict dynamics. One case is South Africa. The international sanctions against the Apartheid regime were among the few mandatory decisions taken by the Security Council during the Cold War. The negotiations that led to democratic elections in South Africa were held between the parties themselves, without the involvement of any international organization. Another case is the Israeli–Palestinian process, which largely was handled by the United States, following the breakthrough created by Norwegian diplomacy. Some time after the breakdown of negotiations in early 2001, a 'quartet' of the UN, the EU, Russia and the USA announced a 'road map' for peace, but in the following years there were no negotiations. A new start was attempted in 2007 and yet another in 2010.

This has illustrated many of the ways in which the United Nations can be useful for peacemaking. Its roles are many. The UN may serve as a framework for action which is driven by other parties. It may also be an actor in itself, handling the settlement process but without losing sight of what member states may want (Weiss et al. 2001). It needs to be recalled, however, that the UN is a membership-directed organization and the members are all states. This strongly affects what it can do. Let us explore this further by analysing collective security through the UN (Section 9.2), agenda-setting (Section 9.3) and UN measures for peacemaking (Section 9.4). The Secretary-General has a role also in mediation. We shall return to this in Chapter 10.

9.2 Collective Security

The UN Charter

International collective security is the primary concern of only one organization, the United Nations. What the UN does is related to this framework, which thus requires some explanation. It normally works for the peaceful settlement of disputes, as stipulated in Chapter VI of the UN Charter. But it can also, by invoking Chapter VII, command the allegiance of the entire organization and its full membership. This is the quintessential meaning of collective security. It includes identifying a breach of international peace and security (Article 39), and then making decisions on measures to be taken by the members. These actions are for the Security Council to take on behalf of the entire organization. Through the Charter all members are obliged to carry out these measures. The Security Council, furthermore, has an extraordinarily powerful composition, as it is composed of the strongest military states. The power of the Council is vested in its position in the Charter and based on an underlying reality of power. This is what makes it unique, when compared to all other international organizations.

The only regional organization that is close to such a powerful position is the European Union and its Council of Ministers. With the ratification of the Lisbon Treaty in 2009, it may take on a larger role in peacemaking than has hitherto been the case (Johansson et al. 2010). Regional organizations are useful in conflict resolution, as we observed in Chapter 8. In addition to the EU, we referred to the OSCE, the AU (following OAU) and the OAS. However, none of them can legally define aggression, but they are increasingly active in conflicts within member states, as witnessed by AU sanctions against unconstitutional changes of government in Africa.

Decisions require the cooperation of all member states, meaning that there is a 'veto' for all. This is often a prerequisite for states to join. Thus, the organizations are not able to identify, publicly and with votes, one of their members as being at fault. The OSCE actually instituted a 'Consensus Minus One' rule to prevent Milosevic's Yugoslavia from blocking the majority. Other organizations lack such procedures. Actions against aggression have been taken either against suspended members (OAS against Cuba) or against non-members (OAU on Apartheid South Africa). In 2000, this exposed the European Union to a severe dilemma, as most member states opposed the Freedom Party's entry into the Austrian government. Its policy on migration and ethnicity run counter to EU norms. At the same time, the government was formed under legitimate democratic procedures. Mild sanctions were imposed for about half a year.

A unique task for the Security Council, thus, is to identify aggression. Article 39 gives three ways of categorizing a particular crisis situation under Chapter VII. It has to be an 'act of aggression', a 'breach of the peace' or a 'threat to the peace'. Mostly, the Council has refrained from using the label 'aggression', even if that is what it had in mind. Iraq's invasion of Kuwait in 1990 was not defined as an 'act of aggression'. The Council preferred the formulation of a 'breach of the peace'. In practice, this made little difference, as the central decision was to invoke Article 39 (Security Council Resolution 660 of 1990). In September 2001, the Council decided that 'any act of terrorism' constitutes a threat to international peace and security (Resolution 1373, building on 1368), giving rise to a major counter-terrorism operation within the UN system.

A further enlargement of the UN agenda was outlined in the World Summit meeting of September 2005, when it accepted the notion of an international responsibility to protect exposed populations against genocide or ethnic cleansing. This responsibility rests primarily with the sovereign government but, if it fails, the international community needs to act. The most dramatic application of this to date are resolutions 1970 of

February and 1973 of March 2011 on the situation in Libya, including an arms embargo and a no-fly zone.

Together, these measures may reduce the independence of individual states. Their only 'protection' as a UN member state, within the confines of the Charter, is that a permanent member can use its veto, or that they can muster the support of at least seven non-permanent Council members. This 'sixth veto' would prevent the Council from reaching the nine votes required for a decision. The major powers have accepted Chapter VII, as they themselves are protected through their own veto. The veto is criticized, but it is also important for smaller states. It provides a guarantee that the UN will not be used by one group of major powers against another. In this way, it makes it possible for neutral or non-aligned states to become members. This is a most important difference between the UN and the League of Nations, which could be used against major powers such as Japan, Italy and Germany. This is why major powers withdrew, or did not even join, as was the case for the United States. In the end it made the organization inoperative.

The armed conflict that the founders of the United Nations had in mind was an interstate conflict, where one state convincingly could be identified as an aggressor. The collectivity of states would then gather under UN guidance to force the aggressor to give up its aggression. In interstate conflict, this is largely a matter of returning to *status quo ante bellum*. In Chapter 5 we saw some examples of that (notably the Gulf War), but also some of the difficulties in arriving at such a shared judgement (for example, in the Iraq–Iran War). This notwithstanding, the UN has a particular function in interstate conflict, especially in those cases where none of the permanent members is directly involved. If a permanent member is one of the fighting parties, the UN will face a problem. It might mean that the UN will not be used at all (blocked by a veto) or that it involves itself on the side of this particular state (with the support of others on the Council). The first option is straightforward and the permanent member will act outside the UN framework, or possibly use some of the escape clauses that exist. Article 51 allows for the right of self-defence, for instance, at least for a period of time. This is a clause that has been invoked by the USA in defending its actions against Iraq in March 2003. It may also resort to the use of a regional organization under Chapter VIII.

In the second option, where all permanent members are in support of action, it may be problematic for other members to determine if this is a strict application of UN procedures or a case of major power cooperation threatening the sovereignty of smaller states. It is a valid concern and raises the question of the representativity and composition of the Council (Russett 1997; Wallensteen 1994b). This argument has been used against Council action, for instance, by Iraq in the Kuwait crisis. In that case it received little sympathy internationally. The invasion of Kuwait was too flagrant and a potential precedent that made other states worried. Nevertheless, the UN Charter builds on the ability of major powers to cooperate. That may, at least in theory, result in policies that are negative for less powerful members or lead to neglect of issues that are important to them.

We have seen that the interstate conflict is not the most typical armed conflict. Instead, the record since the Cold War deals with civil wars and state formation issues, even entangled in regional conflict complexes. Aggression is more difficult to define. Is it the rebels rising against repression who are to be deterred or the government that violated human rights? Are government and/or rebels receiving support from the outside and is that to be seen as aggression? Is the incumbent government merely defending the country's territorial integrity and political independence when it is attacking rebel positions in neighbouring countries? The aggression criterion becomes difficult to apply in a detached analysis. In the Security Council this may be compounded by the positions of member states and the possibility that members do not interpret facts in the same way.

In practice, the Council has defined situations in more general terms, such as 'threat to international peace and security'. Such formulations mean that the international repercussions of a particular conflict are the legal basis for action, notably, the flow of arms, the refugee situation, etc. In the debate, more stringent criteria have been proposed, such as 'genocide', 'mass violation of human rights', and 'ethnic cleansing'. These concepts cover situations with considerable international attention. They push members of the Council to take action, but also lead Council members to find ways to avoid action, when they do not want to act. The Genocide Convention contains strong stipulations for states to act against genocide. In the Rwanda genocide, the United States preferred officially to describe what was going on as 'acts of genocide' in order not to be forced to act. It was not alone among the permanent members in avoiding a description that would result in concrete measures. The mandate for the peacekeeping operation focused on restoring a cease-fire rather than preventing genocide (*Independent Inquiry...* 1999).

There is a definite development in the internationally accepted collective security doctrine. It includes an enlargement of the meaning of security. The definition of the collectivity – whose security is to be protected – no longer includes only states and their survival; the fate of the populations of the states are also of international concern. Concepts such as human security have become important, as are common, cooperative, democratic and preventive security (Åsberg and Wallensteen 1998). The agenda for collective security by the UN has broadened. The endorsement by the World Summit meeting in September 2005 of the principle of a responsibility to protect exposed populations is a further expression of this. It has been noted that the Charter does not mention the word 'democracy', something which would be inconceivable if it were written today (Boutros-Ghali 1996). The shift is not simply one of moving from interstate conflict to intra-state conflict. Also, the understanding of what is problematic in a conflict has gradually shifted. It is not only a matter of bringing parties to cease-fire and negotiations, there is also an increasing commitment to reconciliation, peacebuilding, democracy, equal rights, gender issues and the protection of populations that might be harmed.

UN institutions

There are three bodies that may take actions in the advent of a serious conflict. They are concerned with conflict resolution and with the possibility of collective action, which may, in some instances, involve the use of violence: the Security Council, the General Assembly and the Secretary-General.

Some of the special features of the Security Council have already been noted. Among its 15 members, five are permanent, meaning that they have held this position since 1946, for more than 65 years, while ten are non-permanent members, elected by the General Assembly, for a period of two years. This imbalance in tenure in itself makes clear the difference between these two categories. It is further strengthened, of course, by the veto power given to the five permanent members. We have already noted that there is a hidden veto. If seven of the non-permanent members unite, they can block a decision. For this and other reasons, the permanent members will have to take into consideration the views of non-permanent states. This provides a measure of representativity of the decisions of the Council.

The activation of the Security Council since the end of the Cold War has pushed the more representative body of the UN, the General Assembly, into the background. When the Cold War raged, decisions in the General Assembly gained increasing stature. Its resolutions represented a broad spectrum of world opinion and contributed to some development in international legal thinking. An important decision was the Uniting for Peace Resolution in 1950. It meant that if the Security Council was blocked from acting on a particular issue, this issue could be taken over by the General Assembly. This was a way of bypassing the veto of the Security Council. It was used during the 1950s. For instance, the decisions on the peacekeeping operations following the Suez Crisis in 1956 were taken in the General Assembly. In this case, Britain and France – the countries that had staged the intervention to wrest control over the Suez Canal from Egypt – prevented the Council from acting. Another example is the case of Afghanistan. The Security Council was blocked by a Soviet veto from acting on the Soviet invasion in late 1979. Instead, a resolution was passed in the General Assembly, giving the Secretary-General a mandate to take measures on the crisis.

The crises since the end of the Cold War have not resulted in many vetoes. Thus, it has not been possible or necessary to activate the UN through the General Assembly. The few veto votes that have been cast have been handled differently. The most frequent ones have come from the USA and China: in the former concerning questions on the Middle East; in the latter on issues, which, in some way, have concerned the international recognition of Taiwan. As the latter affected an important operation, it requires some elaboration.

China stopped the prolongation of the preventive deployment of forces in Macedonia, as Macedonia had established relations with Taiwan. The voting had nothing to do with the peacekeeping operation in place, but concerned an issue of great interest to China. It should be noted that the acceptability of the veto is tied to its responsible use, meaning that a permanent member has a commitment to do what is in the interest of the organization as a whole, not only for the member itself. The peacekeeping operation was dismantled as a consequence of China's vote in February 1999, at a time when the crisis was escalating in neighbouring Kosovo. It is necessary to ask if the issue could have been transferred to the General Assembly and, thus, received a mandate for continuation. No such suggestion was made, which is indicative of the new relationship between the Council and the Assembly. The Council has become paramount.

However, reforming the institutions of the UN requires decisions through the General Assembly. The push for reforms of the UN during its 60th session (2005–06) made the Assembly more central than has been the case for a long time. It gave global attention to its President, Ambassador Jan Eliasson of Sweden.

The Secretary-General, as the chief administrative officer of the Secretariat, has an important position. According to Article 99, the holder of the office can call to the attention of the Security Council any emerging threat to international peace and security. This is one of the ways in which the Secretariat works. Sometimes it may be necessary for the Secretary-General formally to invoke Article 99. In July 1960, Dag Hammarskjöld used this to have the Security Council meet on the crisis in the newly independent Congo. This was the first time Article 99 was used explicitly (Nicholas 1971: 179). Within a few days a peacekeeping operation was dispatched to the troubled country. It faced a complicated situation, bordering on what today is described as a state failure. One element was that the richest part, Katanga in the South, sought to secede from the state. This was something that the central government opposed, as did the African states, which all recently had acquired independence and might face similar challenges. It was one of the experiences that made it important for the OAU to establish in 1964 the principle that the colonial borders should not be changed. It became the task of the UN to find a negotiated solution to the attempted secession. In September 1961, the Secretary-General flew to meet the leader of the secession, Moise Tshombe. It was a unique action for a Secretary-General. Hammarskjöld's plane crashed on its way into landing at Ndola, in what is today Zambia. The Congo conflict shows that the Secretary-General will have to build on the support of other states, whether in the General Assembly or in the Council. Hammarskjöld eventually met strong opposition from two permanent members, France and the Soviet Union, but had determined support from the emerging Third World and from the United States. The formal rights of the Charter have to be complemented with the ability to muster support among the member states.

Other Secretaries-General have also invoked Article 99, but seldom found themselves in a drama of such dimensions as Hammarskjöld. Kurt Waldheim did so at the outbreak of the war between Iraq and Iran in September 1980. Javier Pérez de Cuéllar used it in August 1989 to promote an ending to the civil war in Lebanon, something which set in motion a process leading to the peace agreement in 1990 in Taif, Saudi Arabia (Pérez de Cuéllar 1997: 57, 131). With these measures the Secretaries-General have sought to activate the Security Council. These have been situations when the Council has been unwilling or unable to take actions on its own. In the period after the Cold War, the Council has met at an extraordinary frequency, and thus there has not been the same need for the Secretary-General to make it convene.

However, certain innovations have taken place. When Pérez de Cuéllar acted in the Lebanon crisis, it stemmed from dissatisfaction with the inability of the permanent members to take responsibility. Pérez de Cuéllar instituted a new form of cooperation among the permanent members. In January 1987 he initiated regular, informal meetings among the ambassadors of the five permanent members. Later, he noted that only with this initiative '45 years after the founding of the United Nations, did such cooperation become – tentatively, at first – a reality'. The first tangible result was the cease-fire resolution in the war between Iraq and Iran in August 1987 and the cease-fire in 1988 (Pérez de Cuéllar 1997: 152–74). The working arrangement has continued since then and is one factor behind the strong role of the Security Council.

The three organs of the UN are interrelated in ways which actually support the viability of the United Nations. The organization may otherwise have collapsed. For instance, it is remarkable that the Soviet Union chose to return to the Security Council after the Council had voted in favour of a military operation in Korea in 1950, against an ally of the Soviet Union. If it had chosen to stay outside the organization, the UN would have become a Western instrument against the Eastern bloc. This may be why the Soviet Union came back. It upheld the organization. Instead, the result was a deactivation of the Council, as the Soviet Union used its veto frequently. This made the Secretary-General and the General Assembly more important. The Uniting for Peace resolution was significant in an unexpected way, however, as it gave a chance for transferring international action to the General Assembly in the crucial Suez Crisis. The Council was prevented from action by Britain and France, not the Soviet Union. At this and other times, initiatives by Secretaries-General may serve to make the organization responsive to the needs of member states. The roles of the three organs keep shifting, but together they contribute to make the UN relevant for international conflict resolution.

Following the Iraq War of 2003, UN Secretary-General Kofi Annan initiated a reform process that included the main organs of the UN. In December 2004 his High-Level Panel on Threats, Challenges and Changes presented 101 reform items. Many of these were dealt with at the World Summit in New York in September 2005. By January 2006, a new Peacebuilding Commission began to operate as a way of maintaining an international interest in post-conflict situations that earlier tended to relapse into war. It was an attempt to bring together development and security issues as equally significant matters in peacebuilding. Some years later the Mediation Support Unit was created to support the Secretariat's effort as a third party in ongoing armed conflicts.

9.3 The Security Council in Conflict Resolution

The role of the UN in conflict resolution changed during the 1990s. This can be seen most easily from the number of resolutions passed in the Security Council. Figure 9.1 shows the patterns since the Security Council began to operate (January 1946). It also displays the number of resolutions that were vetoed by a permanent member. In the first periods there was considerable activity, then for the early 1950s, at the 'coldest' periods of the Cold War, there were almost as many vetoes as there were resolutions. For the following three decades, a pattern developed where resolutions were passed, mostly as recommendations, that is, under Chapter VI of the UN Charter. The quantitative and qualitative shift came in 1990. It can be timed to the date: August 2, 1990. Upon Iraq's invasion of Kuwait, the Security Council met almost directly and arrived at a clear decision. The invasion was condemned and the Council demanded that the Iraqi forces leave immediately and without conditions. This action put the crisis firmly on the agenda of the Council. It also set a precedent. Many of the conflicts since the Cold War were brought to the Council for action. Thus, the activities of the Council increased dramatically, as can readily be seen in Figure 9.1. The Security Council has become a body that meets continuously and in so doing also makes important decisions. The UN now has a significant role in international affairs.

Figure 9.1 shows that the UN system was remarkably under-utilized during the Cold War. Important conflicts were not brought to the UN, such as the questions over countries and territories that were divided by the Cold War (Germany, Austria, Berlin, China, Vietnam and Korea). Conflicts inside each bloc were barred from entering the UN, for instance, the Soviet invasions of Hungary and Czechoslovakia. Thus, the major power conflagration meant that conflict management became a matter for the direct relations between the major powers. If they dealt with these conflicts at all, it was through bilateral arrangements. As these relationships were at the same time strained by nuclear weapons issues and armament decisions, and coloured by the ideological perspectives of the two sides, many conflicts were not handled in creative ways.

During the Cold War only one reunification was achieved through negotiated means, that of Austria in 1955. Typically, this took place during one

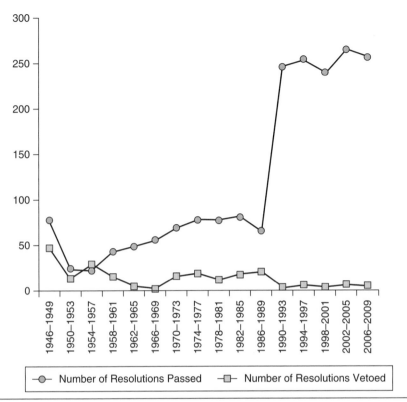

Figure 9.1 UN Security Council resolutions, 1946–2009 (number of resolutions passed and vetoed, four year periods, absolute numbers)

Source: United Nations, *Research Guide*, available at: www.un.org/Depts/dhl/resguide/scact.htm (accessed September 22, 2010), compiled by Rachel Miller.

of the first periods of *détente* between the East and West. It was as a result of such a *détente* period that other solutions were found, beginning in the middle of the 1980s. Mikhail Gorbachev's coming to power in the Soviet Union in 1985 made a significant difference, as mentioned in Section 8.3, but it was also important that his reform policy was received positively by the Western leadership at the time, particularly Ronald Reagan and Margaret Thatcher. The fear that the West would simply exploit a softening of the Soviet system turned out to be unwarranted. Such fears had triggered the Soviet invasions in Eastern Europe in the earlier periods. *Détente*, in other words, was the most important factor in bringing about the remarkable shift in the operation of the Security Council. It illustrates that the Council's continued role is dependent on the relationships between the major powers.

When the crisis of Kuwait erupted, there was an experience of cooperation among the major powers from previous crises. Gorbachev regarded the use of the UN as a way of extracting the Soviet Union from certain international commitments. It was used in ending the Soviet presence in Afghanistan. As a former US ambassador to the United Nations, the US president at the time, George H.W. Bush, had a familiarity with the UN. A framework for consultation had been developed within the Security Council. It was expedient for all sides to turn to the UN for this crisis, and the following ones.

The performance of the Security Council in the Gulf crisis built on the consensus among the major powers. China abstained from the most crucial vote in November 1990, but it did not act to undermine the decision. Thus, Security Council resolutions have been voted throughout the 1990s with the agreement of the five permanent members. There are only a few cases where a permanent member has abstained. The decision on Iraq in December 1999 on a new inspection scheme is unique in that three major powers abstained (China, France and Russia). The same powers, plus the non-permanent member at the time, Germany, united to resist the US and UK draft resolutions on Iraq in February and March 2003, this time joined by a considerable number of other Council members. The drafts were never put to a formal vote. In the Georgia crisis in 2008, however, a draft was presented and received a negative vote from Russia and China, thus limiting UN action in the conflict. The most active peacemaking initiatives instead came from the EU chair at the time, France.

Unity is important. Opponents are likely to look for cracks in the Council membership. During the past decade some leaders have gained expertise in exploiting such disagreements. In his study of some UN missions and the activities of their opponents, the spoilers, Stedman finds major power unity to be essential in enhancing peace processes (Stedman 1997, 1998). Leaders in the Yugoslav and Iraqi crises have understood how to use major power disagreements to their own advantage. Thus, the necessary compromising that takes place in the Security Council should be seen not only as a way of bridging intra-Council disagreements, but also as a way of making policies that can be implemented with the full support of the permanent members in the arena of conflict. Particularly in the aftermath of conflict, this is important so as to maintain international cooperation for reconstruction and post-war peacebuilding. The international reluctance to engage in Iraq after the interstate war of 2003 is indicative of this.

In terms of UN politics, a united Security Council is most desirable. However, it makes other organs lose influence. The Secretary-General finds himself/herself in an entirely new situation. A pattern was set early in the post-Cold War period. The Secretary-General was not involved in the drafting of the key Council Resolution 678 (1990) in the Iraq–Kuwait Gulf crisis (Pérez de Cuéllar 1997: 249). During the first part of the 1990s, on several occasions the Secretary-General had a different preference from the Council and, in the end, had to yield. Kofi Annan was an assertive Secretary-General but faced the problematic US/UK intervention in Iraq in 2003, clearly taking place outside the Charter. His successor, Ban Ki-moon, has taken a low-key approach to the office, but in early 2011 was in the lead in the crisis over Libya and Côte d'Ivoire.

Agenda setting

Among the UN organs, the Security Council has taken the lead since the end of the Cold War. We have also seen that most peace agreements have engaged peacemaking components of the UN. The world body, however, is not necessarily involved in all conflicts. There is a process of selection which sheds further light on how conflicts are handled in the present global system. This leads to the question of agenda setting. Which conflicts are likely to come to UN attention and which ones are not?

With the new role of the Security Council there is likely to be a closer correspondence between the world agenda and the UN agenda. In the Cold War, these agendas were clearly different, as few of the Cold War issues entered the UN system. Today, the concerns of the UN are also likely to be the interests of the world as a whole. Furthermore, once an issue is under Council deliberation it will be of concern not only to Council members but also to all states. There is an agenda-setting function of the UN in general and of the Security Council in particular. Some actors want to have their conflicts on this agenda, while others attempt to prevent it. When the Council defines an issue as a threat to international peace and security, this is a matter to which all states have to attend.

This issue can be approached be studying which comparable conflicts are on the agenda and which ones are not. Tables 9.1 and 9.2 overleaf present data drawn from the Uppsala Conflict Data Program on major armed conflicts. The information covers ten years, 2000–09. The major armed conflicts category is where at least 1,000 persons have died in battle in one year during the course of the conflict. Thus, these are conflicts of such magnitude that they should be noticed and assessed to determine whether they are relevant for international peace and security or not. The main task of the Security Council is to handle matters relating to conflicts and most of its resolutions deal with such matters. The attention given to a particular conflict is reflected in the resolutions passed. The conflicts that are high on this score are likely to be of particular concern to the international community.

Tables 9.1 and 9.2 list the major armed conflicts with the most and the least attention in terms of Security Council resolutions. The ten conflicts with the most attention could easily be identified and described by those who regularly followed the news media during the period. They no doubt draw high universal interest. The seven conflicts, which had received no attention at all, in the form of a Council resolution, might be more difficult for many to describe. Still, the premise is that they all pass the same threshold of human suffering. Furthermore, many were active for a considerable period of time, as is made clear in Table 9.2. Even so, most of them probably received limited interest in foreign ministries or non-governmental organizations beyond the immediate group of concerned states and peoples.

Table 9.1   Agenda setting in the United Nations: the top ten conflicts

Major armed conflict	Number of resolutions
Democratic Republic of Congo	51
Iraq (Gulf War, wars in 2003 and after)	32
Liberia	32
Sudan	29
Afghanistan	28
Somalia	27
Eritrea–Ethiopia	25
USA v. al-Qaida, international terrorism	23
Burundi	13
Angola	11

Note: The table includes the major armed conflicts most attended to, 2000–09 and the number of resolutions in the Security Council dealing with a particular armed conflict.

Source: United Nations Security Council Resolutions, available at: http://www.un.org/Docs/sc/unsc_resolutions.html (accessed September 16, 2010), compiled by Rachel Miller

Table 9.2   Agenda setting in the United Nations: the conflicts least attended to

Major armed conflict	Active 2000–09
Algeria	10 years
Colombia	10 years
India (Kashmir)	10 years
Philippines (Mindanao)	10 years
Uganda	10 years
Russia (Chechnya)	8 years
Sri Lanka (Tamil Eelam)	8 years

Note: The table includes the most 'forgotten' conflicts, 2000–09. The whole period is ten years. Conflicts listed have been active in the period for at least eight years without a resolution from the Security Council.

Source: United Nations Security Council Resolutions, available at: www.un.org/Docs/sc/unsc_resolutions.html (accessed September 16, 2010), compiled by Rachel Miller

This is a way of illustrating that there is a connection between the attention given by the Security Council and the understanding of which conflicts are important. It shows quite clearly that, if a conflict is on the Security Council agenda, it will receive global attention. A 10-year period should suffice to make this conclusion. Are there any systematic variations between the cases in Table 9.1 and Table 9.2? For instance, is there a difference in the level of violence among the top ten and the other seven? Earlier studies suggest that this is not necessarily a strong reason why certain issues come to the agenda of international organizations (Wilkenfeld and Brecher 1984). The seven 'forgotten' conflicts have been very brutal by any standard, even including violence against children. This is not a simple discriminating factor.

Could it be, then, that those with little attention are also of minor importance to regional stability and, thus, are not seen as threats to international peace and security? The conflicts in Uganda, Sri Lanka and Chechnya did not give rise to Security Council resolutions. Some other conflicts in the same regions did, for instance, in Central Africa or Central Asia. Several have resulted in large movements of people within as well as across borders. Several have been connected with armed attacks outside the location of the conflict (kidnappings, murders, terrorism, assassinations, and interventions into neighbouring countries). This has obviously not been sufficient to bring all conflicts that meet these criteria to the Security Council agenda.

There is an important difference which relates to the basic topic of this book. In all the cases that have attracted most attention, there have also been internationally driven peacemaking processes. In fact, most of them have been appearing in the tables of peace agreements. In some cases (Iraq after 2003, Afghanistan after 2001) this was tied to the defeat of the previous regime. This is less so in the case of the seven attracting least attention. Among the top group, furthermore, there were durable peace agreements in six cases. Among the seven at the lower end of attention there were no durable peace agreements, although there were some ceasefire arrangements. Thus, a reason for Security Council attention was to support peace processes, but not necessarily creating them in cases where they might be needed.

This is an interesting conclusion. It could possibly be generalized in the following way: conflicts that enter the Security Council agenda are likely to be those where there is international support for a solution. There is a selection effect. The Council acts when there is some prospect of peace and, obviously, becomes associated with such attempts. If a peace agreement is achieved, the Council attention would be expected to recede as a conflict enters an implementation phase. Crisis or peace process management is no longer required. If not, the issue will stay on the agenda and the UN will increasingly be seen to have failed. In fact, of course, it is the primary parties that have failed. Paradoxically, the onus for the continuation of the conflict often falls on the actor trying to end it, not on the parties pursuing the conflict. Even more remarkable is that armed conflicts which continue without being on the agenda are seldom seen as failures for the UN.

There is one more element that can be seen from the cases which have not come to the agenda in the same period. All seven conflicts in Table 9.2 have been defined as internal matters by the governments concerned. It means that international attention has not been welcomed, unless it has concerned support for the government. In the Cold War period references to Article 2.7 were often made by a major power that wanted to prevent opponents from interfering and creating international interest. In the post-Cold War period major powers may not necessarily play this role. For a conflict not to gain Council attention it would have to involve a comparatively powerful UN member. In the period, this was true of countries such as Russia, India, Sri Lanka, Colombia and Algeria. Whether internationally supported or not, they had the ability to block others from interfering in the conflicts. Only one of these countries was a permanent member; the others were able to prevent such moves due to their regional or international stature.

At some juncture, major powers may positively seek to have conflicts of their particular interest brought to the agenda and not necessarily in conjunction with a peace process. The USA has been the main actor behind three of the conflicts most attended to: Iraq, Afghanistan and al-Qaida/international terrorism. Resorting to the UN has been a way to garner international support for its military actions, although this has led to compromises with other Council members. This, in fact, is why the onset of the Iraq War in 2003 was not on the agenda; the USA, the UK and allies could not muster at that time the same kind of support there was for actions on Afghanistan and international terrorism. Thus, major states can generate attention, but cannot always expect to command the organization.

The reverse is also plausible, that weaker states get more attention. The cases with many resolutions concerned countries whose governments were weak or in transition (new, not established, or failing, as in Afghanistan, Congo, Liberia and Burundi). The same goes for countries that were internationally isolated earlier and were trying to regain international acceptance (Iraq). The importance of this dimension can be demonstrated with two cases not passing the threshold for inclusion in Table 9.1: East Timor and Nepal. The former was on the agenda of the General Assembly in the early 1980s, but Indonesia, having considerable influence in the region and in the Non-Aligned Movement, managed to prevent further attention. East Timor became an international concern again at the time of the massacre in Santa Cruz, Dili, in 1991. This was reinforced when the Nobel Peace Prize was awarded to two East Timorese personalities, Bishop Belo and Mr José Ramos-Horta, in 1996. Still, the Security Council did not pass a resolution on this conflict until May 1999, at a moment when Indonesia's position was dramatically weakened following the Asian economic crisis and the fall of the Suharto regime. This was a time when the chances for resolution were increasing. Similarly for the case of Nepal, where a conflict had gone on for a long time but did not enter the UN agenda until 2007, when the peace process was making significant strides.

The conclusion is that the Security Council gets motivated to act in a conflict when it is urgent to find a solution and when parties are willing to let that happen. Using the vocabulary of Zartman (1989), it means that

Table 9.3   Major armed conflict: UN Security Council (SC) resolutions under Chapter VII and world regions, 2000–09

Region	No. of major armed conflicts	No. of major armed conflicts resulting in SC Ch. VII resolutions	SC resolutions related to the no. of major armed conflicts (%)
Africa	30	10	33
Americas	11	1	9
Asia	14	2	14
Europe	11	3	27
Middle East	7	2	29
Total	72	18	25

Note: Major armed conflict: at least one government is involved, the incompatibility concerns territory or government and at least 1,000 battle-related deaths are recorded in one year during the course of the conflict. Regional divisions are those used by UCDP. Countries with at least one conflict have been counted where this has given rise to a minimum of one Security Council resolution under Chapter VII.

Source: Uppsala Conflict Data Program.

the conflicts on the Security Council agenda are more ripe for resolution than many others. Central to this is the role of the governments. They have to agree that such moments exist and accept international action. If they do not, the conflict is likely to continue. Obviously the government is searching for some form of victory. It needs to make a more sophisticated analysis. For instance, the solution found for East Timor in 1999 would have been possible 10 or 20 years earlier, if the Indonesian government had been open to it. Leadership changes gave new possibilities, but this also illustrated the futility of previous policy. The question can legitimately be asked whether the Council was right to wait so long to take up the issue. This would mean, however, that the Council would change its role and be prepared to act more preventively for conflict resolution.

World regions

In Chapter 8, the significance of the regional dimension was emphasized. Thus, we may also ask if there is a particular regional focus to the Council's attention. Table 9.3 contains information on the uses of Chapter VII since the end of the Cold War.

First, the totals in Table 9.3 show that 25 per cent of all countries with a major armed conflict saw at least one serious decision (in the form of a resolution under Chapter VII) by the Security Council. Next, we can note that the variation among world regions is interesting. More than one quarter of all situations in Africa, Europe and the Middle East reached the highest attention on the Council's agenda. The conflicts in Asia and the Americas showed a different pattern. Very few were brought to the UN in the first place and thus even fewer were likely to have a Chapter VII resolution. This variation deserves some reflection. For instance, there is as yet no Asia-wide organization for peace and security. The UN would thus be a possible alternative framework. It is still not being used. Asia, defined as the area East of the Indus, handles conflict in other ways. This region consists of countries with stronger states, high consciousness about territorial integrity and non-involvement in internal affairs. Its international security system may be closer to the ones described by *Realpolitik* writers, than any other part of the world. Three of the conflicts which received no attention were located in Asia. These were conflicts involving the Philippines, Sri Lanka and India (Table 9.2). All these states were at the time 'strong', as measured by the position of the military in the countries, or the popular bases of the regimes. Thus, they could repulse attempts to bring international organizations into the conflicts of their concern. Indonesia had chosen a similar attitude previously, but, as we just saw, had to yield.

Assuming that these patterns have a certain consistency, we might even suggest that the world presently has three geographically distinct systems for handling international conflict. This would be consonant with some of the observations made in Chapter 8. First, there is a *UN regional security system* with a strong concentration on conflicts in Africa, Europe and the Middle East. Here the UN is highly involved. Eight of the top ten conflicts in Table 9.1 were clearly in this region and the other two (al-Qaida/terrorism and Afghanistan) had strong links to this area. Many of the conflicts have dealt with state formation issues or internal affairs involving issues of identity. This is also the area where much of the campaign against terrorism is taking place. The fears expressed by many in Africa – that their region would receive less attention than during the Cold War – is not borne out by these data. The conflicts in Europe certainly received increased attention but it did not seem to have ended the Council's interest in Africa. Two UN Secretaries-General came from the continent. Both served to remind the Security Council of its duties. In terms of economic relationships, historical connections and conflict involvement, these three regions have unusually strong linkages. It is a remnant, most recently, of European colonization, but the relations go further back.

Second, there is *the inter-American system* with few armed conflicts and, as we have seen before, incompatibilities which did not involve state formation questions. The interstate conflicts have been few and minor. Instead, internal issues relating to military rule, democratization, class struggle, left–right issues, land rights, drugs and, lately, the rights of indigenous people have been central. The regional agenda is markedly different. Furthermore, the OAS, as well as subcontinental initiatives, has been more important, as seen in Chapter 8. The use of extra-regional actors in conflict resolution has been limited. Again, there are strong connections. The role of the USA as the paramount actor serves to highlight the linkages, and the resentments this has created further strengthen the importance of the intra-hemispheric dynamic.

A third system is *the Asian 'non-system'*, consisting of the many countries of South Asia, Southeast Asia and East Asia. It is a set of relationships
where each state is left on its own, to fend for itself. There is *Realpolitik*
concern about arms development, nuclear weapons development, unsettled
interstate conflicts, as well as internal issues, where involvement from the
outside is strongly resented by the governments. At the same time, they
are often prone to claim that these internal conflicts are instigated from
the outside, attributing them to interstate conflicts (for instance, the India–
Pakistan–Kashmir connections, China–India–Tibet, Myanmar–Thailand–
Karen). This non-system contains some subcontinental organizations. They
are often not in a position to deal with conflicts of that particular region, as
we saw in Section 8.2.

The Asian non-system is marked by the strong states which are eager
to avoid international involvement and do not promote stronger regional
bodies. The price is high, however, as few of the conflicts have moved
to any form of settlement. Some of those that have found a peace agreement in the last few years (Cambodia, East Timor, Aceh) have done so with
international concern and intervention. The UN had a large peacekeeping
operation in Cambodia, there was a transitory arrangement for East Timor,
initially based on Australian forces, and EU was involved in the implementation of the Aceh agreement. International action can be of use to these
actors. As the notion of sovereignty is strong and regional major power attitudes add to this, it is difficult to introduce. Asia has strong states, considerable cultural, military and economic independence and modest regional
integration. It has distanced itself from the 'global' politics surrounding
UN operations, dominated by Europe and North America. This self-reliant
attitude may be favourable for economic growth, but it does not seem to be
conducive for the settlement of disputes. Only when strong states weaken
by state mismanagement (or the devastating tsunami of 2004) is international action introduced. This is often very late in a conflict process, and
the tasks of peacebuilding become complex and costly, as witnessed both
in Cambodia and East Timor. Thus, there is now a trend of increased international contribution to peace, but in a more *ad hoc* fashion. A Nordic mission supervised the cease-fire arrangements on Sri Lanka that later lapsed
into renewed war. A non-governmental initiative from the former President
of Finland, Martti Ahtisaari, as well as the EU, played a role in the settlement over Aceh in Indonesia 2005. The peace process between India and
Pakistan, initiated in 2004, so far has not involved external parties and not
yielded results.

The permanent members

What impact do the permanent members of the Security Council have on
attention as well as on conflict resolution? There are contradictory arguments. First, the Council may concern itself primarily with conflict in

which the major powers are *not* involved at the outset. Permanent members may prefer to act on their own in conflicts in which they themselves are parties. The UN would, thus, be limited to conflicts which are not regarded as important to the interests of particular major states. Following this argument, we would expect the Security Council to take up conflicts that are peripheral from a *Realpolitik* perspective. The argument could be turned around, however. The UN may concentrate on *the* questions of the major powers, dealing with the dangers of world war, as presumably was intended at the inception of the organization. As the UN is a place where the major powers can meet, this would also be where they can sort out their disagreements. This would make the Security Council central to major power affairs, leaving out conflicts which are irrelevant to major power politics.

There are very few systematic studies of agenda setting from this perspective. There is much to indicate that the Council is likely to be particularly concerned with conflicts where *several* of the permanent members are involved. This was clearly the case when former Yugoslavia was at the top of the agenda. Also the situations of Iraq, Afghanistan and international terrorism involved the major powers from the beginning of the crisis. The pattern does not fit all cases. In some, such as Angola, Congo, Sierra Leone, Liberia or Burundi, only one of the major powers was historically involved (the USA, Britain and France, respectively), but mostly for economic or historical reasons, rather than strategic military concerns.

This actually means that the Council operates as a forum for major powers to sort out conflicts in which they are involved or even where they are pressured by the larger UN membership to get involved. This is in line with the original intentions of the UN and it may have become more true after the Cold War. However, these years have not seen any cases of a strategic confrontation directly between major powers. It could still be that such challenges are likely to be handled directly between the major powers, as was the case during the Cold War. Disputes over spies and border violations, for instance, have been handled by direct communication. The inability of the Council to agree on a common action on Iraq 2003 is testimony to this: the USA, the UK and their allies chose to act outside the UN framework. Similarly, Russia did not wait for the Security Council to act in Georgia in August 2008. On the other hand, the fact that many conflicts of major power interest have been dealt with in the Security Council may have reduced the likelihood of them turning into direct major power confrontations. There is an increasing expectation that all major conflicts should be brought to the UN. Indeed, for the most recent ten-year period, only seven conflicts had gone on for more than eight years without UN attention; for the previous period of the same length, the number was 11 (Wallensteen 2007).

There is a corollary to this conclusion. For effective action it is important for the major powers to work out a consistent policy. If the primary fighting parties learned to play the major powers against one another, they could expect to benefit from these disagreements. There would be a hope that the decisions would increasingly tilt the UN towards one or the other of the parties. The UN, therefore, instead of being the impartial arbiter, risked becoming just another actor in the conflict, applauded by some, abused by others. In fact, the most serious challenges to UN authority came in this process, particularly during the prolonged crisis over former Yugoslavia in the early 1990s.

The difficulty in handling disagreements among the strongest UN members creates a dilemma for the organization. On the one hand, disregarding the views of a permanent or otherwise important member may mean that this member will act to undermine the majority. There is much that such a member can do, given the resources available to a major actor. It may encourage an actor to resist the UN decision. It may send arms, for instance, disregarding an arms embargo. It may choose more drastic means. From this point of view, it is preferable for the organization to have all important members as part of the consensus. On the other hand, it may result in decision delays and decision obscurity. As discussions take place during an ongoing armed conflict, much can change in a short period of time. The dilemma is between making quick decisions or consensual decisions. It is a difficult dilemma, as the 2003 Iraq War demonstrates. The proponents of military action were impatient with the already agreed avenue of action, the UN inspection team (UNMOVIC) and, instead of allowing time or accepting a consensus decision, chose to move ahead, only later having to return to the organization. It led to a crisis, however, and made the Secretary-General initiate a broad reform process on the UN role in collective security. The World Summit of September 2005 agreed on significant reforms that also concerned UN principles of action.

If there is no agreement but UN operations are under way, the situation becomes acute. The only solution may then be to withdraw, which is likely to make a situation even worse. That happened in the crisis in Rwanda in 1994, playing into the hands of the perpetrators of the genocide. This is an undesirable state of affairs for an international body. It is important to engage so that sufficient consensus develops and as long as there is a chance for coherent operative mandates. The UNMOVIC (led by Hans Blix) and IAEA (led by Mohamed ElBaradei) teams worked on such a mandate but they had to be cut short due to the military actions that were initiated on Iraq in March 2003.

The Council deliberations are not only a matter of bridging differences between democracies and other forms of governments. As most conflicts dealt with Europe, Africa and the Middle East, the countries interested were the European states and the United States. Only in some instances were Russia and China particularly involved. Among the democracies or democratizing major powers there were clashes of interest. They did not risk a major power war, but had an impact on the ability of the UN to act. It is obvious that the three permanent Western members have extensive interests in Africa, Europe and the Middle East. There is a surprisingly high number of conflicts where one or several of the Western countries have been involved and where the issue has been brought to the Council by the permanent member or by other circumstances. It suggests that they have had some confidence in the organization or that their interest in a particular conflict has been less than vital.[1]

What about the two other permanent members? Taking Soviet conflict involvement to the UN was part of Gorbachev's strategy of disengagement. An example is the Afghan conflict, where the UN was used to negotiate and observe the pullout of Soviet troops. By the early 1990s, this strategy had sharply reduced Soviet and Russian international interest and enlarged the UN agenda (Angola, Central America, Afghanistan). Russia limited its interest to a few armed conflicts close to, or within, its own borders (Chechnya, Azerbaijan, Georgia, Tajikistan), apart from the Yugoslav imbroglio. It watched carefully EU and NATO enlargements into areas that were part of the Soviet empire, which resulted in an interest in supporting pro-Russian regimes, for instance, in Ukraine.

A conflict of high interest to China on the Security Council agenda has been the situation in Cambodia. This conflict became solvable following the normalization of relations between China and Vietnam in 1990–91 (Amer et al. 1996). The Paris Peace Treaty opened the route for a major UN operation. At the same time, China took part in the observer mission to Iraq and Kuwait. This suggests an increasing interest from China to use the organization. Many of the conflicts of greatest concern to China, such as those over Korea, Taiwan and the maritime delimitations in East Asia, have not led to major armed conflicts in recent times. They have not been on the UN agenda, nor have they been handled in a regional framework. China's increasingly global economic interests have made it reluctant to support more intrusive UN action in Sudan. Lately, it has demonstrated a greater interest in participating in UN peace operations.

The Security Council resolution 1973 on March 17, 2011 saw a remarkable confluence of forces, when the decision on a no-fly zone over Libya was taken. Russia and China abstained. This meant that a measure based on the principle of a responsibility to protect civilian populations could be taken. No doubt the support for this measure by the Arab League was decisive for their action.

The permanent members are crucial for the UN's ability to function in conflict resolution. Although they sometimes hide behind the UN, as if it were an independent actor, they have to take the responsibility for which conflicts enter the agenda, how these conflicts are handled and how they ultimately leave the agenda. It is unlikely that any permanent member will ever get a decision exactly to its liking. Compromise is a necessity. Almost all resolutions passed under Chapter VII have been taken with the support of the three permanent Western members, and one or both of the other permanent members. No decision in the Security Council has ever been imposed on the leading member of the Western group, the United States. Furthermore, as most of the conflicts dealt with in the UN have concerned three regions of particular interest to the West, the resulting agenda has reflected the concerns of these three countries and their societies. We can take note also of the fact that the Western European group among the UN member states elects two of the non-permanent seats. Furthermore, the East European seat is often allocated to countries in Central Europe with links to the West. Japan and South Korea have often had one of the Asian seats. Together, this demonstrates the strength of the Western, democratic and industrialized world in the Security Council. The agenda reflects this. It also fuels the interest in reforming the composition of the Council.

9.4 UN Action and Peace Agreements

The expectation is that when an armed conflict enters the agenda of the Security Council there will be action. This is also a reason why some actors resist engaging the Council. Since the end of the Cold War there has been an unprecedented set of actions by the United Nations, including sanctions, peacekeeping operations and peace enforcement. The extensive deliberations in the Council have to do with proposed, planned or ongoing actions. What the members can accept becomes the decision. The key problem is whether this is sufficient for dealing with a particular situation. Since 2001, the Council has pursued special efforts to counter international terrorism, including with sanctions. A special 'executive directorate' has been created to monitor the implementation of UN decisions and help member states in capacity building. In the UN reform process, the issue of peacebuilding in post-war situations emerged as a new aspect. Often it means to support peace agreements between the former warring factions. In the World Summit 2005, it was agreed to create a new body, the Peacebuilding Commission, to attend to such matters. It was put in place by January 1, 2006.

The Security Council has some measures at its disposal to bring about or keep peace. One is the use of economic and other sanctions. These are mentioned in the Charter, and there has been a revitalization of this field. A second major instrument is the use of peacekeeping operations to contribute to, implement and sustain a peace process. It is not mentioned in the Charter and is often imagined to be located between Chapters VI and VII (thus, termed 'Chapter 6 ½' measures). It was developed in the 1950s and has added new dimensions since 1989. A third measure is peace enforcement, a novel development. Let us look more closely at these instruments, and then relate them to armed conflicts and peace settlements.

Sanctions

Since 1990 the Security Council has decided on sanctions in 19 armed conflicts and has addressed them at 19 member states under Chapter VII (by May 2011). During the Cold War there were only two cases, against South Africa and Rhodesia. The end of the Cold War resulted in a sanctions decade

(Cortright and Lopez 2000; Wallensteen and Staibano 2005). Sanctions on South Africa were introduced in 1977 and ended in 1994, following the country's first democratic elections. In the Rhodesian case, they were instituted in 1965, came under Chapter VII in 1966 and were lifted following the negotiated agreement ending the Rhodesian crisis, in December 1979. Another five cases were instituted and fully terminated since the end of the Cold War, meaning that by December 2010 sanctions were in place in 14 cases. The rate of success, as well as the contribution to conflict resolution, is what we are interested in here.

In the five cases where sanctions were ended, there was an element of success. In the case of Libya, sanctions were instituted in 1992, in connection with Libya's alleged involvement in two different aircraft bombings. One case came to be associated with the Scottish town of Lockerbie where the destroyed aeroplane hit the ground. The other case, which received much less attention, concerned a French plane exploded by a bomb while in the air over Africa. By 1999, after seven years, the Council determined that Libya had fulfilled UN demands. Two agents accused of planting the bomb in the Lockerbie case were handed over to a Scottish court, temporarily relocated to the Netherlands. One of them was convicted in early 2001. Later, Libya paid compensation to the families of the victims. In this case, the sanctions were the only coercive action going on and they can thus be credited with having had an impact. In a controversial decision, the convicted person was released in 2009 on medical grounds and received a heroic welcome in Libya. In connection with the uprising that began in Libya in February 2011, new sanctions for a different purpose, the protection of citizens from the regime's violence, were imposed.

A second case where the impact of sanctions may have been in the direction desired by the initiators concerned former Yugoslavia. An arms embargo was instituted against all states of former Yugoslavia in 1991, and specific sanctions were imposed on the successor-state, the Federal Republic of Yugoslavia (Serbia and Montenegro), in 1992. These measures were removed in 1996 following implementation of the Dayton peace accords. In this case, the effects of the sanctions were interwoven with the effects of the war. Still, it is likely that the sanctions played an instrumental role, making, in the end, some parties more eager to conclude agreements and establish some degree of 'normal' conditions in their international relations.

In the third case of terminated sanctions, the measures on Haiti were instituted in an unusual on-off pattern. They were imposed in June 1993, suspended in August, only to be reinstituted in October 1993, and then terminated in October 1994, when the previously ousted, democratically elected government had been returned to power. The economic effects in Haiti seem to have been devastating, but the military regime, which took power in a coup in 1991, refused to yield for a considerable time. It was not until it was faced with an invasion from an overwhelming American force that the regime finally yielded. The immediate military threat was decisive.

In the case of Angola and the war on the Horn of Africa, the role of sanctions can be debated. In Angola, the war ended as a result of the killing of Jonas Savimbi, the leader of UNITA, the armed opposition. The sanctions impacted on the economics of UNITA, but the change in leadership made it possible for UNITA to abide by the agreements. In the case of sanctions on Eritrea and Ethiopia, they were instituted to prevent a return to fighting and support peace efforts. The peace agreement was signed in 2000 and the sanctions expired in 2001, thus claiming some impact on ending the war. Ethiopia later did not implement the agreed measures, but the Council chose not to reintroduce the sanctions. Eritrea, however, was exposed to new sanctions in 2009 due to its involvement in the Somalia conflict.

The results in the remaining cases are mixed. In several instances, the conflictual conditions remained or even worsened (Iraq, Rwanda, Somalia, Sudan) but efforts of peacemaking may have been strengthened in others (Democratic Republic of Congo, Côte d'Ivoire, Liberia, Sierra Leone). In the case of the 2005 Lebanon sanctions, the aim was to support the investigation into the assassination of former Prime Minister Rafik Hariri, and thus was not directly related to an ongoing armed conflict (but potentially helped to prevent a new one).

In fact, the inability to achieve the goals has led to a need for the more precise targeting of the sanctions. Significant criticism against sanctions has been that they affect an entire population of a state. In this way, they may serve to undermine the possibility of opponents strengthening themselves against the government. Instead, the government tends to improve its standing, branding the opponents as 'unpatriotic' or as 'foreign agents'. The national crisis means that the government can assume extraordinary powers. The comprehensive sanctions against Iraq in the 1990s were strongly debated because of their humanitarian consequences. The Council tried to smooth the effects on the general population through an oil-for-food arrangement. Iraq was entitled to sell oil under UN control, and to use the proceeds to buy food. It improved the situation for the population, but it also tilted the internal balance of power in favour of the regime of Saddam Hussein, who could control the proceeds. After the US-led invasion in 2003, the sanctions were instead targeted on particular individuals associated with that regime, while the rest of the economy became entirely unrestricted. Documents found in the Iraqi ministries exposed a number of persons, companies and countries that benefited unduly from the sanctions regime. This scandal was investigated by several independent commissions. Most notable was the one headed by Paul Volcker, whose reports in 2005 revealed mismanagement also in the UN itself.

These examples further strengthened the need for more targeted sanctions as well as close monitoring of their implementation. Such a move was already visible earlier, for instance, in the case of Angola, where an oil embargo was specifically instituted against UNITA in 1993. Another example is the sanction regime against Rwanda. Arms trade with the government of Rwanda was allowed but there were sanctions against non-governmental forces fighting the government. Thus, the Council attempted in these cases to shift the strength of the forces inside countries so as to disfavour a particular party. Sometimes this has been stated explicitly, as in the case of UNITA in Angola, other times this follows by implication.

In October 1999, sanctions were also introduced against Afghanistan, directed against the internationally unrecognized Taliban regime. This was done because of the Taliban's unwillingness to take action against terrorism and, in particular, because it had not turned over Osama bin Laden to 'appropriate authorities in a country where he will be arrested and effectively brought to justice' (Security Council Resolution 1267 of 1999). Following the September 11, 2001 attacks on the USA, there was increased support for stronger measures (Security Council Resolution 1368 of 2001). After the war that deposed the Taliban regime, the sanctions remained in place, targeting specific individuals, wherever they were on the globe. These sanctions have become part of the global struggle against terrorism and listing new persons or organizations became a major concern in these sanctions regimes.

Sanctions are obvious demonstrations of the intentions of the Security Council. Targeting particular actors makes them more precise, but also provides opportunities for evasion by the actors, using go-betweens, family or clan members, even strengthening the determination of the ruling clique to keep itself in power. In an imperfect world, it remains, after all, an action with some impact, and it is non-violent at that. In the context of peace negotiations, the lifting of sanctions becomes an additional bargaining chip for which the senders, the outside world, may be able to extract additional concessions. Thus, originally conceived as punishment, in the later phase their ending can be turned into potential rewards. This assumes that the goals of the sanctions are clear and that, as part of a deal, it is possible for the negotiators to ensure that the sanctions actually will be lifted (Doxey 1996: 119–21).

It also assumes that the sanctions are properly implemented. By making sanctions more targeted, the demands on government bureaucracies increase. Now they have to identify commodities going to or stemming from a particular country. It is also required that specific individuals are prohibited from entering a country. Their bank accounts have to be frozen and they are prevented from trading in particular commodities. The sanctions reform process has resulted in a number of reports aimed at improving the use of sanctions, but also enhancing national capacity to carry them out. A result is to demonstrate that sanctions are not necessarily always useful. Furthermore, as individuals are listed in the Council decisions, there are significant human rights aspects to consider (Cameron 2005; Wallensteen et al. 2003). In 2009, the Council finally decided to institute a more transparent system for the listing and delisting procedure.

Among the 19 cases of sanctions, peace agreements were signed, or reactivated, and became durable in 11. The sanctions literature has been more concerned with success and failure of sanctions from the point of view of the initiator, the sender (Wallensteen 2000, 2011b). Their role in a peace process requires a more detailed analysis. Let us make some introductory observations on the topic.

The threat of not lifting sanctions was used to push recalcitrant parties in the several negotiations, for example, Rhodesia and former Yugoslavia. It means that the lifting of sanctions was part of the peace negotiations, either directly as an element in the negotiations or indirectly as a promise to the parties if they agreed. The sanctions clearly contributed to the negotiated outcome in South Africa in 1994. Their impact was a burden on the Apartheid government and worked in combination with pressure from below. Writings on the earlier Liberia peace agreements do not credit the sanctions regime for the outcome (Alao et al. 1999). However, President Charles Taylor had to leave the country in 2003 as his regime was running out of resources to fight insurgents. After this the sanctions, in combination with peacekeeping, helped to lay the ground for the implementation of the peace agreement and the presidential elections in 2005. In the cases of Angola and Sierra Leone, sanctions could not help to maintain the settlements, but together with additional developments (the death of leaders, the presence of international peacekeeping) may have served to return the states to peaceful conditions. Similarly, the peace processes in the Côte d'Ivoire and the Democratic Republic of Congo may have had some support from the sanctions, as they reduced the strength of potential spoilers. The contributions of targeted sanctions to peace settlements are difficult to assess, but this overview suggests that they may constitute a significant element in a broader international strategy to deal with ongoing violence. The combination with peacekeeping may be particularly important.

Peacekeeping operations

In his study of six major peacekeeping operations, Diehl concludes on the role of peacekeeping in conflict resolution: 'What is abundantly clear is that they are not very successful.' The record was clearly better with respect to limiting armed conflict. 'Peacekeeping operations may be best suited for use *after* some measure of conflict resolution, rather than the traditional preresolution deployment' (Diehl 1993: 105–6). Diehl's study concerns the original type of peacekeeping operations. It points, however, to an important element. Peacekeeping operations are basically thought of as measures to be instituted after a peace agreement. They are there to implement what has been agreed. They have an impartial role after a devastating war when the conflicting parties are not likely to be able to cooperate easily among themselves.

The peacekeeping record since 1989 is impressive. The number of new peacekeeping operations, renamed peace operations, using the definition given by the UN, mirrors closely the curve of resolutions passed in the Security Council. A total of 64 peacekeeping missions were mandated by the United Nations from 1948 to 2010. Fifteen were initiated prior to 1989. Thus, three-quarters of all operations belong to the post-Cold War period. Sixteen were ongoing by 2010. Interesting, non-UN actors initiated even more peace missions, defined in the same way as the UN. There were 67 such operations for the 1948–2005 period. The mandate, duration and size of all these operations vary considerably. It is not surprising to find that most UN peace operations were in the three regions which are typical UN areas of operation: Africa, Europe and the Middle East. Non-UN action often meant more regional activities, but the patterns are not sharply different (Heldt and Wallensteen 2006). As could be expected, most of the operations were associated with ongoing or recently terminated major armed conflicts. An interesting exception was UNPREDEP, the preventive deployment in Macedonia, which became an independent operation in 1995 and was closed down in 1999 (Pellnäs 1997). There was no armed conflict going on in Macedonia and the UN mission was meant to prevent the spread of wars from former Yugoslavia. It served to consolidate the newly independent country that was exposed to pressure from Greece (which resisted the right of the new state to call itself Macedonia) and dissent from a sizeable Albanian population. Such preventive measures need a separate discussion (see Section 10.2).

Concentrating on the UN operations, their contribution can be discussed in the terms suggested by Diehl. Do they contribute to a reduction in actual conflict behaviour and lead to conflict resolution? That they have a quick impact in the reduction of armed conflict and that they serve to pacify their immediate area of operation is beyond doubt. However, this is not only to the credit of the operation as such. As it is, in most cases, conceived as a peacekeeping mission, it means that there is some prior accord among the parties. The presence of UN forces makes possible the implementation of what has been agreed. Among the operations that have been terminated, it can be asked whether violence returned among the same parties after the ending of the mission. These would then be the most obvious cases of failure, whereas operations where this did not take place would appear to be associated with a genuine change in the relationships among the contending parties.

Among all the terminated missions in actual conflict situations the same conflict continued in only three cases (Angola, Rwanda and Somalia). In one, Haiti, peacekeepers had to return several years later. In Angola, a peace agreement was implemented, no less than twice, but the war ended only after a leadership change. In Rwanda, the peace agreement of 1993 was never put into practice and in Somalia it was not possible to get credible commitments from the warring factions. The mission was supplemented with a US-directed and ill-fated peace enforcement operation in 1993 (see below). It led to the withdrawal of the American forces. It also made the USA reluctant to get into the ensuing crisis in Rwanda less than six months later. Thus, UN deployments in Rwanda could not carry out the assistance they were supposed to provide to the Rwandan peace process.

These missions could be seen as failures in contributing to a peace process. It is a failure rate that is unacceptable in view of the suffering involved. The blame for violence, of course, has to rest primarily with the parties themselves. It is not likely that the wars would have stopped without the UN presence. The record shows that they all continued after the UN had departed. These UN missions can be seen as lost opportunities for the parties as well as a failure for the UN strategy for conflict resolution. It is not the full picture, however.

In a large number of cases, operations were terminated without further conflict among the same parties. Most of these are associated with durable peace agreements that have been identified in Chapters 5, 6 and 7. This must be seen as a more acceptable outcome than expected. This means that the record for UN peacekeeping in contributing to actually ending armed conflicts is remarkable. The conclusion can be phrased as follows: if there were peaceful conditions when the UN left, it is likely that the peace arrangement was going to be sustained. If, however, the UN left under conditions that were turbulent, its departure was not likely to restore peace to the situation.

Most of the situations have been missions to maintain peace in typical civil wars. Among the terminated operations in the post-Cold War era, only four (Namibia, East Slavonia in Croatia, Georgia, and East Timor/Timor-Leste) dealt with state formation issues. Among the continuing missions, several were in state formation conflicts (Western Sahara and Kosovo). It shows what has been illustrated before, that state formation conflicts are difficult for any international organization to deal with. States have often resisted such engagement; movements for independence have demanded it. These are conflicts on the threshold between internal and international relations. They have an ambiguity which makes them difficult to handle. As they make up half of all conflicts, this underlines the necessity of coming to grips with them.

Most peacekeeping operations, as well as the sanctions issues, treat conflicts in a basic, almost bilateral way. As has been shown in Chapter 8, conflicts may sometimes be part of a regional or global conflict complex, requiring broader approaches. Such measures have rarely been tried. Among the terminated peacekeeping operations, ONUCA for Central America had a regional mandate. So has the oldest ongoing peacekeeping operation, UNTSO, for truce in the Middle East. More typically, conflicts have been conceptually isolated from one another. This is a way to achieve a manageable mandate and a broader consensus. It could still be asked if the time has come to think of regional peace missions, where the UN might sponsor particular regional peace processes.

What we note is that there is a distinctly positive contribution to conflict resolution associated with UN peacekeeping. This, in a sense, qualifies the conclusions suggested by Diehl (1993) for cases during the Cold War. Conditions have changed. In particular, the contributions of peacekeeping are now associated with the cooperative relations in the Security Council.

This has made constructive work possible. It is logical that it would be connected with finding agreements among warring factions. The UN peacekeeping operations are working together with other measures undertaken by major powers. The importance of the Council is that it synchronizes the efforts of interested major powers, generates international support for the missions and, thus, brings out one coherent message to the targeted group.

Peace enforcement

The concept of peace enforcement is one of the new 'instruments' for international organizations. It means that wars are brought to a halt through direct and overwhelming military intervention under the auspices of multilateral organs. There are two examples of military actions that have been outside direct UN control, but had their bases in UN decisions: Korea in 1950 and the Gulf War in 1991. In both cases, the operations were firmly controlled by the USA. In both cases, the situation was seen as one of repelling aggression. The decision on Korea was taken under peculiar conditions. At the time of the North Korean attack, the Soviet Union was boycotting the work of the Security Council. This was due to the fact that the majority refused to allow the government of the People's Republic of China to take China's seat in the Security Council. Thus, the majority consisted of the United States and its allies. The decision to send UN forces to fight the North Koreans was done under circumstances that cannot be regarded as a precedent.

The second situation is more interesting as it involved a wilful agreement of the members of the Council to take concerted action against Iraq. The processes of the Charter were used. In one sense, it was a textbook case of the UN dealing with aggression. It also showed the limits of UN influence. Following Iraq's invasion of Kuwait, the Security Council instituted a series of gradually escalating measures, resulting, on November 29, 1990, in an ultimatum to Iraq. This is found in Security Council Resolution 678. At the same time, there were different negotiation initiatives and compromise solutions put forward. The parallel buildup of forces around Iraq made negotiations less credible. It became increasingly clear that the military option was preferred by the American side and was expected also on the Iraqi side. There was no room for a compromise. Efforts by the UN Secretary-General in January 1991 were doomed. When the Council's conditions were not met, an extensive air campaign was initiated, followed by a short ground operation, all under US command. By the end of February 1991, the Iraqi forces had been driven out from Kuwait's territory. Security Council Resolution 687 laid out the conditions for Iraq's defeat.

The key formulation in Resolution 678 was the granting of the use of 'all necessary means' to the countries cooperating with Kuwait. All military actions were taken by these countries. The UN regained a role through the Special Commission for the monitoring of Iraq's implementation of

Resolution 687, UNSCOM. This was a UN operation, but not peacekeeping. Its mandate was to supervise the conditions laid down in the resolution terminating the war. It had no precedent. The obstructions of Iraq in carrying out the required dismantling of weapons of mass destruction, as well as its capacity to construct and deliver such weapons, led to repeated crises, sanctions and air raids against Iraq.

The formulation 'all necessary means' in the mandate for the Gulf War was repeated in some other conflicts. In the conflict in former Yugoslavia it was used for the protection of humanitarian deliveries. The same was true for the UN commitment to protect six designated 'safe areas'. Necessary means, however, in the form of equipment and troops, were never extended to the UN peacekeepers on the ground. It resulted in the tragedies of Srebrenica, Gorazde and Zepa in 1995. These towns were all 'protected' by the Security Council, but could not be defended by the peacekeepers entrusted with the task. They were easily overrun by Serb forces. It led to a further loss of credibility for UN peacekeeping. An air campaign, under the command of NATO, was launched against the Bosnian Serb positions, shifting the military balance and creating conditions for negotiations and a peace agreement (Holbrooke 1999).

In the Somalia operation, the formulation of 'all necessary measures' was used, but in this case the target was the Somali faction believed to be responsible for armed attacks on UN peacekeepers in 1993 (Security Council Resolution 827 in 1993). This led the USA to deploy a special force in Somalia, resulting in military operations against the warlord defined as most responsible for preventing a peace arrangement. The battle between US forces and Somalis resulted in the deaths of more than 100 peacekeepers, including 36 Americans (Lyons and Samatar 1995: 60). The UN operation was terminated shortly thereafter.

An interesting case is Haiti, where in 1994 an invasion was under way, also under the authorization of the UN, consisting largely of American forces. On the eve of the invasion, the military junta chose to give in to the demands. A peaceful settlement was found. The junta acted under the immediate threat of an overwhelming enforcement mission.

However, the war on Afghanistan in 2001, the aim of which was the removal of the Taliban regime and the bases of al-Qaida operations, was not authorized in this way. The Council resolution of September 28, 2001, reaffirmed the inherent right of self-defence at the same time as it identified terrorism as a threat to international peace and security (Security Council Resolution 1373). Thus, the US war on Afghanistan was seen as a matter of self-defence against the groups that orchestrated the attacks on the USA on September 11, 2001. This war took place with unusually strong international support. The international security assistance force (ISAF) created in December 2001 to support the new government was not a UN peacekeeping operation, but was under NATO command, and it remained in place in 2011.

There are also experiences of peace enforcement outside the framework of the UN. The USA and the UK have bombed Iraq repeatedly. In December

1998, the two escalated the continued disputes over UN inspectors into an intensive bombing campaign, on their own initiative, without achieving the desired change. By early 2001 a new UN body, UNMOVIC, had still not been able to carry out its inspection mandate in Iraq. However, in November 2002, facing increased US military deployments, Iraq agreed to accept UNMOVIC and IAEA inspections to determine the issues of its possible access to weapons of mass destruction. Reports to the Council in January and February 2003 did not satisfy the USA, the UK and other allies, who continued to claim that there were weapons programmes, actually or potentially. Without the authorization of the Council, they intervened to remove the regime in March and the USA proclaimed major military combat to be over by May 2003. However, the war continued in different forms, giving Iraq little chance of peaceful reconstruction, except in the Kurdish-dominated areas. Official US investigators concluded in early 2004 that Iraq possessed no weapons of mass destruction or the capacity to produce them. By that time, the rationale for the war had turned into the construction of a democracy and the elections of 2005 were seen as a first achievement of this. However, the war escalated, only to change by 2007 when agreements were made with particular Iraqi groups. In August 2010, President Obama proclaimed that the USA had met its responsibility and officially ended its combat role. Still, 50,000 US troops remained in the country.

In Kosovo in 1999, the United States chose, together with the United Kingdom, to act entirely outside the UN framework, in a NATO-led air campaign against targets in Kosovo as well as in the rest of Yugoslavia. This was designed to gain Yugoslavia's acceptance of peace conditions laid out by the United States. It was an attempt to prevent the ongoing violence in Kosovo from turning into another protracted Balkan conflict. It also was meant to prevent further expulsion of Kosovo Albanians. The war lasted for more than two months, leading to a vast exodus of Albanians into neighbouring countries and considerable destruction in Serbia as well as in Kosovo. It resulted in the acquiescence of the Yugoslav government, in June 1999, to a NATO-led force, KFOR, stationed in the province. The Kosovo Albanians could return and an international regime was created for Kosovo, although it remained technically a part of Serbia. The Serbs remaining in the area could stay under international protection. Many, however, chose to leave. As we have seen, Kosovo remained under international administration until its declaration of independence in 2008.

In 2008, Russia acted without UN authorization in South Ossetia, repelling an attack from Georgian forces to retake the area that formally belonged to Georgia. The armed conflict was a military disaster for Georgia. Immediately following this, South Ossetia declared itself independent. Abkhazia, another Russian-controlled area in Georgia, did the same. Only four countries recognized these declarations.

These cases of peace enforcement point to a different route for international action from the earlier ones assumed under the UN Charter. The success rate is mixed. In one way it has meant an enlargement of available options. In another way it has led to actions that are of questionable legitimacy. The actions in the

Gulf War, Bosnia-Herzegovina, Somalia and Haiti were all agreed to within the UN framework and, thus, were internationally legitimate. The Afghanistan War of 2001 was defined as a matter of self-defence under Article 51 of the Charter. The actions in Iraq, Kosovo and Georgia require more elaborate arguments to be compatible with the letter of the law. The use of force is normally legitimate only through a decision in the Security Council. In the case of Iraq, it has been argued that earlier resolutions bestowed that right to the United States, the United Kingdom and their allies. However, a new Council resolution had been agreed only in November 2002 on another course of action, first using the inspections. The other possibility is that these actions also constituted self-defence, according to Article 51. Iraq's future capacity of nuclear and other weapons would then be such a threat that it would have to be eliminated. However, it would require a prior establishment of such a threat, where, again, the inspections might provide the evidence. On Kosovo, it might be possible to argue that NATO was acting in self-defence on behalf of the Albanian population that was driven out from their homes in Kosovo. As they could not defend themselves, NATO undertook that task. A third possible argument is to appeal to an emergency. The situation in Kosovo was extreme and military actions were the last resort after negotiations had failed. Such an argument would be difficult in the case of Iraq, however, as oppressive conditions had remained for a long period of time without any international action. A gain from the war, the removal of the Saddam regime, was probably generally appreciated.

To this could be added a fourth argument, that humanitarian concerns now are as legitimate as others for intervention in another country, even against the will of an internationally recognized government. This would be in line with the actions to protect the Kurdish populations that were fleeing from the onslaught of Iraqi forces in March 1991. In its Resolution 688 (1991), the Security Council authorized such assistance. In the parallel situation of Kosovo in 1999, it was thought that the Council was not likely to agree to such actions. A veto by Russia and China was expected. Instead of going along the route suggested with the Uniting for Peace resolution, the Western countries chose to use NATO. A chance to find unquestionable legitimacy was lost. The actions were not in accordance with the letter of the Charter, but may have been in accordance with the spirit of humanitarian priorities. The World Summit in 2005 agreed that such principles, the responsibility to protect exposed populations, could be used in cases where a government does not meet its international obligations to its own population.

In the Georgian cases, Russia used self-defence arguments, claiming that many of the inhabitants in South Ossetia were Russian citizens who needed protection. It did not take the matter to the UN. The following declarations of independence, furthermore, contradicted Russia's position when denying Kosovo the same right.

This means that the no-fly zone instituted by the UN over Libya in March 2011 was the first international use of force built on the principle of a responsibility to protect an exposed population. Upholding the zone required precise bombings of military assets used by the Gadaffi regime to attack opposition strongholds throughout the country. The leadership of the bombing campaign was handed to NATO.

The peace enforcement operations accomplished the immediate goals in the Gulf War, Haiti and Bosnia-Herzegovina, possibly also in Kosovo, Iraq and Georgia (from Russia's perspective). It failed in Somalia. Several of these conflicts, however, still have not been removed from the agenda. Iraq continues to be a problem for the Security Council and the United States. The workings of the Dayton agreement are cumbersome and require revision. For Kosovo, there is hope for a qualitatively improved peace following the declaration of independence. Haiti was off the list of armed conflicts for a period, only to return in 2004. The future of the two new Russian dependencies in the Caucasus is uncertain, as international recognition is unlikely. The record of success for multilateral and unilateral peace enforcement in contributing to durable peacemaking is limited. It may be an instrument that handles a particular crisis, but lasting peace requires very different measures.

In this chapter, we have seen the importance of the UN in many peace processes. There are strengths and there are limits. The UN is not the only one engaged in this, but it has an undisputed legal position in the international system. The UN Secretary-General has a special role both in the early phases of conflict, when prevention is still possible, and in the later stages of conflict and conflict resolution. There are also other actors involved in such processes. Thus, Chapter 10 takes up the role of the international community as a whole in mediation and conflict prevention.

Further Readings

Go to the *Understanding Conflict Resolution* web page at www.sagepub.co.uk for free access to journal articles listed.

Axworthy, L. 2001. 'Human Security and Global Governance: Putting People First', *Global Governance*, 7 (1): 19–23.
Haas, E. B. 1983. 'Regime Decay: Conflict Management and International Organizations, 1945–1981', *International Organization*, 37 (2): 189–256.
Malone, D. (ed.) 2004. *The UN Security Council. From the Cold War to the 21st Century.* Boulder, Colorado: Lynne Rienner.
Wallensteen, P. 1994. 'Representing the World. A Security Council for the 21st Century', *Security Dialogue*, 25 (1): 63–75.
Weiss, T. G. 2005. 'Compromise and Credibility: Security Council Reform?' *Security Dialogue*, 36 (2): 131–54.

Note

1   For instance, UK resistance to bring up Northern Ireland in the UN contrasts sharply with its quick action to have Southern Rhodesia on the UN agenda in 1965, although this conflict was defined as 'internal' and had similar colonial traits. In the Rhodesia case, African reactions favoured internationalizing the issue, while in the Irish case, Ireland was isolated and not likely to get organizational attention to the conflict.

INTERNATIONAL COMMUNITIES IN CONFLICT RESOLUTION 10

10.1 The New Communities

The end of the Cold War meant the dissolution of blocs that had for a long time formed the thinking in international relations. The challenges of violence, humanitarian intervention, protection of exposed populations and peace processes required new goals, new forms of actions and new actors pursuing these goals. Thus, new communities of action have arisen in practice and many more in theory. There are now several distinct and partly competing concepts which give different meanings to international action. Let us look at these emerging, as well as present, communities. Partly, they include the same actors, but give different perspectives on the objectives of international action. Indeed, some actors can choose which community to belong to. Then we will proceed, in Section 10.2 to discuss the possibilities of conflict prevention in the trichotomy of conflicts. After this, it is time to proceed to the role of mediation and negotiation (Section 10.3) and finally, in Section 10.4, to bring attention to questions of structural changes that could reduce the likelihood of armed conflict.

The concept that has been used most prominently, but with little consideration to its meaning, is *the international community*. It is a good starting point for a discussion on emerging communities. The notion of a *global system of states and non-state actors*, which was introduced in Section 4.2, is more general and, in one sense, more comprehensive. In a traditional, realist understanding, it is an anarchic system, made up of autonomous actors with few shared values, some of which are states, many of which are not. The global system is large but it lacks shared values, making it a system rather than a community. A community, in addition to a large number of members, involves shared values and the power to act. With this in mind, we can locate distinct action communities. One possibility is a global security community of many shared values among many actors. It may be an emergent community, and the closest equivalent so far is the international community. Such communities would build on the membership in the UN or see the UN as an important forum for action. Other communities would be those that are more limited, focusing on particular values, regions or powers. Some may be deeper forms of the UN-focused communities, such as the *democratic community*. A contrast is the more limited, integrated *regional security community*, with an ability to act in regional conflict issues. Other alternatives are communities resting on the power of a few actors, as in organized major power cooperation, so called *concerts* building on common understandings (universalism), or on one power, today a US-led community, the *Pax Americana*. This gives us six distinct groupings to observe in matters of international peace and security. They form different types of world order. Let us discuss them as the UN-focused communities and those based on exclusive values or power.

UN-focused communities

The *international community* is a frequently used concept, including in this book. It depicts a group of actors with some coherence, shared purpose of action and moral standing. The international community is particularly concerned with matters of human rights, mass refugee movements, armed conflict and justice-based solutions to conflict. It does not have one identifiable institutional setup but refers to a network of actors. The international community includes, no doubt, actors in the leading Western countries and EU organs, but also international organizations (UN, UNHCR, UNHCHR), popularly based action groups and associations, media and religious societies. Furthermore, the concept extends beyond a confined Western world: it is used, for instance, by democracy-promoting groups in Asia. Thus, there is some common understanding of the international community. It is 'international' and it is also a 'community', as there are similar ways of reacting to particular crises. It expresses widely shared democratic values, and builds on similar reactions to particular situations. This community appears to have been important in setting the agenda for conflict resolution. This includes the activation of the United Nations, particularly its Secretary-General, giving priority to negotiations and peace agreements, and a reluctant, case-by-case support to humanitarian action.

One problem with this conceptually vague international community is its inability to maintain interest in one issue for an extended period of time. There is a volatility which allows attention to shift from one issue to another. What is urgent by necessity gets priority and will result in some action. Unfortunately, such action may be short-lived and unsustainable, particularly as new matters enter the agenda. Since the UN peacekeepers left Somalia in 1994, attention to this conflict in the international community has been minimal. Haiti was central in the mid-1990s, and again came into focus in 2004. Clearly, durable peace requires that institutions be left in place to follow the developments. This has been the argument in favour of the new UN Peacebuilding Commission that began its work in 2006. The devastating earthquake and the following cholera epidemic of Haiti in 2010 reinforced the importance of this, but also demonstrated that action had not come very far.

The UN, along with its specialized agencies is an institutional expression of the international community. Since the end of the Cold War, the agenda of the UN has also been the concern of the international community, as we saw in Chapter 9. However, the UN is not the domain of only one community. It includes an even larger grouping than the international community. It is a *global system* that is partly also represented in the UN. This points to a wider and even more heterogeneous set of actors, not often forming a community. For many states, the UN membership is a way to have their statehood confirmed, but they may not be willing to adhere to other implications of the Charter. Furthermore, this global system is comprised not only of states. There are state-like entities, popular movements, private corporations, armed non-state actors, and forceful individuals acting across state borders. The outer borders of the global system are not easy to depict. Almost any group which is able to act and has an impact on others is part of this system. The only shared value in the system is a desire to retain an element of independence so as to remain an actor. Some of the frustrations experienced in the international community have to do with this. In the Security Council as well as in the General Assembly, there are actors who object to the basic values underlying the actions proposed by members of the international community. Stipulations of the UN Charter may be used to remove a particular conflict from international concern, for instance, with reference to territorial integrity and political independence (Articles 2.4 and 2.7). The reality is often different. This provides an inconsistency for the international community. As we have seen, some conflicts will be attended to, others will not, depending partly on the interest and ability of actors to block action.

The reasons go deeper than the wording of the Charter. The Islamic Republic of Iran would not accept international involvement for the Kurdish population, although such decisions were taken with respect to Kurds in neighbouring Iraq. It might undermine the authority of the government. Iran, however, would want to have Security Council measures protect its borders with Iraq and Afghanistan as this serves to maintain its integrity as an actor and a state. Actors are likely to make calculations of utility and act accordingly, even if it may appear opportunistic. At the same time, it means that Charter provisions cross cultural divides. They express a minimum of agreement in a global system of great diversity. The surprisingly uniform reaction to Iraq's invasion of Kuwait in 1990 indicated such common concerns among states, notably the preservation of territorial integrity. Similarly, there was a uniform condemnation of the terrorist acts on September 11, 2001.

It could be said that the values of the UN are expressed in what the international community aims to achieve, rather than what the global system as a whole finds operative or even desirable. The Preamble to the Charter mentions fundamental human rights, dignity, equal rights, social progress, freedom and tolerance. The UN as an organization, however, has to act in the global system, not only within the international community. Thus, the UN can be caught between the concerns of the global system and the international community. Many violent clashes since the Cold War were fought along this divide. For instance, the sympathetic reading given to popular-based claims for self-determination of national minorities in the international community clashes with the strong emphasis on state sovereignty, incumbent governments and territorial integrity as basic in the global system. This division cuts across states and regions. It makes it difficult to find common ground for peace. The UN is located on an uncomfortable dividing line.

Paradoxically, this particular location may also give the UN a special function as a conflict-resolving body. UN representatives will have to talk to the rogue and shady characters who are real actors in real conflicts. These actors exert power and may be crucial for ending wars. Many of the peace agreements have included such encounters.

Value- and power-focused communities

The UN may have a particular role as a gateway between the international community and the global system. That is not its only role, however. It can be of importance to any community, but in different ways. The idea has emerged of creating an entirely different framework that can more closely mirror a stronger value-based, democratic international community. This is the idea of a *Pax Democratica*, a global association of democratic states. There is such an organization for Europe – the Council of Europe. It requires that states have functioning democratic institutions to attain membership. This body aims at strengthening cooperation among existing democracies and serves to promote democratic institutions in Central and Eastern Europe. It has, for instance, admitted Russia and Ukraine as members, hoping to augment their democratic institutions. An exclusively value-focused community would be one that emphasizes the importance of democracy for peace.

In Chapter 5, we learned that democracies rarely fight wars with each other, and in Chapters 6 and 7 the role of democracy for solutions to internal and state formation conflicts was discussed. Thus, democracy is an important factor in conflict resolution and prevention. It gives support for the idea of a specific community of democratic states. One may ask if a democratic international community would be needed to solve conflicts among the democracies. Most likely, the worst conflicts are to be found outside this group. It is also likely that there will be conflicts between members of this community and states outside it. This might make democratic states supporters for one side against another. To many, NATO's intervention to stop the armed conflict in Kosovo in 1999 was an expression of the ability of the democratic community to act. Certainly, the political support for the actions of the Western powers was strong throughout the democratic world. But it existed elsewhere, for instance, among Muslim societies advocating solidarity with Muslim Albanians. A more reasonable idea might be to create a caucus of democratic states *within* the UN system, rather than a democratic international association as its replacement or complement (Huntley 1998: 153–5). Clearly, this community will be more limited in numbers than either of the earlier two. It would be a novel constellation. The UN system, for instance, does not have special groups building on criteria other than power (Security Council members), geography (regional groupings) or development (the Group of 77 comprising most Third World nations).

There is another understanding of community, building on cooperation at regional or subregional levels. It includes even fewer states or actors, but with a distinct regional and sociological profile. It stems from the concept of a *security community*, developed by Karl W. Deutsch as a result of studies on peaceful interstate relations (see also Section 8.2). The notion has gained increasing saliency, with what Deutsch termed a pluralistic security community having particular relevance. It refers to situations of close cooperation, where states maintain their independence and where they do not expect to use violence among each other to solve mutual conflicts. This requires common values, mutual responsiveness and, possibly, common institutions. It is interesting to note, however, that institution building has not been seen as a necessary condition. Thus, the concept is applicable to areas where states remain independent, do not have the ambition of forming a union, but continue to cooperate and do not have recent experiences of mutual disputes turning into conflicts and wars (Adler and Barnett 1998; Deutsch et al. 1957; Wallensteen et al. 2002).

The Nordic area exemplifies such an alternative, where some states joined NATO or the EU while others remained outside, but they still maintained a tradition of solving conflicts without violence. The European Union is an additional expression of this idea, although it is a much more centralized and institutionalized version. Either way, the examples show that in the concept of security community, the shared values apply to a more narrow group of societies and the values cut deeper into the social fabric than is the case of the international community. It applies primarily to neighbouring countries, constituting subregions in the global system. It is deeper, in the sense that there are shared experiences of dealing peacefully with conflict among the members, thus leading to shared values in conflict management. There are democratic values in the examples given, but they may be more autocratic, as has been the case when building the security community of Southeast Asia.

If developed solidly enough, there would be no reason for the outside world to follow conflicts in these areas at all. The security community would then be self-sustaining in the management of its own crises. As these communities often consist of smaller states, however, the principles of peaceful cooperation may not apply to all kinds of conflict. For instance, they are likely to have difficulties in deterring hostile action from strong neighbours outside the community. The members may also be reluctant to involve themselves in the internal affairs of others. The notion of a security community is very attractive. It suggests that attitudinal shifts inside countries will affect their relationship to the outer world. Countries in a security community could turn into actors on the international scene. Shared values are likely to result in common understandings of international affairs. The Nordic countries illustrate this. Their values place them as a central group in the international community, together with a set of other, like-minded states. In such a constellation we could find Australia, Canada, New Zealand, the Netherlands, but also today's Argentina, Brazil, Chile, Mexico and South Africa, and increasingly, the Philippines, Nigeria, Thailand and South Korea. They need international fora to act, and for many of these countries the UN, the EU or NATO are primary foci.

There is another way by which a limited number of countries may cooperate, but without the term 'security community' being appropriate. Throughout this book, we have seen the significance of major power relations for conflict patterns. When these relations are universalist, cooperation in the form of *major power concerts* prevails. In history, such periods have been identified and labelled, for instance, the European concert of the early nineteenth century or periods of *détente* during the Cold War. It means that the powerful actors are incorporating the security concerns of the others into their own calculations of interest. The avoidance of major power war is an important element, but without fully excluding the possibility of resorting to armed conflict even among the majors. Thus, there may be a shared interest in security, but it does not extend as deeply as would be the case in a security community. We have noted that contentions among these actors historically have resulted in particularism and major war. To some analysts cooperative major power relations may still be the only way the world can be governed, although this is far from an ideal form of governance building on shared beliefs (Gilpin 2001: 402). It is an argument for vesting power with the permanent members of the Security Council and for developing the Group 8 (G8) framework into consolidated cooperation among the leading economies of the world. The global financial crisis since 2008 has given a new role to the Group of 20 (G20), which originally was a meeting of finance ministers. As it incorporates a number of emerging economies, it pulls together countries with economic clout. To many, it is more attractive than the formation of a Group of 2 (G2), meaning the USA and China, as the largest economies.

An additional alternative community is one which is under the determined leadership of one powerful actor. By its strength, it makes other states fall into line. Its values are given prominence and radiated throughout the community. Today, this could be termed a community of *Pax Americana*. Clearly, only one country has the capacity to project force globally – the United States. After the end of the Cold War, European countries have reduced their military expenditures and reallocated resources to matters which more immediately promote the welfare of populations (unemployment support, educational investment, health and social services). There has been a peace dividend. As we have seen, the world has not remained peaceful. New challenges have required unprecedented international action, peacekeeping operations and even peace enforcement. For the time being, the United States is the only country that maintains a capacity to airlift troops to distant regions in a short period of time. Its fleets can provide bases for military actions in many parts of the world. It has ground forces that were used to invade Iraq in 2003. Its satellite systems give the United States more information than any actor for discovering troop movements, other military preparations and general intelligence. In 2003, the USA alone accounted for 43 per cent of world military expenditures, while no other country was above 7 per cent (SIPRI 2010). It has led the USA on a path of unilateralism, where it acts on its own or, as in Iraq, in a coalition of close allies, or in Afghanistan with the help of international organizations. It can also result in multilateralism and a realization of a need for cooperation. The record since the Cold War is mixed. Sometimes the USA has acted in line with the international community at large; sometimes it has pursued its own course, as in Iraq since 2003. Increasingly, however, it has realized the importance of international support for its actions.

The United States is militarily unchallenged on a global scale. However, many of the wars since the Cold War have been highly local, and local opponents have found ways in which they can block action by powerful states. They are in a historical line of resistance movements fighting French and American forces in Vietnam, Soviet forces in Afghanistan, Russian troops in Chechnya and now facing the USA in Iraq and Afghanistan. These struggles involved considerable casualties. Some led to political victories for the opponents. The US actions in October 1993 in Somalia aimed at capturing some of the collaborators of a Somali warlord. It led to the death of US servicemen. The casualties among the Somalis included at least 500 killed (Bowden 1999: 333). Neither the American public nor the government was prepared for American casualties. This event changed the military intervention policy of the Clinton administration. It illustrated the potential military vulnerability of a strong power, whether acting alone or in concert with others.

For the remainder of the decade, no American soldiers were put into ground battle operations. The interventions that followed used air power. In 1995, this strategy achieved a retreat of Serb forces in Bosnia. The opportunity of weakened Serb positions created by the NATO bombardment was seized by Croat and Bosniak forces which quickly pushed forward to conquer more territory. The USA created the conditions. The subsequent peacekeeping mission was done in a multilateral framework with NATO, the OSCE, the EU and the UN. In 1999, the air campaign influenced the Yugoslav leader Slobodan Milosevic to agree to a withdrawal from Kosovo. It was achieved through NATO, but the civil administration of Kosovo was turned over to the UN. All US administrations since the Gulf War used air raids against Iraq to achieve compliance with UN resolutions. In attempts to strike at international terrorism, US missiles hit installations in Afghanistan and a pharmaceutical plant in the Sudan in 1998 – again unilateral moves. Following September 11, 2001, however, the American public was more accepting of unilateral action and American casualties. Thus, US ground forces were deployed in Afghanistan, and an Army of more than 150,000 soldiers invaded Iraq in 2003. The continued wars in Iraq and Afghanistan, however, have led to increased American battle deaths, and thus to an unease in the USA about the wars, their purposes, duration and ending. In Afghanistan, ground forces and air raids have been supplemented with drones, unmanned planes controlled from afar.

The power of the US is extensive, but the results may not appear equally impressive. Years later, the agreements in Bosnia-Herzegovina and Kosovo remained fragile. Saddam Hussein, Osama bin Laden and the Taliban continued to be defiant. The political gains from the air campaigns were often limited. The successful removal of Saddam in 2003 did not create a functioning state in Iraq, but led instead to a protracted war, continuing even as US forces began to leave the area in 2010. Years after the removal of the Taliban from power in Afghanistan, the new government remained brittle and the future uncertain. The effects of the killing of Osama bin Laden in May 2011 remain to be seen. The military arsenal of the United States remains the largest, but its contribution to peacemaking requires international consensus and able local allies.

The political limits of US power not only stem from the military strategy used. The USA is a superpower which often displays acute divisions among its policy-making circles on its role in world affairs. Traditionally, it has been one focusing on isolationism versus engagement. This is too simple a distinction. The internal debate is more complex, less predictable and highly volatile. There is a prominent role for the media, NGOs and special interests, notably the large corporations, as well as for an entrenched military establishment in shaping US policy. The outcomes may in the end be more random than well planned and strategic.

This means that the most likely scenario for the future is not one of a community consciously developed by the United States for a clear idea of *Pax Americana*. Rather it is one of the United States avoiding having to act in isolation. The USA will need the cooperation of other countries. This can be achieved through the United Nations, which gives other countries some influence on the course of action. It can also be done with the construction of international regional organizations that depend on the United States. It would constitute a network which may act outside the UN if necessary. There is a discernable trend in this direction, NATO being an example. NATO enlargement (in 2010 to 28 members), the ISAF engagement in Afghanistan, cooperation within the Partnership for Peace, and the Mediterranean Dialogues, makes NATO a comprehensive network for Europe and beyond (Al-Khazendar 2005). It is typical that the USA chose to hand over to NATO the air campaign against Libya, that began in March 2011. It is conceivable that the USA may support the construction of similar frameworks in other parts of the world. APEC was given prominence in Asian affairs by the Clinton administration. The Bush government, however, preferred direct dealing with leading states as well as to work with the Group of 8 (G8). The Obama administration may have a preference for G20.

There is a need to rethink the issues of global order to find measures which can reduce the number of conflicts, improve the chances for settlements and prevent new conflicts from becoming violent. What we have seen are six different designs for a new world order. They range from a loose, almost anarchical, global system of independent actors occasionally using the UN for particularist interests (the global system) to a closely knit, strategically formulated, superpower-directed world (*Pax Americana*). But the concepts tell us that there are many alternatives. The post-Cold War world is not moulded according to only one framework. There will be many approaches competing for attention and success in the conflict resolution activities in the years to come. Indeed, the alternatives may be even wider, including a world centred on the countries in the South pursuing the North–South divide or on China more specifically, another departing from Christian or Muslim values, one building on the interests of transnational corporations, or one departing from environmental and ecological concerns. The options are many and the results are going to depend on the strength and coherence of the particular concepts. Their clashes and mixing will shape the world, its regions and interactions.

10.2 Early Action and Conflict Prevention

The emerging conflict management communities include new forms of action. We are interested in actions that aim to reduce the number and scale of armed conflicts by finding solutions at an early stage. These ambitions are oftentimes described as conflict prevention. The idea is simple. By observing early warning signs, developing agendas for early action, summoning support, implementing particular measures and sustaining collective action, the chances of reducing suffering increase. The world would be spared more disasters. In order to clarify this line of thought we need to distinguish between structural and direct forms of conflict prevention. The structural aspects we shall return to more fully in Section 10.4. The direct prevention approach comes into play when there are actors, incompatibilities and action, but where violence is still not the dominant expression of the problem. Furthermore, this form of prevention aims to reduce or eliminate violence in a conflict, not necessarily to eliminate the conflict as such. It includes constructive actions taken by third parties to avoid the likely threat, use or diffusion of armed force by parties in a political dispute. This is referred to as preventive action or preventive diplomacy. A broad spectrum of actions is customarily included, even military measures (Cahill 1996; Carnegie Commission 1997; Lund 1996; Malone and Hampson 2001; Stedman 1995; Wallensteen 1998).

Preventive actions are not actions undertaken by the parties themselves to scale down a conflict, but rather those of third parties. This is not normally the perspective held by the primary parties themselves. It is more likely that each regards itself as 'benign' and 'well-intended'. Their actions are taken in order to bring the conflict to a speedy ending, to their own advantage, no doubt. There were comparable concepts in use during the Cold War. They communicate a party-based perspective. Prevention was synonymous with pre-emptive actions by one side before the other side could launch its attack. Prevention was connected to imminent crisis. Preventive diplomacy after the Cold War is one coming from the outside, building on goals such as those expressed in the international community. It serves to reduce tension in a conflict and push the parties towards a negotiated solution. To be effective, it has to be credible by not benefiting one or the other of the fighting parties. Thus, the community to which the actors belong becomes important.

Lately, 'preventive war' has acquired prominence in US strategic doctrine. This is a return to the unilateral concepts of the Cold War era, but focuses today on potential terrorist threats, primarily to the United States itself. The preventive actions dealt with here are those carried out by third parties and emphasize the use of non-military means.

Examples of conflict prevention

The efficiency of preventive actions is difficult to ascertain. How do we know that there was an imminent threat? If there is no crisis, do we know that one was likely? It is easier to establish that preventive actions have failed than to show that they have succeeded. However, history is full of examples of crises that many expected would become serious. The Cuban Missile Crisis is but one case. There are also historical records of the successful management of tension among major powers in previous centuries (Schroeder 2006). Sometimes these have involved third parties, oftentimes the actors have controlled actions among themselves. In fact, it is likely that great powers are reluctant to have other states involved in their conflicts.

There are also examples of preventive action since the Cold War. In chronicles of events, it is possible to find disputes that were regarded as having a potential for violent escalation. Observers and policy-makers may agree on this. The examples of conflict prevention cases often include more interstate conflicts than we would expect from the fact that the armed conflicts of this decade have largely been internal. There have been close to 20 such crises since 1989, most of them well documented in international media and scholarly work. A typical example is the conflict between former Yugoslavia and Macedonia in the early 1990s, when the UN positioned a peacekeeping operation on the border. A number of cases have also been brought to the International Court of Justice or found neighbouring countries as mediators (Wallensteen 2002: 273). A positive reading of this is that there are instruments in place to handle such conflicts. The examples show that such measures are functioning, perhaps even more often than can be expected. A negative reading is that only interstate conflicts receive attention and, as a consequence, they will see more international preventive action.

Either way, this suggests that interstate conflicts can be defused and that this is almost regarded as normal practice. Indeed, there are cases of confrontations where the parties sorted out matters among themselves rather than inviting outsiders. For instance, there were severe tensions between Russia and Ukraine over the division of the Black Sea fleet early in the 1990s. Similarly, the same countries had repeated confrontations over natural gas prices in 2006–09. These issues were solved between the parties with minimal outside involvement. Also, we can see that there are no cases of third parties in major power disputes.

There is likely to be a larger number of internal disputes with serious crises than normally observed. They might have been handled by local actors and thus only reported about locally (if at all). Authoritarian governments are not likely to allow much attention to such conflicts either. Still, some cases can be identified. In the protracted crisis in Zimbabwe, which politically began with the elections in 2002, international action focused on democratization as a possible way to avoid a future civil war. Another case concerned the rights of the Albanian population in Macedonia in 2001, where a peace agreement could be concluded before the level of violence had escalated (Väyrynen 2004). In reality, there are more cases, but governments are not likely to report on such matters, fearful that it would undermine the authority of the state.

Similarly, we might expect an under-reporting for state formation conflicts. In this case, however, there might be groups outside the country which could document what has happened. Some state formation conflicts are also part of regional conflict complexes and, thus, are often more likely to draw outside attention.

Among conflicts contained through preventive measures, the state formation conflict over Palestine has probably received the most attention. In fact, the Oslo peace process saw a series of crises and crisis management. Often, outside parties have been able to undo some of the tension. One situation was sparked by Palestinian President Yassir Arafat's threat to declare independence when the Oslo process formally expired on May 4, 1999. It would be a unilateral action, not based on an agreement with Israel. The threat had credibility and led to a series of diplomatic and political actions. Chief among these were the summit negotiations in October 1998 outside Washington, DC. They saw the participation of the leaders of the USA, Israel and Jordan, together with Arafat. An agreement, the so-called Wye Memorandum, was worked out. It fell apart shortly afterwards as the Israeli cabinet split on the issue. The peace process was frozen but Arafat managed to get promises of support from the EU and postponed his threat. The international engagement to prevent an imminent crisis was impressive and, in effect, successful. No immediate crisis followed; instead, a new Israeli government with a strong commitment to peace came into office.

However, the next crisis did not work out in a similar way. The second Intifada that began in late September 2000 resulted in summit diplomacy. It involved some of the same actors as in the efforts less than two years earlier. This time, the UN and the EU were also drawn in. Again, a sizeable part of the international community acted to prevent the events from escalating and spreading. These efforts did not succeed equally well, neither bringing peace negotiations to an end nor reducing violence. However, it served to keep international attention on the issue. It is not easy to see why efforts worked in 1998 but not in 2000. The same means were tried, but important elements of trust and confidence among the primary parties had evaporated. Not until 2007 was an attempt made to restart the dialogue followed by one more try in 2010. The possibility of a unilateral Palestinian declaration of statehood may again spur the international community into action.

Peacekeeping or other preventive deployments have been part of crisis control efforts, not only in the case of the UN preventive deployment in Macedonia in 1993–99 (UNPREDEP). Another mission was in the Central African Republic 1998–2000 (MINURCA). A special development was the European force under Italian command that was deployed in Albania for some months in 1997 (ALBA). Also, the regional organization, Southern Africa Development Council (SADC), stationed troops in Lesotho in 1998. To set up such operations in a short time indicates a strong commitment and concern about developments. A very special deployment was the EU-led, UN-mandated ARTEMIS mission that was placed in Bunia, in the Ituri region of the Democratic Republic of Congo in September 2003 to deal with the violence among ethnic groups in the area. In these cases, tension was reduced.

In other instances, peacekeepers were already in place when the crisis occurred. This was the case in the 2000 crisis over armed Albanian incursions from Kosovo into southern Serbia. The NATO-led KFOR mission was stationed on one side of this divide. As a result of negotiations, Serb police forces were allowed again to enter the demilitarized zone on the other side of the lines to reduce the danger of escalation. In this case as well as in the one in Macedonia, where the international force also had an impact, conflicts were brewing in areas of considerable international involvement already. The swift actions taken suggested that the international community was unwilling to let the conflict linger. At least militarily, these crises were defused. Similarly, there were peace operations in place in several of the interstate conflicts. These may have contributed to keep tension within limits (Korea, Cyprus and Kashmir).

Predicting escalation

Many of these disputes were well known to decision-makers and analysts. They concerned unsettled borders, minorities with majorities on the other side of a border, claims on islands and historical tensions. Each one required special attention. Many conflicts were 'frozen' in an uneasy state of affairs. To predict that such conflicts are dangerous is not difficult. To specify more exactly when acute danger will arise is less simple.

It is more difficult to predict which internal conflicts are likely to escalate into severe violence at what time and what type of international preventive action they may require. For instance, it is difficult to determine if actions of a particular government towards its opposition will 'work' without leading to a severe crisis internally. The government may feel confident as it takes actions, but it may make a serious error. It will not be easier for outsiders to predict what will happen. Also, a government may fall more quickly than anticipated because the opposition turns out be better organized than expected. The fall of Yugoslav leader Slobodan Milosevic in October 2000 was unexpected, as he himself had called the election. At a crucial moment, it turned out that he no longer had the support of the armed forces. The unarmed opposition could take over and Milosevic had to resign. Was this a crisis which was prevented from escalating, for instance by the sanctions imposed? Or was it a crisis that was not likely to escalate, as the police and military took a neutral stand? The same can be asked of the democratizing Orange Revolution in Ukraine in late 2004 where the actions of the EU High Representative Javier Solana could be interpreted as a successful contribution both to democracy and to the prevention of violence. Others, however, saw these preventive actions as a way of forcing a premature compromise on a non-violent revolution (Cloos 2005; Maksymenko 2005). During the Arab spring, Western countries pressed Egypt's president Hosni Mubarak to resign in February 2011, clearly in the hope of preventing a violent turn of events.

It is likely that most government crises do not result in violence and thus do not warrant international concern. Sometimes deals are made between opponents and governments. The existence of legal structures and democratic forces may be a necessary condition for non-violent change. The fear of intervening when matters are changing through their own dynamics makes international actors reluctant to act. They may even be afraid to stimulate counter-reactions that prevent desirable change. There is a danger that international action will increase tension. When the options are unattractive, the outside will tend to postpone action. But the longer the international community waits to act, the more difficult it will be to intervene at all. As a consequence, for the outside world, the balance will often tilt in favour of taking no action.

These arguments apply even more stringently to state formation conflicts. They threaten the breakup of states. Most external states are reluctant to encourage such prospects. The Palestinian question is special in its international support. It is more typical that the local governments actively and often successfully prevent international approaches to challenging groups. From the incumbent government's perspective, for outsiders to establish relations with such groups is equal to accepting their claims. For the opposition, the reverse is of course true. Early action would be vindication of the 'justice' of the struggle and may further their chances of victory. Thus, we would expect early action from the international community in state formation conflicts to be rare, at least on the open and diplomatic levels. Even if there is an expectation of violence, the interstate system often prefers not to take up the issues. The Palestinian case had been high on the world agenda for more than half a century and is probably exceptional. The regional repercussions, for instance, are well known. Other issues which have drawn attention, such as Tibet in China, Aceh in Indonesia, Corsica in France, Samis in Scandinavia, or Native Americans in the United States, have rarely been the focus of international governmental organizations. However, some situations have been handled on an international level and at an early stage. The OSCE has taken a particular role in European disputes and has been more active than, for instance, the UN. This has been achieved through the office of the High Commissioner on National Minorities. The relatively low-key approach taken may have been highly effective in defusing tension (Kemp 2001).

Prevention departs from an assumption that the parties actually do not want disputes to escalate. They have a preference for finding a solution and the international community can contribute by rewarding that option. However, there are situations when this premise does not hold. These will be the tough cases of prevention, as parties do their utmost to hide their plans. There are some cases that illustrate this. The initiation of large-scale hostilities includes considerable planning and is not made by spontaneous action at the whim of a leader. Thus, interstate armed conflicts sometimes escalate on purpose. Egypt and Syria planned carefully and their attack in October 1973 against Israel aimed at surprising the other side. Information was not available, weapons deliveries were not stepped up but spread over time, troop movements were credibly described as manoeuvres. The initiation of the war was, from that point of view, a success. It was purposefully done so as to avoid pre-emptive action by the adversary or by the major powers. Iraq's occupation of Kuwait on August 2, 1990 had similar features. Clearly, neither the Kuwaiti leadership nor the major powers anticipated this move, although the concentration of Iraqi troops around Kuwait was observed. The actions taken against Iraq in 2003, however, were entirely in the open, as this was a way to pressure its regime. Thus, it left some space for preventive action.

The hope that the weapons inspectors would be able to conclude their work was one element in possibly delaying a war, or even making it unnecessary. The delaying tactics, however, seem only to have increased the determination, primarily of the USA, to act decisively and early.

Surprise situations are also found in internal conflicts. The coup in Romania in 1989 against the Communist Party leader Ceauşescu came as a surprise, although the tensions had been rising in the country for days before. Coup leaders challenging an incumbent government will always have to build on their ability to surprise and, thus, they will camouflage moves that might constitute an early warning. The same is true for the government side, which has its intelligence network in operation and would like to have information as early as possible in order to be able to pre-empt threatening moves. The timing of action will depend on how suspicious the leaders are. It is not uncommon that authoritarian governments claim to have foiled a coup attempt and arrested culprits. Sometimes there is evidence. Whether it would withstand independent court review is another matter. These accusations are seldom put to trial.

Also, state formation conflicts can have such coup-like patterns, either from the side of the challengers or from the government. Many successful rebellions start with complete military failures, as shown by the Easter uprising in Dublin in 1916. The survivors became heroes for the Irish nationalists, but the action did not lead to the victorious ending that the originators had hoped for. It became a starting point, nevertheless, of an armed and political process that gave independence to the Irish Republic in 1922, albeit at the price of dividing the island in two.

The delicacy of early detection means that direct conflict prevention has to be conceived in a different way. It is not there to compete with intelligence planning of the contending sides. The lessons for prevention and early warning are different. Sometimes it may be possible to warn the primary parties of impending events. It is often more certain to point to conditions that enhance the likelihood of violent actions, and ask for remedial measures. This points to situations of human rights violations, lack of democracy and need for transparency. These are matters which have implications for internal and state formation conflicts as well as interstate conflicts. Global human rights monitoring is already an established activity and it is useful also from the prevention perspective.

However, in authoritarian societies, violations of human rights are routine. They are even important for regime survival and the violations may give few clues as to whether a civil war or an interstate conflict is about to break out at a particular time. When repression increases, does it mean tensions in society increase and the escalation of conflict is more likely? Is it instead when repression decreases, and societies open up and more becomes known that the likelihood of conflict increases? Is it more important to identify which groups are targeted by repression and which leaders are harassed? Such questions need to be used in the analysis of particular societies. Too general indicators may imply different things, depending on economic conditions, political situations and other local circumstances.

The issue of direct conflict prevention faces particular challenges. We have seen that there is a record of early action, particularly for inter-state conflicts. There are considerable difficulties for conflict prevention in internal affairs and state formation conflicts. Observing human rights violations, ethnic discrimination, lack of access to institutions and other political measures are useful early indicators of possible conflicts. Among concerned governments there is serious attention to such activities. International organizations are giving more attention to preventive work, notably the United Nations, the OECD and the World Bank. The World Summit in 2005 also emphasized the significance of preventive actions. The difficulties notwithstanding, the idea of prevention is gaining ground as a chief lesson from the conflict experiences of the post-Cold War period.

This can be seen in the new actors who have entered and taken their place in the international community. Some non-governmental organizations have been particularly active. To these belong The Carter Center, International Alert, Conciliation Resources, Search for Common Ground, and the International Crisis Group, among others. They have taken different approaches. Some concentrate on early warnings, others try to bring parties together, using variants of the problem-solving workshops, still others provide analyses of rising situations. University departments have also been a resource for such activities, as seen in the work of the Institute for Conflict Analysis and Resolution, George Mason University, and the Department of Peace and Conflict Research, Uppsala University. It also means that new sources of information are being developed. An example is the European Platform for Conflict Prevention and Transformation in the Netherlands and the Global Partnership for the Prevention of Armed Conflict. Many of these activities have been instrumental in bringing about cease-fires or laying the groundwork for peace agreements. Often, non-governmental activities have a broader purpose than simply preventing a particular crisis from erupting into violence. The aim is to contribute to long-term constructive relations between a broad set of actors who are divided by a particular conflict. To influence government policy is but one aspect of the activities. Dialogue, confidence-building and identifying common interests are as important as finding immediate prevention measures.

As preventive diplomacy is receiving more attention, there are two additional matters to keep in mind. The first is that it is difficult to know whether it actually was the preventive action that worked and not some other factor. It could even be that the parties would say – afterwards – that the threats of escalation or diffusion were never that serious. This is difficult to establish and only an educated guess is possible. Conflict dynamics may be analysed and compared to cases with similar characteristics. We can establish that all major armed conflicts continuing today were relatively minor and insignificant once upon a time. This makes it likely that at least some of the conflicts mentioned here would have escalated if no preventive actions had been taken. Some systematic studies are emerging, however, particularly focusing on what actions might be more conducive for prevention. In 67 ethnic conflicts since 1990, it was established that contacts between the parties had a particular effect in reducing the likelihood of escalation (Öberg et al. 2009). A new database on preventive measures in minor, intra-state armed conflicts 1993–2004 has been published at the Uppsala Conflict Data Program (www.ucdp.uu.se) and is developed further.

The second issue is the question of the ethics of direct conflict prevention. Effective preventive actions are probably agreeable to most. They achieve a reduction in tension that is beneficial to the different sides. But there is a danger that outside actions will be to the advantage of one or the other side in the conflict. It could be that they help to consolidate a situation which in the long run is unsound and necessary changes are prevented, as well as unnecessary violence. This basic normative issue should be part of the discourse on direct conflict prevention. It may, at times, be unethical to intervene too early if this will inhibit a positive long-term development. At the same time, it could be unethical not to act early, when there is a danger of innocent people being victimized. The ethics of intervention and non-intervention are fundamental. There has to be an ethical answer before action is taken.

10.3 Third Parties and Mediation

Since the end of the Cold War third parties have been involved in conflict resolution as a normal state of affairs. It is increasingly difficult for countries to refuse access for the outside community into particular conflicts. However, it is still common that countries decline offers of using the good offices of international secretariats, other governments or even non-government organizations. Thus, Russia has not been prepared to invite outsiders to assist in settling the conflict in Chechnya. In some conflicts it might be possible to find third parties from the country itself. This has sometimes been an assignment taken on by persons with particular status who can transcend the conflict divides, such as individuals with religious roles, retired statesmen or even businessmen.

The United Nations Secretary-General is a resource of global significance. The Secretary-General has appointed a number of Special and Personal Representatives for particular issues or conflicts (Peck 2004). This is done with consent from the parties. A new development is the pressure from non-state actors. During the crisis over East Timor in September 1999, the Secretary-General received thousands of messages calling for action. In this conflict, the Secretary-General served as a mediator, being instrumental in forging the referendum agreement of May 1999. Thus, the outside world can impact the actions taken. The UN Secretary-General may have a more uncontested status as a third party than any other of the

UN collective security institutions. The World Summit in 2005 suggested that this capacity should be further strengthened, and later the Mediation Support Unit was created in the Secretariat. Also, a new development is that countries interested in the promotion of conflict resolution have begun to appoint their own envoys for conflicts of particular interest. There are groups of 'Friends of the Secretary-General' for different conflicts. This means that the options for the primary parties interested in finding a solution are widening. There are competent persons to turn to. Whether a conflict is settled or not no longer depends on the availability of mediation possibilities. The early literature on third parties assumed that such parties would be strategic for turning a conflict from war to peace. The post-Cold War experiences suggest that this is no longer a crucial variable. Parties are increasingly aware of the possibilities of settling their conflict. The decisions are now even more strongly connected to their interest in a settlement. The excuses for not engaging in a peace process are increasingly limited.

In many cases of peace agreements, there is a record of mediation in the process leading to a settlement. Often the parties express their satisfaction with such efforts. Unfortunately, there is also a record of such efforts in conflicts that were not solved. It suffices here to mention the conflicts in Angola and Somalia, which drew considerable efforts during the 1990s, and Sri Lanka during the early 2000s.

Increasingly, mediation has been seen as a process, where a third party enters, acts, coordinates and leaves the scene. This process has been studied with respect to one mediator involved in third party activity during a 30-year period, Ambassador Jan Eliasson (Svensson and Wallensteen 2010). Other efforts have also been studied. Here we single out two issues of particular importance for a third party. The first has to do with the appointment and mandate of the mediator, the second with the approach taken by the third party in dealing with the primary and secondary parties. These issues can be seen in two highly publicized experiences: Bosnia-Herzegovina and Northern Ireland. Both found a settlement in the 1990s, and years later remained in a volatile phase of implementation. Both had considerable international attention. Only one was on the UN agenda.

Entering a conflict

The question of the appointment of a third party is central as it will determine the mandate and the parties' perception of the mediator. The traditional form is a mediator chosen, for instance, by the UN Security Council or the UN Secretary-General. This is a procedure which ensures the impartiality of the mediator, if the Council or the Secretary-General is viewed as impartial. As we have seen earlier, this is not necessarily true for the Council, but is more often the case for the Secretary-General. It is important that the candidacy of the third party, if appointed by the UN, is accepted or not actively opposed by the warring parties. They need to have had a chance to express their opinion on the selection. It does not make sense, of course, for a world organization to appoint a person for mediation if there is no interest among the parties to talk to this particular individual. The UN appointment procedure gives the parties influence on the decision.

The parties may, if they are in direct contact with one another, agree on an appointment without involving the UN or any others. Direct contacts can result in secret negotiations (as is exemplified by the Oslo Channel in 1993) or open ones (as was the case in the Northern Ireland talks). In principle, nothing prevents the parties from making an arrangement of their own.

It can be a complicated procedure, as in the case of Northern Ireland (Mitchell 1999a: 26–7, 48–50). The Northern Ireland independent commission was to have three international chairpersons, drawn so that one was selected jointly by the two governments which initiated the negotiations (Britain and Ireland). They chose former US Senator George Mitchell. Following this, each side chose one person. Similar procedures have been applied in other conflicts. It gives the opposing sides a stake in the process. In this case, it meant that the real contenders, the Northern Ireland parties, had little say on the selection. However, they were not left out. In a remarkable procedure, they were to agree to the international chairpersons taking the presidency in the plenary sessions of the negotiation forum. Thus, all parties involved in the peace process convened and debated this issue for two days. Meanwhile the selected persons were waiting in an adjacent office. When they finally could enter the room, a British officer was sitting in the chair in which George Mitchell, as the leader, was to sit. He was not leaving until Mitchell was about to sit down. The explanation was that, in this way, the opponents could not take the seat, physically preventing the negotiations from starting and, thus, having to be expelled by force! The chairpersons faced an uphill struggle to gain the confidence of these parties. The opposition was directed not at the leadership as such, but at the idea of negotiations. They were the spoilers, who were participating in the process to prevent it from succeeding and, later, when this was not possible, left the forum and tried to wreck the process from the outside.

In other instances, the mediator is appointed by an outside party, with or without consultation. The United States has acted in a number of conflicts. The actors may have been the President, the Secretary of State or high-ranking officials of the administration. They are often seen as 'mediators' and, indeed, perform some of the same functions. In the strictest sense of the word, they often are not third parties. Their appointment is made by American authorities. Ambassador Holbrooke is often described as a mediator in the conflicts in Southeast Europe. In fact, he was the US Assistant Secretary of State for European Affairs when he dealt with Bosnia-Herzegovina, undeniably the most difficult and acute issue of his area of assignment. It may well have been understood from the beginning that this was his role. Nevertheless, he entered into a conflict in a role which is different from the one Mitchell had in Northern Ireland. He could rely on the official support and resources of the United States.

The USA might appear to be a normal third party, but this is not the case. It often has its own interest in the outcomes. It will benefit from the settlement of the conflict, but it also has its own agenda. It may give priority to issues which other parties may not. It may be prepared to exert pressure on some parties, but not on others. There is also the possibility that the USA may resort to military power. This has meant that the United Nations, for instance, has used relatively few American officials as Special Representatives for mediation. The problem of bias can also affect the United Nations, as the Security Council may have its own view on how a particular conflict should be solved. We have seen that this happened during the Iran–Iraq War (Chapter 5). The Security Council was negative to the Islamic government of Iran. Thus, Iran's government preferred to relate to the Secretary-General. The Secretary-General appointed his own special representative. This position was held by the Swedish statesman, Olof Palme, until his assassination in 1986. He was later replaced by a Swedish diplomat, Jan Eliasson (Svensson and Wallensteen 2010). The solution that finally brought an end to the war was made under the auspices of the UN Secretary-General, building eventually on a more balanced position taken by the Security Council. Similar experiences have also been noted for the post-Cold War period. There were efforts by Secretary-General Kofi Annan to defuse some of the crises with Iraq over the UNSCOM inspections. These repeatedly led to threats against Iraq, particularly from the United States. The Secretary-General made a special agreement with the Iraqi leader, Saddam Hussein, in February 1998. This prevented an escalation of that particular crisis while maintaining the inspections. Unfortunately, the relationship between UNSCOM and the Iraqi government resulted in a new crisis later the same year and inspections ceased. From the Iraqi perspective, UNSCOM was not seen as balanced, although Iraq apparently was willing to deal directly with the Secretary-General. In 2003, the situation was reversed, when Iraq was willing to work with UNMOVIC (having replaced UNSCOM), while the USA and its allies did not want to rely on this process. Thus, no space was left for third party action.

Much experience suggests that the parties to a conflict primarily want a mediator who is impartial to their position. It means that the mediator correctly appreciates their interests and correctly transfers information and evaluations between the sides. It does not, however, require an entirely neutral position. Bias can sometimes be useful (Svensson 2009). The fact that a mediator is close to one side can satisfy the other, as it hopes this will bring more pressure on that particular side.

Approaches to mediation

The possibility of issuing credible threats is one of the 'cards' that is uniquely available to the USA in the post-Cold War period. The distinction between

mediators with much power – 'muscle' – and those with little or no physical power is important. Senator Mitchell, when chairing the negotiations on
Northern Ireland, had no such power. Some of the negotiating parties in the
talks had access to sympathetic violent groups. Britain, furthermore, had its
forces as well as its legal preponderance, as it were, controlling the sovereignty of Northern Ireland. Mitchell could rely on the parties with a strong
interest in making an agreement, but the use of force was beyond his realm.
If for no other reason, he was not part of a chain of command. Furthermore,
the parties had agreed to a cease-fire, reducing the pressure of violence on
the negotiations.

Ambassador Holbrooke could act with the certitude of official US support. He was implementing, as well as influencing, US policy. From this
position he could, for instance, encourage some parties to use force in order
to facilitate the negotiations. In the autumn of 1995, Croat and Bosniak
forces were encouraged to take as much land as possible, only with the
warning of not creating large refugee flows. The preconditions of the
negotiations that were to convene at the Air Force base in Dayton, Ohio,
were that they would arrive at a 49–51 formula of territorial division. The
Serbs would have 49 per cent of Bosnia's territory, and the Croat-Bosniak
Federation the rest. As the Serbs held more territory than this, it was important to achieve a territorial division on the ground. The losses of territory
by the Bosnian Serbs in September and October 1995 reduced their share
to the stipulated 49 per cent (Holbrooke 1999: 160, 166, 199). There was a
definite bias in American policy. For instance, the US side was reluctant to
put pressure on the Bosniak leadership. This was the country whose independence the USA was protecting. At a crucial juncture in the Dayton peace
talks, when the American negotiating team felt that some pressure would be
needed also on the Bosniak side, the White House National Security staff
reportedly balked and prevented any such action (Holbrooke 1999: 301).

The experiences from these two negotiations are interesting, as they suggest two distinct forms of mediation. As both negotiators were Americans,
there was no cultural distinction between the two, although their class
background and careers were different. It was the format for the talks that
differed. One was done without power, the other one with power. Let us
look more closely at the two.

The first approach had to work with persuasion, developing confidence
with the parties, finding intelligent propositions and, thus, attempting to
transcend some of the difficulties. It was deal-making, but not only that.
It appears as a genuine search for common agreement. It would, inevitably, take time. Reaching the Good Friday Agreement in 1998 took two
years. The question is whether this would also make the agreement stick.
It is interesting, however, that when the implementation reached a snag on
demilitarization a year later, the leaders of Britain and Ireland tried hard
to reach an agreement but without success. Senator Mitchell was called in
again to make a review. It took 11 weeks of painstaking talks in seclusion
before the parties finally found a way out of this stalemate. Thus, by the

end of November 1999, the agreement's first provisions on self-rule could begin to be implemented. Clearly, it had been a time-consuming task. It may have the advantage, however, of making the parties themselves take control over the process (Mitchell 1999b). A remarkable achievement was noted in May 2007 when Ian Paisley, leader of the Democratic Unionist Party, became First Minister in a Northern Ireland government with Sinn Fein leader Martin McGuinness as Deputy First Minister. The return to war seemed increasingly unlikely.

The second approach requires considerable ingenuity as well. Parties will not subscribe to an arrangement which they fear. However, the use of the threat of force changes the dynamic, particularly when, as was the case in the Bosnia-Herzegovina crisis, the force used by the outside was targeting one side only. There was a clear basis on which the outside power, the United States, made its evaluation of the outcome. It had a preference. It may be one that was shared internationally, but nevertheless it shifted the talks from searching for common positions to finding positions that were compatible with this basic premise. The talks in Dayton lasted for three weeks. It was, in the words of Holbrooke, 'the Big Bang approach to negotiations: lock everyone up until they reach agreement' (Holbrooke 1999: 232). It achieved a permanent cease-fire and a constitution for the Republic of Bosnia-Herzegovina. To implement the agreement a NATO-led force was placed in the country, as was an international police force and an internationally appointed High Representative for civilian affairs. The implementation required close surveillance and these institutions were still in place more than 15 years later.

The results were remarkable in both circumstances. The agreements were detailed, concrete and gave directions for implementation. Clearly, the strong international presence differentiated the Dayton agreement from the Northern Ireland one. This reflects more the differences in the issues that had to be solved, the ferocity of the wars and the magnitude of state-building tasks that lay ahead. It can be asked, however, whether the result in the first process is such that the parties are prepared to take more responsibility for implementation than in the second case. The sharing of power by two parties that were seen as each other's extremes is a mark of this, taking place eight years after the original agreement. Has the second approach resulted in an agreement that is heavily dependent on a sustained international interest? The international development has been scaled down but still remains crucial. The constitution that was part of the peace agreement is increasingly challenged but change appears difficult.

If the first approach had been used in the Bosnia-Herzegovina case, it might have meant that Dayton would only result in a cease-fire agreement, after which the parties were to start to negotiate among themselves. A momentum for settlement would have been lost and the difficulties of keeping the state of Bosnia-Herzegovina together would have been apparent. In the autumn of 1995 there may not have been many viable alternatives to the process selected. A process of the first type requires a somewhat better chance of meaningful dialogue. At the same time, a solution is still needed to provide for a smooth-functioning daily life. The parties may easily walk out as they are not forced into the arrangements. A process of the second type requires considerable and constant pressure, in the end exhausting the participants. It is an expensive approach and the chance of failure is high. Even if the parties cannot walk out, they can procrastinate and obstruct. For both processes, the benefit from success may still be considerable and change their priorities for the future.

The evaluation of the two approaches is important. It is a general question of interest to many types of conflict. Both agreements have remained in place and there has been no outbreak of war. But the quality of the peace can be questioned. The opportunities for economic growth and development are greater in Northern Ireland. Bosnia remains aid-dependent.

We have seen that conflicts increasingly have been brought to international attention. They become issues for the UN, for human rights and conflict resolution organizations, for those fearing genocide, as well as for compatriots spread around the world. A global economy creates global connections for local conflicts. Thus, issues of prevention and mediation become central concerns for the different new communities that are emerging. A final question, then, is this: is the world doomed always to see the rise of new conflicts and wars?

10.4 Structural Changes and Peaceful Conflict

The study into the causes of conflict can yield some insights into broader changes that are required for reducing the danger of new wars. This is consonant with the idea of a structural approach to conflict prevention or peacebuilding (Lederach 1997, Wallensteen 2001a). It means taking a long-term perspective. Conflicts develop from grievances experienced in a society, actions are based on deliberate considerations of gains, and conflicts escalate to levels where they may become violent, as we have seen in Chapter 3. Such a structural approach would have to involve measures to influence this chain so as to allow for legitimate change without the need for violence. It becomes a broad programme and the results are not too easily observable in the course of a particular conflict. The measure of success is seen in an analysis of a conflict over a longer period of time. It would be, for instance, where formerly conflictual interstate relations are no longer tense, once conflict-ridden societies are integrated, and previously divided societies have found ways to cooperate. In short, we are looking for results where historical conflicts are turned into non-conflict or even cooperation.

This is a broad agenda. The peace agreements since the Cold War give some clues to the possibilities. Most of them aim at converting conflictual relations. Many of them are still too fresh to suggest safely that such shifts have taken place. The institutions put in place through the peace agreements include measures that might also be useful for other situations. Chapters 5, 6 and 7 give ideas for a structural conflict prevention programme. Conclusions can also be drawn from studies of the causes of war and the causes of internal war. It gives a role for development cooperation, but also economic planning, political engineering and popular movements for change.

Undoing the effects of war

Peace agreements, particularly those that failed, illustrate the fears and concerns that parties have when they try to end one war in which they are not the victors. A peace accord, of course, will have implications for future relations. In order to avoid the phenomenon of a repetition of war, the war effects have to be undone. Studies suggest that the length of a situation without war is related to a reduction in the likelihood of new internal war (Collier and Hoeffler 2000; Vasquez 2000). This means that peace processes need support in the early phase of implementation to have a chance of success. This might be a way to break historical cycles of violence. We have illustrated such cycles with the Franco-German relations. There are also the more recent experiences of repetitions of war, for instance, Iran–Iraq, Israeli–Arab relations and India–Pakistan. Cycles have also been reported from internal wars, such as between Hutus and Tutsis in Central Africa, or Serbs and Albanians in the Balkans or around the Taliban in Afghanistan.

There are ways in which such cycles can be broken. The return of refugees is an important and concrete aspect. Forceful evictions are not easily forgotten. People in refugee camps are in conditions that daily remind them of their history. Most peace agreements allow for the return of refugees, but in some cases, ethnic cleansing has been the objective of one or several parties. It is possible that the question of the return of refugees is particularly difficult in state formation conflicts. The advance in approaches to war crimes is another important achievement. It serves to make a distinction between those more responsible than others, and thus can reduce stereotyping between the parties. A more difficult, but urgent field of inquiry concerns reconciliation and peacebuilding. Different approaches have been developed, notably government-sanctioned truth commissions (Brounéus 2003; Heyner 2000). Lately, also, the issues of ex-combatants have caught attention and matters of disarmament, demobilization and reintegration (DDR) have come into focus (see Gleichmann et al. 2004; Humphreys and Weinstein 2005; A. Nilsson 2008). Military and police need to be reformed, whether countries are coming out of conflicts or authoritarian conditions, giving rise to programmes on security sector (or system) reform (SSR).

These are measures which, in conjunction with new economic opportunities, may turn countries and peoples away from sentiments of violent revenge and towards developing methodologies for peaceful change. Personal calculations of gain may be changed, as may the self-understanding of one's role in society.

Reducing access to arms

The structural change approach will have to address the question of arms sales. Finding a cease-fire remains an integral part of peace agreements. It can be debated whether it should come early or late in the process of negotiations. In some instances, a small number of determined soldiers with limited military equipment can block the progress of peace talks which may be favoured by the majority on each side. Thus, demilitarization is in the interest of both sides. Furthermore, following the agreement, it is unlikely that it will be maintained if new fears are generated by the previously warring parties accumulating armaments. Since the Cold War there has been a focus on small arms. They are the chief weaponry used in many contemporary wars. Demilitarization thus has been a necessary element to reduce fears after the peace.

This leads to broader implications. It suggests that easy access to armaments may facilitate the initiation of armed conflict. Also in interstate relations, actors tend to be highly concerned about the armaments of other capable actors. It is part of the *Realpolitik* thinking and the interstate security dilemma: armament imbalances, even created for defensive reasons, may inject fear on the other side of a contentious border, thus initiating a series of actions that may result in war. This is particularly true, of course, for nuclear weapons. Thus, the full range of disarmament, arms control and transarmament measures are part of the agenda for structural changes.

There are various measures in place to reduce access to armaments. The Land Mines Convention of 1997 was an important achievement to curtail production of one such weapon with particular effects for civilians. In many conflicts, light arms have been readily available and put to use. This remains an urgent issue. An important concern is how to strengthen arms embargoes (Fruchart et al. 2007).

For the major power relations there are implemented measures, for instance, on conventional weapons in Europe and on confidence-building measures. The Anti-Ballistic Missiles (ABM) Treaty of 1972 aimed at preventing an arms race in the field of anti-ballistic defence between the USA and the Soviet Union. It served to reduce fears in East–West relations. The idea of creating a system of missile defence, as implemented by the United States in the early 2000s, had unsettling effects and the programme has now been scaled back. This applies particularly to the relations between the USA and Russia, and to some extent also China. The treaty on the reduction of strategic nuclear weapons signed in Prague 2010 is also an important measure for tension reduction.

Another important measure of general conflict prevention is the Non-Proliferation Treaty of 1968. The treaty created an international instrument against the proliferation of nuclear weapons. Thus, sinister prognoses made at the time did not materialize. The treaty has a basic flaw in the distinction made between states that have and those that do not have nuclear weapons. Some of the known or new nuclear weapons states are countries that have not signed the treaty (Israel, India, Pakistan). Some states may attempt to develop nuclear capacities clandestinely, threaten to or formally opt out of the treaty (Libya and Iraq prior to 2003, Iran, North Korea). Nevertheless, the Non-Proliferation Treaty has managed to check developments that definitely would have made the planet more unsafe. Similarly, the comprehensive nuclear weapons test ban aims at preventing the development of new nuclear weapons. These are examples of structural prevention. They reduce the risks of escalation and decrease the likelihood of disputes occurring as a result of miscalculation.

Tackling the territorial issues

We have also seen that territorial issues remain pertinent, both for interstate conflicts and state formation conflicts. Grievances over the borders themselves or problems experienced by groups divided by borders are causes of conflict. At the same time, the strict rules in the UN Charter, the AU (OAU) and the OSCE may have acted to prevent parties from raising demands for border changes. There is a normative framework against territorial change by violent means. It is remarkable, for instance, that the demands for border revisions in Europe have been few after 1945 compared to the situation before 1939. The record of forced changes is also limited. Thus, as a preventive measure, the norms enshrined in these international institutions may have been successful. Even in the dissolution of states in the early 1990s, there was an attempt to follow previously drawn lines, albeit internal ones, to reduce the pain of border revisions. There remain in the world a great number of dormant border disputes that very well could have surfaced without these norms and their support by the overwhelming majority of the members of the global system.

Nevertheless, there are cases where territory is an element of conflict. The puzzle for a structural approach is to find ways in which present borders can be maintained, but be made less 'hard' so as to remedy popular grievances. The security of some identity groups rests on the possibility of having access across borders (Albanians, Armenians, Kurds, Serbs, Somalis, for instance). However, softer borders can create new problems. It may result in unwanted movements across the same borders (drug trade, prostitution, human trafficking, organized crime).

A preventive approach may require a regional framework where common interests, such as sharing of water, may serve as an impetus for softening the impact of borders. Using geographical features, cooperative ventures can be found to ameliorate grievances of the local population and worries of governments. In a regional framework, it may even be possible to give one country a say in what occurs on the other side of the border.

This can be a guarantee for minorities, but also for the governments as relations become more transparent. Such arrangements may be attractive for Central Africa, Kurdish-populated areas in the Middle East and Albanian-populated areas in Southeast Europe. If this is coupled with a government renouncing territorial demands, a reasonable trade-off is made. Some peace accords have such arrangements. For instance, the Belfast agreement includes a deal between Great Britain, Northern Ireland and the Republic of Ireland, thus cutting across the borders.

Developing democratic institutions

Democracy has emerged as a factor of significance for all conflicts in the conflict trichotomy. Democratic states rarely fight wars with other democracies, democratic institutions have been used as ways of solving civil wars, and state formation conflicts often have had an origin in the lack of access to authority. Thus, a structural approach would include the support of emerging and fragile democratic institutions. It is closely tied to the promotion of human rights, but is not necessarily the same. There are more countries that have signed the convention on human rights than are democratic. From a conflict prevention perspective, the essence is not a strict electoral process, issues of representation or other constitutional matters. Rather, the key is in institutions that are unbiased and offer the opportunity of having a decision corrected. This is what we have defined as the rule of law. The legal institutions, of course, reflect political decisions, as law is a political matter, but such institutions have a longer duration than political leadership. Laws are maintained even if governments change. The independence of the juridical and administrative institutions is important for predictability and transparency. To be durable, laws have to reflect a degree of consensus in society, meaning that broader governments are preferable when institutions for conflict resolution are created. This is the reason why constitutional changes require wider support than ordinary political decisions.

Democracy, however, is more than institutions. It is a form of governance building on shared values. The viable democracy is one which has the ability to use the conflict resolution forms introduced in Chapter 3 and applied, for instance, in internal conflicts in Chapter 6. It requires that the public at large, as well as various special interest groups, be in agreement on the rules of the society. It builds on an attitude where the democratic machinery is important in itself and worth the protection of the population. This requires a vibrant civil society, the development of which is also part of a structural approach.

It appears that the single most effective way in which democracy can lose its legitimacy is from corruption. The internal security dilemma may stimulate kleptocracy, particularly under authoritarian regimes. Democracy would remove some of these dynamics. However, in any social system whose leadership is mostly concerned with its own enrichment, state institutions are affected. Even a democracy may turn into a kleptocracy that generates new conflict. The inaction of the population to defend the democratic institutions in Pakistan in October 1999 shows the result. The civil society was not willing to challenge the military coup at that time, but in 2007–08 helped to undermine the regime. The first years of the new democracy, however, have not been reassuring on this score. Similarly, ten years earlier Indonesia's road to democracy showed the same rocky start, with a dormant and repressed civil society, but its ability to withstand greed appears stronger. This points to some of the strains the new democracies of Tunisia and Egypt faced in 2011.

The international community may be able to affect this, by making clear that its dealings are expected to be free of corruption. This can be enforced by rules in home countries of transnational corporations and donor agencies.

The promotion of democracy, however, is more delicate. There has to be an ethically and politically viable trade-off between support of democratic institutions and the actual desires of a given population to have them. There is likely to be, in most societies, groups that embrace concepts of human rights, democracy and the peaceful settlement of disputes. There are others who will view such matters from an opportunistic perspective, and still others who regard them as threatening. Normally, democratic institutions have to build on local conditions. The experiences of democracy-building in Japan and Germany following the Second World War are not typical, even though the strong international presence in Bosnia-Herzegovina and Kosovo may have a corresponding impact. Timor-Leste (East Timor) and Liberia seem now to be on paths towards democracy. The future of Iraq remains difficult to predict. It is important that democracy is connected to local beliefs, concerns and issues. Otherwise, it may later come to be regarded as something introduced by international institutions or external forces for reasons other than the genuine concern of the local society.

Finding new state structures

The state is central in our deliberations, and it is likely to remain so. We find the state at the same time to be an actor in conflict and a disputed resource. It gives rise to hope for protection for some and fear of repression for others. This is particularly pronounced in countries with many identity groups. Thus, there is a need to consider alternatives in state-making.

A federal solution may effectively deal with state formation issues within a democratic framework. Many of the large federal states that exist today – the United States, the Federal Republic of Germany and the Russian Federation – were only partly designed to handle such conflicts.[1] Switzerland remains the classical example, but it grew as a federation from below. The different cantons got together to form the state. As we have seen, India made a conscious effort to redraw its internal borders in the 1950s. The record from these five cases is not entirely convincing. The US Civil War of the 1860s is the most devastating war in the country's history. The Russian Federation is young and has faced severe problems, not least with two consecutive wars in Chechnya and an increasingly more dominant centre. India is the more interesting example. Although it has faced several internal state formation conflicts, they are not directly related to the federal structure created in the 1950s. The reforms sought to meet the fears of a bid for secession by the Tamil population in the South and that has not happened. The conflict in Punjab was severe, however, and was not handled in a similarly peaceful way. Switzerland went through a process of dividing one of the cantons in order to alleviate fears of one part of the population.

Federation has been applied in some peace agreements, as we have seen in Chapter 7. Bosnia-Herzegovina is a federal state. The solution to the future status of Kosovo may result in a federal constitution, either within present-day Yugoslavia or with neighbouring Albania and, perhaps, Macedonia and Montenegro. Functioning federal constructions may serve as preventive strategies. Countries which today have considerable potential of state formation conflict may find it appropriate to consider such forms, before disputes become armed conflicts. Some states have embarked on such strategies, for instance, Nigeria and Ethiopia. In these cases, the centre still maintains strict control, in spite of the constitutional setup. States which would benefit from federal ideas are Indonesia and China.

It is possible that the very limited state concept that has been applied throughout the twentieth century needs reconsideration. It has assumed a fairly centralized political unit, which carries out uniform policy within the territory to which it has legal access. Thus, all parts of the state are treated in an equal way. However, we have noted that many states do have interesting constitutional variations: Puerto Rico in the United States, the Channel Islands in the United Kingdom, the Åland Islands in Finland, Zanzibar in Tanzania. Spain has different layers of self-rule for its mainland regions. There is a clash between the uniformity required by existing state structures and the diversity of the populations of these states. Inside the same state, conditions are likely to vary economically, culturally and politically. Thus, there is a need to produce models for alternative state structures. A case in point is finding a solution to the Palestinian conflict. It may require out-of-the-box thinking (Mossberg 2010). Such alternatives will have to find ways of forming governance, protection and welfare for the inhabitants against criminality and other unwanted interference, while meeting the needs for diversity and ease of international connection. These demands are high but not unreasonable. A state has to earn the allegiance of its inhabitants and, thus, it has to be able to respond to such demands.

Assessing the role of power

There is a challenge to the arguments of democracy as a long-term preventive strategy. It has been noted that democratization means that more conflicts will emerge than would otherwise have been the case. It means a weakening of the centre and, thus, opens a number of otherwise dormant conflicts. The transition from authoritarian rule to democracy is troublesome. For many, keeping order becomes preferable, popular and good for the economy. The argument is found also on the international scene. Strong powers maintain order in 'their' regions and perhaps also globally. Might induces fright. This prevents a number of concerns from being articulated, and thus fewer conflicts will arise. There is a parallel argument in favour of the balance of power and deterrence for interstate relations and for intra-state affairs. The democratization of China might make this state as conflict-prone as India or Russia. The fall of the military regime in Indonesia gave publicity to conflicts that had not been heard from in a long time.

A closer analysis reveals, however, that many repressive regimes fall because, in the end, their repression reduces the legitimacy of the regime. In Indonesia, there was considerable resistance, which was met with repression and atrocities during the years of the Suharto regime. Little may have reached mainstream media at the time, but much was still known in society. After the fall of Suharto, there was more conflict behaviour, but there were not necessarily more grievances. In other words, repressive regimes are not able to accommodate the demands from the population and that leads, in the longer run, to their demise. In effect, repression may contribute to escalating conflicts that might otherwise have been dealt with when they were still disputes.

Is the same true on the international level? Did deterrence work as a preventive strategy? NATO was seen as the West's protection against Soviet aggression. There was no such aggression. Does it mean that NATO prevented it from happening? To prove the efficiency of deterrence is as difficult as understanding the effectiveness of prevention and structural change. It requires that we really know what the intentions were, and even if they can be documented with plans, we still do not know how close the decision-makers were in making the decision that was, in the end, not made. In the Cold War, both sides claimed that they were deterring the other from launching an attack. Only by being able to credibly threaten the other with devastating nuclear strikes could the other be made reasonable. Tensions were high. The way out was through negotiations and the reaching of common understandings. The elimination of an entire class of weaponry solidified the confidence that was finally being created through direct contacts between the two sides. In other words, deterrence created its own problems and it took considerable energy and imagination to overcome its effects. Overwhelming power created fear and did not lead to less conflict. We may note that the Cold War consisted of many armed conflicts but they were far away from the central arena of contention. There might have been an effect of displacement of conflict in order to avoid escalation (Singer 1991).

In a more asymmetric power relationship, we cannot exclude the possibility that overwhelming force actually has an impact on the agenda setting of groups demanding a change. There may be fewer such demands, but it may also stimulate a search for alternative violent strategies. Weighty power may be met by actions aimed at the weakness of the powerful. This is often its unprotected bases or civilian population. This has turned into terrorist strategies against the USA since the end of the Cold War. It might be the way some governments plan to meet the conventional strength of the United States (Brackan 1999). Thus, the contribution of terrifying power to structural conflict prevention is debatable, whether it comes from the centre or from the periphery.

10.5 Between the International Community and *Pax Americana*

The peace agreements since 1989 illustrate that there is a profound new world order. It was not constructed deliberately after a major war, as has often been the case throughout history (Holsti 1991; Kegley and Raymond 1999). Instead it has grown out of the unprecedented ending of a major power confrontation, the Cold War. There are some documents that herald the new order, such as the Paris Treaty of 1990, but on the whole it is an order that has developed in a piecemeal and pragmatic way. The peace agreements are one indication of this, the efforts at direct conflict prevention another and ambitions at structural change for conflict prevention a third.

The new order still has no name. It is an international community, with its particular human concerns. It also has elements of *Pax Americana*. The dominant actor is the United States. It has the veto power on multilateral action for international peace and security. What it does not want to participate in, others will be reluctant to undertake. The blessing, tacit support or active involvement of the United States has been common to most of the peace agreements and conflict prevention actions that are recorded.

However, it is also apparent that the United States is not the only power or even the 'omni-power' that can direct all other actors in the global system. International action is modified by other states, be they the permanent members of the Security Council, members of the EU or important regional actors. An increasingly powerful China will have a greater say. Even local actors with limited resources can have an impact on US policy. But clearly no outside actor can force an international agenda on the United States. The agenda is increasingly formulated by this one state and groups that are able to muster its support for particular actions. Non-governmental organizations take on a significance that they have not had before. They can bring international concern into the political debate in the United States, and thus contribute to agenda setting. They are not alone in this. Transnational actors, such as major corporations, also realize the significance of having an impact on the US political scene. Campaign contributions are but one way. Other governments also influence the political scene, but their ways of directly impacting are restricted by laws and tradition. Clearly, developing friendships and connections in Washington, DC, is becoming increasingly important for actors in the global system.

Some issues brought up in this post-Cold War order are novel. The international community has enlarged the agenda. Humanitarian concern, human rights and conflict resolution have a stronger position. This means that engagement in international conflicts is stimulated also by a willingness – even a responsibility – to support victims in conflict before there has been a war (as the human rights concern can do), during a war (the humanitarian concern) or for a just settlement (conflict resolution concerns). These may also seem more important than strategic considerations. Strategic challenges are increasingly rare as the world order rests on a *status quo* that is firmly entrenched from the point of view of the leading actors. The nuclear superiority is one element in this. In practice, conventional forces are more important in upholding peace. Still, strategic considerations will come into play and be part of policies for conflict resolution.

Since the end of the Cold War, US forces have been active in areas previously outside its parameters of action. The interventions in the Balkans have given the USA semi-permanent ground stations in new areas. The 1990–91 Gulf War, the Iraq War, the war in Afghanistan and the confrontations with Iran have led to a major long-term deployment in the Gulf region. Engagements in Africa take the form of supporting African peacekeeping operations. Even in Indochina, US military personnel are again involved. During the East Timor crisis, US warships were stationed off the island. It is present in the Indian Ocean and the Persian Gulf. The US reach has therefore become global and has been challenged only by a few determined actors with limited physical capacity. Attacks on US military installations in Saudi Arabia and Yemen and on embassies in Dar-es-Salaam and Nairobi all testify to the difficulties of protecting diplomatic outposts. But such actions have changed nothing of substance. Similarly, bringing the battlefield to the USA itself, as was done on September 11, 2001, resulted in new American interventionism, not a retrenchment. US reach is not easily undermined. Although China and Russia remain powerful in their particular regions, they are unlikely to seriously challenge the present US military position. The new world order could be one of more dialogue among leading actors, where the EU would also be important. But there are no indications that the United States is likely to lose its pre-eminence in the foreseeable future. The most obvious threat to the USA is that global engagement will result in its own economic and military overstretch.

Predictions are notoriously difficult, but the trends since the end of the Cold War point in unexpected directions. There have been more conflicts in Europe than anticipated and also new forms of involvement by the North in the South. Global terrorism was not predicted. Although this book is based on an analysis of more than 100 conflicts in the past decades, it cannot suggest what conflicts will dominate the concerns a decade from now. Surprises are part of the picture.

The range of actions for humanitarian and strategic causes has become different and wider. There has been an unprecedented resort to economic sanctions, and this instrument is in a phase of rapid refinement. There are new forms of military actions, ranging from drones to clandestine counter-terrorism. There has, however, been a resort to diplomacy, not only coercion or force, particularly in issues not relating to terrorism.

The peace agreements that have provided material for this book give insights into strategies for solving conflicts and preventing violence tomorrow and in the future. Some simple concepts, such as those introduced here, may be helpful in making important distinctions. They are meant to guide analysis and suggest policy. They will need continuous processing. Their use in the real world will provide feedback. The conditions of the new world will affect their uses and consequences. No analysis of the chances for peace is made without an interaction between analysis and reality. In that interaction, both the analysis and the reality may change. This is relevant wherever the world finds itself between an international community of concerned actors and a *Pax Americana* under the firm leadership of one major state. The task is the same: to move the world towards less conflict, less suffering and more human cooperation, democracy and justice. The beauty of the planet deserves just that.

Further Readings

Go to the *Understanding Conflict Resolution* web page at www.sagepub.co.uk for free access to journal articles listed.

Annan, K. A. 1999. 'Two Concepts of Sovereignty', *The Economist*, September 18, pp. 49–50.

Carnegie Commission 1997. *Preventing Deadly Conflict: Final Report*. Carnegie Commission on Preventing Deadly Conflict, Washington, DC.

High Level Panel 2004. *A More Secure World: Our Shared Responsibility*. Report of the Secretary-General's High-level Panel on Threats, Challenges and Change, United Nations.

Lund, M. S. 1996. *Preventing Violent Conflicts. A Strategy for Preventive Diplomacy*. Washington, DC: United States Institute of Peace Press.

Öberg, M., F. Möller and P. Wallensteen 2009. 'Early Conflict Prevention in Ethnic Crises, 1990–98: A New Dataset', *Conflict Management and Peace Science*, 26 (1): 67–91.

Svensson, I. 2009. 'Who Brings Which Peace? Neutral versus Biased Mediation and Institutional Arrangements in Civil Wars', *Journal of Conflict Resolution*, 53 (3): 446–69.

Svensson, I. and Wallensteen, P. 2010. *The Go-Between. Jan Eliasson and the Styles of Mediation*. Washington, DC: US Institute of Peace Press.

Wallensteen, P. 2011. *Peace Research: Theory and Practice*. London: Routledge. pp. 125–42.

Note

1 Other large federations are those of Australia, Brazil and Canada but the statement remains equally valid for them. The status of Quebec in Canada, however, is worth closer scrutiny.

References

Adler, Emanuel and Michael Barnett (eds) 1998. *Security Communities*. Cambridge: Cambridge University Press.

Alao, Abiodun, John Mackinlay and Funmi Olonisakin 1999. *Peacekeepers, Politicians and Warlords: The Liberian Peace Process*. Tokyo: UN University Press.

Al-Khazendar, Sami 2005. 'NATO's Mediterranean Dialogue and Arab States: Themes, Dimensions and Challenges', *Dirasat: Human and Social Sciences*, 32 (3): 637–58.

Amer, Ramses, Johan Saravanamuttu and Peter Wallensteen 1996. *The Cambodian Conflict 1979–1991: From Intervention to Resolution*. Penang and Uppsala: Department of Peace and Conflict Research, Uppsala University.

Arnson, Cynthia J. (ed.) 1999. *Comparative Peace Processes in Latin America*. Washington, DC: Woodrow Wilson Center Press and Stanford, CA: Stanford University Press.

Åsberg, Carl Johan and Peter Wallensteen 1998. 'New Threats and New Security: The post-Cold War Debate Revisited', in Peter Wallensteen (ed.), *Preventing Violent Conflicts: Past Reccord and Future Challenges*. Uppsala: Department of Peace and Conflict Research, Uppsala University pp. 167–202.

Axelrod, Robert 1984. *The Evolution of Cooperation*. New York: Basic Books.

Azar, Edward E. and John W. Burton (eds) 1986. *International Conflict Resolution: Theory and Practice*. Boulder, CO: Lynne Rienner.

Bednar, Jenna 2009. *The Robust Federation: Principles of Design*. Cambridge, MA: Cambridge University Press.

Bell-Fialkoff, Andrew 1996. *Ethnic Cleansing*. New York: St Martin's Press.

Bercovitch, Jacob (ed.) 1996. *Resolving International Conflicts*: The Theory and Practice of Mediation. Boulder, CO: Lynne Rienner.

Bilder, Richard B. 1997. 'Adjudication: International Arbitral Tribunals and Courts', in I. William Zartman and J. Lewis Rasmussen (eds), *Peacemaking in International Conflict: Methods and Techniques*. Washington, DC: United States Institute of Peace Press. pp. 155–89.

Blair, Tony. 2010. *A Journey*. London: Hutchinson.

Blake, Gerald 1999. 'Is the Time Ripe for a Voluntary Register of Boundary Status with the United Nations?', in Julie Dahlitz (ed.), *Peaceful Resolution of Major International Disputes*. New York and Geneva: United Nations. pp. 145–67.

Boutros-Ghali, Boutros 1996. *An Agenda for Democratization*. New York: United Nations.

Bowden, Mark 1999. *Black Hawk Down: A Story of Modern War*. New York: Simon & Schuster.

Bracken, Paul 1999. *Fire in the East*. New York: HarperCollins.

Brecher, Michael 1993. *Crises in World Politics: Theory and Reality*. New York: Pergamon Press.

Broome, Benjamin J. 1997. 'Designing a Collective Approach to Peace: Interactive Design and Problem-solving Workshops with Greek-Cypriot and Turkish-Cypriot Communities in Cyprus', *International Negotiation*, 2: 381–407.

Brounéus, Karen 2003. *Reconciliation: Theory and Practice for Development Cooperation.* A report for the Swedish International Development Cooperation Agency, Stockholm.

Brounéus, Karen, 2008. *Rethinking Reconciliation: Concepts, Methods and an Empirical Study.* Uppsala: Department of Peace and Conflict Research, Uppsala University.

Burton, John W. 1987. *Resolving Deep-rooted Conflict: A Handbook.* Landham, MD: University Press of America.

Burton, John W. 1996. *Conflict Resolution: Its Language and Processes.* Lanham, MD, and London: Scarecrow Press.

Buzan, Barry 1991. *People, States and Fear* (2nd edn). Boulder, CO: Lynne Rienner.

Buzan, Barry and Ole Waever 2003. *Regions and Powers: The Structure of International Society.* Cambridge: Cambridge University Press.

Cahill, Kevin M. (ed.) 1996. *Preventive Diplomacy: Stopping Wars before They Start.* New York: Basic Books.

Cameron, Iain 2005. 'Protecting Legal Rights: On the (In)security of Targeted Sanctions', in Peter Wallensteen and Carina Staibano (eds), *International Sanctions: Between Words and Wars in the Global System.* London: Routledge/Frank Cass. pp. 181–206.

Cañas, Antonio and Héctor Dada 1999. 'Political Transition and Institutionalization in El Salvador', in Cynthia J. Arnson (ed.), *Comparative Peace Processes in Latin America.* Washington, DC: Woodrow Wilson Center Press, and Stanford, CA: Stanford University Press. pp. 69–95.

Carment, David 1993. 'The International Dimensions of Ethnic Conflict: Concepts, Indicators and Theory', *Journal of Peace Research*, 30: 137–50.

Carment, David and Patrick James 1995. 'Internal Constraints and Interstate Ethnic Conflict: Toward a Crisis-based Assessment of Irredentism', *Journal of Conflict Resolution*, 39: 82–109.

Carnegie Commission on Preventing Deadly Conflict 1997. *Preventing Deadly Conflict: Final Report.* Washington, DC: Carnegie Commission on Preventing Deadly Conflict.

Carter, Jimmy 1992. *Keeping Faith: Memoirs of a President.* New York: Bantam Books.

Case, William 2001. 'Malaysia's Resilient Pseudodemocracy', *Journal of Democracy*, 12 (1): 43–57.

Chan, Steven and Moisés Venancio, with Chris Alden and Sam Barnes 1998. *War and Peace in Mozambique.* London: Macmillan.

Cloos, Jim 2005. 'Conflict Prevention as an Instrument in the EU's Security Box', in Anders Mellbourn (ed.), *Development, Security and Conflict Prevention.* Brussels: Madariaga Foundation, The Bank of Sweden Tercentenary Foundation and Gidlunds. pp. 14–23.

Cohen, Saul B. 1999. 'The Geopolitics of an Evolving World System: From Conflict to Accomodation', in Paul F. Diehl (ed.), *A Road Map to War: Territorial Dimensions of International Conflict.* Nashville, TN, and London: Vandesbilt University Press. pp. 271–98.

Collier, Paul and Anke Hoeffler 2000. *Greed and Grievance in Civil War.* Washington, DC: World Bank. Mimeo.

Corell, Hans 1999. 'The Feasibility of Implementing The Hague/St. Petersburg Centennial Recommendations under the UN System', in Julie Dahlitz (ed.), *Peaceful Resolution of Major International Disputes.* New York and Geneva: United Nations. pp. 31–48.

Cornell, Svante E. 2002. *Autonomy and Conflict: Ethnoterritoriality and Separatism in the South Caucasus – Cases in Georgia.* Uppsala: Department of Peace and Conflict Research, Uppsala University.

Cortright, David and George Lopez 2000. *The Sanctions Decade: Assessing UN Strategies in the 1990s.* International Peace Academy, Boulder, CO: Lynne Rienner.

Coser, Lewis A. 1956. *The Functions of Social Conflict*. New York: Free Press.

Coser, Lewis A. 1967. *Continuities in the Study of Social Conflict*. New York: Free Press.

Dahlitz, Julie (ed.) 1999. *Peaceful Resolution of Major International Disputes*. New York and Geneva: United Nations.

Davies, James C. (ed.) 1971. *When Men Rebel and Why*. New York: Free Press.

Deeb, Mary Jane and Marius Deeb 1995. 'Internal Negotiations in a Centralist Conflict: Lebanon', in I. William Zartman (ed.), *Elusive Peace: Negotiating an End to Civil Wars*. Washington, DC: Brookings Institution. pp. 125–46.

Desch, Michael C. 1999. *Civilian Control of the Military: The Changing Security Environment*. Baltimore, MD, and London: Johns Hopkins University Press.

Deutsch, Karl W. et al. 1957. *Political Community and the North Atlantic Area*. Princeton, NJ: Princeton University Press.

Diehl, Paul 1983. 'Arms Races and Escalation: A Closer Look', *Journal of Peace Research*, 20 (3): 205–12.

Diehl, Paul F. 1993. *International Peacekeeping*. Baltimore, MD, and London: Johns Hopkins University Press.

Diehl, Paul F. (ed.) 1999. *A Road Map to War: Territorial Dimensions of International Conflict*. Nashville, TN, and London: Vanderbilt University Press.

Dollard, J., L. W. Doob, N. E. Miller, O. H. Mowrer and R. R. Sears 1939. *Frustration and Aggression*. New Haven, CT: Yale University Press.

Doob, Leonard W. (ed.) 1970. *Resolving Conflict in Africa: The Fermeda Workshop*. New Haven, CT: Yale University Press.

Doxey, Margaret P. 1996. *International Sanctions in Contemporary Perspective* (2nd edn). London: Macmillan, and New York: St Martin's Press.

Duchacek, Ivo D. 1977. 'Antagonistic Cooperation: Territorial and Ethnic Communities', *Publius*, 7: 145–60.

Duffield, Mark 1998. 'Post-modern Conflict: Warlords, Post-adjustment States and Private Protection', *Civil Wars*, 1: 65–102.

Eck, Kristine 2005. *A Beginner's Guide to Conflict Data: Finding and Using the Right Dataset*. UCDP Papers No. 1, Uppsala: Uppsala Conflict Data Program, www.ucdp. uu.se.

Einaudi, Luigi R. 1999. 'The Ecuador–Peru Peace Process', in Chester A. Crocker, Fen Osler Hampson and Pamela Aall (eds), *Herding Cats: Multiparty Mediation in a Complex World*. Washington, DC: United States Institute of Peace Press. pp. 407–29.

Ekstrand, Eric Einar 1944. *Jorden runt på trettio år* (*Around the World in Thirty Years*). Stockholm: Norstedts.

Eriksson, Mikael 2010. *Supporting Democracy in Africa: African Union's Use of Targeted Sanctions to Deal with Unconstitutional Changes of Government*. Stockholm: FOI (Swedish Defence Research Agency).

Esty, Daniel C., Jack Goldstone, Ted R. Gurr, Barbara Harff, Pamela T. Surko, Alan N. Unger and Robert Chen 1998. 'The State Failure Project: Early Warning Research for US Foreign Policy Planning', paper presented at the conference on Failed States and International Security: Causes, Prospects and Consequences, Purdue University, West Lafayette, IN, 25–27 February.

Etzioni, Amitai 1967. 'The Kennedy Experiment', *Western Political Quarterly*, 20: 361–80.

Fisher, Roger and William Ury 1981. *Getting to Yes*. Boston, MA: Houghton Mifflin.

Fisher, Ronald J. 1983. 'Third Party Consultation as a Method of Intergroup Conflict Resolution: A Review of Studies', *Journal of Conflict Resolution*, 27 (2): 301–34.

Fisher, Ronald J. 1997. *Interactive Conflict Resolution*. Syracuse, NY: Syracuse University Press.

Fox, Mary-Jane 1999. 'Somalia Divided: The African Cerberus (Considerations of Political Culture)', *Civil War*, 2: 1–34.

Fox, Mary-Jane 2000. *Political Culture in Somalia: Tracing Paths to Peace and Conflict*. Uppsala: Department of Peace and Conflict Research, Uppsala University.

Fruchart, Damien, Paul Holtom, Siemon T. Wezeman, Daniel Strandow and Peter Wallensteen 2007. *United Nations Arms Embargoes: Their Impact on Arms Flows and Target Behaviour*. Uppsala: Stockholm International Peace Research Institute (SIPRI) and Special Program on the Implementation of Targeted Sanctions (SPITS) Department of Peace and Conflict Research, Uppsala University. 58 pp.

Fry, Douglas P. and Kaj Björkqvist 1997. *Cultural Variation in Conflict Resolution: Alternatives to Violence*. Mahwah, NJ: Lawrence Erlbaum.

Galtung, Johan 1965. 'Institutionalized Conflict Resolution', *Journal of Peace Research*, 2 (4): 348–97.

Galtung, Johan 1969. 'Conflict as a Way of Life', in J. Galtung, *Essays in Peace Research* (Vol. 3). Copenhagen: Ejler. pp. 484–507.

Galtung, Johan 1996. *Peace by Peaceful Means: Peace and Conflict, Development and Civilization*. London: Sage.

Gantzel, Klaus Jürgen and Jörg Meyer-Stamer (eds) 1986. *Die Kriege nach dem Zweiten Weltkrieg bis 1984: Daten und Analysen* (*The Wars since the Second World War to 1984: Data and Analysis*). Munich: Weltforum Verlag.

Gantzel, Klaus Jürgen and Torsten Schwinghammer 2000. *Warfare since the Second World War*. New Brunswick, NJ, and London: Transaction Publishers.

Geller, Daniel S. and J. David Singer 1998. *Nations at War*. Cambridge: Cambridge University Press.

Gibler, Douglas M. 1999a. 'An Extension of the Correlates of War: Formal Alliance Date Set, 1648–1815', *International Interactions*, 25: 1–28.

Gibler, Douglas M. 1999b. 'Alliances That Never Balance: The Territorial-Settlement Treaty', in Paul F. Diehl (ed.), *A Road Map to War: Territorial Dimensions of International Conflict*. Nashville, TN, and London: Vandesbilt University Press. pp. 181–204.

Gilpin, Robert 2001. *Global Political Economy*. Princeton, NJ: Princeton University Press.

Glaser, Charles L. 1997. 'Why NATO is Still Best: Future Security Arrangements for Europe', in Paul F. Diehl (ed.), *The Politics of Global Governance: International Organizations in an Interdependent World*. Boulder, CO: Lynne Rienner. pp. 121–58.

Gleichmann, Colin, Michael Odenwald, Kees Steenken and Adrian Wilkinson 2004. *Disarmament, Demobilisation and Reintegration*. Stockholm: Swedish National Defence College.

Goldstein, Erik 1992. *Wars and Peace Treaties*. London: Routledge.

Greig, Michael J. and Patrick M. Regan 2008. 'When Do They Say Yes? An Analysis of the Willingness to Offer and Accept Mediation in Civil Wars', *International Studies Quarterly*, 52: 759–81.

Gurr, Ted R. 1970. *Why Men Rebel*. Princeton, NJ: Princeton University Press.

Gurr, Ted R. 1993. *Minorities at Risk*. Washington, DC: United States Institute of Peace Press.

Gurr, Ted R. 2000a. *Peoples Versus States: Minorities at Risk in the New Century*. Washington, DC: United States Institute of Peace Press.

Gurr, Ted. R. 2000b. 'Ethnic Warfare on the Wane', *Foreign Affairs*, 79 (3): 52–64.

Hampson, Fen Osler 1996. *Nurturing Peace: Why Peace Settlements Succeed or Fail.* Washington, DC: United States Institute of Peace Press.

Harbom, Lotta and Peter Wallensteen, 2005. 'Armed Conflict and Its International Dimensions, 1946–2004', *Journal of Peace Research*, 42 (5): 623–35.

Harbom, Lotta and Peter Wallensteen 2010. 'Armed Conflicts, 1946–2009', *Journal of Peace Research,* 47 (4): 501–09.

Hauge, Wenche and Tanja Ellingsen 1998. 'Beyond Environmental Scarcity: Causal Pathways to Conflict', *Journal of Peace Research*, 35 (3): 299–317.

Heldt, Birger 1996. *Public Dissatisfaction and the Conflict Behavior of States: A Theory Reconstruction with an Empirical Application.* Uppsala: Department of Peace and Conflict Research, Uppsala University.

Heldt, Birger and Peter Wallensteen 2006. *Peacekeeping Operations: Global Patterns of Intervention and Success, 1948–2004* (2nd edn). Stockholm: Folke Bernadotte Academy.

Henderson, John and Greg Watson (eds) 2005. *Securing a Peaceful Pacific.* Christchurch, New Zealand: Canterbury University Press.

Herz, John H. 1950. 'Idealist Internationalism and the Security Dilemma', *World Politics*, 2: 157–80.

Heyner, Priscilla B. 2000. 'Past Truths, Present Dangers: The Role of Official Truth Seeking in Conflict Resolution and Prevention', in Paul C. Stern and Daniel Druckman (eds), *International Conflict Resolution after the Cold War.* Washington, DC: National Academy Press. pp. 338–82.

High-Level Panel 2004. *A More Secure World: Our Shared Responsibility.* Report of the Secretary-General's High-level Panel on Threats, Challenges and Change. New York and Geneva: United Nations.

Högbladh, Stina 2006. 'Finding a Peace that Will Last – Examining Peace Processes and Peace Agreements', paper presented at the Annual ISA Convention, San Diego, CA, March.

Höglund, Kristine, 2008. *Peace Negotiations in the Shadow of Violence.* Leiden: Martinus Nijhoff.

Höglund, Kristine and Magnus Öberg (eds) 2011. *Understanding Peace Research.* London: Routledge.

Holbrooke, Richard 1999. *To End a War.* New York: The Modern Library.

Holsti, Kalevi J. 1991. *Peace and War: Armed Conflict and International Order 1648–1989.* Cambridge: Cambridge University Press.

Human Security Report 2005: War and Peace in the 21st Century. New York: Human Security Centre, University of British Columbia Press and Oxford University Press.

Humphreys, Macartan and Jeremy Weinstein 2005. 'Disentangling the Determinants of Successful Demobilization and Reintegration', paper presented at the 101st Meeting of the American Political Science Association, Washington, DC, August 31 – September 3, 2005.

Huntington, Samuel P. 1996. *The Clash of Civilizations and the Remaking of World Order.* New York: Simon & Schuster.

Huntley, James Robert 1998. *Pax Democratica: A Strategy for the 21st Century.* New York: St Martin's Press.

Independent Inquiry into the Actions of the United Nations during the 1994 Genocide in Rwanda, chaired by Ingvar Carlsson, United Nations, December 1999.

International Center for Transitional Justice 2005. *Annual Report 2003–04.* Available at: www.ictj.org.

Jarstad, Anna 2001. *Changing the Game: Consociational Theory and Ethnic Quotas in Cyprus and New Zealand*. Uppsala: Department of Peace and Conflict Research, Uppsala University.

Johansson, Emma, Joakim Kreutz, Peter Wallensteen, Christian Altpeter, Sara Lindberg, Mathilda Lindgren and Ausra Padskocimaite 2010. *A New Start for EU Peacemaking? Past Record and Future Potential*. Uppsala Conflict Data Program, Report No. 7. Uppsala University.

Johnson, James Turner 1999. *Morality and Contemporary Warfare*. New Haven, CT: Yale University Press.

Jung, Dietrich, Klaus Schlichte and Jens Siegelberg 1996. 'Ongoing Wars and Their Explanation', in Luc van de Goor, Kumar Rupesinghe and Paul Sciarone (eds), *Between Development and Destruction: An Enquiry into the Causes of Conflict in Post-colonial States*. London: Macmillan, and New York: St Martin's Press. pp. 50–63.

Kacowicz, Arie M. 1994. *Peaceful Territorial Change*. Columbia, SC: University of South Carolina Press.

Kaufmann, Chaim D. 1996. 'Possible and Impossible Solutions to Ethnic Civil Wars', *International Security*, 20 (4): 136–75.

Kaufman, Stuart 1996. 'An "International" Theory of Ethnic War', *Review of International Studies*, 22: 149–71.

Kegley, Jr., Charles W. and Gregory A. Raymond 1999. *How Nations Make Peace*. New York: St Martin's Press and Worth.

Kelman, Herbert C. 2008. 'Evaluating the Contributions of Interactive Problem Solving to the Resolution of Ethnonational Conflicts', *Peace and Conflict*, 14: 29–60.

Kelman, Herman C. and S. P. Cohen 1976. 'The Problem-solving Workshop: A Socialpsychological Contribution to the Resolution of International Conflicts', *Journal of Peace Research*, 13 (2): 79–90.

Kemp, Walter (ed.) 2001. *Quiet Diplomacy in Action: The OSCE High Commissioner on National Minorities*. The Hague: Kluwer.

Khan, Shaharyar M. 2000. *The Shallow Graves of Rwanda*. London: IB Tauris.

Kinzer, Stephen 1999. 'Kurds Sense a Shift Toward Peace after 15-Year War', *The New York Times*, 27 November.

Kolodziej, Ed 1998. 'The Regionalization of International Security', in Roger E. Kanet (ed.), *Resolving Regional Conflicts*. Urbana, IL: University of Illinois Press. pp. 11–42.

Kotkin, Joel 1992. *Tribes: How Race, Religion and Identity Determine Success in the New Global Economy*. New York: Random House.

Kotliar, Vladimir S. 1999. 'The Elements of a "Model Negotiation" for the Settlement of Major Border Disputes between States', in Julie Dahlitz (ed.), *Peaceful Resolution of Major International Disputes*. New York and Geneva: United Nations. pp. 127–40.

Kreutz, Joakim 2010. 'How and When Armed Conflicts End: Introducing the UCDP Conflict Termination Dataset', *Journal of Peace Research*, 47 (2): 243–50.

Kriesberg, Louis 1992a. *International Conflict Resolution*. New Haven, CT: Yale University Press.

Kriesberg, Louis 1992b. *De-Escalation and Transformation of International Conflict*. New Haven, CT: Yale University Press.

Kriesberg, Louis 1997. 'The Development of the Conflict Resolution Field', in I. William Zartman and J. lewis Rasmussen (eds), *Peacemaking in International Conflict: Methods and Techniques*. Washington, DC: United States Institute of Peace Press. pp. 51–77.

Lacina, Bethany and Nils Petter Gleditsch 2005. 'Monitoring Trends in Global Combat: A New Dataset of Battle Deaths', *European Journal of Population,* 21 (2–3): 145–66.

Lacina, Bethany, Nils Petter Gleditsch and Bruce Russett 2006. 'The Declining Risk of Death in Battle', *International Studies Quarterly,* 50 (3): 673–80.

Lederach, John Paul 1997. *Building Peace: Sustainable Reconciliation in Divided Societies.* Washington, DC: United States Institute of Peace Press.

Levy, Jack 1983. *War in the Modern Great Power System, 1495–1975.* Lexington, KY: University of Kentucky Press.

Licklider, Roy 1995. 'The Consequences of Negotiated Settlements in Civil Wars, 1945–93', *American Political Science Review*, 89 (3): 681–90.

Lijphart, Arend 1975. *The Politics of Accommodation: Pluralism and Democracy in the Netherlands* (2nd edn). Berkeley, CA: University of California Press.

Lijphart, Arend 1984. *Democracies.* New Haven, CT: Yale University Press.

Luard, Evan 1986. *War in the International Society.* London: IB Tauris.

Lund, Michael S. 1996. *Preventing Violent Conflicts: A Strategy for Preventive Diplomacy.* Washington, DC: United States Institute of Peace Press.

Lyons, Terrence and Ahmed I. Samatar (eds) 1995. *Somalia: State Collapse, Multilateral Intervention and Strategies for Political Reconstruction.* Washington, DC: Brookings Institution.

Magnusson, Kjell 1999. *Rambouilletavtalet (The Rambouillet Treaty).* Uppsala: Centre for Multiethnic Research.

Maksymenko, Serhiy 2005. 'European Neighbourhood Policy and Post-Orange Revolution Ukraine', in Anders Mellbourn (ed.), *Development, Security and Conflict Prevention.* Brussels: Madariaga Foundation, The Bank of Sweden Tercentenary Foundation and Gidlunds.

Malone, David and Fen Osler Hampson (eds) 2001. *From Reaction to Conflict Prevention: Opportunities for the UN System.* New York: The International Peace Academy.

Marshall, Monty G. 1999. *Third World War: System, Process and Conflict Dynamics.* Boulder, CO: Rowman & Littlefield.

Marshall, Monty G. and Ted R. Gurr 2005. *Peace and Conflict 2005: A Global Survey of Armed Conflicts, Self-Determination Movements, and Democracy.* College Park, MD: University of Maryland, Center for International Development and Conflict Management.

Mason, T. David and Patrick J. Fett 1996. 'How Civil Wars End: A Rational Choice Approach', *Journal of Conflict Resolution*, 40: 546–68.

Melander, Erik 1999. *Anarchy Within: The Security Dilemma between Ethnic Groups in Emerging Anarchy.* Uppsala: Department of Peace and Conflict Research, Uppsala University.

Merrills, J. G. 1999. 'International Boundary Disputes in Theory and Practice: Precedents Established', in Julie Dahlitz (ed.), *Peaceful Resolution of Major International Disputes.* New York and Geneva: United Nations. pp. 95–112.

Migdal, Joel S. 1988. *Strong Societies and Weak States: State–Society Relations and State Capabilities in the Third World.* Princeton, NJ: Princeton University Press.

Mitchell, Christopher R. 1981. *The Structure of International Conflict.* New York: St Martin's Press.

Mitchell, Christopher and Michael Banks 1996. *Handbook of Conflict Resolution: The Analytical Problem-solving Approach.* London: Pinter.

Mitchell, George J. 1999a. *Making Peace.* New York: Alfred Knopf.

Mitchell, George J. 1999b. 'Rebuilding the Path to Peace in Northern Ireland', *The New York Times*, November 20.

Morton, Jeffrey S. and Harvey Starr 2001. 'Uncertainty, Change, and War: Power Fluctuations and War in the Modern Elite Power System', *Journal of Peace Research*, 38: 49–66.

Mossberg, Mathias 2010. 'One Land, Two States? Parallel States and an Example of 'Out of the Box' Thinking on Israel/Palestine', *Journal of Palestinian Studies*, 39 (2): 40–5.

Nicholas, H. G. 1971. *The United Nations as a Political Institution* (4th edn). London: Oxford University Press.

Nilsson, Anders 2008. *Dangerous Liaisons: Why Ex-combatants Return to War. Cases from the Republic of Congo and Sierra Leone*. Uppsala: Department of Peace and Conflict Research, Uppsala University.

Nilsson, Desirée 2008. 'Partial Peace: Rebel Groups Inside and Outside of Civil War Settlements', *Journal of Peace Research*, 45: 479–95.

Nincic, Miroslav 1985. *How Wars Might Spread to Europe*. Stockholm International Peace Research Institute. London: Taylor & Francis.

Nordquist, Kjell-Åke 1992. *Peace after War*. Uppsala: Department of Peace and Conflict Research, Uppsala University.

Nordquist, Kjell-Åke 1998. 'Autonomy as a Conflict-solving Mechanism – An Overview', in Markku Suksi (ed.), *Autonomy: Applications and Implications*. Amsterdam: Kluwer. pp. 59–77.

Öberg, Magnus, Frida Möller and Peter Wallensteen, 2009. 'Early Conflict Prevention in Ethnic Crises, 1990–98: A New Dataset', *Conflict Management and Peace Science*, 26 (1): 67–91.

Ohlson, Thomas 1998. *Power Politics and Peace Policies: Intra-state Conflict Resolution in Southern Africa*. Uppsala: Department of Peace and Conflict Research, Uppsala University.

Ohlson, Thomas (ed.) 2011. *From Intra-state War to Durable Peace: Conflict and Its Resolution in Africa after the Cold War*. Dordrecht: Republic of Letters Publishing.

Olson, Jr., Mancur 1971. 'Rapid Growth as a Destabilizing Force', in James C. Davies (ed.), *When Men Rebel and Why*. New York: Free Press. pp. 215–27.

Osgood, Charles 1962. *An Alternative to War or Surrender*. Urbana, IL: University of Illinois Press.

Owen, David 1995. *Balkan Odyssey*. New York: Harcourt Brace & Co.

Peck, Connie 2004. 'Special Representatives of the Secretary-General,' in David Malone (ed.), *The UN Security Council: From the Cold War to the 21st Century*. Boulder, CO, and London: Lynne Reinner. pp. 325–39.

Pellnäs, Bo 1997. 'UN Preventive Deployment in the Former Yugoslav Republic of Macedonia', in Peter Wallensteen (ed.), *International Intervention: New Norms in the Post-Cold War Era?* Uppsala: Department of Peace and Conflict Research, Uppsala University. pp. 107–14.

Peres, Shimon, with Arye Naor 1993. *The New Middle East*. New York: Henry Holt.

Pérez de Cuéllar, Javier 1997. *Pilgrimage for Peace: A Secretary-General's Memoir*. New York: St Martin's Press.

Pettersson, Thérése 2010. 'Non-State Conflict 1989–2008: Global and Regional Patterns', in Thérése Pettersson and Lotta Themnér (eds), *States in Armed Conflict 2009*. Uppsala: Department of Peace and Conflict Research, Uppsala University. pp. 183–285.

Petterson, Therése and Lotta Themnér (eds) 2010. *States in Armed Conflict 2009*. Uppsala: Department of Peace and Conflict Research, Uppsala University.

Pillar, Paul R. 1983. *Negotiating Peace: War Termination as a Bargaining Process*. Princeton, NJ: Princeton University Press.

Pruitt, Dean G. and Jeffrey Z. Rubin 1986. *Social Conflict: Escalation, Stalemate and Settlement*. New York: Random House.

Prunier, Gérard 1995. *The Rwanda Crisis: History of a Genocide*. New York: Columbia University Press.

Putnam, Robert D. 1993. *Making Democracy Work: Civic Traditions in Modern Italy.* Princeton, NJ: Princeton University Press.

Rabinovich, Itamar 1999. *Waging Peace: Israel and the Arabs at the End of the Century*. New York: Farrar, Straus and Giroux.

Rapoport, Anatol 1960. *Fights, Games and Debates*. Ann Arbor, MI: University of Michigan Press.

Reno, William 1998. *Warlord Politics and African States*. Boulder, CO: Lynne Rienner.

Rohter, Larry 1999. 'In New Role, Venezuela Army Runs Clinics and Shops', *The New York Times*, 13 April.

Rouhana, Nadim A. 1995. 'The Dynamics of Joint Thinking between Adversaries in International Conflict: Phases of the Continuing Problem-solving Workshop', *Political Psychology*, 16 (2): 321–45.

Russett, Bruce M. 1993. *Grasping the Democratic Peace*. Princeton, NJ: Princeton University Press.

Russett, Bruce M. (ed.) 1997. *The Once and Future Security Council*. London: Macmillan.

Russett, Bruce M. and John R. Oneal 2001. *Triangulating Peace: Democracy, Interdependence, and International Organizations*. New York: W. W. Norton.

Safire, William 1999. 'The Skillful Envoy', *The New York Times*, November 8.

Sarkees, Meridith Reid and Frank Whelon Wayman 2010. *Report to War 1816–2007*. Washington, DC: CQ Press.

Schaeffer, Robert 1990. *Warpaths: The Politics of Partition*. New York: Hill & Wang.

Schahczenski, Jeffery 1991. 'Explaining Relative Peace: Major Power Order, 1816–1976', *Journal of Peace Research*, 28: 295–309.

Schelling, Thomas 1960. *The Strategy of Conflict*. Cambridge, MA: Harvard University Press.

Schroeder, Paul W. 2006. 'The Life and Death of a Long Peace, 1763–1914', in Raimo Väyrynen (ed.), *The Waning of Major War: Theories and Debates*. London: Routledge. pp. 33–63.

Sharp, Gene 1973. *The Politics of Nonviolent Action*. Boston, MA: Port Sargent.

Shaw, Malcolm N. 1999. 'Peaceful Resolution of "Political Disputes": The Desirable Parameters of ICJ Jurisdiction', in Julie Dahlitz (ed.), *Peaceful Resolution of Major International Disputes*. New York and Geneva: United Nations. pp. 49–75.

Singer, J. David 1991. 'Peace in the Global System: Displacement, Interregnum or Transformation', in Charles W. Kegely, Jr. (ed.), *The Long Postwar Peace: Contending Explanations and Projections*. New York: Harper Collins. pp. 56–84.

SIPRI (Stockholm International Peace Research Institute), *Yearbook* (selected years). Oxford and Stockholm: Oxford University Press.

Sisk, Timothy D. 1996. *Power Sharing and International Mediation in Ethnic Conflicts*. Washington, DC: United States Institute of Peace Press.

Small, Melvin and J. David Singer 1982. *Resort to Arms*. Beverly Hills, CA: Sage.

Snow, Donald M. 1996. *Uncivil Wars: International Security and the New Internal Conflicts*. Boulder, CO, and London: Lynne Rienner.

Sollenberg, Margareta and Lars van Dassen 1998. 'The Intervention that Never Was: Crises, Politics, and the Refugees in Eastern Zaire', in Peter Wallensteen (ed.), *Preventing Violent Conflicts: Past Record and Future Challenges*. Uppsala: Department of Peace and Conflict Research Uppsala University. pp. 139–52.

Sorokin, Pitirim A. 1937. *Social and Cultural Dynamics* (Vol. 3). New York: American Book Company.

Southall, Roger, Neo Simuntanyi and John Daniel 2005. 'Former Presidents in African Politics', in Roger Southall and Henning Melber (eds), *Legacies of Power: Leadership Change and Former Presidents in African Politics*. Uppsala: The Nordic Africa Institute. pp. 1–25.

Spalding, Rose J. 1999. 'From Low-intensity War to Low-intensity Peace: The Nicaraguan Peace Process', in Cynthia J. Arnson (ed.), *Comparative Peace Processes in Latin America*. Washington, DC: Woodrow Wilson Center Press, and Stanford, CA: Stanford University Press. pp. 31–64.

Starr, Harvey and G. Dale Thomas 2005. 'The Nature of Borders and Conflict: Revisiting Hypotheses on Territory and War', *International Studies Quarterly*, 49 (1): 123–39.

Stedman, Stephen John 1991. *Peacemaking in Civil War: International Mediation in Zimbabwe 1974–80*. Boulder, CO: Lynne Rienner.

Stedman, Stephen John 1995. 'Alchemy for a New World Order: Overselling "Preventive Diplomacy"', *Foreign Affairs*, 73 (3): 14–20.

Stedman, Stephen John 1997. 'Spoiler Problems in Peace Processes', *International Security*, 22 (2): 5–53.

Stedman, Stephen John 1998. 'Conflict Prevention as Strategic Interaction: The Spoiler Problem and the Case of Rwanda', in Peter Wallensteen (ed.), *Preventing Violent Conflicts: Past Record and Future Challenges*. Uppsala: Department of Peace and Conflict Research, Uppsala University. pp. 67–86.

Stedman, Stephen John, Donald Rothchild and Elizabeth M. Cousens (eds) 2002. *Ending Civil Wars: The Implementation of Peace Agreements*. Boulder, CO: Lynne Rienner.

Strandow, Daniel 2006. *Sanctions and Civil War: Targeted Measures for Conflict Resolution*. Uppsala: Special Program on the Implementation of Targeted Sanctions (SPITS), Department of Peace and Conflict Research, Uppsala University.

Su Wei 1999. 'Confidence Building and Efficient Methods for Border Dispute Resolution', in Julie Dahlitz (ed.), *Peaceful Resolution of Major International Disputes*. New York and Geneva: United Nations. pp. 113–25.

Svensson, Isak 2009. 'Who Brings Which Peace? Neutral versus Biased Mediation and Institutional Arrangements in Civil Wars', *Journal of Conflict Resolution*, 53 (3): 446–69.

Svensson, Isak and Peter Wallensteen 2010. *The Go-Between: Jan Eliasson and the Styles of Mediation*. Washington, DC: United States Institute of Peace Press.

Thibaut, John W. and Harold H. Kelley 1959. *The Social Psychology of Groups*. New York: John Wiley & Sons.

Tillema, Herbert 1989. 'Foreign Overt Military Intervention in the Nuclear Age', *Journal of Peace Research*, 26: 179–95.

Tilly, Charles 1990. *Coercion, Capital and European States AD 990–1990*. Cambridge, MA: Blackwell.

Tyler, Tom R. 2000. 'Social Justice: Outcome and Procedure', *International Journal of Psychology*, 35 (2): 117–25.

United Nations 1999. *The Fall of Srebrenica*. Report of the Secretary General, UN General Assembly A/54/549, November 15.

Urquhart, Brian 1994. *Hammarskjold*. London and New York: W. W. Norton.

Vasquez, John 1993. *The War Puzzle*. Cambridge and New York: Cambridge University Press.

Vasquez, John 1995. 'Why Do Neighbors Fight? Proximity, Interaction and Territoriality', *Journal of Peace Research*, 32: 277–93.

Vasquez, John (ed.) 2000. *What Do We Know about War?* Lanham, MD: Rowman & Littlefield.

Vasquez John A. and Marie T. Henehan 2001. 'Territorial Issues and the Probability of War, 1816–1992', *Journal of Peace Research*, 38 (March): 123–38.

Väyrynen, Raimo 2004. 'The Challenge of Preventive Action: The Case of Macedonia', in Anders Mellbourn (ed.), *Developing a Culture of Conflict Prevention*. Brussels: Madariaga Foundation, The Bank of Sweden Tercentenary Foundation and Gidlunds. pp. 91–100.

Wallace, Michael 1979. 'Arms Races and Escalation: Some New Evidence', *Journal of Conflict Resolution*, 23: 3–16.

Wallensteen, Peter 1981. 'Incompatibility, Confrontation and War: Four Models and Three Historical Systems, 1816–1976', *Journal of Peace Research*, 18: 57–90.

Wallensteen, Peter 1984. 'Universalism vs Particularism: On the Limits of Major Power Order', *Journal of Peace Research*, 21: 243–57.

Wallensteen, Peter 1994a. *Från krig till fred: Om konfliktlösning i det global systemet* (*From War to Peace: On Conflict Resolution in the Global System*). Stockholm: Almqvist & Wiksell.

Wallensteen, Peter 1994b. 'Representing the World: A Security Council for the 21st Century', *Security Dialogue*, 25: 63–75.

Wallensteen, Peter (ed.) 1998. *Preventing Violent Conflicts. Past Record and Future Challenges*. Uppsala: Department of Peace and Conflict Research, Uppsala University.

Wallensteen, Peter 2000. *A Century of Economic Sanctions: A Field Revisited*. Uppsala: Department of Peace and Conflict Research, Uppsala University.

Wallensteen, Peter 2001a. 'Reassessing Cases: Direct versus Structural Prevention', in David Malone and Fen Osler Hampson (eds), *From Reaction to Conflict Prevention: Opportunities for the UN System*. New York: The International Peace Academy. pp. 213–28.

Wallensteen, Peter 2001b. *The Growing Peace Research Agenda*. Occasional Paper No. 21, Joan B. Kroc Institute for International Peace Studies, San Diego, CA.

Wallensteen, Peter 2002/2007. *Understanding Conflict Resolution: War, Peace and the Global System*. London: Sage. (Second edition, 2007.)

Wallensteen, Peter 2011a. 'The Origins of Contemporary Peace Research', in Kristine Höglund and Magnus Öberg (eds), *Understanding Peace Research*. London: Routledge. pp. 14–32.

Wallensteen, Peter 2011b. *Peace Research: Theory and Practice*. London: Routledge.

Wallensteen, Peter, Erik Melander and Frida Möller 2011. 'Preventing Genocide: The International Response', in Mark Anstey, Paul Meerts and I. William Zartman (eds), *The Slippery Slope to Genocide: Reducing Identity Conflicts and Preventing Mass Murder*. Oxford: Oxford University Press.

Wallensteen, Peter and Margareta Sollenberg 1998. 'Armed Conflict and Regional Conflict Complexes, 1989–1997', *Journal of Peace Research*, 35: 593–606.

Wallensteen, Peter and Carina Staibano (eds) 2005. *International Sanctions: Between Words and Wars in the Global System.* London: Routledge/Frank Cass.

Wallensteen, Peter, Carina Staibano and Mikael Eriksson 2003. *Making Targeted Sanctions Effective: Guidelines for the Implementation of UN Policy Options.* Uppsala: Department of Peace and Conflict Research, Uppsala University.

Wallensteen, Peter et al. 2002. 'Towards a Security Community in the Baltic Region', in Claes Levinsson and Witold Maciejewski (eds), *The Baltic Sea Region: Cultures, Politics, Societies.* Uppsala: Baltic University Press. pp. 431– 84.

Waltz, Kenneth N. 1959. *Man, the State and War.* New York: Columbia University Press.

Waltz, Kenneth N. 1979. *Theory of International Politics.* Reading, MA: Addison-Wesley.

Wantechekon, Leonard 1999. *Why Do Resource-rich Countries Have Authoritarian Governments?* New Haven, CT: Department of Political Science, Yale University. Mimeo.

Weart, Spencer R. 1998. *Never at War: Why Democracies Will Not Fight One Another.* New Haven, CT, and London: Yale University Press.

Weber, Max 1964. *The Theory of Social and Economic Organization.* New York: Free Press.

Weiss, Thomas G., David Forsythe and Roger A. Coate 2001. *The United Nations and Changing World Politics* (3rd edn). Boulder, CO: Westview Press.

Whitfield, Teresa 1999. 'The Role of the United Nations in El Salvador and Guatemala: A Preliminary Comparison', in Cynthia J. Arnson (ed.), *Comparative Peace Processes in Latin America.* Washington, DC: Woodrow Wilson Center Press, and Stanford, CA: Stanford University Press. pp. 257–90.

Wiberg, Håkan 1976/1990. *Konfliktteori och fredsforskning* (*Conflict Theory and Peace Research*). Stockholm: Esselte Studium (second edition, 1990).

Wilkenfeld, Jonathan and Michael Brecher 1984. 'International Crises, 1945–1975: The UN Dimension', *International Studies Quarterly*, 28: 45–67.

Woodworth, John A. 1999. 'Dispute Resolution in Bilateral Arms Control: The INF Experience', in Julie Dahlitz (ed.), *Peaceful Resolution of Major International Disputes.* New York and Geneva: United Nations. pp. 181–201.

World Summit Outcome 2005. United Nations General Assembly, 15 September.

Wriggins, Howard 1995. 'Sri Lanka: Negotiations in a Secessionist Conflict', in I. William I. Zartman (ed.), *Elusive Peace: Negotiating an End to Civil Wars.* Washington, DC: Brookings Institution. pp. 35–58.

Wright, Quincy 1942/1965. *A Study of War.* Chicago and London: University of Chicago Press (second edition, 1965).

Zartman, I. William 1989. *Ripe for Resolution: Conflict and Intervention in Africa* (updated edn). New York and Oxford: Oxford University Press.

Zartman, I. William (ed.) 1995a. *Elusive Peace: Negotiating an End to Civil Wars.* Washington, DC: Brookings Institution.

Zartman, I. William (ed.) 1995b. *Collapsed States: The Disintegration and Restoration of Legitimate Authority.* Boulder, CO: Lynne Rienner.

Zartman, I. William 2000a. 'Mediating Conflicts of Need, Greed and Creed', *Orbis*, 24 (2): 255–66.

Zartman, I. William (ed.) 2000b. *Traditional Cures for Modern Conflict: African Conflict 'Medicine'.* Boulder, CO: Lynne Rienner.

Zartman, I. William and Maureen R. Berman 1982. *The Practical Negotiator.* New Haven, CT, and London: Yale University Press.

Zartman, I. William and J. Lewis Rasmussen (eds) 1997. *Peacemaking in International Conflict: Methods and Techniques*. Washington, DC: United States Institute of Peace Press.

Zartman, I. William and Alvaro de Soto 2010. *Timing Mediation Initiatives*. Washington, DC: United States Institute of Peace Press and Baltimore, MD: Johns Hopkins University, 51pp.

Websites

AKUF: www.sozialwiss.uni-hamburg.de/publish/Ipw/Akuf/

CIDCM, University of Maryland: www.cidcm.umd.edu

Correlates of War Project: www.correlatesofwar.org

Targeted Sanctions: www.smartsanctions.se

Uppsala Conflict Data Program: www.ucdp.uu.se

Index